Dutch

Dutch

BIOGRAPHY OF A LANGUAGE

Roland Willemyns

OXFORD

UNIVERSITY PRESS

OXFORD
UNIVERSITY PRESS

Oxford University Press is a department of the
University of Oxford. It furthers the University's objective
of excellence in research, scholarship, and education
by publishing worldwide.

Oxford   New York
Auckland   Cape Town   Dar es Salaam   Hong Kong   Karachi
Kuala Lumpur   Madrid   Melbourne   Mexico City   Nairobi
New Delhi   Shanghai   Taipei   Toronto

With offices in
Argentina   Austria   Brazil   Chile   Czech Republic   France   Greece
Guatemala   Hungary   Italy   Japan   Poland   Portugal   Singapore
South Korea   Switzerland   Thailand   Turkey   Ukraine   Vietnam

Oxford is a registered trade mark of Oxford University Press
in the UK and certain other countries.

Published in the United States of America by
Oxford University Press
198 Madison Avenue, New York, NY 10016

Library of Congress Cataloging-in-Publication Data
Willemyns, Roland.
Dutch : biography of a language / Roland Willemyns.
p.   cm.
Includes bibliographical references and index.
ISBN 978-0-19-985871-2 (alk. paper)
1. Dutch language—History.   2. Dutch language—Etymology.
3. Germanic languages—History.   I. Title.
PF75.W55   2012
439.3109—dc23   2012010285

3 5 7 9 8 6 4 2

Printed in the United States of America
on acid-free paper

To Helga, who helped me through this book,

not only as a loving wife but also as a very

competent fellow professional.

NOTHING ENDURES BUT WORDS

Robert Harris in "Lustrum"

CONTENTS

INTRODUCTION

Dutch: Biography of a Language describes and analyzes the Dutch language in all its historical, geographic, social and cultural aspects and variation. It gives an abundantly documented survey of the former and present state of the language, which has 23 million speakers in the Antilles, Belgium, the Netherlands, and Suriname.

This book has three main focuses: the history of the language (chapters 2–5); contemporary development (chapter 6 and chapter 9); and Dutch abroad (or colonial Dutch) and Afrikaans (chapters 7–8).

Intensive research on historical sociolinguistics over the past 20 years has provided not only much new data and information on how the language and the linguistic situation in the Dutch language territory evolved but also new insights into the methodology of how to sociolinguistically interpret and present historical language data. It allows for an interesting and innovative look at how to detect a linguistic hierarchy in societies as far back as the Middle Ages.

Although geographic and social variation is predominant in the contemporary part of the book, it is present in the historical chapters as well. At the same time, there is a strong emphasis on recent variation and developments in contemporary Dutch, both on the micro and the macro level. Destandardization and the genesis and impact of new language varieties such as Poldernederlands (in Holland) and Verkavelingsvlaams (in Flanders), for example, are thoroughly discussed. The book addresses the linguistic situation in both the two motherlands (Belgium and The Netherlands) and also in the other countries where Dutch is an official language (Suriname, the former Dutch Antilles) as well as in former colonies such as Indonesia or countries where Dutch has played an important role in the past such as the United States, Ceylon, and Japan. A whole chapter is devoted to Afrikaans, the only extant daughter language of Dutch. All chapters are conceived in such a way that they can also be used independently.

The story of Dutch is predominantly a story of language contact and conflict, which is the connecting thread in its history: in all the countries where Dutch is an official language, other languages are (and used to be) spoken as well, and some have an official status. Also, from the very beginning, Dutch in the Low Countries has been in intense and permanent contact with other languages both within and outside its borders. Language shift has occurred at the border with French as well as at the borders with Frisian and German, whereas language shift within the territory occurred because of upward social mobility, language planning, or linguistic legislation.

The Dutch language area in Europe is treated as a whole throughout the book, although for reasons based on the actual situation both in the past and in the present, sometimes more attention had to be given to one particular region. Language evolution up to the 16th century is predominantly a southern affair, whereas the 17th and 18th centuries are, on the contrary, dominated by what happened in the northern part. The 19th-century development is, for different reasons, interesting on both sides of the state border. Passion, excitement, a battle for status and prestige, internal and external confrontation, and patriotic emotion: we find these in the 19th-century southern Netherlands, but they are completely lacking in the north, which, for its part, witnessed both the birth of Netherlandistics and the unfolding of the standard language. Even in contemporary history—from the early 20th century onward—there are, in spite of obvious differences, so many common developments that I decided to analyze them in the same chapter, constantly cross-referring and attempting to discover the underlying reasons why reactions to identical impulses may indeed be identical or, on the contrary, completely different.

The picture that emerges across the chapters is that this language, rooted in a territory divided at the end of the 16th century by a state border, is continuously changing since internal and external factors have compelled the language community to sometimes strive for congruence and integration and at other times to favor distance and disintegration. To give these developments due attention, the language is presented here in all its facets: various kinds of Dutch are discussed, including the many dialects that still exist in Holland and Flanders, all of them threatened and some of them on the verge of extinction.

Over the centuries, a standard language has gradually developed. During the Middle Ages a supraregional, more or less standardized variety of the language did not exist, and we have to wait for the 16th century to witness how, very gradually, the foundations for Standard Dutch were laid. Modern Standard Dutch does not derive from any particular older dialect. Instead, it mainly originates from the upper-class sociolects of the 17th-century northwestern provinces (Holland, Utrecht), with a mixture of earlier southern-central forms (Brabant) on a solid base of the medieval southwestern (Flemish) language. From the very beginning this new variety coexisted with the dialects, and the nearer we come to our present time the more the standard gradually prevailed. Then, in the late 19th century and the 20th century, we witness a process of dialect loss, a complex and complicated phenomenon spanning over a long lapse of time. Still, even during the process of loss, two (or more) varieties continued to coexist and to compete, sharing the various communicative functions between them. This explains why, in spite of the progressing dialect loss, throughout the 19th century the dialects remained the habitual medium at home, on the job, and even in many more formal gatherings. It is mostly during the 20th century that the dramatic consequences of that process came to be really felt.

Standard language and dialects are not the only varieties under the Dutch umbrella. Apart from the regional varieties (e.g., dialects, regiolects, Netherlandic, Belgian, Suriname Dutch), there are socially determined varieties called sociolects (i.e., language use typical for a specific social class or group); there are jargons and there is the slang used by young people; there is ethnic Dutch (i.e., Dutch as spoken by nonnative speakers); there are pidgins and creoles; and there is Afrikaans, the only extant daughter language of Dutch. Historically speaking, there is, on top of that, Old Dutch, Middle Dutch, Early New Dutch, 19th- and 20th-century Dutch, and, maybe even 21st- century Dutch already. This whole scope of variation is displayed and analyzed in this book, which attempts to present to a general readership the Dutch language in all its variegated opulence. In addition, the book concentrates on the external history of Dutch, which means that the emphasis is on what happens *with* the language much more than what happens *in* the language. Therefore, the historical, social, political, and economic framework in which the Dutch language has developed is described as well.

Since I published my first book on the history of Dutch (almost 20 years ago), research on several aspects of that history has boomed. Some of its results have already been incorporated in Willemyns (2003) as well as in Van der Sijs and Willemyns (2009), but the full amount of recent research results (e.g., on the Old Dutch period and the 19th century) is displayed here for the first time. The last couple of years also saw an amazing expansion of research on the 18th century. Most of these new findings are summarized here as well. With the exception of 17th-century Flanders, which is still almost virgin territory, we are now in the happy position to have at our disposal a profusion of information on 15 centuries of Dutch.

Obviously, it is impossible to treat every aspect with the same thoroughness. The choices made here are based on two main criteria:

- What aspects are the most interesting in view of the evolution toward modern standard Dutch, as it is used in the language territory at large
- What aspects are the most interesting for nonnative speakers having learned Dutch as a foreign language and for other foreigners taking an interest in Dutch.

Chapter 1, "Who Speaks Dutch and Where?" deals with the widespread confusion as to what exactly Dutch is and where and by whom it is spoken; some terminological issues are taken care of as well. This chapter also deals with the borders of Dutch and the questions of whether and how they have changed over time. The southern language border (between Dutch and French) and the eastern one (between Dutch and German) are discussed in detail, as is the inner border between Dutch and Frisian.

Chapter 2, "Old Dutch: Its Ancestors and Contemporaries," concentrates on the genesis of Dutch: where does it come from and where and when did it come into being? The breaking up of the Indo-European language family is touched upon only very briefly. The real survey starts with the breaking up of Old Germanic into North, East, and West Germanic, the latter being the most important group for us since not only Dutch and English but also Frisian and Low and High German derive from it. We see how Dutch is indeed a language between English and German, as is so often maintained. The final part of the chapter deals with the Franks, the Frisians, and the Saxons, whose languages are the building blocks of Dutch as we know it. The chapter also gives an overview of the earliest documented sources and details the main linguistic characteristics of Old Dutch. Thanks to many recently unearthed sources, we are able to draw a reliable picture of what Old Dutch was like.

Chapter 3, "Middle Dutch: Language and Literature," demonstrates how Middle Dutch has developed a supraregional writing language in its own right. Although each region displays its own characteristics, Middle Dutch texts were more or less intelligible in all parts of the Low Countries and, sometimes, beyond its borders as well. The chapter opens with an overview of the Middle Dutch literary masterpieces that came to us in the 13th, 14th, and 15th centuries. They were written during the heyday of Dutch literature, when it was the leader in Europe in poetry as well as in drama.

This chapter also brings a thorough discussion of the merge of the Low Countries with Burgundy. In many treatises, Burgundy is mentioned (briefly and partly erroneously) as only having introduced bilingualism in Flanders and afterward in the Netherlands at large. Here, we uncover which were the consequences of intensive language contact which French and whether or how bilingual functioning proceeded.

Since the cradle of Dutch is in Flanders, Flemish Middle Dutch is dealt with extensively; it is, after all, the dialect in which more than two-thirds of all documented 13th-century texts were written. Obviously, the main characteristics of the language as written in Brabant, Holland, Limburg, and the northeast from the 12th through the 16th century are described in detail as well.

Chapter 4, "Early New Dutch, 1500–1800," discusses how the 16th century was an age of transition. It saw the renewed interest in all things classic (humanism and renaissance) and experienced a huge religious upheaval (reformation), both of which are reflected in books that can now be printed and reach audiences undreamed of before.

The first half of the century was marked by a shift of the economic and cultural center of gravity from Flanders to Brabant. Scores of people started to reflect on the way the language was used and how to influence (or, as they were convinced, improve) it. Dictionaries, spelling treatises, and grammars shot up like mushrooms. It is during this period that, thanks to the combined efforts of

Flemings, Brabanters, and Hollanders, a written standard language was gradually taking shape.

Most of these efforts, though, were annihilated when, by the end of the century, political events lead to the breaking up of the unity of the Low Countries. De facto from 1585 onward, the Low Countries were divided into two parts (more or less present-day Belgium and Holland): the southern Netherlands, ruled by Spain and forced back to the Roman Catholic religion on one hand; and the Northern Republic, an independent and Calvinist state, on the other. It was to the latter part that the center of gravity of standardization gradually passed. The (socio-)linguistic consequences of the devastating Eighty Years' War are depicted in this chapter.

In 17th-century Holland (the Golden Age), it was increasingly felt that the norm of the standard language was to be found in the idiolect of the upper classes of both Amsterdam and The Hague. This is the start of a long-lived tradition: we see how the social variable unmistakably supersedes the regional one and how, until well into the 19th century, having a regional accent will be deemed less of a problem than having the wrong social accent. The Golden Age also saw the publication of the (printed) *Statenbijbel*, not only a paramount theological but also linguistic achievement, since it turned out to be one of the most important standardization instruments ever.

For the south, on the contrary, the 17th century was one of economic and cultural decline.

Until recently, *boring* and *uninteresting* were commonly used to describe 18th-century Dutch. As for Holland both the literature and culture are considered dull compared with the splendor of the preceding Golden Age.

In Flanders, which became the "Austrian" Netherlands in 1713, the 18th century is mostly remembered as the age in which the gap between the social classes was supplemented with a linguistic component: the upper classes were rapidly switching to French, a language the vast majority of the population had not mastered. This chapter argues that—both in the north and in the south—this rather undiscriminating image seems to be in contrast with what recent research has revealed.

When, in the late 18th century, French revolutionary troops invaded the southern as well as the northern Netherlands, both countries were brought under French influence, be it in different ways.

Chapter 5, "Reunion and Secession: The Nineteenth Century," explains that this is the age in which Belgium was founded, with all the radical changes this would bring about for the south as well as for the north. Previously, after Napoleon's defeat, the north and south were reunited in one United Kingdom of the Netherlands. Until recently, the influence of this reunification had definitely been underestimated, mostly because it was generally believed that King William I's rather rigid language policy had not really been successful. We know now that the opposite was the case. It was a period during which both parts of the Netherlands came to know each other again, lived together, and, most importantly, talked with each other. For the first time ever the Flemings were ruled by an autochthonous king, a native speaker who armed them to survive in their subsequent struggle against the gallicizing policy of the Belgian rulers.

In the north, the 19th century witnessed many changes, such as the beginning of dialect loss and the flourishing of historical linguistics, made possible when Netherlandistics was introduced as an academic discipline.

The norm of the language continued to preoccupy the intellectual part of the population. The question of whether it had to be prescribed or rather described divided both the linguists and the general public. Also, grammars, dictionaries, and spelling treatises not only were written but for the first time ever also received the official approval of the governments of the Netherlands and Belgium. After some hesitation both countries even agreed on an identical, compulsory spelling. The authoritative grammars and dictionaries were (and remained) the same in both countries as well.

The language struggle between Dutch and French that dominated Belgian political life started in 1830. Despite the fact that Dutch speakers constituted the majority of the population, no legal means was provided for their language. The so-called Flemish Movement immediately started a long-lasting, acrimonious battle for cultural and linguistic rights for Dutch speakers. At the same time, we witness a heated discussion on the norm of Dutch between integrationists (in favor of the northern norm) and particularists (in favor of a southern-flavored language).

Chapter 6, "Twentieth Century: The Age of the Standard Language," covers how in the 1900s language development was characterized by a fast-progressing standardization process that established norms and rules as well as by important language planning movements aimed at integrating Flanders and Holland more closely. The chapter opens with a description of the rise and fall of Algemeen Beschaafd Nederlands (ABN), after which special attention is given to variation in Dutch. On the micro level, dialect areas and an impressive wave of dialect loss are discussed. On the macro level (north–south), internal standard language variation in the Netherlands and Flanders is reviewed, and Dutch is described as a pluricentric language, oscillating between convergence and divergence.

As a follow-up to the preceding chapter, the main constitutional consequences of Flanders' struggle in favor of its own language are briefly summarized. This chapter also details the so-called standardization tools and gives a rather extensive survey of the spelling problems the 20th century has endured. Finally, the chapter comments on several destandardization processes that occurred by the end of the century and closes with an overview of the extensive amount of language planning measures displayed in the Low Countries and the institutions involved in the planning.

Chapter 7, "Colonial Dutch," opens with the now mostly extinct Dutch-based pidgins and creoles in former colonies. In four sections, the fate of Dutch in the main colonial possessions of the Netherlands is detailed. We start with Suriname, for which the Dutch had given up New York and other American possessions. Next is an analysis of the situation of Dutch in the Caribbean, from the very beginning until October 10, 2010, which marked a completely new turn in the relationship between The Hague and its Caribbean possessions. The fate of Dutch in Nederlands Indië (Indonesia) as well as how Dutch has fared in what is now the United States and what is left from its presence are also discussed.

Finally, we try to understand why Dutch has not left its mark on the linguistic situation in Asia, the Americas, and Africa in a way comparable to the languages of their former colonial rivals England, France, Portugal, and Spain.

Chapter 8, "Afrikaans," is devoted completely to the genesis, history, and development of the only extant daughter language of Dutch. After relating the history of the Dutch presence at the Cape, we reveal how Dutch gradually evolved into Afrikaans. Linguistic conflicts arose as soon as the British took possession of the Cape and, subsequently, of the independent republics that had been founded by the Boers, eager to escape British rule and language legislation. In the 20th century, Afrikaans' peak coincided with the policy of apartheid. As a consequence, the future of Afrikaans after 1993 was mortgaged, and, nowadays, a fight for its survival is taking place. Before proceeding to concluding reflections, attention is given to Afrikaans in Namibia, an even more Afrikaans-speaking country than South Africa. We end with some remarks on the functioning of Afrikaans in a multilingual and multiethnic South Africa.

Chapter 9, "Progress or Decay? The Future Development of Dutch," covers the institutional embedding of Dutch at home and abroad as well as in the European Union. And the eternally returning question of whether language change equals decay is answered in the negative.

The possible influence of external and internal factors on language change is assessed, after which a number of changes are discussed more in detail, such as the centrifugal developments in the north and south, often called Poldernederlands and Verkavelingsvlaams, respectively. Although they are linguistically unrelated, the fact that they occur simultaneously may considerably influence the evolution of Dutch as a pluricentric language in the course of the 21st century.

A further consequence of the destandardization process is that, for a constantly growing part of the population, both north and south of the border, the conventional norm of the standard language no longer appears to be the target in an increasing number of settings.

Finally, a few short paragraphs address what the future may hold. Not unexpectedly, there is no unequivocal answer to be given.

**

Until now, there is no history of the Dutch language in English. In fact, there is no up-to-date history of the Dutch language in any other language than Dutch. *Dutch: Biography of a Language,* therefore, is purposefully written for an international audience, giving much, yet certainly not exclusive, attention to the Anglo-Saxon world. It is also conceived as a contrastive story, stressing the similarities and differences with the other West Germanic languages, especially English and German.

In Dutch departments of over 250 foreign universities all over the world, thousands of students are studying the language and its literature to become scholars of Dutch or teachers and interpreters and translators of that language or to use it for business or other purposes. All of them are eager to finally have at their disposal a book that tells—in English—the story of the language in which they are interested. The same goes for a large number of scholars, students, and other interested people involved with other Germanic languages, not the least of which is Afrikaans, spoken as a first or a second language by more than ten millions of South Africans and Namibians.

The book is intended for academic specialists as well as for advanced or graduate students in the field of the Dutch language. Furthermore, it will appeal to undergraduates and postgraduates whose background is in Dutch but who have little previous knowledge of linguistics. As a reference book, it collects together and summarizes all the information available in the area of the history of and variation in Dutch. That area is covered comprehensively. It can, moreover, also be used as a textbook for students of Dutch all over the world.

The book has also been designed for all those in other disciplines having to do with the Low Countries (e.g., art history, history, theology, business). As in my previous books published in Dutch, it is my firm intention to reach out to a broad general audience interested in the Dutch language and culture.

**

I am deeply indebted to the late Jan W. de Vries as well as to Peter Burger and Nicoline van der Sijs, my coauthors of *Het verhaal van een taal* and *Het verhaal van het Nederlands,* respectively. Many discussions and a very pleasant and productive cooperation gave me insights and ideas, many of which have found their way into this book as well.

For help and advice or comments I am grateful to Hugo Baetens Beardsmore (Brussels), Helga Bister Broosen (Chapel Hill), Bruce Donaldson (Melbourne), Martin Durell (Manchester), Ilse Feinauer (Stellenbosch), Paul Roberge (Chapel Hill), Gijsbert Rutten (Leiden), Gerald Stell (Brussels), Nicoline van der Sijs (Leiden), Wim Vandenbussche (Brussels), and Rik Vosters (Brussels), and, of course, the two anonymous referees who read part of my manuscript on behalf of the publisher.

Dutch

1 }

Who Speaks Dutch and Where?

What Is Dutch?

DUTCH IN PARADISE

In his book on the *Origines Antwerpianae*, published in 1569, Joannes Goropius Becanus (born as Jan van Gorp), a physician from Brabant, claimed his Dutch mother tongue to be not only the best but also the oldest language in the world, since, as he maintained, it was the language spoken by Adam and Eve in paradise (Hagen 1999, 11–12). One of the "arguments" to prove this claim was a pseudo-etymological one: the name of the language, Duyts, was to be pronounced *doutst,* which means "the oldest."

At that time, people like Becanus were not considered eccentric or weird, and many other very serious scientists and "language experts" in several countries propagated similar convictions as far as their respective vernaculars were concerned. Simon Stevin, the famous mathematician, engineer, and humanist from Brugge, not only readily accepted Becanus's assertion but also thought Dutch to be the language most fit for science, since it has the largest amount of monosyllabic words. To his count, Dutch had 1,428 monosyllabic nouns and 742 monosyllabic verbs, whereas Greek had only 220 and 45, respectively, and Latin had fewer still (Hagen 1999, 16–18). Although the relevance of the argument is not obvious, it went unchallenged, not only in the 16th century but also a long time thereafter. According to Knowles (1997, 78–79) it was Becanus's work that started the continental interest in the Germanic peoples in general and the English interest in the Saxons in particular.

As opposed to Becanus's 16th-century contemporaries, no modern reader is likely to take this seriously. Also, they might wonder why Becanus calls his language *Duyts,* a name that nowadays is reserved for German. This is only one of many examples proving that the terminological confusion as to what Dutch really is has existed for ages.

It may seem strange that, for example, the language (and the people) of a country called the Netherlands or Holland should be called Dutch, a word many will recognize as being cognate with *Deutsch,* the word the Germans use to call their own language. After all, even in Dutch the word *Duits* now means "German."

Also, isn't it intriguing that English uses two different words to designate the language of the Low Countries (*Flemish* and *Dutch*), whereas three are used in both French (*Flamand, Hollandais, Néerlandais*) and German (*Flämisch, Holländisch, Niederländisch*). Reassuringly, in Dutch only *Nederlands* now refers to the language, which is the native tongue and the official language of almost 23 million people in Belgium and the Netherlands as well as the official language of Suriname and the (former) Dutch Antilles. It is appropriate, therefore, that the first chapter of this book opens with the question of what Dutch is and where it is spoken.

Furthermore, the borders of Dutch will be dealt with as well as the question of whether and how they may have changed over time. The southern language border (between Dutch and French) and the eastern one (between Dutch and German) as well as the Dutch–Frisian border will be discussed in detail.

The borders of Dutch overseas are not geographical but are of a sociolinguistic nature. The relationship of Dutch to Sranan in Suriname and to Papiamento or English in the Caribbean will not be discussed here but is explained in detail in chapter 7 on colonial Dutch.

WHAT'S IN A NAME?

Dutch is a West Germanic language, as are English, Low German, High German, Frisian, Afrikaans, and Yiddish.

Since Dutch is the official language of various countries, it is a *pluricentric language,* in the (widely accepted) sense of Kloss (1978, 66–67), where it means a language with several interacting centers, each providing a national variety, with at least some of its own norms. Clyne (1992, 2) quotes the examples of Standard German in Austria, Standard French in Canada, and Standard Dutch in Belgium, all of which he labels as "a variety of a standard language limited to a certain national area." Bister Broosen and Willemyns (1988) developed the notion of *peripheral varieties,* as opposed to the variety of the center of gravity of standardization. Here, too, Standard Dutch in Belgium and Standard German in Austria are explicitly mentioned. For historical reasons, Dutch in the Netherlands is often called *Hollands* (Hollandic), whereas Dutch in Belgium, in colloquial speech, is often called *Vlaams* (Flemish). This has led to the persistent misconception that we are in the presence of two different languages. In spite of regional differences, the Low Countries have only one single language, called Nederlands (Dutch in English, Niederländisch in German, Néerlandais in French).

The confusion as to the name of the Dutch language is old and may partly be explained by the scattered history of the Low Countries. One of the first names ever used for the non-Romance languages of Western Europe derives from the Old Germanic word *theudisk*, an adjective that meant "pertaining to the language of the people, as opposed to Latin." In the first text in which it is found, dating from 784, *theodiscus* refers to the Germanic dialects of Britain. Diets and Duits (in Dutch) as well as Deutsch (in German) are its modern cognate forms. The fact that in English the language of the Low Countries was (and is) called Dutch (derived from Deutsch) or that Pennsylvania Dutch is not Dutch but German is proof enough of how confusing this could be.

In the early medieval, multilingual empire of the Franks, *theudisk* was coined to put an end to a terminological confusion that came into being because the name Frenkisk (meaning the Germanic language of the Franks) was also used by the Gallo-Roman population to indicate their own Romance language. This Romance Frenkisk was later to become "Français."

However, in coining *theudisk*, a new confusion was created: the Franks and their successors lived not only in the Low Countries but also in what was to become Germany. Since they all used Duits or Deutsch to refer to their own language, it was soon clear that it might be advisable to differentiate. In the Netherlands, therefore, Duits was often further specified as Nederduits (Low German), which obviously was not a real improvement since Nederduits was also what was spoken in the whole northern part of what was eventually to become Germany.

The first time the language was called by its present-day name of Nederlands was in 1482.[1] Although this appeared to be unambiguous enough to end the confusion, it did not succeed in becoming really popular and by the 18th century had virtually disappeared. It started a new life in the 19th century, first in the Netherlands and shortly after in Belgium. During the 18th century Nederduits, however, was the everyday name, used 72 percent of the time and Nederlands only in 19 percent of the cases (De Vreese, 1909).

Vlaemsch (Flemish) originally meant "pertaining to Flanders"; it was an adjective, the first occurrence of which was found in an English text from 1080, where it was spelled Fleminsce (Gysseling 1975). From the 13th century onward we see how Vlaemsch, as a noun, gradually acquires the meaning "the language spoken in the County of Flanders" (Gysseling 1971). Since that was the culturally and politically leading part of the Netherlands, it is no wonder that the first name for the language originated there (De Schrijver 1987). The language of Brabant, Limburg, or Holland was never labeled Vlaemsch. The use of this term to refer to the Dutch language as it was used outside of the county of Flanders is attested for the first time around 1500, when a bilingual dictionary had on its title page that it provided translations from *romain* (French) into

[1] Based on the texts that came to us; we have 56 more references in the period preceding 1550.

flameng (Flemish) or from *walsch* (French) into *vlaemsch*. Thereupon, we witness how *flameng* in that particular, new meaning increasingly appeared in French texts. It was this French habit that probably was the direct source for the use of its Dutch equivalent Vlaemsch (in later spelling systems also Vlaamsch and Vlaams) in Dutch texts as well. From the early 19th century on, Vlaamsch is increasingly used to refer to Belgian Dutch. As a consequence, we see how Vlamingen (Flemings) gets a new meaning as well, in that it referred to Dutch-speaking Belgians. Until then, people had always differentiated between Flemings, Brabanters, and Limburgers.

Hollands referring to the variety of Holland is found for the first time in 1550. However, only shortly thereafter—from 1610 on—it also turns up as a synonym for Dutch in general (Van der Sijs 2004, 2006). How confusing all of this really was can be deduced from the words of the famous Dutch linguist Lambert ten Kate who, in 1723, tells his readers that the "Belgian or Dutch" language (Belgisch of Nederlandsch in his words), as it was used in the Dutch Republic and two centuries before that still went by the name of Flemish (Vlaamsch), was then also called Hollandsch. This language, Ten Kate boasts, is spoken to perfection only in Holland. Our Belgian language (*onze Belgische taal*), he adds, now proudly carries the name of Hollandsch.[2]

Very often in essays and books on language the terms Noord-Nederlands and Zuid-Nederlands are used to refer to the northern and the southern variety of the standard language as it is spoken in Holland and Belgium, respectively.

In view of all this, how could we ever blame foreigners for not knowing what name to call the language of the Low Countries (box 1.1)?

BOX 1.1 } Case and Brode in England

In 1302, during the prewar troubles preceding the Guldensporenslag, a lot of Frenchmen were killed by the Flemings in the so-called Brugse Metten. Legend has it that to be able to tell friend from enemy during that nightly raid suspects were required to say, "Schild ende Vriend." Those with a French accent didn't live to regret their linguistic incompetence.

Some 80 years later, the Flemings were apparently treated the same way in England. "In the 'Peasants' Revolt' of 1381 we are told that 'many fflemmynges loste here heedes...and namely they that koude nat say Breede and Chese, But *Case and Brode*'" (Baugh & Cable 1978, 187, italics in original).

A TERMINOLOGICAL CHAOS

Finally, we still have to address the question of how to refer to various variants of Dutch and to various regions and their inhabitants.

---

[2] Throughout the book, all translations of Dutch quotes are mine unless otherwise indicated.

In Dutch an inhabitant of Antwerp, Brussels, The Hague, and Leiden is called an Antwerpenaar, Brusselaar, Hagenaar, and Leidenaar, respectively. Someone who lives in Amsterdam or Groningen is an Amsterdammer and a Groninger respectively. Almost all inhabitants of cities can be referred to by using the suffixes -(n)aar and –er; a Bruggeling, who lives in Brugge, is one of the few exceptions to this rule.

In English there is no way to name the inhabitants of our cities. In various previous publications I have used Brusseler, and, although it may be clear and self-explanatory enough, as would be, for example, Amsterdamer, these names are not found in dictionaries. Both Donaldson (1983) and Paul Vincent, the British translator of Brachin's (1985) French language history of Dutch, use Amsterdammer, Brusselaar, and similar Dutch words in their English text. Apart from that, referring to the people living in other Belgian and Dutch cities (as well as many German cities) is simply impossible unless you use the paraphrase "the inhabitant(s)/citizen(s) of...."

Whereas a Fleming lives in Flanders, there is no way to designate somebody who lives in Brabant, Holland, or Limburg. Consequently, for the provinces as well as for the major dialect areas there is no possibility of naming those who live there or use the dialects in question. The Dutch words Brabander,[3] Hollander,[4] and Limburger have no counterpart in English, although they do have one in German and in French.

Bruce Donaldson, the only native speaker of English to ever write a history of Dutch in his mother tongue, naturally faced the same problem. Finding no solution that really suited him, he finally "opted for leaving such Dutch words untranslated" (Donaldson 1983, viii). Consequently, he (as well as Vincent) uses words such as Brabants, Hollands, or Limburgs in their original Dutch form. In most cases I followed his example. Occasionally, though, I opted for another solution. Even if the words I use (e.g., Hollanders, Hollandic, Brabanders, Brabantic) are not in dictionaries, I reckon they'll be self-explanatory enough to be understood by my readers, be they native speakers of English or of any other language.

Finally, a word on the way a lot of cities in the Low Countries are referred to in English: England has apparently always looked at the Continent through French glasses. With only a few exceptions (Antwerp, Brussels, Ghent, The Hague) English has taken over the names used in French. Consequently, Brugge becomes Bruges, Leuven Louvain, and 's Hertogenbosch Bois-le-Duc. By the same token, Germany's Aachen is referred to by the totally incomprehensible French name Aix-la-Chapelle and *Köln* by Cologne.

---

[3] The title of Bredero's play *De Spaanse Brabander* is often translated as *The Spanish Brabanter,* yet Brabanter does not exist in "normal" English speech. Still, Vincent (Brachin 1985) also occasionally uses Brabanters when referring to people from Brabant (e.g., 17, 22).

[4] *Dutchman,* as in *The Flying Dutchman,* is of no use here, since that refers to a citizen of the Netherlands, not of the provinces of Holland, although the original title given by Wagner is *Der fliegende Holländer.*

Whereas the inhabitants of the two latter cities probably don't mind being called those names in English, those living in the Low Countries, and particularly in Flanders, are more sensitive. As a consequence of centuries-long Francophone endeavors for dominance, calling a Flemish city by the name given to it by the Walloons looks very much like taking sides and is therefore not really appreciated very much.

The Hollander Pieter Geyl, a famous professor of history at University College in London during the early years of the 20th century, who wrote extensively on the Low Countries, felt very uneasy with this habit and tried to change it in that he kept the original denominations in his English publications: "I found it impossible to confirm to the English custom of calling all western continental towns by French names" (Geyl 2001, 21).[5] Some decades later, though, he had to confess that it was impossible for an outsider to try to change the linguistic habits of speakers of a foreign language. Although "I still think that it is unfortunate that the English should be addicted to the use of French geographical names for non-French-speaking countries on the Continent," he says, "I have come to realise that it is presumptuous, and in any case a hopeless undertaking, for a foreigner to try to improve the English language" (297).[6]

What Geyl didn't manage to "improve," Google and an increasing mobility did. People traveling through Europe are confronted, be it on maps, on their GPS, or on traffic signs, with the names in the language of the country they're in. Also, if you're looking for information (e.g., on Google), you have to use the original names as well. Most foreigners nowadays (including the British) have no idea anymore that Bois-le-Duc or Furnes used to be Anglo-French for Den Bosch and Veurne. Therefore, I adopted the same solution as Vincent: "For most geographical and place names in the text the official spelling in the country or area concerned has been used. Exceptions have been made for, e.g. Antwerp, Brussels and The Hague...where it was felt that departure from current English usage would be distracting" (Brachin 1985, vii).

Finally, Geyl copied by many others in Belgium and Holland, for obvious reasons also attempted to coin the word Netherlandic or Netherlandish instead of Dutch. It did not have the desired effect and has been given up altogether.

The Dutch Language Territory

Not only the name of the Dutch language but also the borders of its territory in Europe are problematic. These borders delimit the area where Dutch is an official language, and one of them runs through one of the Dutch provinces, namely, Friesland. Although on a European scale this isn't really an exceptional

---

[5] Quote originally in the first edition of 1936.
[6] Quote originally in the Preface to the second edition (1961).

occurrence, it has to be noticed that it is not a real border, since all Frisians also speak Dutch.

The border that separates Dutch from its neighbor, German, almost runs parallel to the state border between Holland and Germany, although it also cuts off a small part of Belgium. It has been stable for some time now, although until the early 20th century German was used in some parts of Limburg,

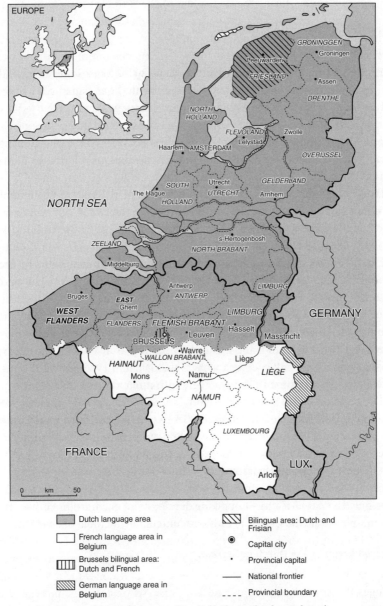

FIGURE 1.1 Dutch Language Area (Courtesy of Ons Erfdeel vzw, Flanders, Belgium)

whereas Dutch still had some functions in some German areas close to the border.

The most legendary language border, though, is the Dutch–French one, the crash barrier in Belgium that separates Flemings from Walloons. It is internationally famous for the cohabitation problems both peoples have had and are still struggling with up to the present day. A small part of that Dutch–French border is situated in France (fig. 1-1).

THE DUTCH–GERMAN BORDER

Dialect Borders

It has never been possible to identify a clear-cut border between the dialects spoken on both sides of the Dutch–German border that share such important features (not existing in the Dutch standard language or in the more Western dialects) as the so-called Saxon common plural (see chapter 2), morphological umlaut alternations in the building of the diminutive or of the plural (chapters 2 and 3), or the tone opposition (*stoottoon* >< *sleeptoon*) shared by Limburg and the bordering German Rhineland.

However, when dialect speakers on both sides of the border, whose dialects are almost identical, read a book or write a letter, the Dutch one will read and write standard Dutch, whereas his German counterpart will read and write standard German (Donaldson 1983, 11).

Due to dialect decline and the ever-increasing penetration of the respective standard languages on both sides of the border, what used to be a dialect continuum is rapidly falling apart into two different language areas. Studies published in Bister-Broosen (1998) detail all aspects of this evolution and demonstrate how the differing standard languages finally even affect the dialects themselves. Even so, the borderline between the Dutch- and German-speaking parts hasn't always been what it is today: in the course of the centuries some (smaller) adjustments did occur in both directions.

The region situated around the river IJssel used to be part of the so-called Saxon (i.e., Low German) territory, but from the 14th to 15th century onward, its urban centers (Deventer, Zwolle, and Kampen as well as Zutphen and Doesburg) were increasingly influenced by the Westerly flavored written Dutch and became a linguistically mixed area (Barbour & Stevenson 1990, 85).

From the 17th century onward, it was gradually integrated into the Dutch language territory. An almost opposite development occurs in the Lower Rhine region, one of the most ancient cultural centers and a cradle of Old Dutch

The Last Remnants of Dutch in Germany

Starting in the 16th century we witness how, as a consequence of political changes, the Lower Rhine region gradually loses its Western ties and is integrated into the German-speaking territory. The same development occurred in some territories to the north of the Lower Rhine, where Dutch used to be an important language in such domains as religion, education, city administration, and was sometimes even used as the prestige language of the upper layers of urban society. The language used in Kleve has been regarded for a long time as one of the important varieties of Dutch (Muller 1939, 69). The more Dutch and High German both developed into widely used languages of writing and culture, the more clear-cut the language border became. The process was gaining momentum, as the regional vernaculars on both sides were increasingly influenced by their respective standard languages.

Nevertheless, even as of today, a lot of Dutch is still present in the dialects in question. In Krefeld, for instance, we find phrases like *He het et dröck* (Dutch *hij heeft het druk* [he is very busy]) or *Ech kann net mihr Papp segge* (Dutch *ik kan geen pap meer zeggen* [to be dead beat]) or words like *aantrecke* (Dutch *aantrekken* [change into]), *schnöppe* (Dutch *snoepen* [eat sweets]), and both *quiesel* (Dutch *kwezel* [bigot]) and *schlonz* (Dutch *slons* [slut]), all of which are incomprehensible to the average speaker of German but pose no problem at all for speakers of Dutch (Bister-Broosen 1998). On the other hand, since dialect usage has become almost extinct, the whole Lower Rhine region is an integral part of the German language territory now, and the bonds with Dutch are hardly felt anymore, even though the state border is not far away.

In the more northern border regions, the evolution has been different, although the outcome eventually was the same. The fact that Dutch continued to be used east of the border, in some cases until the end of the 19th century, must be explained by the influence of religion. The religious controversies between Roman Catholics, Lutherans, and Calvinists left their marks on the language map from the north (East Friesland) to the south (Lower Rhine). However, the exact role played by each religion was not predictable and varied from region to region.

In Emden, already a refuge for Calvinists in the 16th century, both Dutch and Low German dialects were favored to the detriment of High German. In the major Lower Rhine city of Kleve, where Dutch already had a long tradition throughout the Middle Ages, Dutch profited from the fact that the Catholic majority heavily opposed the High German of the new Prussian, Lutheran rulers. In protestant Bentheim, it was the Calvinists who preferred Dutch over the language of Martin Luther's bible. However, in Gronau, where Dutch Calvinist *dominees* (preachers) were active from the 17th century on, a curious form of triglossia lived on till the end of the 19th century: the local Low German dialect was the habitual means of oral communication, whereas both Dutch and High German enjoyed specific and well-defined functions as the languages of education, church, and administration. Lingen finally changed both religion and nationality a couple of times; in 1648, with the Treaty of Westphalia, it ended up a Roman Catholic, Dutch enclave in German territory, and Dutch was the only official language. The language situation didn't change when, in

1702, it was transferred to Prussia, yet in 1810 under its next ruler, Hanover, Dutch was quite rapidly traded in for High German.

These days, hardly anything is left of the Dutch past of those regions and language use is regulated, as everywhere else, by the German–Dutch national border.

German-Speaking Belgium

Apart from Flanders, there is yet another territory in Belgium where a Germanic language is spoken. It is divided into two parts known in linguistic literature (though not in any administrative sense) as Neubelgien and Altbelgien (New Belgium and Old Belgium). The former is Belgium's official German-speaking part, whereas in the latter German has by now become a minority language in an officially French-only speaking territory. Both areas are situated in the eastern part of Belgium, adjacent to Germany and Luxembourg (fig. 1.1).

In the 13th century, the Land van Overmaas (Goossens 1998), to which all these territories belonged, became part of the Duchy of Brabant and shared its general and linguistic fate for a long time. By the end of the Ancien Régime, a triglossic situation had developed: Dutch was the language of the administration; High German was the language of the school and the church; and the population communicated by means of a local dialect from which it is impossible (and also futile) to determine on the basis of linguistic criteria whether it was (or is) a Dutch or German dialect (Nelde 1979, 69). From the split of the Low Countries onward the region underwent the same Frenchification process that occurred in Flanders at large.

At the Congress of Vienna in 1815 the region was split: part of it (later known as New Belgium) went to Prussia; the rest (Old Belgium) remained in the United Kingdom of the Netherlands and after 1830 in Belgium. In 1839 the larger part of the latter returned to the Dutch King William I and has been known ever since as the Grand Duchy of Luxembourg. As a result of the Frenchification policy of the Belgian authorities and of the loss of four-fifths of its speakers to Luxembourg, French gradually superseded German in all official and formal domains in Altbelgien. Since it is geographically situated within the Walloon part of Belgium, the Frenchification never stopped; as of today French is its sole official language, and German, if still used at all, has become limited to the private domain (Darquennes 2005).

The fate of New Belgium was completely different. During the time it was part of Prussia (later the German Empire), German was firmly established not only as its official language but also as the habitual means of communication of the population. The situation changed dramatically, though, when after WWI the Versailles Treaty allocated the region to Belgium as war booty. The Belgian authorities provided for no autonomy or linguistic protection whatsoever, and both the habitual Frenchification policy and the usual mechanisms of upward social mobility accomplished that French became both the language of administration and also increasingly a language mastered and used by the upper social strata of the population. However, the inhabitants eventually profited from the struggle of the Flemings against francophone dominance. Linguistic legislation in 1963, which installed the territoriality principle, upgraded German to an official language of the area, which, as a consequence of the subsequent constitutional changes became an autonomous region. The Deutschsprachige Gemeinschaft, as it is now officially called, comprises the cantons of Eupen and Sankt Vith (some 65,000 people on 867 square kilometers) and has qualifications identical to those of the Flemish and Walloon communities. Having its own parliament and government, its population now constitutes, as Héraud (1989) observes, "probably the best protected linguistic minority in Europe." German is the official language of the administration, education, and the judicial system, and it is the everyday language of those who live there.

THE DUTCH-FRISIAN BORDER

The only indigenous minority language in the Netherlands is Frisian, which has regional official status in the province of Friesland (approximately 4 percent of the Dutch population) (fig. 1-2). A total of 340,000 of the 650,000 inhabitants are mother-tongue speakers of Frisian, and 460,000 in all claim to have "at least reasonable proficiency" (Gorter 2001, 231). Frisian is in limited official use as a language of provincial and city administrations, of education, of the media, and of the courts. There is some active promotion of the language by the regional and almost none by the national authorities. Although no real census figures exist as to the mastery and the use of Frisian, a lot of statistical information has recently been made available by the province of Friesland, based on a large-scale quick scan carried out in 2006. The most important figures have been published in *Provincie Fryslan* (2007), and all can be accessed at http://www.fryslan.nl. According to the quick scan, some 94 percent of the Frisians can understand Frisian, 73 percent can speak it, 75 percent can read it, but only some 26 percent can write it. Whereas the understanding and speaking ability has hardly changed since the first inquiries in the sixties, the reading ability has made light progress, whereas the writing competence increased significantly from 10 to 26 percent.

Active usage of the language is mainly concentrated in the domains of the family and the neighborhood, and the patterns of usage reveal that it is the habitual tongue of some 70 percent of the rural population and of only some 40 percent of the town dwellers (in Friesland's capital Leeuwarden, less than 40 percent of the population claim to have Frisian as a mother tongue; Provincie Fryslan 2007, 15). Its use in the educational system is still very limited. Since 1980 it has become an obligatory part of the primary school curriculum (Ytsma 1995), and since 1993 it has "obtained a modest place in

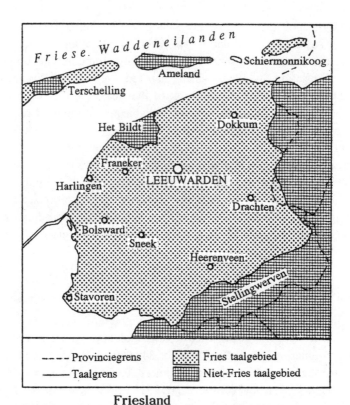

Friesland

FIGURE 1.2 "Friesland" = Map of the Frisian Language Territory
Legend: "Provinciegrens" = Province border; "Taalgrens" = Language border; "Fries taalgebied" = Frisian Language Territory; "niet-Fries taalgebied" = non Frisian Language Territory.

the first three grades of secondary school" (Gorter 1996, 1155). The use of Frisian in the educational system is considered one of the spearheads of language policy, which is mainly coordinated by the Fryske Akademy, a mostly scholarly body engaged in both status and corpus planning. The publication of a scientific dictionary (with normative authority) is one of its major projects, and the 25 volumes of *Wurdboek fan de Fryske taal/Woordenboek der Friese taal* (WFT) were officially put online by Queen Beatrix on July 6, 2010 (http://www.fryske-akademy.nl).

The spelling system the Fryske Akademy has devised has been officially authorized by the provincial government in 1980. There is no prescriptive grammar yet; Tiersma (1999²) is a reference grammar written in English. The history of Frisian literature is detailed in Oppewal et al. (2006).

The Dutch authorities have always been insecure and often rather hostile in dealing with the Frisian situation. Most of the time they have been reluctant to grant official rights to Frisian speakers, and as of today the official policy is mainly one of tolerating rather than of promoting or supporting the Frisian language. After the Netherlands ratified the European Charter for Minority Languages, it automatically accepted the task of promoting the Frisian language. On February 12, 2011, the Minister van Binnenlandse Zaken (Home Office) Donner declared on Frisian radio that a new language law is in the making, guaranteeing that all inhabitants of the province will have the right to choose whether to use Frisian or Dutch in court and in communication with the authorities. A Council for the Frisian Language will be installed, meant to stimulate, and thus guarantee, the use of Frisian.

Even so, Frisian has been on the loser's side for centuries: it has been and still is losing territorially, functionally, and socially. Frisian used to be the habitual language of a much larger territory than it is now, such as in Groningen and the northern part of the province of North Holland, from which it has gradually vanished since the Middle Ages. Its social prestige has diminished considerably as well, since Dutch is undoubtedly the prestige language and functioning monolingually in Frisian has become impossible, even within Fryslân, as the province is now officially named. Still, Gorter (2001, 230) feels that "things have, on the whole, not gotten worse for Frisian." The diglossic situation of old is disappearing since Dutch has entered "the intimate spheres of the home, friends, family and neighbourhood" (Gorter 2001, 231). On the other hand, "Frisian has made inroads in areas where it was not used 50 years ago," such as education, media and public administration" (ibid.). "However," Gorter adds, "as a written language Frisian has remained quite marginal, thus there still is a diglossic distribution between spoken and written language functions" (ibid.).

A number of structural processes work against the use of Frisian, and, on top of that, Frisian is increasingly influenced by Dutch to the point that "the quality of the language is deteriorating and Frisian may at a certain point run the risk of dissolving into Dutch" (Gorter 2001, 231). This contact not only affects the language itself but also still gives way to language shift, mainly in the upper social strata and the urban population. Frisian is the native tongue of the majority of the population of Friesland, but even they do not always speak Frisian but have to switch to Dutch for specific functions and on specific occasions. Consequently, Frisian is seriously in danger of losing an increasing number of functions to Dutch, its more prestigious rival.

Finally, the migration pattern (with some 25,000 Frisians yearly leaving the province and approximately an identical number of non-Frisian Dutch immigrating) is potentially threatening for the use and eventual survival of Frisian.

THE DUTCH–FRENCH LANGUAGE BORDER

As far as the Dutch–French language border is concerned, we have to differentiate between the smaller part in France and the larger one in Belgium.

The Dutch–French Language Border in France

A small group of native speakers of Dutch exists in northern France, and although language shift has reduced the number dramatically during the last two centuries it is still common practice to locate the westernmost part of the Romance–Germanic language border in the French Département du Nord. Native speakers of West Flemish dialects are concentrated in the so-called Westhoek, in the *arrondissements* of Dunkirk (Dutch: Duinkerke) and of Hazebroek. This piece of northern France used to be part of Dutch-speaking Flanders until 1678, when it was annexed by the French crown as a result of the Treaty of Nijmegen. It remained under French rule forever more and is (colloquially) known as Frans Vlaanderen (French Flanders) (fig. 1-3).

At the moment of its annexation by France, the Westhoek was monolingually Dutch speaking (Ryckeboer 2002). Although the language shift process started almost right away, it gained momentum only after the French Revolution as a consequence of a concerted Frenchification policy and legislation on the part of the French authorities. The Jacobin philosophy that all power had to be concentrated in and should emerge from Paris could be effective only on a one country, one language basis. Also, it was believed that French was the only language fit to propagate and diffuse the ideals of the French Revolution. Consequently, French had to supplant all national and regional idioms, and in 1806 the major towns of Dunkirk and Gravelines (Dutch: Grevelingen) appeared to already be intensely gallicized, as can be seen from a linguistic inquiry carried out by Coquebert de Montbret (Brunot 1905–1979, vol. 9, 525). The same inquiry also reveals that in the remaining Westhoek Dutch was still the habitual language of everyday communication in all but some 10 villages. Every subsequent investigation (all listed in Pée 1957) documents further language loss.

The most recent as well as the most complete and reliable data available were collected between 1935 and 1939 by the dialectologist and professor of Dutch linguistics Willem Pée. His main conclusion was, "Should industrialization not be stopped instantly, then my prediction is that, in a rather near future, Dutch will be pushed backward toward the Belgian border, where it may still survive for quite some time in a few border villages" (Pée 1957, 57). Industrialization was, on the contrary, intensified even more.

Nowadays the use made of Dutch has become so restricted that in France the language border in the habitual sense of the word has actually ceased to exist (Ryckeboer 2002). Although this does not mean that Dutch has completely vanished from the Westhoek we are witnessing one of the ultimate stages of *language death*. Monolingual Dutch speakers are completely extinct, and only a very limited number of senior citizens still have Dutch as their habitual tongue. Hence, it is impossible that the mastery of the language, or even its passive knowledge, may be handed down to the next generations.

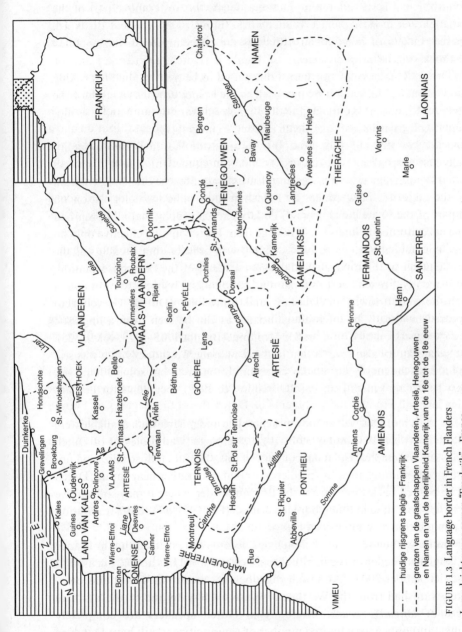

FIGURE 1.3 Language border in French Flanders

Legend right upper corner: "Frankrijk" = France

Legend left lower corner: "huidige rijksgrens België-Frankrijk" = contemporary state border Belgium-France; "grenzen van de graafschappen Vlaanderen, Artesië, Henegouwen en Namen" = county borders of Flanders, Artois, Hainault and Namur

Within the map:

- - - - - huidige rijsgrens belgië - Frankrijk

- - - - - grenzen van de graafschappen Vlaanderen, Artesië, Henegouwen en Namen en van de heerlijkheid Kamerijk van de 16e tot 18e eeuw

Summarizing, we see how Frenchification was initiated by political events that have disconnected parts of Flanders from the motherland. Consequently, the inhabitants lost contact in a number of domains of which language is probably the most spectacular one. Through annexation by France, the language variety in use in these parts became roofless (in the sense of Kloss 1976). This entailed functional as well as structural loss and, hence, reduced its communicative value decisively.

Theoretically, a language can survive for a long time even under the circumstances just mentioned. Subsequent extralinguistic factors, though, may be the prelude to almost complete attrition. Conscious discrimination through linguistic legislation is one of them. Another is growing industrialization and a considerable internal migration (in both directions) that annihilates the linguistic homogeneity of the region and, consequently, the usability of the minority language. Social integration took care of the rest: mastery and usage of the majority language appear to be so indispensable for upward social mobility (and social life in general) that they easily overcome solidarity factors such as cultural and linguistic loyalty.

The combination of all these factors hardly ever allows for more than a short transitional period of bilingualism. The minority language, structurally and functionally impoverished and no longer supported by innovating injections from a genetically related standard language, stands no chance against the domestic majority language and thus gradually vanishes. The only lasting consequence of the cultural heritage in these parts may lie in the field of foreign language acquisition and mastery: since Dutch is now again available as a subject in French schools and since a considerable number of private Dutch classes also have emerged during recent decades, it may be assumed that French Flanders will produce more students of Dutch than other regions of France, where it is not part of the cultural heritage. Together with a considerable amount of place and family names this may be, in the not distant future, the only remnant of the Dutch past of French Flanders.

The Dutch–French Language Border in Belgium

Belgium (11 million inhabitants) is a trilingual and federal country, consisting of four different entities constituted on the basis of language: the Dutch-speaking community (called Flanders; 58 percent of the population); the French-speaking one (called Wallonia; 32 percent); the small German-speaking community (0.5 percent); and the Dutch–French bilingual community of Brussels (9.5 percent). Since regional governments have legislative power, the frontiers of their jurisdiction, being language borders, are defined in the constitution.

Although the language border has existed for centuries, no solid information prior to the 19th century is available as far as the territory of present-day Belgium is concerned. In 1846, the recently established Kingdom of Belgium started conducting censuses including a question on language usage that provided statistical information until 1947 (De Metsenaere 1998). For various reasons the information gathered this way is often inaccurate: the exact wording of the questions was changed from one census to another. More important still, two basic requirements for reliable information gathering, namely, honest intentions and scientific support, were hardly ever met, as has been convincingly demonstrated by Gubin (1978).

The most important insight yielded by the first census in 1846 is that the administrative division of the country into provinces, *arrondissementen* (counties), and even communes had been carried out without taking into account the language border at all and that it had never been the intention to provide for more or less linguistically homogeneous administrative entities. Also, the information yielded perfectly allowed to draw a language map showing a borderline neatly separating the French-speaking (i.e., Walloon dialect) and the Dutch-speaking (i.e., Flemish dialect) communities. For almost one century (and in spite of the deficient methodology) there were (with the exception of Brussels) no significant differences from one census to another (Martens 1975), a fact demonstrating the remarkable stability of Belgium's linguistic communities.

A dramatic change occurred in 1932, the year in which the language border became a political issue. A century of struggle by the Flemish Movement (see chapter 6) in favor of the promotion of Dutch in a country up to then dominated by French speakers had finally resulted in extensive linguistic legislation bringing about the de facto acceptance of the territoriality principle (McRae 1975; see box 1.2), which implied that Flanders was to be governed exclusively in Dutch and Wallonia exclusively in French. To implement this decision, though, a precise legal description of the delimitation of these territories, in other words of the language border, was needed. Although the 1932 laws did not provide such a description, they held a provision that communes with a linguistic minority of at least 30 percent were to be governed bilingually and that, should a minority become the majority, the linguistic status of the commune was to change accordingly. This seems to be fair enough, were it not that the only means of acquiring the information needed was the census that thus, unfortunately, acquired important political significance (see chapter 6 for a more detailed analysis).

The first census with these political implications was scheduled for 1940 but was postponed because of World War II, and when in 1947 it was finally carried out it resulted in an outburst of political commotion. Contrasting heavily with the stability the returns had shown for more than a century, it appeared that this time not only were notorious shifts registered but also they all went in the same direction: many Dutch-speaking villages appeared to harbor so many French speakers that they turned into either bilingual or even French-speaking communes (Martens 1975). Since fraudulent maneuvering by (local as well as national)

BOX 1.2 } Personality and Territoriality Principle

Multilingual countries mostly regulate the use of their official languages according to either the personality or the territoriality principle (McRae 1975). The personality principle means that all citizens, regardless of where they live, can decide for themselves in which language they want to communicate with the authorities. This implies that the government has to guarantee that all its services are made available in every official language all over the country (Canada is an example). The territoriality principle means that the place where citizens live decides in which language they are addressed by the authorities. People living, for example, in German-speaking Switzerland or French-speaking Belgium are addressed by their federal government in German and French, respectively, regardless of their own linguistic preference. The language border is the legal means of delimiting the areas in which a particular language is the official one. In Belgium, the legislator has rearranged all domestic administrative divisions into monolingual entities. Both the language border and the territoriality principle are defined in the constitution.

Often there is some kind of combination of both principles. In Brussels, for example, the territoriality principle was not workable, for lack of a geographically delimitation of the languages spoken in the officially bilingual capital.

authorities was very apparent, the Flemish reaction was extremely vigorous, and the government was finally forced to skip language questions from future census questionnaires altogether and to look for a political solution that might, once and for all, determine the language border between the communities.

A law to this effect came into being on September 1, 1963, and since its underlying philosophy was to produce linguistically homogeneous administrative entities, several adjustments had to be made, transferring 25 communes with 87,450 inhabitants from Flanders to Wallonia and 24 communes with 23,250 inhabitants from Wallonia to Flanders (detailed information in Martens 1975; Verhulst, De Metsenaere, & Deweerdt 1998).

Another provision of the 1963 law was the installment of communes with so-called *faciliteiten* (linguistic facilities; De Schryver 1998), meaning that if a community harbored a considerable linguistic minority (on the date of September 1, 1963) provisions were to be made enabling this minority to communicate in its own language with communal authorities and to obtain possibilities for instruction in its own language. This status was allotted to a restricted number of communes on both sides of the language border. This was a paramount blunder, jeopardizing the functioning of an otherwise perfectly working system. The major provision, though, meant to put minds at rest, was that after September 1, 1963, changes in the linguistic status of communes and provinces became virtually impossible and could be brought about only through a very complicated procedure of changing the constitution. On top of a two-thirds majority required for any constitutional change, those with linguistic implications require a majority within both language factions of the Belgian parliament. Almost everywhere this peace of mind was indeed brought about, with two notorious exceptions: the so-called Voerstreek and the Brussels suburban region (the so-called Randgemeenten) (fig. 1-4).

THE VOERSTREEK

The Voerstreek is part of the so-called Land van Overmaas, a small territory situated between the major cities of Aachen (Germany), Maastricht (the Netherlands), and Liége (Wallonia, Belgium). During the Ancien Régime Dutch was the language of instruction and administration in the whole Overmaas territory (Goossens 1998), but subsequently both a Germanifying and a Frenchifying tendency had become apparent. Also, it has always been nearly impossible to distinguish between Dutch and German dialects in the region on the basis of purely linguistic criteria (Nelde 1979, 41).

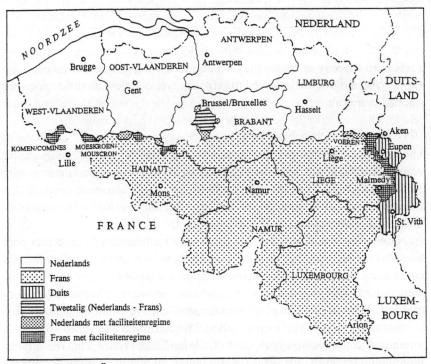

Taalgebieden in België

FIGURE 1.4 "Taalgebieden in België" = Language Territories in Belgium
Legend: "Nederlands" = Dutch; "Frans" = French; "Duits" = German; Tweetalig (Nederlands-Frans)" =
Bilingual (Dutch-French); "Nederlands met faciliteitenregime" = Dutch with linguistic 'facilities' for
French speakers ; "Frans met faciliteitenregime" = French with linguistic 'facilities' for Dutch speakers

From the end of World War I onward, when the Eupen region, a former Prussian possession, was annexed by Belgium, the 17 Overmaas communes were part of three different linguistic regimes (Goossens 1998), two of which (Old Belgium and New Belgium) were previously dealt with.

This leaves the six communes of the Voerstreek, which gained political celebrity and a wretched reputation during the final decades of the 20th century (Murphy 1988). Subject to both the Frenchification process, which also affected the other communes in the region, and (mostly) to Walloon immigration they turned out a linguistically mixed region with a French-speaking minority. For that reason the 1963 law transferred them from the Walloon province of Liége to the Flemish province of Limburg. Since, however, they are not geographically linked to the latter province and were dependent, for various economic functions, on Liége, some of its inhabitants were not very happy with this transfer. This uneasiness has been exploited by Walloon activists, causing political commotion for a long time. Still, both Flemish determination and changes in the constitution that put the Voerstreek firmly under the authority of the autonomous government of Flanders seem to have lessened political tension a good deal. From 1964 through 2000 the political faction advocating a return to the francophone province of Liége managed to secure an ever diminishing majority in the local city council (Vandermeeren 1996). From October 2000 on, though, the opposite faction came into power. Consequently, a return to Liége is no longer on the political agenda of Voeren's city council and of the majority of its inhabitants. Linguistic unrest in the region has stopped ever since.

THE BRUSSELS SUBURBAN REGION

The 1963 law also affected the status of some suburbs in the Brussels region where the officially bilingual territory is restricted to 19 communes that together constitute Brussels as a political entity. Ongoing Frenchification of Brussels also affected some of its suburbs. Mostly because of immigration of French speakers some of these communes lost their former exclusively Dutch-speaking character, and pressure was put on consecutive governments to annex them to bilingual Brussels (Sieben 1986). Yet surrendering to francophone demands was politically unfeasible and, afterward, made constitutionally impossible. Some of these suburbs, though, appeared to harbor not only important French-speaking minorities but in some cases even de facto majorities. Six of them—Drogenbos, Kraainem, Linkebeek, Sint-Genesius-Rode, Wemmel, and Wezenbeek-Oppem— officially received a *faciliteiten* system (De Witte 1975; Witte 1993; De Schryver 1998) but remained part of Flanders and, consequently, officially Dutch speaking. This way the risk of Francophone overspill to other than these six communes had been considerably diminished. The constitutional change of 1993 also provided for the split of the province of Brabant from January 1, 1995, into the province Vlaams Brabant (Flemish Brabant) and the province Brabant

Wallon (Walloon Brabant), cutting the Brussels periphery for good from the capital (Detant 1998). This furthered the increasing homogeneity of the language territory through assimilation of minority language islands but has not yet appeased the situation in the six *faciliteiten* communes. Prolonged governmental crises in 2007 and 2010–2011 are mainly due to that problem. A new change of the constitution is part of the government program of the six-party coalition government that was sworn in on December 6, 2011, after tortuous negotiations lasting 540 days. It guarantees the split (both administratively and judicially) of the Flemish communes of the cantons Halle and Vilvoorde (including the six *faciliteiten* communes) from Brussels, with which they used to form one entity and one constituency. This split was approved in parliament in July 2012.

As a result of the aforementioned changes, we are now in the presence of a firmly monolingualized Belgium, divided into autonomous communities based on linguistic homogeneity and determined to reduce the political consequences of language contact at their borders to a strict minimum. In so doing the language border has become the most important internal boundary to which all preexisting administrative delimitations were subordinated.

In Belgium at large the language border is no longer a mere linguistic notion but a legal, administrative and political reality. This evolution has completely changed the nature of the coexistence of the country's various linguistic communities—firmly embedded in their own monolingual structures—and has also demonstrated how decisive the implications of language planning activities can be (Willemyns 2002) (box 1.3).

One problem though, has never been solved (and isn't even as of today): that of Brussels, the only part of Belgium where the comforting territoriality principle is not applicable.

BOX 1.3 } The Language Border Stinks

> In one of Belgium's leading newspapers *De Standaard* on October 16, 2000, a Flemish government official is quoted as saying, "Since we are understaffed we have no means of preventing illegal crossing of our borders at night." This newspaper article is not about people trying to illegally enter Belgium; the border the official is referring to is the language border. Flanders and Wallonia appear to have a different legislation on the treatment of manure, and apparently some Flemish farmers are transporting their excess manure to Wallonia. Although language is not involved at all, it is very significant that the term *language border* is used in the title of the article: "*Mest steekt's nachts illegaal de taalgrens over*" [Manure is illegally crossing the language border at night]. This is one striking example of how very real the notion of language border can become.

Brussels

Until the 19th century, Brussels shared its linguistic fate with other Flemish cities: an important part of the social elite was bilingual and used French for most of the traditional culture and social language functions. The majority of the population spoke a dialect of Dutch. Since Frenchification was stopped and eventually reversed in Flanders but not in Brussels, an explanation can be found only in factors specific to the Brussels situation.

Ever since the start of the Burgundian period in the 15th century (see chapter 3), Brussels has been a capital, and consequently the number of courtiers, noblemen, and influential government officials and civil servants has always been larger than elsewhere. It is precisely in these groups of people that the influence (and usage) of French has always been the most important. Frenchification after the annexation by France was more intensive here than elsewhere in Flanders, not the least because of the presence of an influential group of French immigrants.

After 1830, Brussels emerged as a symbol of Belgium, and here the one country, one language principle appeared to be more appropriate than elsewhere. The strongly centralizing Belgian policy resulted in a disproportional high concentration of the country's financial and industrial power in the Francophone milieu of the capital. Since power and wealth essentially used to derive from Walloon industry, it is hardly surprising that the elite particularly favored this region and its language.

On rather short notice, Brussels became a pole of attraction to numerous immigrants. Between 1830 and 1840 the population quadrupled (De Metsenaere & Witte 1990, 3). Flemish immigrants mostly consisted of lower-class and poor people, whereas Walloon immigrants mostly were upper-working-class and middle-class people (De Metsenaere 1998). The latter immediately fortified the Francophone population. As to the former, "The pressure from the top social stratum to adopt its French language filtered down through the middle-classes and from them into the 'labour aristocracy' of skilled workers, but generally stopping short at the lowest categories of service personnel and day labourers, made up to a large extent in the nineteenth century of Flemish immigrants to the capital" (Baetens Beardsmore 1990, 2). Consequently, until far into the 20th century, being Flemish (and speaking Dutch) used to be associated with being poor or even being socially and culturally retarded.

An additional handicap for both immigrant and autochthonous Dutch-speaking Brusselers was that their habitual language was a dialect, that is, a variety with a very limited social prestige. Consequently, the majority of the lower middle and working classes tried to acquire mastery in the only language that appeared to make upward social mobility at all possible. Hence, the attractiveness of the French educational system was immense in a period of rapid development of mass education. The unprofessional and fraudulent censuses in Brussels (Gubin 1978) showed an enormous increase of the statistical amount of allegedly French-speaking inhabitants, and the judicial consequences of censuses were very real.

An additional reason that the development in Brussels was different from Antwerp or Ghent was that most of the linguistic legislation either did not apply to Brussels or, worse still, had to be paid for by concessions intensifying the Frenchification of the capital. This situation changed as soon as the major struggle in Flanders was over and the Flemish Movement could start paying attention to the capital as well (Witte & Van Velthoven 1998, 2010).

The turning point appears to have been when Flemings agreed to give up the advantages of their numerical majority in the country at large in favor of parity in administration for Brussels. This implied, among other things, that Dutch-speaking Brusselers, even after having become a minority group, were nevertheless allotted half of the high-ranking civil servants in the administration of Brussels' 19 communes (Willemyns 2002). Several measures taken by the federal government guarantee Dutch speakers in Brussels a position on all kinds of levels, which they never could have extorted by virtue of their sole numerical strength.

Education in Brussels is a story of its own. From the late 1970s onward, there has been a constant increase of the population of Dutch schools as opposed to the decrease of the school population in the country at large and in French schools in Brussels in particular. The reinstallment of the so-called freedom of the head of the family meant that, rather unexpectedly, many heads of French-speaking as well as foreign families use their freedom to choose Dutch education for their children. Pupils in Brussels' Dutch schools increasingly originate from linguistically mixed or homogeneously French-speaking households. In recent years nonnative speakers of Dutch constitute the majority of the pupils in many Dutch-speaking schools (Janssens 2007; Mettewie 2007).

Flanders' increasing economic resources made it possible to put up structures in Brussels that enabled "the individual to function as a monolingual. Schools, hospitals, welfare services, cultural instances, recreational facilities have all been set up to service either community in its own language" (Baetens Beardsmore 1990, 5). It enabled the Brussels Flemings also to profit maximally from the gain in prestige Dutch had acquired in the country at large.

Finally, the rapidly expanding population of foreign origin accounts for the fact that for more that one-third of the capital's citizens none of Belgium's languages is their mother tongue. Yet, for the majority of those, French is their first Belgian language. The importance and use of English is rapidly growing as well, and in private business many important jobs and positions are occupied by trilinguals, that is, people who are proficient in English, French, and Dutch (Mettewie & Van Mensel 2009).

2 }

Old Dutch: Its Ancestors and Contemporaries

Indo-Europeans and Germani

THE INDO-EUROPEAN LANGUAGE FAMILY

Dutch is a Germanic language as are, for example, English, German, or Danish. French, on the other hand, although a neighboring tongue, is not a Germanic but a Romance language. That does not mean that they are unrelated: they both descend from the so-called Indo-European language family.

We call Indo-European a group of related languages that used to be spoken in Europe and Asia. Apart from Germanic and Romance languages, the Celtic and Slavic languages are also part of this group as well as, for example, Sanskrit, Hittite, or Avestic, all predecessors of languages now spoken in Asia.

Sir William Jones, a British judge stationed in India, established that Sanskrit bore a striking resemblance to two other ancient languages of his acquaintance, Latin and Greek. He was not the first to notice similarities, but no one before Jones had studied them systematically. The Sanskrit language, he announced to the Asiatick Society on the evening of February 2, 1786, shared with Greek and Latin "a stronger affinity than could possibly have been produced by accident" (McCrum, Cran, & MacNeil 1987, 51). It is obvious, he said, that they have sprung from some common source, which "perhaps, no longer exists" (ibid.). Two centuries of linguistic research have only strengthened Jones's basic proposition.

"When we notice that *father* corresponds to Dutch *vader*, Gothic *fadar*, Old Norse *faðir*, German *Vater*, Greek *pater*, Sanskrit *pitar*...or that English *brother* corresponds to Dutch *broeder*, German *Bruder*, Greek *phrater*, Sanskrit *bhratar-*, Old Slavic *bratu*, we are led to the hypothesis that the languages of a large part of Europe and part of Asia were at one time identical," Baugh and Cable (1978, 18) observe, and they add: "the extensive literature of India...preserves features of the common language much older than most of those of

Greek or Latin or German. It is easier, for example, to see the resemblance between the English word *brother* and the Sanskrit *bhratar-* than between *brother* and Latin *frater*."

There are no written records of the common Indo-European language. By comparing the oldest extant forms of its more important descendants, 19th-century scholars were able to reconstruct some of the essential features of its vocabulary and inflection. Declensions and conjugations showed a rich variety of inflexional forms, and such a highly complicated inflexional system points to a long period of development. The period of time over which this process is spread is impossible even to estimate.

As far as numbers are concerned, the Indo-European language family appears to have been the most successful on Earth. The languages of about one-third of the human race come from this common source. In the top 10 languages with the largest number of native speakers, 7 are from Indo-European stock: English, Spanish, Hindi, Bengali, Russian, Portuguese, and German. The remaining three are Chinese, Arabic, and Japanese.

THE GENESIS AND GROWTH OF GERMANIC

Who the first Indo-European tribes were, and when and where exactly they lived, is a hotly disputed mystery. It is mostly assumed that Indo-European was the language spoken by a group of people pertaining to the so-called Kurgan culture. It is generally believed that this specific culture developed during the fifth millennium BC in a region north of the Caspian Sea. Some 1,000 years later, the Kurgan peoples were drifting in the direction of Europe, and still another 1,000 years after that they had arrived in Scandinavia, the Low Countries, and Northern Germany. In the course of time the Indo-European community split up, for reasons we do not know. As far as the disintegration of the Indo-European community (if ever community there was) and the development of separate languages is concerned, Chambers and Wilkie (1981, 15) are probably right that the process was "a very complex one, different for each language and probably impossible to reconstruct in any detail."

One of the first signs of Germanic[1] gradually building an independent language group marking them off from other Indo-Europeans is the so-called accent shift, that is, the gradual fixing of the accent on the root syllable of the word as opposed to the former varying position for stress in related words or different forms of the same word (as is, e.g., the case in present-day English *photo*graph and pho*to*grapher). In so doing, initial stress has become one of the

---

[1] It is important to distinguish between *Germanic* and *German*. Yet, as Chambers and Wilkie (1981, 17) rightly observe, "There is no good English equivalent of '*Germanen*' to designate speakers of Germanic dialects." I will mostly go by their solution and "use the Latin form *Germani* or such phrases as 'Germanic tribes', 'Germanic peoples.'" (ibid.).

major characteristics of Proto-Germanic. An everlasting consequence has been the gradual disintegration of the complicated Indo-European case system. Since the final syllable of many words was no longer being stressed, much of the valuable information it contained was gradually getting lost (compare Latin where the sound difference between *servi* and *servo* indicates the case: genitive as opposed to dative). As soon as the final vowel becomes a muted ə (*schwa*), it is no longer possible to determine the case and, consequently, the case system gradually disintegrates.

The Proto-Germanic language is distinguished above all else by a phonological structure that sets off sharply from Indo-European. Those sound changes go under the heading *the Germanic sound shift,* and although the vocalic structure was also modified the most dramatic changes involved the consonants. In the consonant system, all Germanic languages share the reflexes of the so-called first consonant shift (better known as Grimm's law, since Jakob Grimm was the first to formulize those changes). This stipulates that certain series of Germanic obstruents correspond to related series in Indo-European. For example, the Indo-European voiceless stop series /p, t, k, kw/(as in Latin *piscis, tres, cornu, quando*) correspond to Proto-Germanic (also called Common Germanic, Dutch Oergermaans)/f, þ, X, Xw/ as in present-day English *fish, three, horn, when.* When this fricative series occurred in syllables that did not bear the main stress in Indo-European, they were additionally subject to voicing in Germanic: Gothic *broþar* (brother) as opposed to *fadar* (father) (this is called Verner's law). Also the "f" of Latin *frater* (brother) and *flos* (flower) developed into a "b" (cf. Gothic *broþar* and *bloma*). In the same way some other consonant strings changed as well. We don't know how long such changes took to complete, but we know that it was finished before the Germanic peoples established contact with the Romans in the first century B.C. The Goths left the Germanic homeland circa 150 A.D., and the extensive Gothic texts that came to us show the first consonant shift complete. Consequently, the whole thing probably has taken place between 500 B.C. and 150 A.D.

Among the other changes that distinguish Proto-Germanic from Indo-European are a number of vowel changes (e.g., a/o convergence, umlaut); disintegration of the system of *sonants*; the development of a second, weak declension of adjectives; and the development of weak verbs (Van Coetsem 1970). The strong verbs were organized according to a specific Proto-Germanic system called *ablaut,* which is based on a regular alternation of vowels as shown in the following example: Gothic *bindan-band-bundans,* Dutch *binden-bond-gebonden,* German *binden-bant-gebunden,* English *bind-bound-bound.* Details on all of this can be found in many books on the development of Indo-European and Germanic languages.

Of the territories where the Germani found a new home, some were bare and some were not and were settled by other peoples who, with or without their consent, have eventually been integrated in the tribes of the conquerors. Although some of their linguistic habits may have survived (as a substrate or in the form of loanwords and place names) their languages as such disappeared, sometimes even without leaving a trace. For example, according to the famous linguist and toponymist Maurits Gysseling, the Low Countries were, in Julius Caesar's times (from 58 B.C. onward), settled by tribes who spoke a language we don't even have a name for (for practical purposes he labeled it Belgisch [Belgian]) (Van Durme 2002). Some traces, he says, can still be found in place names and in an occasional Dutch word such as *pink* (little finger). It was only afterward that the Celts came; they were shortly after conquered in their turn by Germanic tribes. The Celtic languages had previously spread over much of southern and western Europe, including modern France, northern Italy, and Spain, in the first millennium B.C. The names of some Celtic tribes survive in modern names: for example, the name of the Belgae survives in the name of Belgium. The name Gallia survives in the adjective Gallic, referring to the French.

The cradle of what were to become the Germanic languages was located in a territory comprising southern Scandinavia and bordering Schleswig Holstein. It is from there that the Germani are believed to have started their trek in mostly southern and southeastern directions. This is how Van Coetsem (1970) describes it: somewhere around 750 B.C. northern Germany from the Ems to the Vistula (Weichsel) rivers was inhabited by Germanic tribes. Some two centuries later they were also found considerably more to the south, both on the Vistula and Elbe as well as on the Rhine side. The northern half of the territory between the coastal region and the Danube had by then been conquered by Germanic tribes. At that very moment their southwestern neighbors were the Celts and their southeastern ones the Illyrians, the Venetics, and later the Baltic people who in turn had Slavic people as their neighbors.

What we are witnessing here is a trek that lasted for centuries. The whole Germanic world seems to have been in fairly constant turmoil, whole tribes and confederations of tribes moving very long distances at remarkable speed. It eventually brought the Germanic peoples right where they are to be found nowadays. These impressive Great Migrations, though, eventually also put an end to the relative uniformity of the Germanic language.

BLOND AND BLUE-EYED BARBARIANS

The mysterious, nebulous realm inhabited by Germanic tribes was known to the Romans although they had no firsthand information. Their interest grew, though, as soon as an ambitious warlord directed his legions to the north in 58 B.C. In that year Caesar started his conquest of Gaul, or Gallia Transalpina, which is present-day France and Belgium. Being not only a gifted general but also a shrewd demagogue, he made sure his compatriots were informed of his exploits through his *De Bello Gallico*, his very own and obviously embellished account of his campaign in Gaul. In so doing, he was the first to give the Low Countries a place in historiography and millions of school children a Latin text much easier to understand than the language of Caesar's more sophisticated contemporaries. One of his many opponents were the Belgae, a people he deemed to be "the bravest of them all" (*horum omnium fortissimi sunt Belgae*).[2] To the north of the Belgae, on the opposite bank of the Rhine, were the Germani, valiant warriors who constituted a permanent threat to the Romans and their newly conquered territories (Van Loon 2010). The Roman historian Tacitus gives a description of them. Although he had never been in Germania himself and had only secondhand information at his disposal (from prisoners of war and slaves), he depicts them as tall, blond, and blue-eyed barbarians, brave and virtuous but addicted to dicing and booze. They live in a land with dreadful forests and horrible swamps. At any rate, they were the forbears of the present-day speakers of Germanic languages: the Scandinavians, the Germans, the inhabitants of the Low Countries, as well as the English.

In their new province of Gallia Belgica, the Romans built villas and most of all strategic highways and fortresses. The habits and costumes of the conquerors were mixed with those of the natives, who also eventually traded in their own language for the "vulgar Latin" of the Romans. Some of the Gallo-Roman settlements as Tongeren, Maastricht, and Nijmegen grew into opulent cities. Attempts to conquer the lands on the opposite bank of the Rhine failed.

Roman influence, consequently, is also visible in the many loanwords in the Germanic languages. Not only Roman politics and civilization as in *keizer* (Caesar), *villa, muur* (murus), and *straat* (strata) but also even plain everyday words such as *kaas* (caseus), *boter* (butyrum), *wijn* (vinum), and *ezel* (asinus) and many, many others found their way from Latin into most Germanic languages and are still with us today.

As late as roughly the second or first century B.C. the first faint historical allusions to the Germanic tribes occur. Although we must wait another six centuries for documents written in any of their languages, we begin to find references to the people in the writings of Roman and Greek historians, and—from the early Christian centuries onward—we have valuable testimony of the runes: letters carved on bone, stone, and metal by the Germanic people themselves. It is on the basis of all available information that we have been able to roughly reconstruct the account of the earliest migrations of the Germanic tribes that left their Scandinavian homeland.

Speakers of Germanic languages entered present-day Dutch language territory from the second century B.C. onward, and the path they followed can be quite adequately mapped, thanks to intensive and detailed studies of place names. Germanic tribes entered mostly by water, that is, via the Vlie, the IJssel, and the Vecht, descending from the coastal region of northern Germany and Groningen (Van Durme 2002). The area they occupied was huge, yet in many places linguistic enclaves persisted, often for centuries.

---

[2] A sentence proudly quoted very often in Belgian schools, whereby the fact that these Belgae have nothing whatsoever to do with present-day Belgians is mostly concealed.

In time, the northernmost part of the land, as far south as present-day Zeeland and Noord-Brabant, gradually developed into a Germanic-speaking territory. In what is now Belgium and northern France, the Germani were temporarily stopped by Caesar's legions. Eventually, though, Germanic tribes took possession of the land even there, since starting at the end of the third century Franks poured in en masse.

Variation in Germanic

How the various Old Germanic dialects came into being we don't really know, since no primary sources have come to us. It is assumed, though, on the basis of archaeological and other nonlinguistic evidence that at the end of the B.C. period five large confederations of Germanic tribes may be discerned. The Northern group is composed of those who remained in Scandinavia; the Eastern group includes Germani who had emigrated from Scandinavia and settled between the Oder and the Vistula rivers (e.g., Goths, Vandals, Burgundians). And the Western group, one of them the forbear of Dutch, is usually subdivided in three more groups (the North Sea, the Rhine Weser, and the Elbe Germani).

The first documents in the Germanic dialects appear at very different dates. Some Scandinavian rune inscriptions may go back to the end of the second century A.D. The first continuous text in any Germanic language is the Gothic (fragmentary) bible translation by Bishop Ulfilas (311–383; better known as Wulfila). It has come to us in a copy dating from the sixth century, written in silver letters on purple parchment—hence its name Codex Argenteus.

Gothic, on first sight, seems to be a strange mix of familiar and exotic words. The first lines of the Lord's Prayer go like this (þ is pronounced as the "th" in *thousand*):

> *Atta unsar, þu in himinam, weihnai namo þein.*

Word for word this means: "Father our, thou in (the) heaven, hallowed (be) name thine." Gothic *atta* (for father) is also found in the name of the ferocious King of the Huns, Attila, which is the diminutive form of *father*.

Apart from supplying the first continuous text in any Germanic language, Gothic is also our only representation of the East Germanic dialects, which became extinct a couple of centuries later. Although for a time the Goths played a prominent part in European history, including in their extensive conquests of both Italy by the Ostrogoths and Spain by the Visigoths, their language soon gave way to Latin. Even elsewhere it seems not to have maintained a very tenacious existence. For sure, Wulfila's Gothic is a relative yet not a direct parent of Dutch and the other West Germanic languages: Gothic is an aunt, not a mother. It's a very precious aunt, though, since she is our sole link to previous generations of Germanic.

The real parent language of Dutch is Proto-West-Germanic (Van Coetsem 1970). We are not absolutely sure how it looked since there are no sources to document it, but we know that it had a number of other extant languages as well: English, for example, but also Low German, Frisian, and High German. The Roman historian Tacitus (ca. 55–118), who thought he knew a lot about the Germani, tells us in his *De Origine et Situ Germanorum Liber* that what we now call the West Germanic tribes used to worship a God called Mannus, who had three sons who gave their names to the three different parts of the West Germanic lands: "Manno tris filios assignant, e quorum nominibus proximi oceano Inguaeones, medii Herminones, ceteri Istvaeones vocentur" (Mannus was assigned three sons, and they gave their name to [the inhabitants]: in the coastal region Ingweonen, in the center Herminonen, the remaining ones Istweonen).[3]

During the 19th century, philologists used Tacitus' terminology to distinguish among the three groups the West Germanic tribes were supposed to be divided into:

- The Ingweonen, or North Sea Germanic tribes, living in the coastal region—for example, Frisians, Angles, and Saxons
- The Istweonen, or Rhine-Weser Germanic tribes, Franks and Hessians, occupying present-day Franconian territory in Germany, the Netherlands, Belgium, and northern France.
- The Herminonen, or Elbe Germanic tribes, later Alemannics and Bavarians in the southern and southwestern parts of present-day Germany.

It is generally assumed that by the beginning of the Christian era the Proto-Germanic language community had broken up into several dialect areas. Written evidence supporting this assumption, however, is long in coming. Therefore, it is not at all sure that the linguistic division went along the lines just sketched and based on Tacitus. It is for lack of more and better information that we stick to the traditional terminology. In spite of the fact that dialectal differences were developing and threatened to break up the assumed unity of Proto-West-Germanic, a strong similarity persisted and a strong resemblance actually continues up to the present day.

Still, during the first half of the first millennium some fundamental changes occurred along the lines of the three great tribal confederations already mentioned. A few examples of common West Germanic changes (as opposed to North or East Germanic) are as follows (Van Coetsem 1970):

- Consonant gemination: in West Germanic every single consonant (except r), when followed by j and, to a lesser extent, by r, l, w was

---

[3] Here too we have a terminological problem. Since in most cases no English terms appear to have been coined, I will either use the Latin or the Dutch equivalents: Ingweonen, Istweonen, Herminonen.

doubled. Examples: Gothic hafjan >< Dutch heffen; ON sitja >< OE sittan

- Rhotacism, whereby [z] > [r]: Germanic wæzun >< OE wæron "were"; Gothic Dius >< OS dier, OE deor, OHG tior[4]
- Final Germanic -s is usually dropped in West Germanic (*dags-dag; fisks—fisk; gasts—gast*—Gothic as opposed to Old Saxon)

The next phase in the history of Dutch is the extensive period in which West Germanic eventually split up into different languages, viz. Old English (or Anglo-Saxon), Old Frisian, Old Saxon (or Old Low German), Old Dutch (or Old Low Franconian), and Old High German. Old English—or Anglo-Saxon, as it is mostly called—is the language as it developed in England after its conquest by the Angles, Saxons, and some other West Germanic tribes who set off from the continent in the fourth and fifth centuries. All other West Germanic languages were born and raised on the continent and are therefore called Continental West Germanic (Dutch: Continentaalwestgermaans). They were spoken in what are now the Frisian, Dutch, and German language territories.

From our present point of view, we can observe how a series of long-lasting language changes eventually resulted in conspicuous differences between them. We will have a closer look at two of those changes. The first one originates in the northern part of West Germanic in the shape of a west-to-east movement. The latter started in the south and slowly worked its way in a northern direction.

The west-to-east changes are labeled Ingvaeonisms[5] (or North Sea Germanic). This is an umbrella term for innovations originating in the western, coastal region of Continental West Germanic (and in Britain) and slowly worming their way in an eastern direction. They are to be found, albeit to a very different degree of intensity, in (Old) English, (Old) Frisian, (Old) Dutch, and (Old) Low German.

A very revealing example is the loss of a nasal consonant before a fricative, with a lengthening of the preceding vowel. Compare English *mouth* and *muide,* as it used to occur in Dutch dialects—still to be found in the place names IJmuiden, Diksmuide, and Arnemuiden—to German *Mund.* The source was Old Germanic **munth.* In Standard Dutch the change did not occur in this word (it is *mond,* not *muid* or *muide*). In place names farther to the east this Ingvaeonic feature is missing as well: Rupel*monde,* Dender*monde,* Roer*mond.* English *goose* is *gans* in Dutch (*Gans* in German), but in the place name Goes

---

[4]Rhotacism also occurs in Old Norse.

[5]Although English probably is the Germanic language with the largest amount of Ingvaeonisms, the term is hardly ever used in treatises on the history of the English language. It is very popular, though, in the history of Dutch (Ingweonismen) as well as of German (Ingwäonismen). Donaldson (1983) calls them Ingwaeonisms. There appears to be no agreement on the spelling either: as opposed to Donaldson's Ingwaeonisms, Paul Vincent (Brachin 1985) prefers Inguaeonic, whereas Ingvaeonic is what we find in Barbour and Stevenson (1990). Ingvæonic is the "original" solution used by Buccini (2010).

(in Zeeland) or in the street name Goeseputstraat in Brugge, the Ingvaeonic form is still alive. In *vijf* (five), on the other hand (from **fimfe*) and *zuid* (south) (from **sunth*), the loss of the nasal consonant does appear in Standard Dutch. *Us* or *uus* (English *us*, as opposed to Standard Dutch *ons* and Standard German *uns*) is very common in Low German dialects. *Uus* is also found in the westernmost West Flemish dialects.

Another Ingvaeonic characteristic is the presence of *h-* pronouns, that is, personal pronouns beginning with an *h*. They can be found in Dutch and English (*hij, hem, haar, hun; he, him, her*) but not in High German (*er, ihn, ihr, ihnen*). They also occur in Frisian and Low German. *Ingvaeonic palatalization,* on the other hand, occurs solely in English and Frisian: velar stops adjacent to front vowels have become palatal and change into either fricatives or affricates: hence English *church* and *cheese* and (north) Frisian *serk* and *tsiis* as opposed to Dutch *kerk, kaas* and German *Kirche, Käse*.

In sum English, Frisian, Low German, and coastal Dutch display the largest amount of Ingvaeonic characteristics (box 2.1). Since there are none in High German, we have northwestern West Germanic (English and Frisian, with a considerable amount of Ingvaeonisms) on the one side and southern West Germanic (High German, displaying none of them) on the other. In between there is the rather extensive transitional area of Dutch and Low German, characterized by a variable amount of Ingvaeonisms.

The south–north movement that should be briefly mentioned is the *High German sound shift*, also known as the second sound shift and described by Jakob Grimm along with the first or Germanic sound shift as part of Grimm's law. It originally affected exclusively Upper German (probably from the fifth or sixth centuries onward) and gradually made its way northward, having less and less effect as it progressed. This change, by which West Germanic *p*, *t*, and *k*, for example, were changed into other sounds, took place sometime between the fifth and the eighth centuries A.D. in the southern part of the Germanic area. Some examples of the changes in question are *pfund* (Dutch *pond;* pound;), *swartz* (Dutch *zwart;* black), and *mahhon* (Dutch *maken;* make) (Sanders 2010, 92–95). It was carried through consequently only in the southernmost part of the Upper German territory, as is witnessed by present-day Bavarian and Alemannic dialects.

BOX 2.1} English and Dutch

An interesting observation on the relationship between the Germanic languages was made by McCrum, Cran, and MacNeil (1987, 58): "The similarity between Frisian and English, both with strong Germanic roots, emphasizes how close English is to German, Dutch and Danish....The evidence...suggests that if that linguistic cataclysm, the Norman conquest of 1066, had not occurred, the English today might speak a language not unlike modern Dutch."

On its way up north, a considerable part of Middle Germany was eventually affected, although the High German sound shift lost some of its strength en route. It did not reach the Low Franconian (Dutch)[6] and the Low German parts of the continent, and until this very day the second sound shift is considered to be the language border between Low and Upper German dialects.

The division into more northern and more southern forms of speech on the basis of the previously described characteristics appears to be highly complex; in fact only English and Frisian have all the "northern" characteristics and only some southern German dialects have all the "southern" features. Also, it is striking that none of the various dividing lines corresponds to the modern boundaries between the different West Germanic languages. These complex dialectical divisions arose centuries before the modern standard languages began to develop.

As far as the transition zones in the Germanic territory at large are concerned, it is, as already observed, tricky to determine the boundaries not only on the basis of linguistic criteria. Matters are complicated still because, due to the historical evolution, contact (and conflict) between the Germanic languages was so intense that it influenced their linguistic relationship significantly. In the course of history, Frisian lost a considerable part of its territory to Dutch, which also absorbed part of the Low German area (the so-called Saxon area in the northeast of the Netherlands). On the other hand, it lost some territory in the Lower Rhineland (the Low Franconian area on the German side of the present-day state border between the Netherlands and Germany; see chapter 1).

Finally, due to the gradual loss of prestige of Low German, it could not hold up its role as a roofing language for the northern *plattdeutsche* dialects in Germany, and as a standard language it was gradually and completely replaced by High German.

The Genesis of Dutch

FRANKS, FRISIANS, AND SAXONS

"The identity of the Germanic peoples remains an enigma," Knowles (1997, 20) quite rightly observes, and he adds: "we have no reason whatsoever to assume that these or any other tribes spoke only one language" (ibid.). As language historiographers we have to learn to come to terms with these awkward truths, the more so since, in our case, we have to deal with at least the Franks, the Frisians, and the Saxons, whose languages are the building blocks of Dutch. Their sociolinguistic interplay determined the importance of the part they

---

[6] With the exception of a very small part of the province of Limburg in the Netherlands (the region around Kerkrade and Vaals) that underwent some of the changes.

played. It was their relative strength on the battlefield, much more than the structure of their language proper, that was decisive.

The Dutch language territory gradually took shape as Germanic tribes succeeded in either supplanting the beaten Celts or integrating them into their tribes. At the same time there was the influence of the invading Romans, who brought their languages[7] and culture with them. The end of the third century A.D. saw Germanic tribes flooding en masse over the Low Countries. Most of them were Franks, who appear not to have been a single tribe but rather a confederation of tribes, originally centered on the middle Rhine. Historians traditionally differentiate between (Lower Rhine) Salian and (Mid-Rhine) Ripuarian Franks (Dutch Salische and Ripuarische Franken)—but on which grounds is not certain. Their speech was West Germanic, but there surely were quite some internal differences.[8]

It was the Salian Franks who spearheaded the invasion of Gaul. By the end of the third century, they had settled in the Betuwe and the Scheldt areas and during the fourth century also in Texandrië, all regions comprising the south of the present-day Netherlands and the north of present-day Flanders. As Roman allies, they defended the frayed *limes* against other Germanic tribes, some of which—probably Franks as well—eventually joined them.

All of this was the prelude to the Great Migrations, when all of Europe was a seething chaos of peoples and tribes trying to push aside and displace each other. The year 375 saw Huns from the steps of Central Asia turn their ponies toward Europe; Goths, Vandals, Angles, Saxons, and Franks invaded en masse; and the Western Roman Empire collapsed under the weight and pressure of the peoples that invaded its territory.

After that, the Franks, by conquest or peaceful annexation, gradually drew together under their dominion all the Germanic peoples of continental Europe, culminating in Charlemagne (king, later emperor from 768 through 814). It started somewhere around 430 when Chlodio, one of the Frankish kings, broke the contract that linked him to the Romans who had vacated this region in 402. In no time he subdued a huge region comprising a part of present-day Belgium. After the Battle of Soissons in 486, another king of the Franks, Chlodowig (aka Clovis), conquered the Roman part of Gaul and in so doing expanded the realm of the Franks as far as the Loire. Clovis, a Salian Frank and the founding father of the dynasty of the Merovingians (he was king from 481 through 511), also was the first Frankish monarch who succeeded in rallying most of the Frankish tribes under his crown. With his conversion to Christianity and that

---

[7] "...The soldiers who fought with the Roman army no more came from the streets of Rome than the Canadians and Gurkhas who fought with the British army came from the streets of London"(Knowles 1997, 20).

[8] Today the dialects of their home territory range from Low Franconian (i.e., Dutch) to Upper Franconian, the Upper German dialect of the region around Würzburg and Nuremberg (Barbour and Stevenson 1990, 40).

of his subjects also came literacy. After that, the main remaining rivals and adversaries of the Franks were the Frisians and the Saxons.

In Roman times the homeland of the Frisians was situated between the Rhine and the Ems estuaries. During the seventh century they succeeded in increasing their influence in a southern direction considerably, according to some scholars as far south as the Zwin (near to Knokke in Belgium). The Saxons originally were at home in Holstein, from where, starting in the fourth century, raiding expeditions brought them not only to England but also to the shores of Gaul. They reached the Flemish coast by sea, whereas other Saxons drove out the Frisians from Groningen and the Eastern Netherlands and maybe pushed as far as Utrecht. In the seventh century the border between the Franks and the Saxons in the Netherlands was the IJssel River. Therefore, even as of today, the dialects of Groningen, Drenthe, Overijssel, and Northern-Gelderland are labeled Saksisch (i.e., Saxon).

Franks, Saxons, and Frisians were the three confederations of tribes that played the main part in the genesis of Dutch, and all three ruled over part of what is now the Dutch language territory. They also happened to be quite belligerent people, yearning to expand their territory and their influence. Since this meant that they would have to fight each other, the decisive battles that opposed them in the course of the eighth century came as no surprise. They ended as total victories for the Franks.

Since at that time the Frisians and the Saxons still adhered to their "heathen" convictions of old, the Franks loved to mask their lust for power as religious wars against the infidels. The Saxons opposed the Franks vehemently. However, their king, Widukind, was finally defeated in 785, and he and his people were forced to convert to Christianity and to accept the Frankish rule. For both the Frisians and the Saxons the Frankish conquest had not only religious but also linguistic consequences. The Saxons, more so than the Frisians, were exposed to Frankish linguistic influence, which appeared clearly in the texts that came to us but may have been not so apparent in the spoken language. Thus, with the Frankish conquest of north Germany, southern speech characteristics became more fashionable and gradually moved northward since, as Barbour and Stevenson (1990, 42) quite rightly observe, "from the end of the eighth century onwards, there was established a political, economic and hence cultural and linguistic, hegemony of the south in continental West Germanic, in which the more southern areas and their speech forms were generally more prestigious."

In the (Old) Dutch territory, increasing Frankish influence brought about, among other things, a substantial decrease of Ingvaeonic elements. Regarding the de-Ingvaeonization of the western dialects of Old Dutch, some scholars detect at least two waves of Frankish invasions, resulting in a Frankish superstructure being placed above the original Ingvaeonic one and thus changing the language from mainly Ingvaeonic to mainly Frankish (Heeroma 1965, 1972).

Scholars were (and are) intrigued by the rather astonishing fact that Dutch appears to have no umlaut of long vowels (as it used to be called).[9] This means that as opposed to, for example, German *Käse, süß,* and *grün* and English *cheese, sweet,* and *green* Dutch has forms without palatalization of the long vowel: *kaas, zoet, groen* (pronounced [ka:s], [zut], and [Xrun], respectively). The umlaut of long vowels (or secondary umlaut, as it is now called; Goossens 1989) exists in both the eastern (High and Low German) and western (English and Frisian) varieties of West Germanic, and it is therefore really astonishing that it does not occur in Dutch, a language with a very characteristic mixture of eastern and western elements. Adding to the "strangeness" is that the phenomenon does (and did) occur in eastern (dialect) varieties of Dutch (in Middle Dutch there are eastern forms such as *gruun, suut, were,* and *greve* as opposed to their western counterparts *groen, soete, ware,* and *grave*).

Some of the most prominent philologists of the preceding generations (including Gysseling, Heeroma, and Van Loey) have tried to solve this intriguing riddle. Yet the really small amount of excerpts (mostly gathered by Van Loey 1961) they discovered could hardly lead to a convincing solution, and, consequently, the more or less generally accepted hypothesis was based on conjecture much more than on facts. Even so, it does not solve the problem at hand but makes it only more intriguing: how could the fact that Ingvaeonic dialects, displaying secondary umlaut, were deeply influenced by Franconian dialects (displaying secondary umlaut as well) possibly lead to the outcome that secondary umlaut completely (and mysteriously) disappears?

It is at this point that Buccini (1992) started his investigations, and in his dissertation he makes the first serious effort in a long time to solve the riddle. Basically, the solution he proposes is that, probably at the moment of Franconization of the Ingvaeonic coastal dialects, secondary umlaut was not yet part of the phonemic system of Low Franconian (meaning that palatalized and not palatalized long vowels were still part of the same phoneme). By using the *transfer theory* devised by his advisor at Cornell (Van Coetsem 1988), he tries to make the whole procedure more plausible. Yet Buccini's theory, a summary of which can also be found in Buccini (2010), is as proofless as those of his predecessors. One thing seems to be clear enough: since hardly any sources have come to us, the only possible solution, if at all, will have to be sought using other than intern-linguistic methods, such as

---

[9] We are talking here about the so-called i-umlaut, of which Milroy (1984, 7–8) gives the following description: "Of the various vowel changes that took effect within the [Old English] OE period, the most important is 'i-umlaut' or front mutation. This was pre-literate in date and had, among other things, the effect of creating new vowel alterations within noun and verb paradigms: thus OE mūs (mouse) > mys (mice); fōt (foot) > fet (feet). I-umlaut operated when, in Germanic, [i] or [j] followed in the succeeding syllable: under these conditions a low or back vowel in the root syllable was raised and/or fronted. All other extant Germanic languages (except Gothic) have i-umlaut, but they appear to have implemented it independently."

sociolinguistic ones. But to find out how the language really evolved, we would have to know what happened to the people who spoke it. And this is where we are stuck.

This is all very unfortunate, since the problem we are talking about here is not some small detail in the evolution of West Germanic but is a substantial and specific development that has shaped the phonological (and even morphological) structure of Dutch as it is now. Both Goossens and Buccini agree that what the latter calls the abnormal development of i-umlaut in the Low Countries is essential in defining the place of Dutch within the neighboring Germanic languages, since this specific effect of i-umlaut is essentially what separates Dutch from English, German, and Frisian.

Old Dutch (Old Low Franconian)

EARLY BEGINNINGS: WHERE AND WHEN?

Old Dutch is a language in which not much was written, and most of it has not withstood the centuries. Even so, we know that it was used for more than just translating psalms, baptizing children, or hailing heroes. We shouldn't forget that, like any other language, it was a medium of communication and was used to speak much more than to write. It was a language used to pray and to curse, a language in which songs were sung and obscenities were yelled, a language in which children were comforted, a language to whisper terms of endearment into the ear of beloved ones or complain about one's neighbor's bad behavior, a language to answer questions or make quips, a language to be used in the very same way it is used today. It may have sounded differently, but there is no reason at all to assume its functions were all that different as far as the spoken language goes.

The oldest documented words and sentences in Dutch are from the eighth century, and, consequently, that is when the history of Dutch begins. On the other hand, as is the case with all other (Germanic) languages, we know for sure that Dutch was spoken long before anyone ever wrote something down in that language. We even know something about that not-yet-written language, since the reconstruction methods allow us to find out a lot about all undocumented old Germanic languages. Our story of Dutch, therefore, can definitely start before the eighth century, although the question of how long before is very hard to answer and is partly from a terminological rather than from a linguistic nature.

West Germanic, which we identified as one of the language groups descending from Proto-Germanic, itself an offspring of the Indo-European language family, is certainly not to be regarded as a homogeneous, independent language but had broken up into several dialects. Rather soon we witness how, in their turn, they evolved into the different languages we know today, spread over the whole West Germanic area, viz. English, Frisian, Dutch, Low German, and Upper German. We have no way of knowing when exactly they ceased to be geographical variants of West Germanic and can rightfully be considered to be languages in their own right. Therefore, it is best to stick to the facts without addressing the chronological issue.

Also, we should never forget that the state borders, on which names like Dutch and German are based, did not exist, and talking about Old Dutch or Old (Upper and Low) German is, strictly speaking, a projection back in time of a division that came into being only much later.

MANY WORDS, FEW TEXTS

In secondary schools, Old Dutch is not part of the curriculum, yet most pupils in Holland and Belgium are familiar with one small sentence that, as their teachers usually insist, is the oldest one ever written in Dutch:

> *Hebban olla uogala nestas [h]agunnan*
> *hinase hi[c] [e]nda thu*
> *uu[at] umbida[n] [uu]e nu*[10]

This sentence was discovered in 1932 in the Bodleian library in Oxford by the English scholar Kenneth Sisam. It is supposed to have been written around 1100 by a West Flemish monk in the abbey of Rochester in Kent.

There is no doubt that the oldest documented Old Dutch sentences are considerably older, but the *Hebban olla uogala* myth is hard to destroy. We will come back to that small sentence later on; first we'll look at the real beginnings of Dutch as a written language. We are in a lucky time: the last decade has seen a boost of research into Old Dutch, resulting, among other things, in a brand-new *Oudnederlands woordenboek* (Dictionary of Old Dutch), edited by the Institute on Dutch Lexicology (INL; Instituut voor Nederlandse Lexicologie) in Leiden and now available online.

Inscriptions in runes from the early fifth century and found in what is now the northeast of the Netherlands are generally regarded to be Frisian. As already mentioned, the borders between adjacent languages tended to be rather blurred. There is one exception to this—an inscription in Dutch on a sword found near the village of *Bergakker* in the province of Gelderland: *haþuwas ann kusjam loguns.* The first word is a name, and there is no real agreement among specialists on the third and the fourth word. As to the second word, though, there is no dispute: *ann* is a form of the verb that in Middle Dutch is *annen* or *onnen*, meaning to grant [with the prefix *ge-* it accounts for present-day Standard Dutch *gunnen*]. So the first and oldest documented word in Dutch is *ann* [I grant]. The harvest may seem meager, but then very little has come to us in any West Germanic dialect from a

---

[10] Letters within brackets are reconstructed. Literally the text means, "All the birds have started building their nests except for you and me; so what are we waiting for?"

time as early as the fifth century. The next catch comes from the Lex Salica, the law code of the Salian Franks that was written in Latin at the end of the reign of King Clovis (509–511). In one specific version, Latin legal terminology is commented upon in so-called glosses in Frankish words. This manuscript is known as the Malbergse Glossen (a *malloberg* was a hill on which justice was administered). Although the copy that came to us was made in the mid-eighth century, it is generally believed that the glosses were already present in the earliest texts. Examples of Old Dutch words figuring in the Lex Salica are *hano* (rooster, Dutch *haan*), *'hengist* (stallion, Dutch *hengst*), and *fogal* (fowl, Dutch *vogel*). The richest harvest is a short sentence, a legal formula pronounced during the procedure of freeing a serve: *Maltho thi afrio lito* (I tell you: I am setting you free, serve).

Apart from a considerable amount of eighth-century glosses and other words inserted in Latin texts, a few short sentences came to us as well, the best known of which are the *Utrechtse doopbeloften* (baptismal vows from Utrecht) consisting of questions and answers during the baptismal ceremony (Van der Sijs & Willemyns 2009, 152–153). The following is a sample:

> *Q. gelobistu in got alamehtigan fadaer.* (Do you believe in God, [the] almighty father?)
> *A. ec gelobo in got alamehtigan fadaer.* (I believe in God, [the] almighty father.)
> *Q. gelobistu in crist godes suno.* (Do you believe in Christ, God's son?)
> *A. ec gelobo in crist godes suno.* (I believe in Christ, God's son.)
> *Q. gelobistu in halogan gast.* (Do you believe in [the] Holy Ghost?)
> *A. ec gelobo in halogan gast* (I believe in [the] Holy Ghost.)

Furthermore, samples of Old Dutch vocabulary are hidden in the names of places and people still existing today. An example is Eewijk (documented in 855): *ee* is a river; *wijk* is a settlement. Other Old Dutch words discovered this way are, for example, *cachtel* (foal, West Flemish *kachtel*) and *varkin* (pig, Du *varken*).

CONTINUOUS TEXTS

Anglo-Saxon continuous texts have come to us from as early as the late seventh and eighth centuries. Old Saxon and Old High German begin approximately in the last quarter of the eighth century, and texts in both languages become more and more frequent toward the end of the "old" period.

The following incantation, meant to cure horses, came to us from the end of the ninth century (Van der Sijs & Willemyns 2009, 153):

> *Visc flot aftar themo uuatare.*
> *uerbrustun. sina uetherun.*
> *tho gihelida. ina. use druhtin.*
> *the seluo druhtin. thie thena uisc gihelda.*
> *thie gihele. that hers theru. spurihelti.* AMEN

Translation: "a fish was floating over the water with broken fins. Then it happened that our Lord cured him. May the Lord, who cured this fish, also cure the paralysis of this horse. Amen." Today we believe it to be Old Dutch, but not so long ago many scholars assumed it to be Old Saxon (Old Low German). This proves not only that we know less than we would like about the older stages of our languages but also that the difference between them is not so easy to determine and that the boundaries were rather frayed. Even nowadays the dialect of a citizen of Venlo (in the Dutch province of Limburg) may be hard to distinguish from that of an inhabitant of Straelen (the first village on the German side of the border). And, in fact, why do they have to be distinguished? What is actually spoken there are two almost identical language varieties that happen to be used in two different countries and that only scholars want to categorize as one being Dutch and the other being German (see chapter 1). Today and—with even more reason—15 centuries ago, the speakers themselves quite rightly don't and didn't bother. Also, of course, 15 centuries ago, those state borders didn't exist. The urge to draw borders between language varieties— whether geographical or temporal—doesn't add to our knowledge or understanding of the language varieties at stake.

Although there are less documented texts in Old Dutch than in most other West Germanic languages, three longer texts are mentioned in every treatise and should therefore not be missing here either. Most of the texts written in an old Germanic dialect were religious in nature—the church was involved in widespread evangelism of the "pagan" Germanic tribes—and Old Dutch was no exception to that rule. The most extensive text that has come to us is a fragmentary psalter that, in the Low Countries, goes by the name of *Wachtendonckse Psalmen*. Furthermore, there is the *Leidse Willeram*, a Dutchified version of the Song of Songs by the Bavarian abbot Williram von Ebersberg, dating from about 1100. And finally we have the *Mittelfränkische Reimbibel*, a Bible translation on rhyme dating from the first half of the 12th century. The latter text is believed to have originally been written in Dutch and afterward transposed into southern German. That is exactly the opposite of what happened to the Leidse Willeram, which was originally written in Eastern Franconian around 1065 and then transposed into Dutch, in the abbey of Egmond in North-Holland (Sanders 1974). The copier replaced the High German words as well as prefixes and suffixes by Dutch ones and adapted the conjugational and phonetic systems to those of Dutch. He did a very thorough job, and in some cases words that have become very common are attested here for the first time.

The most important and most useful text undoubtedly is the Wachtendonckse psalmen, a manuscript that came to us in a fairly unique way. These psalms are an adaptation in Old Dutch of an originally Old High German translation of the psalms, dating from the late ninth century. The translator, whom we don't know by name, wrote the translated text underneath the original Latin verse, adopting the Latin syntax and consequently making his Old Dutch text unfit for syntactical research. Here is an example of what such a translation looks like (Psalm 54:6–7; in modern numeration Psalm 55:5–6):

> *Forchta in biuonga quamon ouer mi in bethecoda mi thuisternussi*
> *In ic quad uuie sal geuan mi fetheron also duuon in ic fliugon sal in raston sal*

The King James Bible reads: "Fearfulness and trembling are come upon me, and horror hath overwhelmed me. And I said, Oh that I had wings like a dove! [for then] would I fly away, and be at rest."[11]

The way the Wachtendonckse psalmen came to us is probably exemplary for what happened to many old manuscripts. From the original Old High German translation of the psalms, not one copy has survived, and the text of the first translator is missing as well (burned, ransacked, eaten by mice, thrown away, used later as binding of a book?). So what do we have? We know that in the 16th century the famous Flemish humanist Justus Lipsius spotted the manuscript in Liege in the library of the cannon Arnold Wachtendonck (hence the name). He was so excited that he had a copy made, yet even that is not the manuscript that came to us. To make a long story short, what has survived the ages is a fragment of the psalm translation found in the early 19th century in Berlin (the von Diez manuscript) as well as a list of 670 words drawn up by Lipsius and found among his papers in the Leiden University Library in 1880. Since both the von Diez text and Lipsius's glosses display the same copying errors, their source must have been identical. Comparing Lipsius's glosses with the von Diez manuscript reveals that originally our monk must have translated all the psalms and several hymns. Although what has come to us is only part of that original translation, it is very useful since it is our main source of Old Dutch.

The only thing we know about the Old Dutch adaptor is that he probably was a monk, originating from what is now the border region between Limburg and the German Rhineland, somewhere between Venlo and Krefeld. When exactly this adaptation was made we do not know.

Let us now return for a moment to the famous small sentence, *hebban olla uogala.* . . . No other 13 words have ever elicited such extensive commentaries (Kettenis & Meijer 1980). As we can see from other things scribbled on the same piece of parchment, we are in the presence of a *probatio pennae*, which were texts monks used to write down when trying out new goose feathers and freshly made ink. One of them wrote the now famous sentence, accompanied by a Latin translation of his "poem":

> *abent om[ne]s uolu[cres] nidos [in]c[ep]tos*
> *nisi ego et tu*
> *quid expectamus nu[nc].*

---

[11] Dutch: *Vrees en beving kwamen over mij en duisternis bedekte mij en ik zei: Wie zal mij vleugels geven als duiven, zodat ik weg kan vliegen en een rustplaats kan vinden.*

A very extensive analysis of the linguistic form of the poem reveals that it must have been written in a West Flemish dialect. According to the most widely accepted of the many hypotheses, the text was written by a West Flemish monk.

Since it means "While all the birds are making nests / Still you and I demur / What are we waiting for,"[12] it looks like a love poem. Yet we're not completely sure what this is all about. Is it an indecent proposal, or is it a proposal for marriage? Is it a song of love or of lust or both? One thing is for sure: it was not the first song on that topic in a language that was soon to turn into Middle Dutch.

In 1130, in the monastery of Munsterbilzen situated in that same border region between Venlo and Krefeld, somebody composed a list of the monks and nuns living there and finished with the comment, *Tesi samanunga was edele unde scona* (This community was noble and precious). It is the last sentence in Old Dutch that came to us (Goossens 1999). From then until approximately 1200, all we have are glosses, names, and single words in a Latin context. In the text quoted, we find *edele* with an unstressed final *e*, while *scona* has a "full" final vowel *a*. Most likely this illustrates that during that particular period of time the unstressed full final vowels were gradually changing into a muted ə (*schwa*)[13]; the latter were usually considered the characteristic par excellence to mark the end of Old Dutch and the beginning of Middle Dutch. It probably occurred during the second half of the 12th century and was very soon also expressed in the spelling.

WHAT DID THE LANGUAGE LOOK LIKE?

Now we come to the final and probably most difficult question: what was Dutch really like in the Old Dutch period? Perhaps the most distinctive feature of this period is the absence of a standard language. If you happened to meet someone from elsewhere (something that admittedly didn't happen that often), the only possibility was to try to understand the way they handled the language, their way of speaking, their accent, their dialect.

Actually, we know very little about the mutual intelligibility of Old Dutch dialects, and here again we should realize that something like Old Dutch, Old Saxon, or Old High German did not really exist. These are categorizations made afterward, not present in the consciousness of the speakers of that time. For them, the only difference of importance was between strangers they managed to understand and those they couldn't. Language standardization is the result of

---

[12] English translation borrowed from F. van Oostrom's article "The Middle Ages Until Circa 1400" in Hermans (2009, 5).

[13] According to Goossens (1999, 185–186) the change into a muted *e* had occurred already but was still so new that an agreement on how to spell the sound had not yet been reached. A bit later the *e* emerged as the uniform way of spelling. Goossens's article also features a photo of the relevant page with the sentence in question.

language contact, of mingling, and can therefore start and develop only when people meet and try to accommodate to their respective ways of speaking.

Although there used to be, as we have seen, impressive migrations of tribes and groups of people during the early centuries A.D., it would still take a very long time before meeting and mingling of individuals started to occur on a more or less regular basis. It is no coincidence that the real start of language standardization coincides with the invention of book printing, which made some kind of language contact possible without actually meeting other people. In view of all this, most of the following is strictly speaking true only for the documented language specimens. Yet extrapolation to other forms of Old Dutch is certainly permitted.

Old Dutch looks much simpler than its Indo-European or Old Germanic ancestors. Declensions and conjugations had both suffered a drastic reduction in inflexional forms. The lost forms had been or were being replaced by prepositional phrases, compound tenses (i.e., made with auxiliary verbs), or other devices. As opposed to Old High German, the consonant system knew only minor changes. A lot of change, on the contrary, is witnessed in the sound system (e.g., primary umlaut, monophthongization, and diphthongization), though only some of them were actually written down. As to syntax and vocabulary, Old Dutch as it is recorded is a language of monks and clerics, and we have virtually no record of the living speech of the common people.

The Old Dutch dictionary lists all words in the texts already mentioned here as well as many others. It has some 4,500 entries. It demonstrates, among other things, that variation existed in Old Dutch, an umbrella term for the dialects spoken at that time. For all we know, they may have been as diverse as the modern ones. All the texts having come to us (and the many ones that never did) were written in the local dialect of the author, translator, or copier.

This brings us to the last item to be discussed in this chapter: how did the language really look, how related were its dialects, and how did they differ from other West Germanic dialects? The easiest way to start is to distinguish between what may be called negative and positive characteristics. The former don't appear in Old Dutch, whereas the latter do appear.

One *negative characteristic* is the Saxon uniform plural (Dutch *Saksische eenheidspluralis*): all endings in the plural indicative are equal, either *-en* or *-t*. We find it in Low German (Old Saxon) but not in Old Dutch. Consequently, this feature sets Dutch apart from Old Low German. Also missing in (Old) Dutch is the second sound change (discussed earlier), which sets it apart from Old High German.

Positive characteristics that appear in Old Dutch but not (or differently) in other West Germanic dialects include the following:

- The secondary umlaut seems to be absent from Old Dutch (as well as from subsequent Middle and Standard Dutch), which sets it apart from all other Old Germanic dialects: compare Dutch *groen, zoet,* and *kaas* with English green, sweet, cheese and German *grün, süß,* and *Käse*.

- In Dutch in the sequence *a* or *o*, followed by *l* + dental the l is vocalized, which sets apart Dutch *oud* or *goud* from English *old* and *gold* as well as from German *alt* and *Gold*.[14]
- The lengthening of short vowels in open, stressed syllables was completed by the end of the Old Dutch period. In German it occurred gradually (and in some cases not at all) during the Middle period: *Măgeþ > māged* (Dutch *Maagd*, German *Magd*) but *măkkon >* Dutch *māken*, German *machen*.
- Germanic *đ* and *þ* have become *d* in Continental West Germanic but not in English, which explains the difference between *doorn–thorn* and *vader–father*.
- Word final devoicing (*Auslautverhärtung*): Dutch *hoed, hand*; German *Hut, Hand* (all pronounced with a voiceless [t]) >< English *hood, hand* (pronounced [d]) eventually distinguished Continental West Germanic from Anglo-Saxon (and English).

Further characteristics are as follows:

1. Consonant changes:
   — *hs* turns into *ss*; for example, German *Ochsen* and *Flachs* to Dutch *ossen* and *vlas*
   — *ft* changes into *cht*; for example, German *Kraft* and *Luft* to Dutch *kracht* and *lucht*.
   — Word initial *f* turns into *v*: German *fiel, falten*—Dutch *veel, vouwen*
   — /g/ in word initial and intervocalic position turns from plosive into fricative: German *geben* and English *give* (with occlusive /g/) as opposed to Dutch *geven* (with fricative /g/).
2. Vocal changes—monophthongization:
   — *ai > e;* for example, German *Bein* and *Fleisch*; Dutch *been* and *vlees*
   — *au > o*; for example, German *Baum* and *Laub*; Dutch *boom* and *loof*[15]
3. Ingvaeonic characteristics:
   — *Nasalschwund*: German *fünf* and Dutch *vijf*
   — *h* pronouns: German *er, es,* and *ihm*; Dutch *hij, het,* and *hem*[16]

---

[14] This, as well as the preceding characteristic, does not occur in all varieties of Dutch. Nowadays, they are characteristic of Standard Dutch but are absent in some of its more eastern dialects.

[15] In this, as well as in some other cases, the situation in some Dutch dialects differs from that in Standard Dutch.

[16] Most of these characteristics have been discussed earlier in some more detail.

Through these and some other characteristics we are able to differentiate bet-ween Old Dutch, on one side, and other Continental West Germanic dialects on the other. We should keep in mind, though, that not all changes (or the lack thereof) occur in the territory at large or at the same moment. Consequently, only the combination of many characteristics enables us to geographically determine a specific West Germanic text. Even so, the borders between Old Continental West Germanic languages often remain very blurred.

Middle Dutch: Language and Literature

The Cradle of Dutch

Even as of today the famous medieval animal epic *Van den Vos Reynaerde* (Reynard the Fox) is still considered by many to be the most outstanding piece of literature ever written in Dutch. It was originally created during the 13th century in the County of Flanders, the southwestern part of the language territory, and consequently, it was written in Flemish, the then most prestigious variety of Dutch.

Unlike some other Germanic languages, there are not that many written records of Dutch prior to the 12th century (see chapter 2). Although Dutch was definitely used in writing earlier than that, we have to wait until the second half of the 13th century to see the beginning of an uninterrupted written tradition. In spite of the fact that the earliest Dutch documents that came to us originate from the eastern part of the language territory, it is definitely Flanders—with important cities like Brugge, Ghent, and Ieper—that emerges as the cradle of Dutch: E meridie lux, as Brachin (1985, 10) says.[1] When in the course of the 13th century Latin was gradually replaced by Dutch as the overall administrative language in the Low Countries, it appeared that Brugge, "the New York of the Middle Ages" (Sternberg 1999, 53), rapidly emerged as the paramount center of the written language (box 3.1). In the field of literature, too, the two most successful authors during the initial period of Middle Dutch literature were both Flemings: the prolific and encyclopedic poet Jacob van Maerlant; and Willem, the author of Reynard the Fox.

The Middle Dutch period ends somewhere between the beginning and the end of the 16th century (depending on which part of the territory we have in

---

[1] Willemyns (1971, 16–19) gives a nutshell overview of all the available 13th-century texts.

BOX 3.1} Freckled Mary or Crazy Jane?

Accounts of Brugge in the 15th century regularly list prostitutes and brothel keepers having been fined for carrying out their profession. The interesting thing about that is that many hookers are listed by name and nickname. Many of them had their home base in—predictably—the Quade Herberghe (the bad inn), and the choice was plentiful.

Those who wanted to go by origin could choose Tannekin de Schottine (the Scottish) or Calle van Muenekereede (Brugge's harbor). French women were very sought after, and, therefore, Margriet de Waelnede (the French) may have been very popular.

Looks, of course, were decisive as well. Probably Trinne Metten Pockepitten (Pockmarked Catherine) was less patronized than Marie Metten Sproeten (Freckled Mary). Marie Metter Muus (with muscled arms) probably attracted a special class of whore-hoppers, and those who liked large breasts surely considered Griete Metten Tuten (Margaret with the large tits).

Even as early as the 15th century, prostitution may have been a side job for some, as we can see from the sobriquets some girls carried. With Calle de Melkeghe (the milk maid) the profession is clear. For those who fancied something savorier, Lysbette de Biertappeghe (the alewife) was available. Matte Stovejoncwijf (from the bath house) must have had some experience in her main profession already.

Many girls were characterized by an epithet. Cleen Callekin (small Callekin) as opposed to Vette Losie (Fat Losie) is a question of taste. Those who knocked at the door of Leepe Griete (Canny Margaret) or Dulle Jenine (Crazy Jane) could not complain, since they were sufficiently informed as to their specifics. Black-haired girls were supposed to be extremely lascivious, and therefore a good time was to be had with Zwarte Mine (Black Mine). Finally, those anxious not to catch diseases could always opt for Proper Jehanekin (Clean Joan).[2]

mind) and displays an enormous amount of variation. From the very beginning a linguistic contrast between an easterly and a westerly shaped variety[3] can be witnessed. The most salient feature of the east–west opposition was the presence (east) or absence (west) of the *secondary umlaut* and the completely different inflectional systems that resulted from it (see chapter 1), giving way to structurally differing language varieties (Goossens 1989). The overwhelming majority of all texts display decidedly western language features and the written language of the Middle Dutch period was firmly Flemish in its roots even in the non-Flemish parts of the language territory.[4] In the course of the 16th century,

---

[2] Based on Dupont (2004).
[3] West are Flanders, Zeeland, and Holland; East are East Brabant, Limburg, the Lower Rhine region, and (later) the northeast. West Brabant and Utrecht are in between.
[4] Van Loey (1937) lists some of the eastern regional characteristics that were gradually abandoned in Brabantic texts of the 13th and 14th centuries, due to the influence of the more prestigious Flemish (western) writing tradition.

though, the economic and political center of gravity of the Dutch language area shifted to Brabant. Antwerp, Mechelen, and Brussels developed into the more important centers of trade and culture. It was during this period that a standard variety of the written language was gradually taking shape.

The Earliest Middle Dutch Texts

The earliest work of literature in Middle Dutch known to us dates from between 1160 and 1170. It is the biography of the patron saint of Maastricht, *Sint Servaes*, written by Hendrik van Veldeke, a nobleman from Maastricht in Limburg. Because Veldeke moved afterward to what is now Germany, he has his place in the history of German literature as well and is considered by many as one of the most important Minnesänger (troubadours). Until not so long ago he was even often claimed by German literature historians to be a German poet because many of his works have come to us in adaptations made by Middle High German copiers and because modern state borders did not yet exist in those days. Veldeke exercised a strong influence on Middle High German literature and became the man who really established the tradition of the love lyric there. He was regarded as "the master" by German poets such as Wolfram von Eschenbach and Gottfried von Straßburg and was mentioned and praised by several of his German successors as an innovator of poetic technique. Still, it was in his Middle Dutch Limburg vernacular that he wrote his poetry as well as his famous *Sint Servaes* (Goossens, Schlusemann, & Voorwinden 2008).

In the *corpus Gysseling*, which contains text editions of all Middle Dutch texts written prior to 1300 (Gysseling 1977–1987), we find seven texts originating from the Limburg–Lower Rhine region, plus six from Brabant and four from Flanders: two love songs (*minneliederen*) from Brugge and two books by Jacob van Maerlant, viz. his *Der Naturen Bloeme* (The Best of Nature) and the *Rijmbijbel* (Rhyme Bible). Originating from Holland are fragments of the Arthur novel *Perchevael*. There is no doubt that older Middle Dutch texts have existed, but they did not come to us (box 3.2).

BOX 3.2 } Manuscripts that Came to Us: A Never-Ending Story

Middle Dutch language and literature have been neglected for a long time and were only rediscovered in the early 19th century. Unfortunately, by then many manuscripts had been lost. Many are gone forever, and some surfaced again either by chance or as the result of purposive searches. In some cases even originals were unearthed.

Although obviously manuscripts can travel far (De Vreese 1962), the most obvious place to look for them is close to where they were written and exactly where we would expect to find them: in libraries, archives, and museums but also of course in private attics and basements. Often, old parchments were cut into pieces to make hard covers for bound books, or pages were glued together to get the necessary firmness. A hitherto unknown fragment of *Reynaert de Vos* (Reynard the Fox) had been used in exactly that way until it was found in 1972 in Monaco.

One of the most recent thrilling adventures occurred in 2008, when a parchment scroll was discovered in the cover of 15th-century city accounts from Mechelen (http://www.mechelen.be/archief). The scroll measured 1.5 meters and probably was written around 1325. It contains an amazing and unknown poem of some 200 verses, with all kinds of erotic suggestive remarks in the form of riddles as well as political allusions to the German emperor and the French king. Included in the discovery were paper pages with 400 verses from the romance of chivalry titled *Jonathas & Rosafiere*, a rather strange medieval story of incest. Those pages outdate the hitherto oldest known fragment by almost a century.

The Flemish nobility knew French (a considerable number of them were French). Whenever they felt like listening (most of them couldn't read) to troubadour poetry or chivalric literature, it was no problem to have the French original read or sung to them. In Brabant, Limburg, and the Lower Rhine, mastery of French in the nobility was considerably lower, which may explain why the "first" Middle Dutch romances come from the latter region rather than from the west.

Still, the fact that some of the eastern manuscripts that came to us were copies of works originally written in Flanders (fragments of the *Reynaert,* for example) is proof in itself that literary activity existed there as well. Also, in the course of the 13th century the political and economic balance of power changed considerably. The towns of Flanders were flourishing, and very soon at least three of them—Brugge, Ghent, and Ieper—were part of the major cities of Europe. Many patricians in those cities had no knowledge of French and felt the urge to enjoy culture in their own language. It is in this Flemish Middle Dutch that some of the masterpieces of European literature were written.

Writing in the Vernacular instead of Latin

Middle Dutch, obviously, was used not only in literature. Encyclopedic texts were written to satisfy the thirst for knowledge of the burgesses of the Flemish cities (the *poorters*), who had no access to Latin. Moreover, the growing need for records in the vernacular gradually convinced even the skeptics that it was perfectly possible to use the mother tongue as a chancellery language, in which all kinds of administrative texts could be drafted. Consequently, in the course of the 13th century, all over Europe Latin gradually lost its monopoly position in the town hall chanceries and even, albeit considerably later, in the ecclesiastic world of monks and other clerics. In Flanders Latin was replaced not only by Dutch but also for some time by French because the Counts of Flanders were foreigners and the habitual language of their chancelleries and their nobility was French. Having the French king for a liege certainly enforced the influence of French still.

Ghent appears to be the mother tongue pioneer. The Statute of the Leprosarium (*Gentse leprozerie*, 1236) is the very first administrative text in Dutch that came to us, followed shortly by the Dutch translation of the originally Latin city statutes (between 1237 and 1240). Beginning with the year 1253 all city records in Ghent were drafted in the vernacular. Next comes the rural administration of Velzeke, with the famous *schepenbrief van Boechoute* in 1249 (fig. 3-1), the first Dutch record we know of. Ieper followed suit in 1253.

Within the Flemish context, Brugge was a late starter: the first Dutch record was dated 1262, but immediately thereafter it firmly took the lead. With the sole exception of the city accounts that were drafted in Latin through 1302, every document emerging from its city hall was henceforth written in Dutch. Brugge took the lead: more than two-thirds of all the 2,100 Dutch administrative texts that came to us from the 13th century were written there (Gysseling 1971).

After Flanders, the second county to switch to the vernacular was Holland-Zeeland. The city statute of Middelburg (on the island of Walcheren in Zeeland) from 1254 came first. In the Duchy of Brabant smaller cities took the lead: Kortenberg as of 1266. Brabant's larger towns, especially Brussels and Leuven, continued to write in Latin for much longer. In Limburg the very voluminous

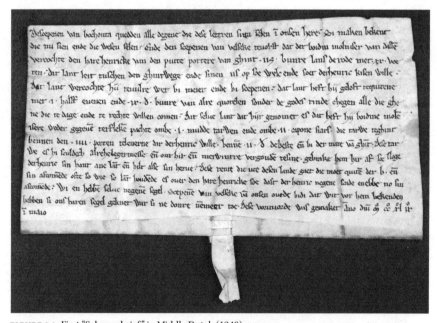

FIGURE 3.1 First "Schepenbrief" in Middle Dutch (1249)

property register of Aldenbiezen in 1280 and a charter from Tongeren in 1277 were drafted in Dutch, but apart from those Limburg didn't part from Latin until the mid-14th century. Utrecht started switching to Dutch in 1278, whereas the northeastern parts produced their first vernacular text as late as 1300 (in Deventer).

As far as the Fachliteratur (scientific texts) are concerned, it is Limburg that is on the fore: the Limburgse gezondheidsregels (diet rules) were written down in 1253 in the margin of a Latin calendar.

In summary, of the 2,100 documents written prior to 1300, 70 percent were drafted in Flanders, 15.5 percent in Holland, 10 percent in Brabant, 1.5 percent in Zeeland, and 1.3 percent in Utrecht; the remaining regions shared the small percentage that was left. It is abundantly clear that the cradle of Dutch stood in Flanders, where the language was also to grow up and to mature.

Literature and Culture

THE 13TH CENTURY

The bulk of medieval Dutch literature[5] originates from the southern part of the Netherlands, that is, from Flanders, Brabant, and Limburg. Holland remained a backwater for a long time and did not come out of its cultural isolation until the 14th century. The earliest literature of the Low Countries displays a rich variety of genres and has contributed a few masterpieces to European literature.

The authors of *Renout van Montalbaen, Ferguut, Walewein,* and the *Lancelot compilation* (some 10 smaller Arthur tales) are unknown to us, but they surely gave us proof of their literary talent and of their mastery of the Dutch language, even if their adaptation of the British–Celtic chivalric literature and the Arthur romances was mostly based on French examples.

All in all, many works of the 12th and 13th centuries were adaptations from the French. Even the odd original among them, such as *Karel ende Elegast,* is influenced by the French literary tradition. There are some notable exceptions though: the most outstanding of which is the animal epic *Vanden Vos Reinaerde,* the first literary product of that typically individualistic culture that was growing up in the Flemish cities and that was to exert such a strong influence on the shaping of intellectual life in the Netherlands at large later on. Although that cynical fable builds on a 12th-century tradition, it is the undisputable literary masterpiece of the Dutch—and even European—13th century. Of the author we know only the name: Willem. The story is based on a French example, but there is no doubt that Willem's epic is not only an original work but also

---

[5] Ample information on every title and author mentioned here (and on a lot more) can be found in Meijer (1971) and Hermans (2009), my two main sources for medieval literature.

BOX 3.3 } Reynaert

Willem's *Vanden Vos Reinaerde*[6] is an animal epic, or a mock epic, and as such it is the only one of its kind in Dutch. Willem had no predecessors in the strict sense of the word, and his poem stands alone. He used some literary materials available to him during that time, but he arranged them in such a way that it is fully justified to regard this as an entirely original piece of work.

One of these materials is the Latin poem *Isengrimus,* attributed to Magister Nivardus of Ghent and dating back to the middle of the 12th century. Poems such as these must have been the sources from which the authors of the French *Roman de Renart* drew their material. One of its episodes, a poem known as *Li Plaid* (The Court Session), in its turn became the source of the Dutch *Vanden Vos Reinaerde.* But the Flemish author used his source so freely and independently and gave the story such a personal twist and purpose that it became a completely new poem, and a masterpiece at that.

Vanden Vos Reinaerde describes the attempts of Bruun the bear, Tibeert the tomcat, and Grimbeert the badger to bring Reynard to the court of King Nobel. The efforts of Bruun and Tibeert are defeated by their own greed, but Grimbeert seems successful. Reynard follows him to court and is sentenced to be hanged. While the gallows is being erected, he embarks on a long story of treason and conspiracy, introducing a hidden treasure and accusing bear, cat, and wolf of plotting against the king. By speculating on King Nobel's cupidity and stupidity, Reynard gets away with it and is set free. Crime pays off handsomely, injustice triumphs, and the stupid are left to pay the piper. It has the tone of a light-hearted cynic who is cool and detached but has a razor-sharp sense of humor and deep psychological insight and laughs at the stupidities of the world. *Vanden Vos Reinaerde* is an accomplished masterpiece, and Willem, whoever he was, must be regarded as one of the major poets of the European Middle Ages.

Probably he wrote his *Reinaert* around 1200 in what is now the province of East Flanders. In Willem's poem the animals behave like humans but still retain their animal characteristics. In the sequel, *Reinaert II,* on the other hand, the animals are simply humans who walk on all fours but in whose behavior there is nothing left of the animal. *Reinaert II* became the basis (unfortunately, one might say) of the Reynard stories in English and German. The prose version of *Reinaert II,* the Gouda edition, was translated into English by William Caxton and published by him in 1481. The Low German *Reinke Vos* (1498), later adapted into High German by Goethe, also goes back to *Reinaert II.*

one of the best ever literary works in Dutch. It is assumed that Willem wrote other works previous to the Reynaert. None of them has come to us though, although one at least is known by name: *Madoc* (box 3.3).

---

[6] The main sources of information in all the boxes on literature (in this and the other chapters) are Meijer (1971) and Hermans (2009).

Jacob van Maerlant also stands out. He was a West Fleming who lived between 1235 and 1291 near Brugge, probably in Damme, where a statue is dedicated to him. He is the first poet whose almost entire oeuvre has been preserved, and that oeuvre was huge. Maerlant started out as an author of epic romance, such as *Alexanders Yeesten* (The Heroic Deeds of Alexander) and *Historie van Troyen* (History of Troy). Later on he switched to mostly didactic poetry, such as *Der Naturen Bloeme* (The Best of Nature), *Spieghel Historiael* (Mirror of History), a world history from creation up to 1250, and *Rijmbijbel* (Rhyme Bible), all of them adaptations of Latin works.

Maerlant shows himself a better poet in his *Strofische Gedichten* (Strophic Poems), which are full of social criticism. *Der Kercken Claghe* (The Complaint of the Church) is a courageous and passionate attack on abuses in the Church, and *Vanden Lande van Oversee* (Of the Overseas Country or Outremer) is an exhortation to a new crusade. Maerlant's popularity was enormous and his influence was long lasting. Both Willem and Jacob van Maerlant, the former from the northeastern and the latter from the northwestern part of Flanders, contributed immensely to making the Flemish variety the model par excellence for the Middle Dutch literary language at large.

Mysticism was another popular genre in the 13th century, mostly in Brabant. The genre's master was the poetess Hadewijch. In the second and third quarter of the century she demonstrates her familiarity with mystical thought and her ability in handling the Dutch language both in verse and in prose (visions and letters). The story of *Beatrijs* (by an anonymous Brabant author) originated in the world of monks and abbeys, strongly influenced as it is by the mystical tradition, yet it was almost certainly aimed at a secular audience.

THE 14TH CENTURY

Throughout the 14th century we see the continuation of the didactical tendencies initiated by Maerlant, which apparently accommodated the inquisitiveness of the patricians (Dutch: *poorters*), an increasing number of which became literate themselves. The societal influence of people not belonging to the aristocracy gradually increased. What we see is not a revolutionary change of the system but rather a shift of accent, the forerunner of a more profound change still to come.

An outstanding political event in this context is the Guldensporenslag, a battle that was fought in Kortrijk on July 11, 1302, opposing (mostly) Flemish artisans and burgesses and the bloom of the French knights. The latter were sent out by Flanders' liege, King Philip the Handsome of France, to bring to "reason" the Flemish cities that had come to view the French as a hindrance to their economic and commercial flourishing. The defeat of the French army by Flemish military amateurs caused a sensation in contemporary Europe and was filed in the collective memory of the Flemings. Even as of today, July 11 still is Flanders' national Holiday in remembrance of the Guldensporenslag, which 19th-century romanticism had blown up as the victory of the Flemings over anything French. It goes without saying that this was not what was really at stake in the battle of 1302.

Still, 14th-century resistance to the French rule was omnipresent, since trade and cooperation with the English, France's enemies, is what made the Flemings prosperous. Simultaneously, and for basically the same reasons, the Flemish leaders felt that a narrower cooperation with Brabant and Limburg might be advantageous to all. That too was not possible as long as Flanders had a French liege. The rest of the Dutch-speaking territory, mainly the northern Netherlands, still remained out of the unionizing tendencies, which were paramount in the parts where economic and cultural blossoming were the largest and the urge for real political power the most intense: the Southern Netherlands, dominated by Flanders, its industrially most developed region.

In literature, two pieces of literature must be mentioned: the didactic *Rijmkroniek van Vlaanderen* (Rhyme Chronicle of Flanders), a huge compilation written by various authors; and the *Brabantsche Yeesten* (History of Brabant) by Jan van Boendale, who also authored *Der Leken Spieghel* (Laymen's Mirror), a poem of more than 20,000 verses. For the first time Holland contributed to (the didactic) literature as well, with the *Rijmkroniek van Holland* (Rhyme Chronicle of Holland) by Melis Stoke in 1305.

The undisputed grandmaster of 14th-century mysticism was Jan van Ruusbroec from Brussels. Writing in prose, he impressed amateurs of the genre, and some of the words he coined are still part of everyday Dutch. Examples are *indruk* (impression), *invloed* (influence), *binnenste* (interior), *neiging* (inclination), *wezenlijk* (substantial), and *werkelijk* (really). Thanks to the many Latin

BOX 3.4 } Ruusbroec (1293–1381)

In the moralistic–didactic literature of the 14th century, the literature of mysticism has its special place. Its great representative, Jan van Ruusbroec, who wrote prose exclusively, was born in 1293 in the village near Brussels from which he derives his name. As a priest he spent most of his life in an abbey close to Brussels. During his lifetime important parts of his work were translated into Latin by several authors. In this way Ruusbroec's work overcame the linguistic barriers, gained fame in Europe, and exercised a strong influence on the German mystics as well as on the mystic movements in France, Spain, and Italy.

His best-known work is *Die Chierheit der Gheesteliker Brulocht* (The Adornment of the Spiritual Espousals), a book on the theory of mystical aspiration. As a means of literary expression, Ruusbroec's achievements received unanimous praise.

Other translations followed after 1440, a time in which a renewed interest in Ruusbroec and the Rhenish mystics developed. In 1552 his complete works were translated into Latin.

translations of his works, Ruusbroec influenced the whole European mystical movement considerably (box 3.4).

Of equal importance were the secular poetry and drama produced in the 14th century. Most of it has come to us in two miscellanies: the *Gruuthusehandschrift;* and the *Hulthemse handschrift*. The former manuscript (now in the Royal Library in The Hague), composed on behalf of the influential Lords of Gruuthuse in Brugge, is a collection of songs, ballads, and lyrical poetry, some of which are still part of the collective memory of the Netherlands at large, such as *Egidius waer bestu bleven* and the *Kerelslied*. The ballade *Heer Halewijn* is also still popular today.

The Hulthem manuscript (kept in the Brussels Royal Library) is one of the most important medieval miscellanies and contains (among many other things) a remarkable set of four plays, the *abele spelen* (noble or beautiful plays), together with six farces, all dating back to the middle of the 14th century. These plays give the Low Countries another important first in the history of medieval literature: they are indeed the very first specimens of serious secular drama in European literature. Three of these plays—*Esmoreit, Gloriant,* and *Lanseloet van Denemarken*—are romantic stories, dealing with love as an irresistible force in life. The origin of the genre as such is not the only puzzling thing, since the genesis of the plays themselves is also surrounded by mystery. We have no idea who wrote them, nor do we know whether they are the work of one author or of several. It is also possible that these plays formed the repertoire of a traveling company of actors, as the presence in the manuscript of six farces, which were performed after the serious plays, would indicate. The language of the plays points to Brabant around the middle of the 14th century.

THE 15TH CENTURY: THE BURGUNDIAN NETHERLANDS

Of all societal changes having influenced the linguistic situation during the Middle Dutch period, the paramount one was, without the shadow of a doubt, the coming into power of the House of Burgundy, which would gradually unite the Low Countries and, in so doing, exert a far-reaching influence on its language proper as well as on the sociolinguistic variables determining how, where, and when it was used. The ensuing change was profound, multifaceted, and enduring, both in the northern and in the southern Netherlands. In the latter the consequences continued to exist, in a way, up to the present day.

The Growth of Political Unity in the Netherlands

Philip the Bold (1342–1404), Duke of Burgundy, managed to win Margaretha van Male, the daughter of the Count of Flanders, for a wife in 1369. As a consequence of this very advantageous marriage, the prosperous County of Flanders fell to Philip as the inheritance of his wife in 1384. Thus was created one of the most powerful and culturally outstanding lands in the late Middle Ages. During the 15th century Brugge was the most flourishing trade capital of that empire and by far the most important and trendsetting city of the Netherlands. Eventually, Philip the Good (1396–1467), the grandson of Philip the Bold and Margaretha van Male, added Holland, Zeeland, Brabant, Hainault, Namur, and Luxemburg to the family property.

At the moment Flanders merged with Burgundy, the Netherlands at large counted some two and a half million inhabitants. Gradually the old centers of prosperity, Ghent and Brugge, sadly decayed. The silting up of the Zwin could be checked no longer, and after some time Brugge was unable to keep up its former status. Simultaneously, the industry of Ghent and Ieper fell behind in their competition with the English. The three great towns still possessed much ancient wealth, but their guilds had lost much hold on economic life and struggled in vain against unemployment.

It was first and foremost Antwerp that became the heir to Brugge. Both Portuguese and Spaniards made Antwerp their headquarters for trade with the north. The German and Italian bankers established offices there. "In the Europe of its own time," Geyl (2001, 29) says, "it made an imposing appearance and in European commerce the place it occupied was unique." In 1430 Brussels was elected as one of the major residential cities of the Dukes of Burgundy, and Mechelen was made the seat of government (the *Hoge Raad*); in 1425 the first university of the Netherlands had opened its doors in Leuven, another Brabantine city.

Even so, at about the middle of the 16th century, Flanders still contributed more to the treasury than any other province, its share being about one-third of the total amount. Brabant paid a little less than Flanders, Holland half of Brabant, and Zeeland one-fourth of Holland. The share of the Walloon provinces was not more than one-fifth. But Holland and Zeeland were on the way up, and the steady growth of trade in both provinces is one of the most noticeable phenomena in the economic history of the Low Countries (Blockmans & Prevenier 1997).

In the state as it grew under Charles the Bold (1433–1477), the Dutch-speaking Netherlands (though still without the Saxon and Frisian provinces) were all united, yet "the Netherlandish country was linked up with a jumble of French and German lands with which no union on a sound national basis was conceivable" (Geyl 2001, 29–30). Also "the Netherlanders…had never been able to recognize themselves in their rulers" (ibid., 36).

After Charles the Bold's death in 1477 the Burgundian state permanently altered its composition. More than half of the French possessions (including their land of origin, the County of Burgundy itself) were lost, and Burgundy became essentially a Netherlands state. Flanders and Brabant, owing to their wealth and the economic importance of their great industrial and trading towns, were now the only true centers of gravity of the realm. In 1543 Gelderland was added as the 17th province under Habsburg rule, more than a century and a half after Flanders, more than a century after Brabant, Holland, and Zeeland had fallen to the Burgundian Dukes.

In November 1549 Charles V (popularly known as *Keizer Karel* in the Low Countries) carried a most important measure that was calculated to consolidate Habsburg rule in the Netherlands even more than the formation of the *Bourgondische Kreits* (Burgundian Circle). All the States and the town assemblies swore fealty to his son and heir, Philip, while at the same time they ratified a uniform regulation of the succession, notwithstanding all ancient privileges and customs as might conflict therewith. It was called a *pragmatieke sanctie* (pragmatic sanction), and it held, among other things, that the lands of the Burgundian Circle were never to be separated and that future rulers would always and exclusively be the male or female successors belonging to Charles's family. Finally, and not in the least, it promised that Dutch would be forever the official language of these new Netherlands.

Burgundian rule also marked the increase of administrative bilingualism in the Netherlands and thus of the kind of Dutch–French language contact that was going to characterize the linguistic situation for centuries to come (Armstrong 1965). This was of little consequence to the common people: they continued to use their dialects of old. Even as far as the nobility was concerned, there was no real change, at least not in Flanders. Even before the Burgundians took over, they were already used to a French liege, a French count, and a French-speaking court and had accommodated wholeheartedly to all that.

In 1299 Holland had merged with French-speaking Hainault under the House of Avesnes, and from then onward, there also French enjoyed a prominent position as the language of the nobility. In 1433 Jacqueline of Bavaria, countess of Holland, Zeeland, and Hainault, transferred her lands to her cousin, Philip of Burgundy. As a consequence of this incorporation of Holland into the Burgundian personal union, the importance of French increased as it became the de facto language of communication with the supraregional government. Yet Philip the Good had assured the people that Holland, Zeeland, and Friesland would be governed by "captains, with whom the good people will be able to speak and whom they will understand" (Armstrong 1965, 395–396). The Burgundian duke kept to his promise: the official language in the *Staten van Holland*—which executed everyday government and jurisdiction in the county— was Dutch. However, after the Burgundian takeover, proficiency in French offered access to the highest levels of government and thus acquired a new aura of power. It was to keep some functions at the court in The Hague until 1890.

In Brabant, on the contrary, it was only after Anthony, the brother of the Duke of Burgundy, became Duke of Brabant (in 1406) that, for the first time ever, they got a French-speaking prince. But Anthony was, as Armstrong (1965, 394) puts it, quick to acclimatize himself linguistically. With the extinction of

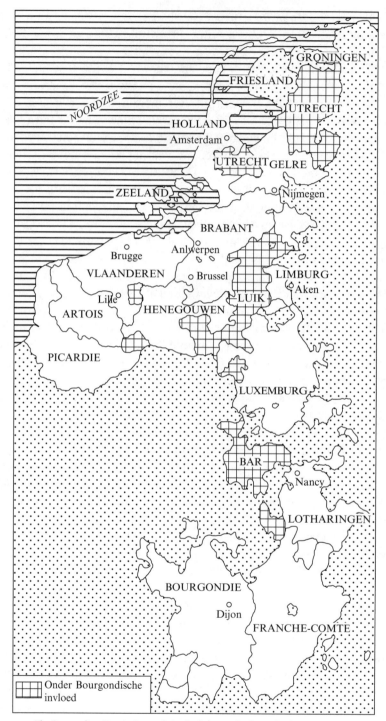

FIGURE 3.2 The Burgundian Empire Legend: Onder Bourgondische invloed = dominated by Burgundy

the junior branch in Brabant in 1430, the senior branch of the Burgundian dynasty, represented by Philip the Good, succeeded to the duchy (fig. 3-2).

He Who Pays the Piper Calls the Tune: Language (Conflict) under Burgundian Rule

In the pre-Burgundian period, Dutch was the language of local administration in both Flanders and Brabant, and it was the language the lands and cities used in their mutual communication. Having French-speaking counts and the French king for a liege, the influence of French in Flanders was important. The situation in Brabant was completely different. The lieges of the Dukes of Brabant were the rulers of the Holy German Empire, and, consequently, French had hardly any function at all in Brabant, even as part of the duchy was French speaking. The medieval duchy extended over what are now the Dutch province of Noord-Brabant and the three Belgian provinces of Antwerpen, Vlaams-Brabant (including Brussels), and Brabant Wallon. Dutch was the language of both the ducal and the city administrations.

Language policy as we know it today is very recent in the history of the Low Countries: prior to the 20th century political boundaries were not influenced by language, and trying to achieve a political unity based on a common language never occurred. Consequently, when Burgundy came into power, no language policy for governing Flanders (or the other Dutch-speaking parts) was devised. Language usage was regulated by the regional constitutions inherited from the pre-Burgundian feudal lords. As far as local government was concerned, Burgundy agreed to respect the native customs.

Still, the House of Burgundy was French, and French was the language of its court and its administration. The incumbents of all senior positions in the Burgundian hierarchy belonged to the nobility or the higher bourgeoisie. In the parts of the Low Countries the Burgundians acquired, the vernacular continued to be, at first, the language of the land, but very soon practical problems arose and in the early years the Burgundians tried to "solve" those by imposing French as the language of administration and government. It appeared that this was workable only on the level of communication with the duke and his entourage. Internal communication within Flanders and, later, with the other Dutch-speaking lands pertaining to Burgundy continued to take place in the vernacular, not in the least because they lacked a sufficient number of officials competent in French.

After some time, though, we see how the Burgundian attitude gradually changes. As the Low Countries advanced, more and more as the center of gravity of the Burgundian possessions, the dukes behaved increasingly as Netherlandic princes, partly because that was what they wanted and partly because their subjects forced them to.

The language question evolved into a recurrent item in all negotiations with the dukes and was used as a weapon in the continuing struggle for power between the centralizing ducal administration on one hand and the cities as well as the Staten of the lands on the other hand, which wanted to keep and protect their privileges of old; language was certainly part of them. At the coronation of John the Fearless (Dutch: *Jan zonder Vrees*) in 1405, the duke was forced to make considerable concessions, including in the field of language. For one, he had to promise that all communications addressed to him as count of Flanders would be in Dutch and that he would move the Council of Flanders from the French-speaking city of Lille into the center of his Dutch-speaking lands.

Geyl (2001, 31) characterizes the Burgundian policy as follows: "When they wanted to ingratiate themselves with the men of Ghent or Brugge, the Dukes knew perfectly how to speak Dutch. When they wreaked their vengeance, when they chastised and humiliated, the language that made the Flemings tremble was always French." This explains why, in 1409, when John the Fearless felt that his authority was well vested, he withdrew most of the concessions he had made four years earlier and continued the typically Burgundian policy of admitting Dutch at the regional level and preserving French for the central government. Still, the attempts of his subjects to make the central government subordinate to the Staten and the cities continued, and when in 1477 Mary of Burgundy succeeded to her father Charles the Bold, who had been killed in a battle he lost, her "good subjects" took advantage of her rather weak position to extort from her a series of concessions that were more radical than ever before. As far as linguistic demands are concerned, Mary was forced to agree that, forthwith, all senior governmental positions would be granted exclusively to *gheboren vlaminghe, vlaemsch sprekende ende verstaende* (born Flemings, able to speak and understand Dutch; Degroote 1956).

This is a paramount example of the fact that linguistic demands were to be understood as a symbol of the opposition against the centralizing Burgundian authority. In all three orders of society, Dutch speakers deliberately used their mother tongue when they wished to advertise their opposition to the Burgundian power. In 1477, as well as previously in 1405, Armstrong (1965, 396) says, "The centralizing and gallicizing procedure of the Dukes aroused the particularism of Flanders to protect itself by imposing the native speech upon the comital administration." French had become associated with a foreign, autocratic rule. Whenever the Netherlanders wanted to emphasize their privileges of old, they made sure to do so in Dutch instead of in French. The more the Burgundians were assimilated and acted like Netherlandic princes, the more they also accepted the language of the Netherlands of which, starting with John the Fearless, they all had a good command. Also, Armstrong concludes, "...More tolerant than later European governments, it [Burgundy] never interfered to teach its subjects what language they should speak or write" (ibid., 409).

Multilingual Skills

Coping with continuously changing working languages and linguistic regula-tions is possible only when there are sufficient officials fluent in the languages at stake. During the Burgundian reign (and, as far as the County of Flanders is concerned, even before that), we see that a class of bilingual (French–Dutch) politicians and high-ranking officials did indeed exist. In fact, they were trilingual, since Latin was still playing an important role as well.

It is strange and, for the language historiographer, rather unfortunate that we have no contemporary sources relating whether bilingual officials were mostly Dutch speakers with a knowledge of French or whether the opposite occurred as well and how often. Only one thing we know for sure: the (courteous) habit of Dutch-speaking city administrations to answer incoming letters in the language they were written in did not exist in the French-speaking parts. Walloon city officials corresponded exclusively in French or in Latin.

On the other hand, the fact that a number of high-ranking Netherlanders were fluent in French certainly doesn't tell how widespread bilingual competence really was. We have ample evidence that many Flemish tax collectors, for example, encountered severe problems when the Burgundian Accounting Office made it compulsory for them to draft their accounts in French (Coutant 1994). Henceforth, a lot of accounts happen to be written in a very odd mixture of Dutch and French, and for some of them the burden was too heavy altogether. The collector of Belle, for example (ironically nowadays part of France and called Bailleul), told his superiors that he was sorry not being able to comply with the new ruling, since he de *Walsche tale lettel oft niet en verstaet* (has little or no knowledge of French). For sure, he cannot have been the only senior official unable to cope with the strange and sometimes very complicated Burgundian language regulations.

The Social Advancement of Dutch

As mentioned before, the dukes understood quite well that it was important for them (and their entourage) to be able to use the language of their subjects, and, when no power struggle was involved, they happily complied. John the Fearless even chose a Dutch motto, and in a letter to his father in 1394 he mentioned proudly that he had conducted negotiations with his interlocutors in Flanders "even in Dutch."

Part of court live took place in Dutch, even when the duke was involved. John the Fearless made sure that his successors Philip the Good and Charles the Bold were raised Netherlandic princes and spoke Dutch fluently. When the daughter of the latter, Mary of Burgundy, married the future German emperor, Maximilian of Austria, he too immediately took to learning Dutch since, he professed, a prince ought to know the languages of his subjects. His teacher, he revealed in a letter, was his mother-in-law, the English princess Margaret of York, the dowager Duchess. Maximilian was convinced that the popularity he thought he enjoyed in Flanders was due to his fluency in the vernacular (Armstrong 1965). When, a few years later, the people of Brugge took him hostage for a long time until he was eventually bailed out, he may have started to doubt his popularity, but surely his linguistic prowess allowed him to converse easily with his jailers.

It was at the coronation of his wife (in 1477) that the Flemings forced her to accept the *Groot Privilegie* (Grand Privilege), a general constitution for the Burgundian Netherlands. Not only did it restore a considerable amount of urban and provincial powers and privileges that had been lost previously, but it also mentioned explicitly that the local vernacular, Dutch, was and would always remain the official language of the land (Blockmans & Prevenier 1997).

Also, during the reign of Philip the Good (1396–1467), the amount of official documents had become so huge that it was no longer possible to have them all translated into French; consequently, even the central administration could not but work with the Dutch originals. In some manuscripts we find the French translation of an occasional word in the margin.

Finally, when Philip the Handsome (Dutch: *Filips de Schone*; 1478–1506) was coronated Duke of Brabant in 1494, a new paragraph was added to the ancient privilege called the *Blijde Inkomst* (Joyous Entry) of 1430, a constitution of Brabant of sorts, which all dukes of Brabant had to swear to uphold and protect. The additional text meant to safeguard Dutch as the official language of Brabant forever and exclude any possible arbitrary ruling on the part of their sovereigns. It reads, among other things, that all official *ordonnances* and edicts, promulgated by the Staten in the name of His Majesty, would henceforth be drafted in the language of the recipients. It is because of this constitutional provision that, until the annexation by France in 1795, the working language of the Staten of Brabant has always remained Dutch.

Summarizing, one can say that shortly after the Burgundian seizure of power the duchy at large had to be governed bilingually even if occasionally some senior official had to concede not being able to cope with the bilinguality rule. As a striking example, in 1434 the Pensionary of Brussels was given the right to refuse all business at court that had been done in French (Armstrong 1965, 405). As a rule, though, from then onward senior functions were reserved for officials with bilingual skills.

The Standardization of Dutch under Burgundy

Burgundian rule was also characterized by an increasing movement toward linguistic standardization of Dutch, partly because the Burgundian form of state gave way to an internal migration on a much larger scale than ever before. For the first time ever Dutch speakers from all over the land met and established a speaking contact that was new and resulted in a growing familiarity with differing regional varieties spoken in the language territory at large. Interestingly, the increasing mobility and the population mix were not restricted to the higher layers of society but also materialized in the common people. The example of Brugge is more than convincing: only 20 to 25 percent of the construction workers employed there were recruited from the County of Flanders. Up to 30

percent were "guest workers" from Brabant, and a considerable amount originated from such "faraway" places as Holland, Gelre, and Utrecht.

The mobility of the higher strata, including the nobility, also increased,
mainly as a consequence of the Burgundian form of government. Their bureaucracy, instead of being swayed by purely local interests, envisaged the country
as a whole. They raised up a high nobility that was similarly free from provincial prejudices. Philip the Good's institution of the Order of the Golden Fleece
"was a stroke of genius; it was remarkably successful in giving a national out-
look to the magnates who were employed as stadtholders of provinces or in the
Prince's Council" (Geyl 2001, 31). Also, as a rule, a nobleman did not fill the
stadtholder's office in his native province or in the province where the bulk of
his estates were to be found. Consequently, the high nobility was a unifying
factor in the Netherlands community (ibid., 39). Urbanization, of course, is an
additional important factor furthering standardization and was very prominent
in the Netherlands. The rate of urbanization in Holland was 45 percent, in
Flanders 36 percent, and in Brabant 31 percent. All three of them were to be
the prominent centers of the immanent language standardization in the Low
Countries (Blockmans & Prevenier 1997).

As far as language development and functioning are concerned, the paramount conclusion undoubtedly is that during the Burgundian reign institutional and societal bilingualism became the rule, not only with the nobility but
also among a large group of officials. The influence and the use of French for
administrating Flanders, Holland, and Brabant were very large. Also, it is
obvious that the prestige of French—the personal language of the dukes—
increased considerably. Simultaneously, there was a boost as far as the elaboration and standardization of Dutch were concerned as well, partly stimulated by
the fact that it was a language used by the central administration and partly by
the intensification of the contacts between political and administrative entities
throughout the Netherlands at large. Finally, internal migration resulted in a
more frequent and intense personal contact between speakers of Dutch
belonging both to the elite and to the lower social classes.

Cultural Life

It is paradoxical that during the reign of the French House of Burgundy, literature
and culture in the Netherlands gradually turned loose of French influence and
developed a distinct originality of their own. Painters like Jan van Eyck, Rogier
van der Weyden, Hans Memlinc, and others found new ways of expressing themselves, and the same applies to architecture (Gothic of the Netherlands) and music
(polyphony with, among others, Johannes Ockeghem and Jacob Obrecht). In all
of these fields the Low Countries were leading in Europe. The same happened in
literature, although often the language was a handicap on the way to international
fame. The most remarkable characteristic was that secular theater flourished,
partly thanks to an institution that was very specific for the Netherlands, the

BOX 3.5 } Rederijkers (Chambers of Rhetoric)

Camers van Rhetorica were play-writing and play-performing literary societies that were very popular and very prestigious all over the Netherlands; being a member could generate substantial social prestige. Since all new ideas, literary experiments, and innovations originated from the southern parts of the Dutch language territory, the center of Rederijker activity was in the south as well. The internal organization of the *rederijkerskamers* was copied from the guilds.

The most revealing Rederijker work of the 16th century, Matthijs de Castelein's *De Const van Rhetoriken* (The Art of Rhetoric), was published in 1555. It was the first full-blown *ars poetica* in Dutch, written at about the same time as the first rhetorics in English appeared, such as Richard Sherry's *A Treatise of Schemes and Tropes* (1550) and Thomas Wilson's *The Arte of Rhetorique* (1553).

Plays such as *Elckerlyc* and *Mariken van Nimweghen* show that the Rederijkers were capable of better things than just the verbal fireworks for which they are notorious. They practiced the same three types of religious plays as their French and English contemporaries: mystery, miracle, and morality plays.

Rederijkerskamers (Chambers of Rhetoric), convivial and literary confraternities covering a wide social range from burgess to artisan (box 3.5).

Camers van Rhetorica, as they were called by the contemporaries, appeared for the first time in 1441 in the small East Flemish town of Oudenaarde, but there is no doubt that they existed before that. On the normal repertoire we usually find religiously inspired plays, followed by farces (called *cluten* or *sotternien* or *boerden*).

Along with the unifying policy of the dukes of Burgundy, the *rederijkerskamers* were another factor strengthening the language standardizing tendencies, since they performed not only at home but elsewhere as well, mainly as a consequence of the play contests they organized in various places called *landjuwelen* (land jubilees). Since (most probably) every chamber performed in its own regional variety, a lot of spectators were confronted with a language form they were not normally familiar with. The most famous contests entailed large festivities that could hold the population of the organizing cities spellbound for days, in exceptional cases even for weeks. The dukes supported the *landjuwelen* enthusiastically, since they were convinced that such gatherings did strengthen the unity of the country and give cohesion to the peoples of the Netherlands, who were not all solidly forged politically together yet. One of the most famous land jubilees was held in Antwerp in 1498 and brought together the unheard amount of 28 chambers competing for the prizes in an atmosphere of popular fair, banquets, and merriment (Pleij in Hermans 2009, 96).

As far as literary quality is concerned, the performances of various chambers were very unequal. Experimentation with form became one of their main concerns, and almost all were very much interested in playing and experimenting with verse form and language. Occasionally this generated intellectual fireworks, but also very often the result did not exceed gruff mannerism (Meijer 1971). In general, the author's ability to cope with (very high) technical standards was valued more than his inspiration and creativity. On the other hand, these very Rederijkers created two masterpieces of European (play) literature: *Elckerlyc* and *Mariken van Nimweghen.*

Mystery, miracle, and morality plays were the three genres most cherished by the Rederijkers, the latter usually being rather dull and of poor quality. Still, it is in this genre that one of the greatest plays ever was written: *Den Spyeghel der Salicheyt van Elckerlyc,* or simply *Elckerlyc.* The author, Pieter van Diest, was from Brabant, and, together with his name, that is all we know about him. He wrote the play around 1470, and in 1485 it was awarded the first prize at a land jubilee in Antwerp. Ten years later it appeared in print, and that was the key to international renown. It was translated into English as *Everyman,* and from then onward its theme was one of the most cherished in European playwriting and literature in general (Pleij in Hermans 2009, 121–123) (boxes 3.6 and 3.7).

As a notorious exception to the usual anonymity of most Rederijkers, we may mention Anthonis de Roovere (from Brugge), a playwright who was rather famous during the second part of the 15th century. Apart from satirical plays and poems, he is the author of *Vander Mollenfeeste* (The Feast of the Moles), a

---

BOX 3.6 } Elckerlyc

The morality play *Elckerlyc,* known in English as *Everyman,* was written about 1470 and was first printed in 1495. For 60 years, English and Dutch literary historians fought over the play's origin and translation. In 1939, the Englishman E. R. Tigg finally proved that the Dutch *Elckerlyc* must have been the original play. *Elckerlyc* is clearly the work of a Rederijker, but a moderate one who preferred a simple and sober style to superficial brilliance. We know his name as Pieter van Diest, a Brabanter about whom we know nothing else.

In the play, the main character, Elckerlyc (Everyman), has neglected to set aside part of his fortune for the performance of good deeds. God decides to punish him and commands Death to go and summon him. Everyman desperately seeks help from family and friends, but none of them wants to come to his aid. Finally Charity agrees to accompany him on his journey toward death.

The success of *Elckerlyc* was great not just in the Low Countries but also abroad, as can be seen from its many translations and adaptations. The English translation was the first and must have been made shortly after the original play was written; it remained popular in England for a long time. In 1536 it was translated into Latin as *Homulus,* and this translation served as the basis for later freer adaptations. In 1911, Hugo von Hofmannsthal published *Jedermann,* in which he transformed the allegorical figure into a realist character based on the English *Everyman* and the German version by Hans Sachs.

BOX 3.7 } Mariken van Nimweghen

The most outstanding example of the miracle play in Dutch is *Mariken van Nimweghen* (Mary of Nijmegen), commonly regarded as the masterpiece of medieval drama in the Low Countries. The author is not known by name; all we know is that he probably was an Antwerp Rederijker.

The central figure in this play is a young girl who lives in a village near Nimweghen (present-day Nijmegen) with her uncle, the village priest. After a lot of adventures she becomes the devil's pupil and mistress, and together they travel through the country. Finally, after many years of penance in a convent, a miracle happens and Mariken is forgiven.

The play is written not in the elevated style of *Elckerlyc* but in a much faster moving, far more colloquial, and very uninhibited idiom. The Rederijkers' touch is clearly recognizable, but the author was not suffering from any obsession with form for form's sake. The (unknown) author of *Mariken* was a first-rate dramatist with a keen sense of how to keep his play moving and how to obtain optimal effects.

dance macabre that established his fame (Pleij in Hermans 2009, 123–127). Almost a century later his cocitizen and fellow Rederijker Cornelis Everaert left us an autograph with his own complete work, comprising a large amount of plays. An autograph is an original manuscript written down by the very hand of the author, and it seldom happens that we are lucky enough to find one.

Rederijkerskamers were active in the northern Netherlands as well, but the center of their activities and success lies in the south, where everything mentioned so far was written. Northern literature was much more conservative and stayed closer to the tradition of the 14th century than did the south. Experiments with language and form fail completely.

Finally, it has to be mentioned that through the invention of the printing press a considerable amount of popular books were edited and printed during the second half of the 15th century and were almost exclusively adaptations in prose of earlier chivalric romances. One of the very first ones was a *Historie van Reinaert de Vos*, clear proof of the everlasting extreme popularity of the story. The English printer William Caxton translated the Dutch story into English and printed it himself (*The Historye of Reynart the Foxe*), thus contributing to spreading its popularity all over Europe.

Linguistic Characteristics of Middle Dutch Dialects

VARIATION IN MIDDLE DUTCH

Little is known on the mutual intelligibility of the Middle Dutch written dialects. Can we take it for granted that someone from Maastricht could understand easily the writings of an inhabitant of Amsterdam or Brussels, even bearing in mind that literacy was infinitesimally low? People who could read, though, were mostly professionals: monks and clerks, for example, practiced in reading other languages and dialects.

It is not simple to give an unequivocal answer to that question, since there is little evidence we can fall back on. One of those professional writers, Jacob van Maerlant (1235–1291), when commenting on the poet's handwork, pointed out that it is often necessary to look for rhyme words in other dialects. One has to *om de rime soucken misselike tonghe in bouken,* is how he put it (Hellinga 1938, 346). This presupposes not only that the poet is familiar with other dialects but also that he is confident that his readers will understand them. In some cases he spells out the differences very clearly, as in the following example in which he gives the name of the hedgehog in "Dietsch" as opposed to "Flemish."

> Een eghel heet ment in Dietscher tale
> In Vlaemsche een heertse, dat wetic wale.[7]

On the other hand, we can safely assume that, then as well as nowadays, attitudes played an important role. It is obvious that more people were able to understand (or believed they would understand) a text written in the prestige dialect of Brugge than one written in the variety of, say, Maaseik or Helmond.

Metalinguistic comments, unfortunately, are rare, and even when they occur they are not always easy to interpret. For example, in the 14th century the monks of the West Flemish abbey of Ter Doest wrote a letter to the famous Brussels mystic writer Jan van Ruusbroec asking to send a translation in Latin of his famous work *Die gheestelike Brulocht* (The Spiritual Espousals), which they claimed not to understand in the original. Whether they really had problems understanding Ruusbroec's language or whether they had other reasons is not sure. Anyway, in his answer Ruusbrouc states that he wrote his book in *theutonico brabantino* (Brabantine Dutch). He admits that Brabantic and Flemish are different (*flandriae brabantieque ydiomatum dissonantium*), yet he also stresses the *loquele vicinitatem* (language similarity) between Brussels and Brugge (Hellinga 1938, 345).

Probably the most clarifying practice as far as the mutual intelligibility is concerned is the behavior of clerks and copyists. A medieval copyist was not a mere transcriber whose intention it was to reproduce a text in just one more copy. He was—on the contrary—almost always keen to accommodate as much as possible the patron, who commissioned the job, since he depended on him for a living. Consequently, the output of a Brabantic text, having gone through the hands of a copyist from Ghent or Ieper, often looked more Flemish than Brabantic, as it originally was. Terminology and phrasing, sometimes even the

---

[7] It is called an *eghel* in Dietsch, whereas in Flemish, as I know well, it is called a *heertse.* Dietsch is used here for all the non-Flemish varieties of Dutch.

rhyme, were often adjusted, and we may safely assume that the copyist would not have taken this trouble if he had known for sure that his patron would have had no problems whatsoever with the original phrasing of the text. Also, a transcriber not only took care of regional variation but also eliminated archaic language. Language is continuously changing, and Middle Dutch from the 13th century could be quite different from the variety as it was written in the late 15th century. Thus, a copyist in the 15th century would certainly eliminate words such as *baraet* (cunning), *goem nemen* (to take care), *quedden* (greet), and *wigant* (hero), which were still frequently used by 13th-century writers but had vanished completely two centuries later.

ORTHOGRAPHY

It is often said that in the Middle Ages everyone used to write his or her own dialect. In truth, this occurred considerably less than generally assumed. Admittedly, there was no such thing as a standard language during the Middle Dutch period, not even a normalized written language in any present-day sense of the word. The same goes for the other European languages as well: there was no standard English, German, or French. The language spoken in various parts of the territory was a local or regional variety. It would be erroneous, though, to presume that this variety was used unchanged in writing. For one, a language that is written always differs from the language as it is spoken, not only because of the discrepancy between casual and more formal style but also because some regionalisms are difficult to write. As an example, we may safely assume that in certain regions the word for *paard* (horse) used to be pronounced (as it is still today in, for example, Brussels) [*pje:t*], with a rising diphthong. Nobody, however, has ever attempted to render this particular pronunciation in writing: it has never been found in any document. Even the limited amount of orthographical uniformity prohibited the rendering of "extreme" dialect features in writing.

   Also, an elucidating practice is the way to distinguish between long and short vowels. To indicate a long vowel in a closed syllable two letters were used, obviating a possible confusion between *been* (bone) and *ben* (I am) or *veel* (much) and *vel* (skin). From the 14th century onward, this system has been used all over the language territory. Which letter is chosen, though, to indicate the length of the vowel (Dutch: *lengteteken*) is regionally different. Sometimes, as in the example quoted, the letter is repeated. To indicate a long *a* or *o*, though, there were various possibilities. The use of *ae*, as in *jaer* (year) or *staen* (stand), was common yet originated in Flanders, where it remained in general use. In other regions more to the east, *jair* could be used. *Oick* was common practice in Limburg, Brabant, and (sometimes) Holland yet was completely absent in Flanders.

   On the other hand, it is well documented that regional characteristics presenting no spelling problems were indeed used again and again. In Flanders and Holland, *duer, of,* and *vier* (through, of, fire) were used almost exclusively for what easterners knew only as *door, af,* and *vuur*. Conversely, easterly flavored documents feature *were, greve,* and *gruun* (were, count, and green) instead of *ware, grave,* and *groen*, as used in the coastal regions.

It is fascinating to observe how sometimes people are hesitating and doubting what to write. In the west, *wuenen* and *vueghel* (to live, bird) reflect the usual (and still existing) pronunciation for words that are, time and again, also spelled *wonen* and *voghel*. What in Brabant was orally produced as *gruun* and *suut* (green, sweet) often (but not always) became *groen* and *zoet* as soon as it was written down, even by writers from Brabant. It is obvious then that certain orthographic representations were considered to be "better" or more "fitting" than others—that some were more "respectable" and carried more prestige. In a 15th-century chronicle in Brugge, the author chose *cueninck* (king) when referring to the winner of an archery contest, whereas he used *coninck* when talking about the sovereign. If *coninck* is more prestigious than *cueninck*, there can be no doubt that cultural influence already existed, even if it might have been weaker than in the ages to come. In 15th- and 16th-century Brugge, we have been able to identify at least three language layers, their differences based on such sociolinguistic variables as the social status of the writers, the text sort, the formality grade of the text, or even the intended audience (Willemyns 1997, 190–196).

Despite the wide individual spelling variation (the same word could be spelled differently not only from one region or one person to the other but also even by one and the same author in different parts of the same text), a considerable amount of conformity has existed and has only increased over the centuries. From the earliest Middle Dutch times onward there has been an orthographic tradition and not a spelling chaos, as is often assumed. On the other hand, writers of Middle Dutch had the same difficulties all languages experience when attempting to write down the sounds of one language using the alphabet of another. The beginning of the written word in the Low Countries, as in the rest of the Germanic world, was an attempt to record a Germanic language with the letters and according to the tradition of the Latin (or sometimes French) alphabet.

In building up their own tradition, the clerks used their previous experience with the orthography of those foreign languages. From the very beginning of Middle Dutch writing, we see how an *h* is inserted between a *g* and the following palatal vowel (e.g., *ghingen, gheen*). This is understood as interference from French spelling habits, where this particular insertion was meant to avoid a possible palatal, sibilant pronunciation of the *g* as [ž]. Useful and efficient as this may have been in French, it is hard to see which function it could possibly fulfill in Dutch. Thus, this kind of preoccupation that clerks and other writers had with the spelling system demonstrates that they were really interested in spelling convention and had no intention of giving in to chaos. The first real spelling treatises did not appear until the middle of the 16th century, and it wasn't until the early 19th century that the notion was born that spelling should be uniform.

REGIONAL VARIATION

From the very first Middle Dutch texts that came to us, a linguistic contrast between an easterly and a westerly variety can be witnessed. According to Goossens (1989), the main feature of the east–west opposition was the presence (east) or absence (west) of the secondary umlaut and the completely different inflectional systems that resulted from it, giving way to structurally differing language varieties (see chapter 2). The written language of the Middle Dutch period was firmly western (specifically Flemish) in its roots, even, as already mentioned, in the non-Flemish parts of the language territory.

Obviously our understanding of dialect features in Middle Dutch depends exclusively on what we can extract from written sources. Those sources are either literary or administrative texts, and although they are very different, both have merits as well as limitations. Administrative texts came later than literary ones, but they are usually dated and the place of origin is known. Consequently, they can be better used to determine what the language of a particular place at a particular time was like. Two handicaps of such texts are that the language is mostly unnatural and that the writer is very often unknown. On the other hand, the literary texts are almost never autographs but rather copies (or copies of copies). Copies are, necessarily, younger than the original and very often adapted to the language use of the copyist and his patron. It is also often impossible to determine the precise date and place of compilation, and even here the author is commonly unknown. The main advantage of literary texts is rhyme, since that is a reasonable guide to how certain sounds were pronounced. Although ideally information of both kinds of sources should be combined, administrative texts are generally more reliable.

Boundaries between dialects or groups thereof are seldom clear-cut. Between various centers of gravity, there is always a large zone of transition. When a feature is labeled Flemish, Brabants, or Hollands, this means only that it is often found in texts written in Flanders, Brabant, or Holland, respectively. In many cases it is not possible to carry the geographical determination any further, since the shibboleths are few. One example to clarify this is that we know that the auxiliary *zullen* in Holland very often turns out as *sellen*, in Brabant as *selen*, in Limburg mostly as *solen,* and in Flanders nearly always as *sullen*. Still, exact boundaries between the various regions cannot be determined.

A typical example is a feature known as *spontane palatalisering* (spontaneous palatalization), occurring in coastal Middle Dutch. We find it in words featuring Old Germanic *ŭ* in open as well as closed syllables. Examples of the former are [ø] (mostly written as *ue*) in words as *bueter, vueghel,* and *suele* (butter, bird, and sole) and [ʌ] in a closed syllable, as in *up, busch,* and *wulf* (up, bush, and wolf). In certain cases the palatal vowel is unrounded; examples are *pit* (pit), *stic* (part, piece), and *dinne* (thin). The equivalents of all these in more easterly colored Middle Dutch are *boter, voghel, sole; op, bosch, wolf;* and *put, stuc, dunne.*

In present-day family names like Antheunis-Anthonis, Demeulenaere-Demolenaere, Dewulf-Dewolf, Debuck-Debock, Vandenbussche-Vandenbossche, and Vandepitte-Vandeputte we see how this west–east contrast lives on. Due to the apparently sedentary nature of the inhabitants of the Low Countries, even present-day telephone guides still bear witness to this centuries-old linguistic contrast: the large majority of the Dewulfs and the Vandenpittes are found in the west; the Dewolfs and Vandeputtes abound in the east. That spontaneous palatalization is found in the whole west doesn't mean that geographical variation within that region did not occur. In Holland and Zeeland, for example, we often read *suemer* (summer), whereas in Flanders *somer* is in exclusive use. Conversely, *meulen* (mill) was used more often in Flanders than in Holland, where *molen* was more popular. The word *kueghel* (bullet; Dutch *kogel*) is exclusively to be found in the far southwest (present-day French Flanders), whereas the palatalization to be expected in words as *sloter* (key; Dutch *sleutel*) and *borgher* (burgher; Dutch *burger*) is missing in a large part of West Flanders. The isogloss of *mosselen* (mussels) shows *musselen* in only one part of present-day West Flanders, whereas the rest of the territory presents us with doublets *mussel* and *mossel.*

In general, the coastal regions from Friesland in the north to (present-day) French Flanders in the south are linguistically closely related and also have a lot in common with the English territory on the other side of the Channel, most of all the Ingvaeonic features.

MAIN DIALECT GROUPS

It is customary to differentiate among three larger Middle Dutch dialect groups: coastal, southeastern, and northeastern (Willemyns 1979).

Coastal Middle Dutch

This is the umbrella term mostly used for the dialects of Flanders, Zeeland, and Holland. The paramount writing dialect during the largest part of that Middle Dutch period was Flemish. One of the most famous Flemish shibboleths is the weak position of the phoneme/letter *h*. It is often dropped where expected and, conversely, appears where it seems to have no function (hypercorrection). Consequently, we often read *ondert* and *ant* (hundred, hand) and *hesele* and *hu* (easel, you).

Some characteristics gradually disappeared over time. An interesting example is the loss of nasal consonants before fricatives (already mentioned in chapter 2 on Old Dutch). Compare English *mouth* and *muide* as it used to occur in Dutch dialects—still to be found in the place names IJmuiden, Diksmuide, and Arnemuiden—to German *Mund*. The source was Old Germanic **munth*. In Standard Dutch the change did not occur in this word (it is *mond*, not *muid* or *muide*). In place names farther to the east the nasal is present as well: Rupel*monde*, Dender*monde,* Roer*mond*. In *vijf* (five; from **fimfe*) and *zuid* (south; from **sunth*), the loss does appear in Standard Dutch. Then again, *uus* (as apposed to Standard Dutch *ons* and Standard German *uns*) is found only in the westernmost part of West and French Flanders. *Goes* (goose; Du *gans*) is still found in the name Goes (a town in Zeeland) or in the street name Goeseputstraat in Brugge but does not exist in the dialects anymore.

More or less along the same lines is what happed to the prefix of the past participle. The prefix *ge-* as we know it in modern Standard Dutch (e.g., *gelopen, gedaan*) and German (e.g., *gelaufen, getan*) did not occur in the Northern part of the Dutch language territory. Also, in parts of Holland past participles like *lopen* and *daan* (without *ge-*) frequently occurred. In the southwestern part of the territory in early Middle Dutch times, the prefix *e-* or *i-* was very common. During the 13th century, participles such as *idaen* (done; Dutch *gedaan*) or *ezeit* (said; Dutch *gezeid*) or even nouns like *imet* (a land measure; Dutch *gemet*) or *iselle* (companion; Dutch *gezel*) were common in Flanders. Starting in the early 14th century, they were gradually pushed back, only to survive as a relic in the southwest of West Flanders and a small part of French Flanders, where they still exist today.

Very characteristic for coastal Middle Dutch is the differentiation made between a short /u/ (written as *ou*) and a long, slightly diphthongal /u:/ (written as *oe*) where the representation of Old Germanic *o* is concerned. Depending on the consonant that follows we'll find *voet* and *boer* (foot, boor) before dentals as opposed to *bouck* and *roupen* (book, call) before velars. This is not a mere spelling differentiation; the opposition still exists in present-day West Flemish dialects and still has phonological consequences (discussed in detail in Willemyns 1997). In Holland this feature does not occur.

Familiarity with the present dialect is very useful in interpreting older linguistic features. A very convincing case is *h-* dropping. Nowadays, it exists in almost all southern Dutch dialects: *ondert* (hundred; Dutch *honderd*) or *ant* (hand; Dutch *hand*). We can learn from the medieval sources that initially the h- dropping occurred only in Flanders and not yet in Brabant and Limburg. The use of *e* for *i* or *i* for *e* as in *blent* (blind; Dutch *blind*), *zelver* (silver; Dutch *zilver*), *inghel* (angel; Dutch *engel*), or *bringhen* (bring; Dutch *brengen*) was (and is) restricted to Flemish as well.

Some other characteristics appear to be more frequent and to last longer in Flanders than in the northern part of the Coastal Middle Dutch area. One example is the *ie* (from West Germanic *iu*) in *dier* (dear, expensive; Dutch *duur*) and *kieken* (chicken; Dutch *kuiken*). Another example is the scherplange *ê* (the phoneme developed from OIld Germanic *ai*), as in *cleen* (small; Dutch *klein*), *eeck* (oak; Dutch *eik*), *eeschen* (demand; Dutch *eisen*) or the fact that *a* is rounded and closed mostly when *f* or *ch* are following, as in *sochte* (soft; Dutch *zacht*), *brochte* (brought; Dutch *bracht*), *of* (of; Dutch *af*), and *ofvol* (offal; Dutch *afval*).

Holland shares most of its characteristics with Flanders. Some others, though, are more or less exclusive to that region: for example, palatalization of *a* in a closed syllable such as *sel* (shall; Dutch *zal*) and *blet* (leaf; Dutch *blad*); or diminutive forms ending in *-tgen* and *-tgiaen* such as *straetgen, wechtgen,* and *sticketiaen* (small street, way, and piece, respectively).

The Holland variety of coastal Middle Dutch also presents us with a very specific development of the scherplange *ê*, such as *stien* (stone; Dutch *steen*), *vliesch* (flesh; Dutch *vlees*), or the spelling *-uy-* preceding *r* as in *verhuyeren* (lease; Dutch *verhuren*) and *schuyer* (barn; Dutch *schuur*). Another one is vocal change before *r* + consonant, more specifically *ar* where Flemish features *er:hart, parsen* (heart, press; Dutch *hart, persen*) or *i* in *mit and him*, as opposed to Flemish *met* and *hem* as well as *tusken* or *visken* for Flemish *tusschen* and *visschen* (between, to fish; Dutch *tussen, vissen*).

Almost a shibboleth for Holland is the fact that, as opposed to almost the entire western and middle part of the language territory, the evolution of *ft* to *cht* does not occur (compare Dutch *lucht* and *kracht* with German *Luft* and *Kraft*). In Holland we frequently read *graft* (gracht) and *vercoft* (verkocht). In Amsterdam it was not until the 18th century that we finally saw the famous *grachten* replace *graften*.

Southeast

Southeastern Middle Dutch consists mostly of the dialects of Brabant and Limburg. Today's provinces of Noord-Brabant, Vlaams Brabant, Brussel, and Antwerpen together build the Brabantic dialect region, whereas the two provinces both called Limburg (one in the Netherlands and the other in Belgium) constitute the Limburg dialect region. Parts of the Lower Rhine (e.g., Kleve) used to belong to it as well.

As a consequence of the very consequential west–east opposition already mentioned, Brabant has considerably more similarities with Limburg than with Flanders or Holland, whereas Brabant and Limburg share a lot of linguistic features that are absent in the west. On the other hand, Flemish has colored many a Brabantic text. Mainly in the 13th and 14th centuries, we see how Brabant borrows features from the more prestigious Flemings, to the detriment of characteristics that are part of their own spoken dialects. One of the most salient examples is the secondary umlaut, very much present in spoken language but omitted more often than not in writing. That's why we often find *backer, groen,* and *soet* instead of the indigenous *becker, gruun,* and *suut*. Even so, the use of the length marker *i* in words like *voight, dair,* and *voir* (tutor, there, for; Dutch *voogd, daar, voor*) is omnipresent in Brabant (as well as in many other regions) but is completely absent in Flanders. Typical Brabanticisms are furthermore *o* for *u* in *locht* and *vrocht* (air, fruit; Dutch *lucht, vrucht*) or syncope of intervocalic *v* in *hoot* (< *hovet*), *heet* (<*hevet*) (head, has; Dutch *hoofd, heeft*).

Brabant is also generally considered to be the center of gravity of the diphthongization of Old Germanic long *i* and *y* to (present-day) *ei* [ɛ.i] and *ui* [œ.y] as in *rijk, wijn* and *huis, buik*. Although we know for sure that the process of diphthongization had already begun during the Middle Dutch times, it is not easy to pinpoint in texts since it took a long time for the former spelling (*rijcke, wijn, huus, buuc*) to change. For a long time it was thought that Brabant was the birthplace of diphthongization and gradually passed it on to Holland (known as the Kloeke theory). Nowadays, though, we see diphthongization as a polygenetic phenomenon, having started almost simultaneously in Brabant and Holland. West Flanders and the largest part of Limburg and the northeastern dialects continue to use the old monophthongs even today. East Flanders adopted diphthongs, under Brabantic influence, in the course of the 18th and 19th centuries.

Because Brabant is a large territory it is not surprising to find variation within the Brabantic written language. Forms with *ft* instead of *-cht-*, as already signaled for Holland (*gecoft, after, graft*), regularly occur in Brabant's northern parts (Breda, Grave, Helmond) but never in the major southern Brabantic cities Brussels, Mechelen, and Leuven. Palatalization like in *brueder* (brother; Dutch *broeder*) frequently occurs in Antwerp but rather sparely in the rest of Brabant (Goossens 1980).

The languages used in Limburg and Brabant were very similar, and the major differences between them are not in the linguistic features themselves but rather in the frequency of their occurrence. Since Flemish influence in Limburg has been considerably less prominent than in Brabant, a feature like secondary umlaut has never been suppressed; therefore, forms like *weer* (were; Dutch *ware*) and *grevynne* (countess; Dutch *gravin*) are abundant. Flanders and in its footsteps (though to a lesser extent) Brabant write *gravinne* and *ware*.

In Limburg too, of course, internal variation is found; an interesting example is that the number of words subject to the second sound shift (e.g., *ich, ooch*) grows larger the nearer we come to the river Maas. The same holds true for *wir* for *wij* (we) and *der/de* for *de/die* (the, this).

More or less omnipresent in Limburg are the transition of *a* into *o* in, for example, *jor, worheit* (year, truth; Dutch *jaar, waarheid*) and the apocope of *t* in *nach* (night; Dutch *nacht*) and *wich* (baby; Dutch *wicht*).

Consonant doubling in word final position—*dorpp, onss, brieff* (village, us, letter; Dutch *dorp, ons, brief*)—occurs not only in Limburg but also in the northeast and in Holland. In Brabant this feature is considerably less frequent, whereas in Flanders it does not exist.

Scherplange ê is almost always rendered *ey/ei*, not only in cases where Flemish has *ee* (*cleyn, eyck* vs. *cleen, eeck*) but also where Brabant and later

Standard Dutch have *ee*, resulting in *vleisch, bein,* and *stein* instead of *vleesch, been,* and *steen.*

Finally, we observe that vocalization of *l* between *a/o* and a dental consonant, a distinguishing feature of Dutch overall, does not occur in the largest part of Limburg and the northeast. Consequently, *olde, solde, wolde,* and so forth are predominant, although in some places *aude/oude, saude/soude,* and *waude/woude* (*old, should, would*) appear as well.

Northeast

Northeastern dialects are used to the north of Limburg and to the east of Utrecht: in today's terminology, the provinces of Gelderland, Overijssel, Drenthe, and Groningen, the territory that originally was close to the Low German territory but that, from the 14th century onward, was gradually integrated into the Dutch language territory, with Utrecht the intermediary for the influence from Holland. It is obvious, therefore, that the number of Saxon characteristics used to be considerable. An interesting example is the Saxon uniform plural (Dutch: *Saksische eenheidspluralis*); that is, all endings in the plural indicative are equal, either *-en* or *-t*.

At the same time, this territory shares a lot of features with Limburg since they are both part of the eastern periphery. Once again, the major differences are found not in the linguistic features themselves but rather in the frequency of their occurrence. Consequently, we find a larger number of secondary umlaut cases still, more *ald-* and *old-* forms in words with *al, ol + dental consonant,* and more often *ee f*or *ie* in words like *breef, de* (letter, this; Dutch *brief, die*).

More specific for the northeast are *a* for *o* in words like *a*pen (open) or *baven* (*boven*) as well as a short vowel in open syllable (lengthened during Old Dutch times in the rest of the territory) as in *etten* for *eten* (to eat). Finally, the pronouns *oer* and *oen* (him, her; Dutch *hem, haar*) should be mentioned as well as *de, we* (this, we; Dutch *die, wie*) and the proposition *to* (at; Dutch *te*).

Practically none of these are ever found in the remainder of the Dutch language territory, although they frequently occur in the directly adjacent territory of present-day Germany.

4 }

Early New Dutch (1500–1800)

Preliminary Remarks

Prior to the 16th century, there had never been a political entity "Netherlands," nor had there ever been a political structure consisting exclusively of Dutch-speaking countries. It was the state building policy of the House of Burgundy that gradually brought the Netherlands together (see chapter 3). Under Charles V (aka Keizer Karel), born in Ghent in 1500, the entire Habsburg Netherlands were united in the *Bourgondische Kreis* (Burgundian Circle) in 1548, which was linked (very loosely) to the rest of the Habsburg empire. For the first time ever, the Netherlands became more or less a political entity of its own, including also some French-speaking parts.

It was also in the 16th century, after the shifting of the economic and political center of gravity from Flanders to Brabant, that a more or less uniform, written variety of the language gradually began to take shape (Van den Branden 1956). It was mainly based on the language varieties of Flanders and Brabant. This process, though, would very soon change its course dramatically as a result of the Eighty Years' War, the revolution of the Netherlands against its Spanish Catholic rulers, which Geyl described as "the 16th century's paramount catastrophe, which was a brutal disruption of a centuries long development" (Geyl 2001, 18). The political split of the territory, which occurred as a consequence of that war, dramatically impacted the evolution of Dutch. From 1585 onward, the Netherlands was divided into two separate parts, each with its specific political, cultural, religious, and social structures and development.

The 17th century in Holland is known as the Golden Age, reflecting both economic and cultural prosperity. Influential writers such as Vondel, Hooft, Bredero, Cats, and Huygens (see boxes) coined the writing standard for ages to come in a republic that had developed into one of the superpowers of its time (box 4.1). The southern regions, on the contrary, stagnated culturally, economi-

BOX 4.1 } The Golden Age

The qualification *Golden Age* applies only to the northern part of the Low Countries, for which the 17th century was indeed a period of unprecedented wealth and prosperity, economically as well as culturally. For the southern provinces the 17th century was anything but golden.

To the world at large, the most spectacular feature of the Dutch Golden Age is the work of the painters. The names Rembrandt, Frans Hals, Johannes Vermeer, Adriaan van Ostade, Jan Steen, Adriaan Brouwer, and many others are known everywhere, and examples of their art can be seen in most countries. Similarly, the achievements of scientists like Anthonie van Leeuwenhoek and Christiaan Huygens, of Hugo Grotius, the founder of international law, and of the philosopher Spinoza became famous throughout the civilized world. But with the writers it was a different matter. The language barrier was powerful and prevented most of them from becoming more than local celebrities. Five of them (the Golden Five) are usually regarded to be the outstanding authors whose literary achievements colored the Golden Age: Breedero, Cats, Hooft, Huygens, and Vondel[1].

cally, and intellectually. In the north, the standardization of Dutch, although still strongly influenced by the southern tradition, gathered momentum in a specifically Holland-flavored way. In the south the Dutch language gradually lost a number of its functions mainly to French, and its contribution to the elaboration of the Dutch standard language decreased and eventually stopped for a long time.

As a result of the Spanish War of Succession (1702–1713), the southern "Belgian" territories were passed on from the Spanish to the Austrian branch of Habsburg, which ruled through the end of the 18th century. The consolidation of French as the more socially acceptable tongue continued. In the north the glory of the Golden Age faded and gave way to what is generally known as the *Pruikentijd* (an age of dullness).[2]

At the end of the period related here, the northern and southern parts of the Netherlands were separately conquered by the victorious armies of the French Revolution. The linguistic impact of the French occupation in the north and south differed.

The 16th Century: The Age of Lexicographers and Grammarians

In summer 1585, Alessandro Farnese, the Italian commander-in-chief of Philip II's Spanish army, captured Antwerp, the last of the important cities of the

---

[1] The main (but not the only) sources of information in all the boxes on literature (in this and the other chapters) are Meijer (1971) and Hermans (2009).

[2] Translated as the Periwig Period by Paul Vincent in Brachin (1985).

Netherlands to return into Spanish hands, after they had previously freed themselves. As far as the history of Dutch is concerned, this was the paramount event of the 16th century (and probably of all the centuries to come). From that point on, Dutch was de facto (although de jure only from 1648 onward) a language spoken and used in two different countries, with the sole exception of the short intermezzo from 1814 to 1830, during the United Kingdom of the Netherlands (see chapter 5).

Apart from that event, which will be dealt with extensively later on, the 16th century is in many respects, also as far as the language is concerned, an age of transition, sitting between the Middle Ages and modern times. Middle Dutch is gradually evolving into Early New Dutch and a new era starts, although it is impossible to pinpoint when one ends and the other emerges, the more so since it is definitely different depending on region. Without a doubt, though, the 16th century saw the beginning of language standardization and of the language planning efforts needed to set it in motion and sustain it. There are no known purposeful attempts in the direction of language planning aimed at unifying written Dutch prior to the 16th century.

The shift of the economic and cultural center of gravity from Flanders to Brabant is what drew attention to linguistic diversity and variation. One of the triggers of language planning may have been the need, also created by the Reformation sweeping over the Low Countries, to produce texts that could be understood by as large an audience as possible in various parts of the territory. The popularization of the printing press helped make this possible. In general, the awareness of this need—the necessary prerequisite for standardization attempts—was present from the early 16th century onward. During that time, and continuing throughout the 17th and mainly the 18th centuries, efforts were made to regulate and uniform the language by means of corpus planning devices, such as dictionaries and grammars.

In the 16th century, Dutch, as De Vries, Willemyns, and Burger (2003, 59) put it, "c[a]me of age: a language to speak and to write, to praise God, to pursue science, alongside with being the language of poets and administrators it had been for centuries before." The lingua franca on the European level, though, continued to be Latin, and one of the most famous Netherlanders ever, Desiderius Erasmus (who died in 1536), wrote his books in that language. Yet more and more people in Europe overall and in the Low Countries in particular urged the use of the mother tongue in as many domains as possible. Jan Gymnich from Antwerp is the first we know of (in 1541), and many others soon followed suit. Nevertheless, broadening the domains of the vernacular also led to the awareness that it needed some "refinement and uniformization," as Van den Branden (1956) calls it in the title of his book, to be able to assume the variety of functions previously performed by the classical languages, who had long been thought to be "intrinsically better" than the vernaculars. The *Naembouck,* a dictionary published by the Ghent printer Joos Lambrecht (1551), was one of the very first corpus planning instruments. He and many of his successors had commercial motives as well: the more people can read a particular language variety, the larger number of books that can be sold, which explains why so many printers were involved in the language-regulating business. By the same token, Lambrecht, as all those coming after him, enjoyed condemning and stigmatizing loanwords from other languages, especially French. Jan van der Werve, another language regulator, put it this way: "help me, I ask you, to raise up our mother language, which now lies concealed in the earth like gold, so that we may prove how needless it is for us to beg for assistance of other languages."[3] The printer Jan de Laet, who totally agreed with Van der Werve, suggested that in the absence of an adequate equivalent (to avoid a foreign word) one should rather have recourse to German as a sister language.

Status planning was provided by famous scientists writing their treatises in the vernacular. The famous botanist Rembert Dodoens from Mechelen published his *Cruijde Boeck* (Book of Plants) in 1554 and the Ghent surgeon Carolus Baten his treatises on medicine in 1589 and 1590. By far and large the most productive linguistic innovator of his age, though, was the famous humanist Simon Stevin from Brugge, a mathematician, musicologist, engineer, astronomer—in short an all-around scientist (see chapter 1). Having fled to the north, he was the first professor to teach in his mother tongue (instead of Latin) at the University of Leiden, and he published almost all of his scientific books in Dutch as well (Van der Wal 2004). As mentioned in chapter 1, he was convinced that Dutch was the language most fit for science, since it has the largest amount of monosyllabic words. By his count Dutch[4] had 1,428 monosyllabic nouns and 742 monosyllabic verbs, whereas Greek had only 220 and 45, respectively, and Latin fewer still (Hagen 1999, 16–18). Although the relevance of the argument is not obvious (Stevin mentions the ease with which compound words may be formed, its great flexibility; Brachin 1985, 15), it went unchallenged, not only in the 16th century but also a long time thereafter.

On top of that, Stevin invented many Dutch words for scientific terminology that previously existed only in Latin; many of them survived through the ages and are still used today. A few convincing examples are *middellijn* (diameter), *driehoek* (triangle), and *aftrekken* (substract). He is responsible for the fact that the Dutch terminology in mathematics and physics deviates from the international terminology existing in most of the European languages. The name of his science itself *wiskunde* (*wiskonst* was how he called it) has replaced mathematics in Dutch (Van der Wal 2004). That Dutch, the language of his hometown of Brugge, was the best language in the world was not only Stevin's conviction; it was shared by many a scientist, and the idea that languages have

---

[3] *Tresoor der Duytsche tale* (1553). English translation in Geyl (2001, 47).
[4] In his *Uytspraeck van de Weerigheyt der duytsche tael* (Statement on the dignity of the Dutch Language), 1586.

intrinsic qualities was rather common. In 1569, Joannes Goropius Becanus, the author of the *Origines Antwerpianae,* claimed Dutch to be not only the best but also the oldest language, since he was convinced that it was the language spoken by Adam and Eve in paradise (Hagen 1999, 16–18). At that time, people like Becanus were not considered eccentric or weird, and many other very serious scientists and language experts in several countries propagated similar convictions regarding their own vernaculars.

Creating some kind of general Dutch, a variety understood by as many people as possible, was the dream not only of the book printers but also of those propagating the "new faith," Martin Luther's and John Calvin's religious reforms. They wanted to be understood in a territory as large as possible and tried to convince people to read the bible by themselves. Both the preaching and the bible reading necessitated some kind of standardized language variety, and, out of necessity, some of the preachers turned into linguists, trying to create a standard language. After all, Luther in Germany had proved that it could be done. Some even tried to create a mixed language that would be understood in both the Dutch and the Low German areas.

Even Catholics had bible translations, such as the Delft Bible (1477), one of the very first books printed in the Netherlands, and the Leuven Bible (1548).

At the onset of the protestant bible tradition, Luther's Bible was adapted, first known as the Liesveldt Bible (1526–1542) and subsequently reworked as the Deux-Aes Bible (1562). Most bible translations aimed at being comprehensible in the Dutch language area as a whole. More ambitious still was the project of the Fleming Jan Utenhove, who created for his translation of the New Testament, a language designed to be understood from Dunkirk to the Baltic Sea. The Frisian Menno Simons and the German Melchior Hoffmann tried their hand at a language variety based on both Eastern Dutch and Low German. On the other hand, the Fleming Petrus Dathenus (from Kassel in today's French Flanders) wrote his famous translation of the Psalms in 1566 for a Calvinist audience in pure Flemish, and it was read and used in the north for centuries to come.

In general, though, the need for a common language for the Low Countries as a whole was strongly felt, and in 1592 the Staten of Holland entrusted to Marnix van Sint Aldegonde the task of translating the whole Bible "using the most general, clear and correct language" (Brachin 1985, 14). Marnix was not able to bring this project to fruition, but it was taken up and achieved a little later. It took until 1637 for the *Statenbijbel* not only to create but also to implement and spread a standardized language that influenced modern standard Dutch more than anything else (Van Dalen-Oskam & Mooijaart 2000).

At the same time, the 16th century is the period in which scores of grammarians (*spraakkonstenaars,* as they were called) struggled with spelling and grammar, considered by most to be one and the same. Joos Lambrecht, already mentioned as the first lexicologist, was also the author of the first spelling treatise: his *Nederlandsche Spellijnghe* was published in 1550. Nevertheless, in the realm of spelling and grammar the ideal of a common language was less obvious, and most of the *spraakkonstenaars* were looking for a norm in their own dialect. The most important, though not necessarily the most influential, one was Pontus de Heuiter from Delft, whose *Nederduitse Orthographie*, published in 1581, was one of the very few based on an intentional general language instead of a particular dialect. Although appreciated by present-day linguists, it was not very popular with his contemporaries. The most influential 16th-century grammar is the *Twe-spraack vande Nederduitsche Letterkunst*, written by Spiegel and published by the Amsterdam *rederijkerskamerDe Eglantier* in 1584 (Hagen 1999, 14–16). Although the author does not try to hide his Amsterdam origins, he emphasizes that his language, and therefore his norm, is not that of the common Hollander but the idiolect of the cultivated and educated classes. This marks the beginning of a new approach in the standardization debate: as far as the elaboration and implementation of the norm are concerned, the social variable grows ever more important, to the detriment of the regional variable. This will run as a leitmotiv through language planning in the northern Netherlands.

Also, the author of the *Twe-spraak* readily accepts the then general idea that the richness of a language depends on the richness of its forms; consequently, it is Spiegel's main ambition to reshape the Dutch language according to the rules of Latin grammar, which of course had no lasting effect on the language. Still, there can be no doubt that Spiegel's *Twe-Spraack* has been both a popular and an influential grammar, very often seen as the real beginning of the tradition of prescriptive grammars in Dutch.

Lexicology in the 16th century prospered even more than grammar. After Joos Lambrecht's *Naembouck,* some real professionals appeared on the scene. The Antwerp master printer Christoffel Plantijn wrote as well as commissioned very important and innovative dictionaries (Claes & Bakema 1995). His own *Tetraglotton*, a quadrilingual dictionary combining Latin, Greek, French, and Dutch, was probably partly composed by Cornelis Kiliaan, his editor. Kiliaan was the author in his own right of one of the most famous dictionaries ever, the *Etymologicum Teutonicae linguae sive Dictionarium Teutonico-Latinum*, first published in 1574 but best known in its revised third edition of 1599 (Van Rossem 2007) (fig. 4-2). Kiliaan not only described the vocabulary of Dutch but also included etymological comments and indicated in which regional dialects the listed words were used. Finally, he added the translation in both High German and Latin. He produced the first scientific dictionary of a vernacular, second to none in Europe and "the Etymologicum is a treasure-house on which scholars are still drawing" (Brachin 1985, 15). Obviously, this is also the paramount status planning instrument of the Dutch language in the field of lexicology; Spiegel's *Twe-Spraack* has to be attributed the same status in the field of grammar (fig. 4-1).

Twe-spraack
vande
Nederduitsche
Letterkunst/
ofte/
Vant spellen ende eyghenscap
des Nederduitschen taals;

uytghegheven by de Kamer
IN LIEFD BLOEYENDE,
t'Amstelredam.

TOT AMSTELREDAM,
By Hendrick Barentsz. Boeckvercoper/
inde Warmoesstraat/int verguldè
Schryf-boeck. 1614.

FIGURE 4.1 Title page of Spieghel's "Twe-spraack"

kw 393 F10

ETYMOLOGICVM
TEVTONICÆ LINGVÆ:
SIVE
DICTIONARIVM
TEVTONICO-LATINVM,

PRÆCIPVAS TEVTONICÆ
LINGVÆ DICTIONES ET PHRASES
Latinè interpretatas, & cum aliis nonnullis linguis
obiter collatas complectens:

Studio & Opera
CORNELII KILIANI DVFFLÆI.

Opus Germanis tam superioribus quàm inferioribus,
Gallis, Anglis siue Anglosaxonibus, Italis, Hispanis,
& aliis lectu perutile.

*Quid hîc præstitum sit, Præfatio ad
Lectorem docebit.*

Editio tertia, prioribus auctior & correctior.

ANTVERPIÆ
Ex OFFICINA PLANTINIANA,
Apud Ioannem Moretum.
M. D. XCIX.

FIGURE 4.2 Title page of Kiliaen's "Etymologicum"

By the time both books were published, another event had already started that would change the evolution of Dutch more decisively than any language planning effort ever: the Eighty Years' War, the revolution of the Netherlands against their Spanish Catholic rulers. Previously, the socioeconomic situation in the Low Countries had changed considerably. The first half of the 16th century was a period of amazing economic development for the Netherlands, but not all the provinces had an equal share. In Flanders the old centers of prosperity were slowly decaying. Since the silting up of the Zwin could no longer be checked, Brugge lost its harbor and its position of old. The industries in Ghent and Ieper had fallen behind in competing with the English. The three great towns still possessed much ancient wealth, but their guilds had lost all hold on economic life and struggled in vain against unemployment. Antwerp had become the heir to Brugge, and, says Donaldson (1983, 101) "by the middle of the 16th century Antwerp had developed into the most important city in Europe north of the Alps....It formed the economic hub of a world-wide trading empire."

During the reign of *Keizer Karel*, reformation reached the Low Countries. The ideas of Luther and, mostly, Calvin, were very appealing and spread like fire, first to Flanders. The official persecution of the "heretics" by the Inquisition was very unpopular with the people and broadened the gap between the local authorities and the central government. The political and religious system was weakening, and the state of the economy was very bad, mostly because Flanders' traditionally strong textile industry was not faring well. Also, gold and silver imported from the Americas fueled inflation. The gap between the rich and the poor was getting larger and larger, most of all in Flanders, where the rural population was reduced to poverty.

This collective displeasure lit the fuse of the rebellion powder keg during the reign of Philip II, who had succeeded his father, Charles V, in 1555 as the ruler of the Netherlands. An ever-increasing part of the nobility joined the rebellion against the Inquisition and the monarch and so did the poor, who had nothing to lose. The iconoclastic fury (Dutch *Beeldenstorm*), starting in 1566 in southern Flanders, marked the beginning of the Eighty Years' War. Alva's repression, culminating in the public beheading of the counts of Egmond and Hoorne, only made things worse.

On April 1, 1572, the *Watergeuzen*[5] took the small beach town of Den Briel, the first, albeit completely unexpected, victory of the rebel army. Finally, as a result of the uprising, the rather passive north gained its independence, whereas the south was eventually recaptured by Spain. Dutch Protestantism, born and raised in the south, was repressed with the power of Spanish arms but became the state religion of the north, which at first had been rather slow at taking sides.

---

[5] *Geuzen* is the name the freedom fighters called themselves.

After the fall of Antwerp in summer 1585, the country was officially split, and the massive exodus of southern Netherlanders toward England, Germany, but mostly the northern Netherlands climaxed. Antwerp emptied: in a few years, its population decreased from 100,000 to 42,000. By the same token Amsterdam's population increased from 50,000 to 100,000 by the end of the century and to 150,000 by 1650. A census in 1622 revealed that one-third of Amsterdam was of southern origin; in Haarlem it was 50 percent and in Leiden even 67 percent. As to their social status, the immigrants were not only skilled craftsmen but also important merchants and in 1611 made up half of the total of 310 in Amsterdam (Van Leuvensteijn 1997). Holland became the economic and cultural center of Europe, but the glory of Holland's Golden Age was also paid for by money from Flanders and Brabant.

The massive exodus was also a brain drain, emptying the southern Netherlands of its influential philosophers, scientists, and artists. Many of them were "men of words": theologists, clergymen, professors, teachers, authors, printers, civil servants, diplomats etc. So the people of Holland were taught by southerners, heard southern sermons in their churches and were entertained by southern Rederijkers in their theaters. The spoken word in Holland was heavily accented with a southern flavor and a lot of that Flemish and Brabantic influence was there to stay in Standard Dutch forever, be it mostly in the more formal written variety.[6]

We may conclude that, although the 16th century bubbled with language planning activities, it is not easy to identify an explicit norm for the standardized language or to understand how exactly the language was built up and what its main components were. Yet we may get an idea of an implicit norm if we look at the practice of the book printers. Willemyns (1997) gave an extensive analysis of the methods of the Antwerp printer Jan van Ghelen who in 1562 printed a selection of the work of the West Flemish playwright Anthonis de Roovere. Since much of De Roovere's work has come to us in manuscript form as well, a comparison is possible. In De Roovere's manuscripts the language is decidedly West Flemish in flavor. In Van Gheelen's printed book almost all West Flemish forms are gone and have been replaced, interestingly enough, not by their Brabantic dialect counterparts but by more or less unmarked forms, which still exist in the present-day standard language. Since an extensive list is to be found in Willemyns (1997, 189), a few examples will suffice: *almueghende–almoghende; vul–vol; stick–stuck; beede–beyden; hoogheblic–ooghenblick; roupen–roepen; selver–silver.* The first form always is De Roovere's manuscript form, the latter the equivalent in Van Gheelen's edition.

---

[6] See later in the chapter for a less traditional view expressed in Boyce Hendriks and Howell (2000).

FIGURE 4.3 Title page of the "Statenbijbel" (courtesy of Ons Erfdeel vzw, Flanders, Belgium)

The 17th Century: The Golden Age

Of the seven northern provinces, Holland was far and away the most prosperous one. Between 1585 and 1685, the built-up area of Amsterdam increased
from 106 to 726 hectares. Leiden was proud of its university, founded in 1575;
The Hague was the seat of the Prince of Orange (the Stadtholder) and of the
court. The language of the province of Holland won the day without imperi-
alist designs or resistance. According to Brachin (1985, 16), "After 1600 the
language written by a Groningen syndic, or a Gelderland chancellor loses its
eastern stamp."

At the same time, it is remarkable that a lot of new language features
appeared in Holland during the 17th century—too many actually to believe
that every so-called new feature would indeed be due to language change. This
indicates that we are not sufficiently well informed about the language used in
Holland during the preceding centuries. Until the 17th century many texts
written in Holland were written (as far as we know) following the southern
norm of the written Dutch language. A good many other features must have
existed in (spoken) Hollands and never found their way to written or printed
texts. To establish what real Hollands during the previous centuries was like, it
will be necessary to go back to the sources to look for more materials, unused
so far.

On the other hand, we know that, as Taeldeman (2007) observes, Hollands
after the Middle Dutch period went through a process of de-Ingvaeonization,
meaning that a lot of Ingvaeonic features it used to have in common with the
other western dialects in Flanders and Zeeland gradually disappeared.
According to Taeldeman influence from Brabant may have been decisive here.

During the 17th century, the newly won self-consciousness demolished barriers that previously may have hampered the use of the vernacular as it really
was. Two different developments seemed to occur simultaneously: the (re)
appearance of real Hollands, as we find it, for example, in many plays by Bredero
(box 4.2); and the almost immediate repression of that popular vernacular to be
replaced, this time not by the southern writing tradition but by a new cultivated
language, the language of the rich and the powerful, the courtiers and nobility
of the court in The Hague, and the wealthy merchants of Amsterdam, *regenten*
all of them. Consequently, the emergence of a "real Hollands" was short-lived.
The new cultivated Dutch (the forerunner of *Algemeen Beschaafd Nederlands*,
or ABN), on the other hand, was there to stay.

From the very first decades of Holland's Golden Age we witness the appearance of a large number of treatises on grammar and spelling. The most influential one, *De Nederduytsche spraec-konst ofte tael-beschrijvinghe* (1633), was
written by Christiaen van Heule. The main objective of those grammars was to
prescribe a norm and change the language accordingly and not the other way

BOX 4.2 } Gerbrand Adriaenszoon Breedero (1585–1618)

In the year of his untimely death, Breedero (aka Breero), the son of a shoemaker, gave us the play *De Spaansche Brabander* (The Spanish Brabanter), a kind of revue, a series of scenes held together by the two central characters, Jerolimo and his servant Robbeknol. Jerolimo is a gentleman swindler from Antwerp who boasts in flowery language of his former grand life in Brabant, continually extolling the virtues of that country while sounding off at the Hollanders. Breedero's conception of Jerolimo, the Spanish Brabanter in the play, is the revolt of the Hollander in him. Another of his very popular plays was *Moortje* (The Moorish Woman; 1615).

After his death in 1618, Breero's poems and songs were published under three headings: Boertigh, Amoureus, and Aendachtigh Groot Lied-boeck (Comical, Amorous, and Religious Great Songbook).

In the years 1612 and 1613, Breedero wrote three short comedies: *De Klucht van de Koe* (The Farce of the Cow); *De Klucht van de Molenaar* (The Farce of the Miller); and *De Klucht van Symen sonder Soeticheyt* (The Farce of Simon without Sweetness).

around. In addition, the acclaimed writers of the time were, of course, influential in their own right. Jacob Cats contributed to general Dutch by successfully mixing elements from Zeeland (his province of origin) with those from Holland and Brabant (box 4.3). Still, Cats (and Bredero for that matter) were not really concerned with linguistic matters, neither practical improvement nor theoretical speculation. Both concerns, though, were present to a high degree in Huygens (box 4.5), Hooft (box 4.4), and Vondel (box 4.6).

The cities of the north became melting pots for Netherlanders from all over the Low Countries. The prosperity that accompanied Holland's mercantile enterprise is undoubtedly one of the most important reasons that the language of that region would form the perfect basis for the (future) standard language (Donaldson 1983, 101).

The language standardization referred to here is the work of a particular elite and was achieved gradually. According to Vondel, the prestigious poet whose parents had fled Antwerp for religious reasons, the norm of the language was to be found in the sociolect of the upper classes of both Amsterdam and The Hague. Once again we see how the social variable supersedes the regional one: the old Amsterdam language, Vondel states, is too ridiculous, and the old Antwerp language (both dialects were used by the common people) is too coarse and insufficiently clear to be able to function as the basis for a civilized standard language. Until well into the 20th century, having a regional accent was deemed less of a problem than having the wrong social accent. The only variety Vondel deemed fit for civilized usage was the language "at present spoken most perfectly in The Hague, at the States-General and at the court of the Stadtholder, and in Amsterdam, the most powerful commercial centre in the world, by people of good education."[7]

A less traditional view of language change and standardization during the Golden Age was expressed by Boyce Hendriks and Howell (2000). They write in the final sentence of their article: "Given the fact that traditional linguistic histories have paid little attention to social history, we believe that the history of Dutch in the early modern period needs to be rewritten" (274). In this article they challenge the traditional view of language development in 17th-century Holland in general and the importance of the influence of southern refugees on the future Dutch standard language in particular: "we have introduced evidence arguing that the depiction of the southern Dutch migration in the linguistic histories of Dutch is incomplete at best, and totally distorted at worst" (ibid.)

BOX 4.3 } Jacob Cats (1577–1660)

Maybe the least talented yet most popular and influential of the Golden Five, this Zeelander of the regent class has served as Grand Pensionary (*Raadspensionaris van Holland*) for a number of years. Father Cats, as he is commonly known, produced a huge amount of verse in didactic poems, such as *Trouwring* (Wedding Ring; 1637), but was at his best in the brief and usually short-lined pieces of his *Spiegel van den ouden en nieuwen tijd (*Mirror of the Old and New Time), a collection of aphorisms subjoined by pictures and emblems with explanatory inscriptions, published in 1632.

According to Pieter Geyl (2001, 519), "as late as the 19th century all respectable protestant households possessed, alongside the Bible, a copy of his *Collected Works*." Some of his aphorisms are now part of the Dutch language such as:

Al draagt een aap een gouden ring
Zo is het doch' een lelijk ding
or
Als de wijn gaat in de man
Leit de wijsheid in de kan

Since his favorite subject, the morality of love and marriage, was of interest to everyone, his print runs were incomparably larger than those of any other writer of his time. A total of 50,000 copies of one title were no exception (on a population of around one and a half million). Vondel, Hooft, Huygens, and the others could only dream of such a circulation.

---

[7]"*Deze spraeck wort tegenwoordigh in 's Gravenhage, de Raetkamer der Heeren Staten, en het hof van hunnen Stedehouder, en 't Amsterdam, de maghtighste koopstadt der weereld, allervolmaeckst gesproken, by lieden van goede opvoedingen ... want out Amsterdamsch is te mal en plat Antwerpsch te walgelijck en niet onderscheidelijck genoegh*" (quoted in Hagen 1999, 27). Brachin (1985, 18) gives an English translation of this famous quotation, part of which I used here.

BOX 4.4 } Pieter Cornelisz Hooft (1581–1647)

In 1609, Hooft, the most cerebral and aristocratic of the Golden Five, had been appointed to the position of Drost (sheriff) at Muiden.

Of his plays, only one has stood the test of time: *Warenar* (The Real Fool), but the lyric poems he wrote in his youth rank with the finest ever produced in the Dutch language. However, from about 1618 onward poetry was no longer his prime concern. Instead he devoted all his energy to writing historical books. In so doing, Hooft carried the culture of his time to a pinnacle. *Nederlandse Historiën* (1556–1584), his account of the Eighty Years' War, is, according to Geyl (2001, 523), "the revolt seen by a libertinist, by an aristocrat who believes in the mission of his class to defend liberty not only against the foreign despot, but against the stupidity of the mob and the unscrupulousness of the fanatic."

The highest Dutch honor for literary achievement today is called the P. C. Hooft Prize.

Since my own experience with traditional linguistic histories in other periods has almost always led to the conclusion that the history of Dutch in the periods in question needed to be rewritten, I completely agree that it would be a good idea to compile as much new information based on as many primary sources as possible to exactly determine how language change occurred and evolved during the Golden Age. With Boyce Hendriks and Howell (2000, 274), I am convinced that "in order to determine which social factors led to the success of certain linguistics variants and to the failure of others" it is indeed "crucial to trace the social history of a given city [or region or country, RW] in the greatest possible detail." As to the substance of the question, which cannot be fully discussed here, Van der Sijs (2004) agrees with Boyce Hendriks and Howell and others that southern influence is considerably less important than is mostly assumed. Taeldeman (2007, 105), on the other hand, concludes on the ground of very solid arguments that "the South, and mainly Brabant, had a decisive influence on the language standardization in 16th and 17th century Holland." His own research, he adds, leads to the conclusion that southern influx and influence are not a "myth" at all (as Van der Sijs calls it) and that the many "highly qualified and rich Brabanters" carried a considerable weight on language change in progress between 1570 and 1600, due to the high social prestige of Brabants. Anyway, at the moment when the language of Holland is about to acquire its full historical importance, it is still neither fixed nor homogeneous but undergoes many transformations in the first decade of the century, as mentioned already.

The eventual "perfecting" of the language (as Brachin 1985, 18 says) would be long in coming. It was the work of a particular elite and was achieved very gradually. A consensus was finally established among those called to debate in public assemblies, to administer justice, or to speak from the pulpit.

The public reached by the grammarians was a limited one, and their impact, when they had any at all, was slow working. The most influential language-planning instrument by far, however, was the Statenbijbel (Bible of the States), named so because it was financed by the Staten-Generaal, which also made sure it was checked for both religious orthodoxy and the linguistic north–south balance. The executive body of the northern protestant state, the Staten-Generaal, commissioned a translation of the Bible at the Synod of Dordrecht in 1618, and the translation, made from the original Greek and Hebrew texts, was published in 1637. The motive for doing this was not only scientific accuracy but also that the advent of Calvinism made it preferable to sidestep the Lutheran precedents and to go back to the original languages (Donaldson 1983, 99).

The principal concern, to arrive at a usable text for all regions, is evident from the choice of translators: two came from Friesland, two from West Flanders, one from Zeeland, and one from Holland. The "revisers" came from

BOX 4.5 } Constantijn Huygens (1596–1687)

Son of a Brussels father and an Antwerp mother yet born in The Hague, he was secretary to the Prince of Orange from 1625 onward; Huygens was a prodigious child and a language genius. At the age of 11 he wrote poetry in Latin, and throughout his life he wrote and published in eight different languages. Apart from that, he painted and felt very comfortable in the exact sciences. Huygens played various instruments and composed over 800 pieces of music. He studied in Leiden. His real job, though, was that of a diplomat, and in that capacity he made frequent trips to England, which had a profound influence on his work. He wrote his John Donne translations in 1630.

Most of his poetry was collected in *Korenbloemen* (1658), but his total oeuvre was huge. Some of his best-known publications are *Ogentroost* (1647); *Hofwijck* (1653), his most voluminous work of almost 3,000 lines; and *De Zeestraat* (1667). Although all of this was didactic, he excelled in *'t Kostelijk Mal* (The Expensive Stupidity), satirical poems on fashion (1622).

His only play, *Trijntje Cornelis* (1653), describes the adventures of the wife of a barge skipper from Holland who goes on a spree in Antwerp and finds herself the morning after robbed of all her clothes and penniless, lying on a dung heap. Huygens proves to be very fluent in the Antwerp dialect of his mother yet equally so in the dialect of his native The Hague. The play, which is an excellent piece of theater, delights in farcical situations and scabrous detail and shows with great candor the down-to-earth, crude, and sometimes vulgar side of Huygens's personality, which was just as real as his aristocratic sophistication.

Huygens came closer to the Renaissance ideal of the *uomo universale* than anyone else in the Netherlands. He counted among his friends and correspondents such people as John Donne, Francis Bacon, Daniel Heinsius, René Descartes, Ben Jonson, and Pierre Corneille.

BOX 4.6 } Joost van den Vondel (1587–1679)

Both in his times and today, Vondel was always referred to as the prince of Dutch poetry. Although he is generally regarded as the greatest Dutch literature man (the Shakespeare, Goethe, or Cervantes of the Low Countries is what he is often called), his works are hardly read anymore. There is no doubt, however, that his influence used to be substantial.

For one, Vondel, who belonged to the Amsterdam middle class, was indisputably the greatest dramatist of the 17th century. His father, a hat maker, left Antwerp in 1582 for religious regions. Young Joost was born in Cologne. The family finally settled down in Amsterdam in 1596, when Vondel was nine years old. The father opened a shop in the Warmoesstraat, the center of the Brabant community in Amsterdam. In 1637 a new theater was built, the Schouwburg, the first proper theater in the Netherlands. Its opening ushered in a new area in which plays written by individual authors were performed by professional actors. It was inaugurated in the same year with what was to become Vondel's best-known play, *Gysbreght van Aemstel*, a tragedy about the destruction of Amsterdam that for centuries has always been performed in the Amsterdam Schouwburg on January 1. Although well versed in other genres as well, Vondel was the leading Dutch playwright of the 17th century and has 33 plays to his name. He was a member of the (Brabant) Chamber of Rhetoric Het Witte Lavendel, mainly frequented by nonnative Amsterdamers. *Lucifer* is Vondel's most baroque and praised play. Vondel was deeply involved in political life in the republic and particularly in Amsterdam. One of his ways to express this was by writing political satires, mostly between 1618 and 1630. At the same time, he was a nationalist who wrote poems glorifying Amsterdam, the nation, and its language.

Both his political views and disastrous stock speculation, mainly by his son, were responsible for the fact that Vondel, who grew uncharacteristically old for his time, suffered a rather unhappy and almost penniless old age.

---

all parts of the Low Countries. As a result, the language of the Statenbijbel—actually created for that purpose—carefully combined northern and southern characteristics and became the basis of the northern written language and writing tradition, thus preventing northern and southern varieties of the language from growing too far apart (Van der Sijs & Willemyns 2009, 234–239). Adopted by almost all Protestants, it remained in use until 1951. Read and reread for three centuries in churches, schools, and homes, it made a significant contribution to the unification of the language. In excluding the pronoun *du* as well as the double negation (as in *ick en heb dat niet ghedaen*; I didn't do that), it eliminated simultaneously a prominent eastern ("du") and a western (double negation) feature from the standard language (fig. 4-4).

During the truce with the Spaniards, the northern republic seemed to explode from within and at one stage came dangerously close to civil war over issues of internal politics and religion. The trial and execution of Johan van

The Low Countries after the Peace of Munster (1648)

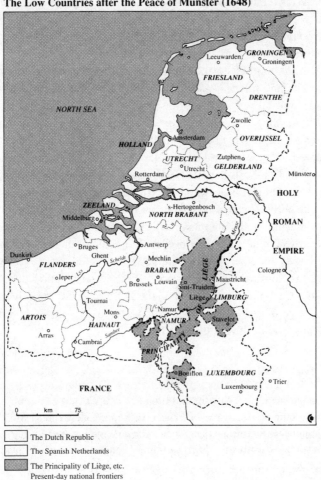

FIGURE 4.4 The Netherlands after the Treaty of Münster (1648) (courtesy of Ons Erfdeel vzw, Flanders, Belgium)

Oldenbarnevelt, one of the ablest Dutch statesmen and architect of the truce, is an indication of the seriousness and the bitterness of the conflict. In 1621 the truce expired and war was resumed. The Peace of Münster in 1648 finally concluded this war, which had lasted 80 years. After 1648 the republic came into conflict with several other European countries, and the war list is impressive, particularly for a period that has become known as a Golden Age: between 1652 and 1654 the first of a series of Anglo-Dutch sea wars was fought; in 1658 the Republic intervened in the conflict between Sweden and Denmark; between 1665 and 1667 the second war with England took place, while on land the Dutch were locked in combat with the Bishop of Münster; from 1672 until 1678 there was almost continuous warfare with France, England, and the

Bishops of Münster and Cologne, while from 1688 through 1697 the Republic was at war with France again. In other words, for more than half the century the Netherlands was on a war footing with one or more other countries, and it is tempting to ask what was so golden about all this.

Still, in sharp contrast to the south, the cultural climate of the north was one of freedom and tolerance. The Erasmian spirit had taken firm root in the Netherlands, and although from time to time powerful factions managed to suppress those they did not agree with, the general atmosphere in the Netherlands was far more liberal than in the surrounding countries. This attitude attracted refugees of all kinds: Jews, French Huguenots, the Pilgrim Fathers, and such famous men as Descartes, Locke, and Bayle. Naturally, the tolerance of the Dutch authorities benefitted not only the refugees but also the republic. The influx of scholars from many different countries brought an element of internationalism and sophistication to Dutch intellectual life. Also, the comparative freedom of the press made Leiden and Amsterdam the publishing centers of the liberal world: Galileo was printed in the Netherlands, as were Descartes, Spinoza, Richard Simon's Bible criticism, and Locke's *Epistola de Tolerantia*. Certainly the prestige of the Dutch did not entirely match that of the language of the country where it was spoken, but it unquestionably reached its high point during this period.

THE SOUTH

What happened to Dutch during this time in the area that had remained under Spanish rule? Cut off from the Northern provinces, devastated by 80 years of war, weakened by the emigration of a considerable part of its elite, and economically strangled by the closing of the Scheldt estuary, the southern Netherlands went through an extremely difficult period in the 17th century (Brachin 1985, 22).

Not only depopulation and the brain drain but also political and religious repression were responsible for a slowly progressing but profound decline of the once so prosperous regions of Flanders and Brabant. In Antwerp, which remained the most important trade center of the southern Netherlands, it was felt later, since the powers that be wanted to turn the city into the northernmost display window of Roman Catholicism and Contra Reformation. Consequently, with the aid of famous artists like Rubens and Van Dyck, the pretence of a still blooming cultural life could be upheld for some time.

After the Peace of Münster of 1648, however, the year considered to be the official year of birth of present-day Netherlands, the Scheldt was definitively closed and in Antwerp the lights went out as they had done earlier in the rest of the country (Geyl 2001, 442–445). Interestingly, there are no indications or worries that the new political and religious situation was expected to change the linguistic situation of the Netherlands at large.

So the South, as opposed to the North, had little to offer during the 17th century. The literary peers of its famous painters Rubens, Jordaens, and Van Dyck did not exist, and we may hold the Roman Catholic church and its Inquisition responsible for creating a literary and intellectual desert in a region that for centuries had been one of the most creative and revolutionary in Europe. It may logically be assumed that the Counter-Reformation and the Inquisition were suffocating most attempts at literary (and other) creativity. The Jesuit Poirters is one of the very few names still remembered, albeit not read. The most important southern poet in the early years of the century was Justus de Harduyn, who wrote a volume of typical Renaissance poetry under the title of *De Weerlycke Liefde tot Roosemond* (The Profane Love for Roosemond), full of reminiscences of the Pléiade poets and important because of its elegant diction and a mastery of the sonnet form, which was unusual in the early years of the century. The volume was completed in 1605—though not published until 1613—and it clearly shows that in those early years of the Golden Age a writer like De Harduyn was still ahead of most of his northern contemporaries.

During the 17th century the activities of the southern Rhetoricians hardly diminished, but the output showed a lack of quality hardly witnessed ever before. The only one who stood out was Michiel de Swaen from Dunkirk, a region (French Flanders) that had been conquered by the French never to return to Flanders (and the Dutch language) again. His best-known play, *De Gecroonde Leersse* (The Crowned Boot), is still occasionally performed. After that, the literature of the south went into hibernation until the middle of the 19th century.

All in all, much more research is needed to find out how the language fared in the 17th-century South.

LOSS OF TERRITORY

The last quarter of the 17th century also saw an important territorial loss for the Dutch language area. Its westernmost part in what is now French Flanders used to be part of Dutch-speaking Flanders until 1678, when it was annexed by the French crown as a result of the Treaty of Nijmegen. It remained under French rule forevermore, but for a long time native speakers of West Flemish dialects were concentrated in the Westhoek, in the *arrondissements* of Dunkirk (Dutch: *Duinkerke*), and of Hazebroek. Eventually this part of northern France was almost completely gallicized (see chapter 1).

The 18th Century: The Dull Age?

Until recently, *boring* and *uninteresting* first came to mind when the 18th century, an age called the *Pruikentijd* in Holland, was mentioned. Both literature and culture as well as the general atmosphere are dull compared with the splendor of the preceding Golden Age.

The 18th century, Donaldson (1983, 113) says, was "a period of stagnation," and Brachin (1985, 24) explains why: "one might say that after the magnificent endeavors of two or three generations, the Netherlands were content to rest on their laurels." Generally speaking both are probably right, yet in very recent years new insights have come to us as far as the linguistic history of the 18th century is concerned.

As for Flanders, the 18th century is mostly remembered as the age in which the social gap between the haves and the have-nots was complemented with a linguistic component: the upper classes were gallicizing rapidly, whereas the linguistic repertoire of the vast majority of the population was restricted to dialects. Willemyns (2003) argues for the first time that this rather undiscriminating image seems to contrast with the activity of a lot of grammarians, having published scores of books on the spelling and grammar of Dutch. In a sociolinguistic situation as previously described, it is not very clear who the potential recipients of these books might have been. The prudent conclusion, therefore, was that the traditional picture of the linguistic situation in 18th-century Flanders was too black-and-white.

The received opinion in linguistic history also held that the southern situation in the 18th century was one of language decay, since Dutch in Flanders had been replaced by French in most domains and its function had been reduced to that of a mere dialect, spoken at home by the lower classes. This is the situation as it is pictured, for example, by Wils 2003[3], 33)[8] or De Vooys (1952, 147).

In various studies on spelling, grammar, and grammarians, young scholars from Leiden and Brussels (Gijsbert Rutten and Rik Vosters) have now shed new light on what has really been going on, both in the north and in the south. Their very thorough analyses of the spelling, based on primary sources hardly ever used before, very often appeared to be revealing.

Rutten (2011) and Van der Horst (2004, 73) agree that the situation as depicted by Wils (2003[3]) and De Vooys (1952) is a myth or, more accurately two: namely, the many norms myth; and the orthographical chaos myth (both terms introduced by Rutten & Vosters, 2011). Not only did uniformity of language and spelling not exist in the north (Vosters, Rutten, & Van der Wal 2010; Rutten 2011), but we also see how the south displays, in the same way the north does, a coherent and lively discussion on norms and, toward the end of the century, even a norm tradition characterized by a large amount of uniformity.

An interesting example of their approach is their analysis of the most important Southern grammar of the time, Jan Des Roches's *Nieuwe Nederduytsche spraek-konst* (New Dutch Grammar; 1761), often disparagingly characterized as a mere grammar of the Antwerp dialect. A study of the sources and the contents of Des Roches's grammar by Rutten (2009) reveals that the author produced a

---

[8]Wils (2003[3]) is based on Wils (1956).

comprehensive compilation of linguistic ideas taken from the works of southern Dutch predecessors (e.g., Verpoorten and Bincken), northern Dutch normative grammars (Moonen and Sewel), a Dutch introduction to Latin as well as the French grammatical tradition. Rather than a mere amateur, Des Roches appears to have been a rather learned and creative grammarian. It is clear from the publications of Rutten, Vosters, and some others that other grammarians, more deprecated than Des Roches still, are equally entitled to much more indulgence and praise than they used to receive. The reappearance of the (anonymous) grammar *Snoeijmes der Vlaemsche tale* (The pruning knife of the Dutch language), for example, adds to the growing body of evidence pleading for a more positive appreciation of 18th-century grammarians. Rather than "a considerable divergence between the written language of North and South, . . . confirmed by the numerous grammars, which in turn were also greatly at odds with one another," as Wils (1956, 528) suggests, Vosters and Rutten (2011) discovered an elaborate and well-informed work, dealing with issues of linguistic awareness, purism, spelling reform, and education, very much in line with contemporary grammaticographical practices in the southern Netherlands and in the Low Countries at large. An analysis of the sources and the themes featured in the *Snoeijmes* revealed a clear embedding in the southern linguistic conventions of the time while at the same time retaining strong ties with the northern tradition of good usage, especially on the discursive level. The work does not display any sort of normative chaos but must be seen as part of the growing and increasingly focused southern normative tradition, closely related to the north, which is further consolidated in the second half of the 18th century.

Apart from what has already been outlined, it is generally thought that the impact of 18th-century grammarians on the evolution and standardization of northern Dutch was rather limited. However, quite a few influential grammarians may be mentioned. Among the early northern 18th-century grammarians, two groups can be discerned (Rutten 2011): Vondel-adepts, who combined the norm of the language with a more sophisticated style (e.g., Petrus Francius, Arnold Moonen, Willem Sewel, and Balthazar Huydecoper); and linguists, who were interested in language historical research (Adriaen Verwer and Lambert ten Kate are the most famous among them).

The *Nederduitsche spraekkunst* (1706) by Moonen was very popular (there were at least four reprints) and was, according to its author, following the Greek and Latin grammatical tradition as well as being inspired by the work of the famous German grammarian Justus Georg Schottel (De Bonth et al. 1997, 367). Shortly after that, a no less famous *Nederduytsche Spraekkonst* (1708) was published by Willem Sewel. It differed from former as well as contemporary grammars; Sewel explicitly stated that, in his opinion, Hollands was definitely the "best" kind of Dutch (ibid.).

Although 18th-century grammarians generally were as obsessed as their predecessors with regulating the Dutch language, we also witness the breakthrough of a new and inspiring grammatical principle, viz. that grammarians ought not to invent rules but only propagate those that can be derived from real language usage. Consequently, more attention must be paid to the spoken than the written language, and different stylistic levels must be distinguished. Ten Kate first formulated these points of view in his internationally acclaimed *Aenleiding tot de kennisse van het verhevene deel der Nederduitsche sprake* (1723).

From today's point of view, it was definitely Ten Kate (the first comparative-historical linguist in Europe) who proved to have the best insight in language change and linguistic evolution in general.[9] Less gifted colleagues of his, however, were the most successful and influential. They deepened the gap between the spoken and the (overly formalized) written language, and their linguistic views came to be known as *language despotism*. Its most famous representative was Balthazar Huydecoper, who, in his *Proeve van taal- en dichtkunde* (1730) even criticized the "ungrammatical" language used by Vondel (De Vries, Willemyns, & Burger 2003, 99).

Thanks to Ten Kate, we also know that in the early 18th century a more or less general spoken Dutch did definitely not yet exist. However, in the course of the 18th century, Van der Sijs (2004, 207) observes, a civilized/cultivated pronunciation gradually developed in educated, well-to-do circles and was supposed to serve as the norm. That norm, though, was not generally accepted, and regional differences continued to exist. Ten Kate and some of his colleagues do point out that the language differs from province to province and even from city to city (quoted in De Bonth et al. 1997, 363). There was, Ten Kate says, also a vivid stylistic variability, and he distinguishes between at least four varieties of Dutch.

The first variety, which he calls *De hoogdravende of Verhevene* (the elevated, the sublime), is the glorious language of our ancestors. Some of the less experienced language users may be able to understand it yet not use it. The second one is the *Deftige of Statige* (stately, solemn), being nearer to everyday language yet formal and completely respecting the rules of regularity, order, and *deftigheid des gezegs* (upper-class style). The third variety, which Ten Kate calls *De Gemeenzame Stijl* (familiar, colloquial), is the one for everyday usage, without minding too much *de uiterste geregeldheid en opschik* (extreme regularity). Although his enumeration stops here, he also mentions a fourth variety (without attributing the number 4 to it) called the *platte Spreek- en Straet-tael* (coarse street language), which, he observes, is good enough for *'t onkundigste gemeen*, or the ignorant rabble, the mob. Here again we see the overruling importance of the social variable in the assessment of language usage.[10]

---

[9]Ten Kate was also the first linguist to discover the regularity of the system of strong verbs in the Germanic languages and one of the pioneers of historical linguistics, as it boomed in the 19th century.

[10]*Aenleiding tot de Kennisse van het verhevene deel der Nederduitsche Sprake*, Amsterdam 1723, vol. 1, p. 334; quoted in the original in Van der Sijs and Willemyns (2009, 243).

At the end of the century we find something similar yet phrased in a much more humorous way, in the *Ironisch Komisch Woordenboek* (Ironic and Comic Dictionary; 1797) in which Fokke Simonsz treats us to an example of various styles of speaking. He expresses the Dutch equivalent of the sentence "Nothing is more shameful than to see a people despising its own mother tongue and preferring a foreign language" in three different "styles":

- *"Niets is schandelijker, dan dat een volk deszelfs eigene moedertaal veracht, en een vreemde boven dezelve stelt"* (exalted language).
- *"Niets is abominabeler, dan dat eene natie derzelver moedertaal meprissert, en eene aliëne daarvoor praediligeert en anteponeert"* (administrative language).
- *"Der is gien leelijker ding, als dat ien volk zen eige moers taal veracht, en ien vreemde veurtrekt"* (language of the street).[11]

In the second half of the century, language-planning activities regain some of the popularity they enjoyed during its initial decades. Kornelis van der Palm (1730–1789) was the first to publish a real school grammar (in 1769), one intended for schools and teachers. In the south we find an identical combination of linguistic and pedagogical interest a little earlier—in the work of Verpoorten (1706–1773) or Jan Des Roches (ca. 1740–1787). The final decades of the 18th century have not yet been researched as far as this aspect is concerned. We are not yet familiar with linguistics as practiced in literary societies or in magazines, which is the more regrettable since it is in those circles where, in the north, the forerunner of Standard Dutch must have been elaborated, the language variety codified by Siegenbeek and Weiland shortly thereafter (see chapter 5). One of the most important of these societies is the *Maatschappij der Nederlandsche Letterkunde* (founded in 1766), a Society for Dutch Literature, in which the study of literature included that of language and continues to exist until the present day.

Meanwhile, and as a result of the Spanish War of Succession (1702–1713), the "Belgian" territories were passed on from the Spanish to the Austrian Habsburgs, both of which used to rule their Dutch-speaking lands and citizens in French. They remained the subjects of a foreign and distant monarch, represented by governors with French backgrounds, like the "Austrian" governor Charles de Lorraine, who managed affairs for 40 years on behalf of the emperors and empress in Vienna. Although Dutch was still spoken and written by the large majority of the population and used for administrative purposes on a local level, it had lost prestige and functions (Deneckere 1954) and, for lacking contact with the north, no longer participated in the language standardization process that took place there.

---

[11]Quoted in Brachin (1985, 28). Examples one and two are clearly parodies.

The Austrians inherited a country consisting of two language territories: a monolingual Walloon part; and a Dutch-speaking part harboring an upper class that was either gallicized or had at least a fair command of French. French was not only the prestige language of the whole country but also a language not understood by the majority of its subjects; these two basic factors determined both the general and the linguistic policy of the Austrians (box 4.7).

The continuing activities of rhetoricians and grammarians demonstrate that Dutch continued to be a language that was written, printed, and read. Nevertheless, they also hint at the fact that the language and the linguistic situation did not fare as well as they hoped for and that changes were needed. Most of the southern grammarians advised their readers to conform to the northern norm, although the southerners had no way of knowing how language was developing in the northern parts. The same, obviously, applied to the grammarians themselves.

Only a few treatises on language or grammar have come to us from the initial decades of the 18th century. A notorious exception is *Nieuwen Néderlandschen voorschrift-boek* (Steven, 1784) by Andries Steven, who was born in Steenvoorde (present-day French Flanders) around 1676; from 1704 onward he was a schoolteacher in Kassel, in the same region (Rutten 2009b). Although this is essentially a book teaching the youth how to behave morally and ethically, it also contains comments on language and spelling. The first edition dates from 1714, and the immense popularity of the book accounts for many reprints, some even in the 19th century. Most editions were published unchanged, but in the 1734 edition there was a Byvoegsel (supplement) on language, in which the author gets more explicit still as to the themes he addressed in the former editions.

Although some characteristics of his West Flemish mother tongue are found in his *Voorschrift-boek*, its language in general meets the norms of the written

---

BOX 4.7 } *Usum non habet linguae flandricae*

During the Austrian regime, prelates were appointed by the emperor, after which they were confirmed by the pope. The archives of the government (Geheime Raad) demonstrate that sometimes the Austrians valued proficiency in the language of the people (so that the prelates could communicate with their sheep) whereas at other times contacts with the upper classes were valued more, in which case proficiency in Dutch was not necessary. In most cases the latter consideration prevailed, since appointing bishops was a sure way of winning the political support of the aristocracy.

The German Earl of Frankenberg, who was appointed cardinal in 1759, learned Dutch, but many other prelates didn't. Frankenberg's predecessor, Cardinal d' Alsace, had to send his suffragan to larger ecclesiastic festivities in Brussels' cathedral since, as the latter observed in a dry tone, his boss "*usum non habet linguae flandricae*" (is not proficient in Dutch).

language as they were accepted in both the Northern and the Southern Low Countries. Steven, indeed, explicitly advocates a common language for the Netherlands at large, although he also allows for regional divergence. It is this combination, Rutten (2011) says, that makes Steven's *Voorschrift-boek* a crucial publication for the language history of the Southern Netherlands.

Probably more influential still was Jan des Roches, mentioned earlier. This former teacher was the secretary of the Imperial Academy of Sciences in Brussels and the most important advisor of the Austrian rulers in the fields of language and education. He published both a grammar (*De nieuwe Nederduytsche Spraekkonst*, 1761) and a French–Dutch dictionary (1782). His spelling system was the first ever to be officially promulgated by any government in the Netherlands, viz. in 1777 (De Groof 2003).

In the 1750s, the Antwerp schoolteachers J. D. Verpoorten and P. Bincken published basic Dutch reading and writing books. Both implicitly criticized one another, and they put forward their own book as the better one. As a result of this competition, the grammatical part of subsequent publications was professionalized. The professionalization mainly consisted in linking up with the northern normative tradition, showing that not only active knowledge of this strong tradition but also the willingness to consider it as normative for southern speakers existed in the southern Netherlands (Rutten & Vosters 2010).

The two most important documents describing the linguistic situation in Flanders in the 18th century were not grammars but essays: one by the merchant Willem Verhoeven from Mechelen (Smeyers 1959, 295–323), *Oordeelkundige Verhandelingen op de noodzaekelijkheijd van het behouden der nederduijtsche taele, en de noodige hervormingen in de schoolen* (1780); and the other, more prominent and still famous today, by the lawyer J. B. Verlooy (Smeyers 1959, 324–359; Smeyers & Vandenbroeck 1979), *Verhandeling op d'onacht der moederlyke tael in de Nederlanden* (1788). Both denounce the linguistic policy of the Austrian officials and the upper classes, neither of which is interested in supporting the mother tongue of Flanders and Brabant and they complained about the governmental *Franschdolheyd*, a word probably used there for the first time. It meant (and still means) Gallomania, an idolatry of French and its use to the detriment of the language of the people. The Dutch language, Verlooy explains, is not only being neglected but also being held in contempt.

Verlooy was also the first to formulate a strategy that became widely accepted in the 19th century: to enforce as much as possible the linguistic ties with the northern Netherlands to be able to use the prestige of that variety for domestic purposes in the south. The Netherlanders from north and south are, Verlooy proclaimed with pan-Dutch enthusiasm, "*het zelve volk, 't zelve in tael, imborst, zeden en gebruyken. Laet ons gezamender-hand ons gevoegzaem Nederduytsch handhaven, eeren en versieren*" (one people, identical in language, character, costumes and traditions. Let us combine our efforts to defend, honor, and adorn our common Dutch language). Both Verhoeven and Verlooy agreed that the authorities ought to play an important role in defending the local language and culture. Here again, they introduce a strategy that became very popular among the supporters of the Flemish movement in the 19th century.

One of Rutten's (2011) most interesting general findings is that the way grammarians were preoccupied with language runs parallel in both the north and the south. His analysis demonstrates how gradually a real coexistence of two varieties evolves. During the last decade of the century the idea of the one and only language area, comprising the north and the south, is partly abandoned and replaced by the idea of two coexisting varieties within the larger entity of the Dutch language area. In the south, the prestige variety is that of Brabant. If it had not been for the reintroduction of the northern norm during the United Kingdom of the Netherlands between 1814 and 1830, Des Roches would have become the Siegenbeek and Weiland of the south, Rutten remarks.

Summarizing, we have found that, in lieu of the traditional image of cultural and linguistic decline in the 18th-century southern Netherlands, there appears to have been a very vivid normative, linguistic awareness and southern grammarians are constantly reflecting upon and comparing with the north and the northern norm. During the first half of the century there is a strong understanding of uniformity. During the second half, though, both the north and the south display a growing awareness of a proper identity.

In the north this leads to a national language codified by Siegenbeek and Weiland. But in the south as well, convergence and standardization are the specific characteristics of 18th-century language development (Rutten 2011). Although the grammarians constantly keep in touch with the northern development we see how Dutch gradually evolves into a pluricentric language. Apart from the northern Randstad, there is a second center—Brabant, more specifically Antwerp. During the final decades of the 18th century it is Des Roches's (1761) *Nieuwe Nederduitse spraakkunst* that sets the standard for the language use in the southern Netherlands. And here again, it is the reunification into one United Kingdom of the Netherlands that puts an end to the linguistic solo play of the south. In the next chapter we will discuss many other fundamental consequences of the short-lived reunification of the Low Countries.

Then Came the French

Almost simultaneously with the French Revolution, the southern Netherlands had a small revolution of its own, labeled the Brabantse Omwenteling (Brabant Revolution). Emperor Joseph II, son of Maria Theresia, is known as an enlightened despot. He had come under the influence of the ideas of the Enlightenment, and it was clear to him that in "his" Netherlands many existing outdated and outworn structures required elimination. The fact that he chose to handle things rigorously explains the second part of his epithet.

The local authorities, members of the Staten of Brabant and Flanders, opposed Joseph's proposed changes vigorously and, in doing so, started the Brabantse Omwenteling (1789–1790). There were two factions: a progressive minority, led by Jan Frans Vonck, that advocated the ideas of Enlightenment and democracy; a conservative group, led by Hendrik van der Noot, that wanted to preserve the privileges of the nobility, clergy, and local authorities. Thanks to the support lent by the rural gentry and the Church, they also enjoyed the support of the lower classes. A small army of the Staten defeated the sparse emperor's troops, busy as they were at that time trying to keep the Turks out of Vienna and consequently not in a position to strike back immediately.

After the deposition of Joseph II by the rebels, the ties uniting the various provinces gradually loosened. For practical purposes they created a confederation called the Vereenigde Nederlandsche Staeten (United States of the Netherlands; in French Etats Belgiques Unis), but actually they didn't want to cooperate at all. The conservative policy of Van der Noot was a big disappointment to Vonck's supporters; this is one reason the Belgian Federation was short-lived. At the end of 1790 the Austrian authority was reestablished, but even that did not last much longer. In late 1792, the Austrian Netherlands was (with the exception of Luxemburg) overrun by French troops, and after the decisive French victory in the battle at Fleurus in June 1794 it was annexed by France.

Although language played no part in all of this, it is interesting to observe that Van der Noot (1731–1827), who belonged to a primarily French-speaking noble family in Brussels, mostly spoke and wrote in French, although he also used Dutch in his correspondence with some of his collaborators. Jan Frans Vonck (1743–1792), a Flemish lawyer living in Brussels as well, published most of his works in Dutch, and many of his letters to Van der Noot were written in Dutch as well. However, the division between both tendencies was ideological, not linguistic.

When on July 14th, 1789, the people of Paris stormed the Bastille, a shock went through Europe and ended the Ancien Régime. Every important societal change eventually influences linguistic conditions, but in the case of the French Revolution the influence was extremely decisive, since both the early leaders of the revolution as well as Napoleon afterward had firm and rather "revolutionary" views and ideas on language and governmental language planning (Deneckere 1954; Willemyns 2005).

The linguistic policy of the French leaders, who shortly after their revolution started to invade a considerable part of Europe, was mainly based on the linguistic situation in France itself. For the first time they realized that their homeland was, in fact, a multilingual country, harboring a considerable amount of languages, to the point that more than half of its citizens didn't even speak French (Duvoskeldt 1999, 41).

The revolutionary leaders wanted to remedy that situation. A more generalized competence of French would benefit the unity of the country and, therefore, had to be propagated, the more so since, to their firm conviction, the ideals and principles of the French Revolution could not possibly be explained and understood in any other language than French. Also, the Jacobin philosophy held that all power had to be concentrated in and emerge from Paris and could, therefore, be effective only on a "one country, one language" basis. Consequently, the previous system of translations (official French texts used to be translated for the benefit of non-French-speaking French citizens) had to be terminated. Since it was the vocation, the mission even, of revolutionary France to "liberate" Europe, it was in the interest of everyone to learn and to know French. *Mieux vaut instruire que traduire* (instructing beats translating) is how, in 1794, Barrère, the spokesman of the Comité de Salut Publique, summarized the strategy to follow. Grégoire added an ideological motivation as well: *L'unité de l'idiome est une partie intégrante de la révolution* (language unity is an integral part of the revolution; Willemyns 2003, 172). Still, at that moment, neither Barrère nor Grégoire intended to force the French to learn French. Compelling measures were not taken until Napoleon issued them in 1804.

The consequences of the French policy were felt not only in France proper but also in many European countries that were overrun by French troops. Part of those were the northern as well as the southern Netherlands, albeit it in different ways.

In the north, the French made no conscious effort to rule out the vernacular language. After French soldiers had occupied Utrecht in February 1795, a *Bataafsche Republiek*, a French vassal state, was founded that same year. In 1806 it was replaced by the Kingdom of Holland, of which Louis Napoleon, one of Bonaparte's brothers, was the king. Consequently, the language policy in the north was specific, and no attempts were made to replace Dutch with French. In 1810 Louis's kingdom was abolished, and Holland was finally annexed to France.

We know that in Holland pronunciation, by the end of the 18th century, was anything but standardized. The dialect, the usual means of communication of the large majority of the population, interfered with even the formalized language of individuals and groups. When, in 1796, the National Assembly (Dutch: *Nationale Vergadering*) of the Bataafsche Republiek met for the first time, it appeared that the chosen representatives of the people coming from all parts of the country, had a lot of trouble understanding each other, even though many of them were highly educated people. "The deputies from Holland," Brachin (1985, 28) assumes, "smiled at the language of their colleagues from other regions."

As opposed to what happened in Flanders, the political changes during the French time in Holland were, as De Bonth et al. (1997, 369) state, "beneficial to the standardization of Dutch." In 1807 Louis Napoleon ordained that all official papers had to be drafted in Dutch that, consequently, kept the status of an official language, alongside French. A year later he founded the forerunner of the Dutch Academy of Sciences (Dutch: Koninklijke Nederlandse Akademie van Wetenschappen), and the famous Rijksmuseum as well as the Royal library (Koninklijke Bibliotheek) were installed.

In 1809 the metric system was introduced; like in other European countries, its terminology was based on French: *gram, kilogram, meter, centimeter, liter, milliliter.* Previous measurement terms like *duim* (inch) and *el* (yard) disappeared together with the things they stood for. Only *ons* (ounce) for 100 grams and *pond* (pound) for half a kilo have remained until the present day.

In 1811 all inhabitants had to register with the Burgerlijke Stand (Registry Office, a French invention), something the Flemings had been compelled to do in 1795. This accounts for, among other things, a different way of spelling family names (Kok vs. De Cock; De Rijk vs. De Ryck, Maas vs. Maes), since between those two dates Siegenbeek's spelling change had occurred (Van der Sijs & Willemyns 2009, 259).

The French period also saw the real beginning of Netherlandistics as a scientific–academic discipline, and its two pioneers were Matthijs Siegenbeek (1774–1854) and Petrus Weiland (1754–1842), the authors of the official and authoritative spelling and grammar: Weiland's grammar (*Nederduitsche spraakkunst*) was published in 1805 and Siegenbeek's orthographic treatise (*Verhandeling over de spelling der Nederduitsche taal en bevordering van eenparigheid in derzelve*) a year earlier, in 1804. Like all of his predecessors (and most of his followers, for that matter), Siegenbeek believed that orthography was supposed to reflect the civilized and cultivated (*beschaafde*) pronunciation: *Schrijf zoo als gij spreekt*, although he knew, as well as we do, that this was possible only for the happy (very) few. Weiland's point of view was a conservative one as well. A striking example is that, although in spoken Dutch cases had disappeared a long time ago, he wanted written Dutch to adhere to a system in which (as in Latin) various functions or meanings were conveyed by various cases.

In the south the situation was completely different. During the early years of the revolution Austria was France's main enemy, and, consequently, the first European country the French attacked was the part of Austria at their very borders. In 1794 the southern Netherlands was occupied, and a year after that it was annexed by France. Their inhabitants were now considered citizens of the French Republic, and the linguistic jurisdiction devised for France proper was valid here as well. Also, for the first time ever, there was an official attempt to change the linguistic habits of the masses by suppressing the Dutch language (Deneckere 1954). Recent research has revealed what exactly the consequences of the French annexation of Flanders have been, and they have turned out to be quite different from what was previously thought (De Groof 2004; Vanhecke 2007).

We now know that the decrees issued in the fields of administration, jurisdiction, and instruction were impossible to implement for lack of a sufficient number of civil servants, magistrates, lawyers, and teachers (not to mention pupils) proficient in French. In 1798, the French reintroduced Dutch in a number of cases, and a central service in Paris started to provide Dutch translations of laws and other regulations. In other words, in the initial revolutionary period, as De Groof (2004, 113) discovered, most of the intentions never lead to enactments.

Napoleon, on the other hand, devised a more pragmatic policy. Because large parts of his realm used languages other than French, it was hard to control what really went on there, which cannot be tolerated in a totalitarian system. Public life, therefore, had to be conducted in French in France at large, domestic as well as conquered. Still, he understood that it was impossible and not necessary to gallicize all his subjects to reach that goal: it would suffice if the bureaucracy and the leading classes were. From 1804 on every official use of any other language than French was legally prohibited. Since the huge majority of the Flemish population had no command of French, it could not comply with Napoleon's language regulations either. This was also the case in many town halls of (mostly) smaller places, and it is the main reason the language policy of the French partly failed. Also, in many primary schools, Dutch continued to be the language of instruction, since neither teachers nor pupils with a sufficient command of French could be found. Also, in Flanders at large 77 percent of the children didn't attend primary school at all. But even so, Dutch was losing in prestige and in official functions (De Groof 2004).

The principles underlying Napoleon's linguistic policy could have entailed much more damaging consequences, but the period of implementation has been way too short, which is why it ultimately failed. Many previous researchers of that period have been misled by the texts of the decrees and the principles they were based on and forgot to check how or even whether they were implemented. That explains the received, erroneous impression, even among insiders, that the period of annexation by France had profoundly gallicized the southern Netherlands.

In French Flanders, though, the situation was more favorable to an irreversible gallicization of more and more social strata and an increasing number of townships and villages (Pée 1957; Ryckeboer 2002; see also chapter 1).

Final Remarks

If we are looking for adventure, suspense, struggle for survival, multilingual contact and conflict, language planning and legislation, the southern Netherlands is the place to be.

In the north the language is chugging along, frugally and sparingly, because it was unchallenged. The language isn't threatened and never becomes the object of passion. From time to time there is some civilized commotion when spelling reforms are presented, but apart from that practically nobody bothers to get excited as far as the language is concerned.

Passion, excitement, hard battle for status and prestige, internal and external confrontation, patriotic emotion: that's what we find in the 19th century in the southern Netherlands and is completely lacking in the linguistically dull northern Netherlands.

5}

Reunion and Secession: The 19th Century

The United Kingdom of the Netherlands (1814–1830)

In anticipation of the Vienna Congress, the victorious anti-Napoleon coalition decided to reunite Belgium and Holland as one United Kingdom of the Netherlands, meant to be a fortress on France's northern border. Northern and southern Netherlands were to be united "so close and complete as to let both countries become one single state" (De Jonghe 1967). On May 30, 1814, the Paris Convention ratified the reunification of the Netherlands.

The *Gazette van Brugge* exclaimed enthusiastically, "*Wy worden eyndelinge eene natie, na zoo veel jaaren slaverny*" (We are finally becoming one nation, after so many years of slavery). William I was very proud to be the king of this new country, and he did not fail to stress the reunification aspect in his acceptance speech in parliament on March 16, 1815: "*Een geheel volk, reeds vooraf door zijn zeden, taal en nijverheid en door zijn herinneringen met ons ver-broederd, komt ons tegemoet*" (It is a whole people, that comes to join us, already fraternized with us through its traditions, its language and its industry as well as through its memories).

After Napoleon's defeat the liberated peoples all over Europe, who had suffered from the French and their language tyranny, obviously considered the free use of their own language to be the very sign of their newly won independence. This new feeling for the symbolic worth of the mother tongue marked the start of the modern national movements in Europe. King William, too, decided to use the common language as the cement for the union; consequently, Dutch was proclaimed the *landtaal* (the language of the country) (fig. 5-1). After all, 75 percent of his subjects were Dutch speakers, 2,314,000 of them in the North and 2,351,000 in Flanders.

By Royal Decree, on September 15, 1819, Dutch was declared the compulsory language in public life in the Dutch-speaking southern parts (including

FIGURE 5.1 King William I

Brussels), as of January 1, 1823. This legislation was of the king's personal making and was more radical than any of his advisors had ever suggested. As far as Wallonia is concerned, an agreement was made to try to enhance the prestige of Dutch, but no measures were taken to introduce—let alone make compulsory—the use of Dutch in the French-speaking parts (Janssens & Steyaert 2008). Still, the king expected teachers in the southern provinces of the realm to promote Dutch among the French-speaking population. This led to the production of a large number of Dutch grammars, pronunciation guides, phrase books, and dictionaries all in French and all intended to serve French speakers. This vast body of textbooks also included literary histories and (bilingual) anthologies.

Since the decree was binding only in a territory where Dutch had of old been the language of the people, a transition period of four years was more than sufficient. Real problems with people not being able to cope with the new language regulations, although predicted by many, did not occur either in the administration or in the judiciary. It appeared, on the contrary, that a lot of magistrates and city administrators were eager to switch to Dutch even before it was compulsory (Vanhecke 2007). The fact that civil servants and magistrates alike possessed the competence to use Dutch in administration and court, after 20 years of annexation by France, may seem intriguing but corroborates the findings of the preceding chapter, namely, that this competence had never really been lost.

As far as education is concerned, Dutch was introduced as the exclusive language of instruction in both primary and secondary schools. Here, too, William was very successful: every year a new class has switched to Dutch, and by 1829 the first generation of students that had been educated completely in Dutch had left high school.

The primary school situation in the south was dramatic. Education was in Dutch (even under the French),[1] but it was so miserable that it hardly served any purpose: in 1815 some 54 percent of the population was illiterate. Since the amount of literacy was socially conditioned, this means that in the lower classes some 75 percent must have been illiterate (Vandenbussche 2002).[2] William rightly thought that for the well-being of the population as a whole it was urgent to improve the quality of education drastically. Even apart from the linguistic goals, this would have been quite a challenge. Nevertheless, in a very short time the government succeeded in improving the whole system of education immensely and spent a lot of money to assure its efficient functioning. One of the (many) novelties was the elaboration of pedagogical academies (called

---

[1] In Flanders at large, 77 percent of the children didn't attend primary school at all.

[2] During French dominance, 84 percent of the lower class in Brugge was illiterate (Ruwet & Wellemans 1978, 96).

normaalscholen and later *kweekscholen*). One in the north (Haarlem) and one in the south (Lier) did ensure that competent teachers were soon available.

Until recently, the generally accepted opinion was that King William's language policy eventually failed since the reunification ended with French being completely reinstalled immediately after the Belgian defection in 1830. However, recent findings have established that the king's language policy, in spite of the initial skepticism, was fully carried out and implemented (De Groof 2004; Vanhecke 2007). There can be no doubt that William's objectives were completely met: as far as official and public language use are concerned, Flanders did function in Dutch indeed. This is an extremely remarkable achievement, the more so since he had so little time at his disposal to devise, promulgate, and implement his language decrees (Willemyns & De Groof 2004).

When, from 1825 onward, the opposition against King William's general policy gradually increased, the linguistic legislation was not included in the items objected to. Only 10 percent of the 378 petitions sent to parliament claimed freedom of language. All the others claimed freedom of religion, education, and the press (François 1992). The freedom to say and print whatever one wanted, which is very dear to the liberal party, was of no interest to the conservatives and the clergy, who did not care even about freedom of religion since their real ambition was to restore the monopoly position of the Roman Catholic religion, even in education. As far as language proper was concerned, the clergy mainly opposed the "Hollands" variety of Dutch, which was often seen as a Trojan horse, smuggling in Calvinism by means of language.

In an attempt to make his southern subjects react more favorably toward the regime, decrees were published in 1829 and in 1830 granting new possibilities for the use of French. Flanders reacted indifferently: hardly anybody was interested in making use of these new opportunities (François 1992; Vanhecke 2007). By then Flanders' elite had accommodated to the fact that Dutch was their official language. Although French still kept an important function as a language of social contact among the well-to-do, even they understood and accepted that Dutch was the career language (Van Goethem 1990).

During the final years of King William's rule, the two main political forces of the south, the liberals and the Catholics (the latter strongly supported by the clergy, who had never felt at ease with the northern protestant state) concluded what was rightly called a *monsterverbond* (monstrous alliance). It enabled them to join forces and more effectively oppose the king's policy for various (and very often opposing) reasons of which language was no part.

THE DEFECTION OF THE SOUTH

On September 26, 1830, a strange graffiti appeared on the walls of Brussels: the letter *W* written 12 times. Everybody knew that it stood for the subversive, alliterating rhyme:

Wij Willen Willem Weg
Wil Willem Wijzer Worden
Wij Willen Willem Weer.[3]

A threatening start, good advice in the middle, and a soothing finale that didn't materialize. In which way William should or could have become "wiser" isn't obvious, the more so since it was utterly clear that the clergy didn't want him back at all.

The proximate cause for the secession was an opera performed in Brussels, telling the story of a revolt in Naples. When the tenor intoned the aria *Amour sacré de la patrie* (sacred love of the fatherland) the audience mixed up Naples with Brussels and started to provoke riots that marked the beginning of the secession. In truth the whole thing was rather an accident: an *opera buffa* instead of a real opera, the result of which was completely unexpected, because even the political opposition required only reforms, not the disintegration of the country. According to Bouveroux (2011, 205) it was mainly the "poor and hungry masses" that took up arms against their "own" rich bourgeoisie, which then, to avoid worse, made sure to turn the mutiny of the people into one for independence.

The driving force behind the Belgian opposition was the middle class, which judged William's policy as either too reactionary (the liberals) or too progressive (the Catholics). The church made sure the ignorant lower and poorer classes supported the upheaval. Mostly because of King William's indecisiveness, stubbornness, and misjudgment of the situation, a fait accompli was soon created, which after some hesitation was grudgingly consecrated by the (former) allied forces against Napoleon.

Being attacked from two sides ultimately sealed William's fate, the more so since he didn't receive the support he needed from his northern subjects either: "the North was lamed by its endless priggishness and had reached a record low in its history; therefore it was not in a position to understand William's greatness and, consequently, it failed to be attractive" (De Jonghe 1967, 267). Pieter Geyl (1930b, 24) said, "The king had the faculty of sight, whereas so many Hollanders were blind.... He believed that his people had a mission to fulfill at the time when his people only wanted to be left alone."

It took some time to find someone suitable and acceptable to all to climb the Belgian throne. In 1831 Leopold von Sachsen-Coburg (1790–1865), the widower of the English princess Charlotte Augusta, daughter of the future King George IV, was finally sworn in. In 1839 a peace treaty was signed in which the Belgians gave up the present-day Dutch province of Limburg (east of the river Maas) as well as the German-speaking part of Luxemburg.

A question almost completely neglected in all publications on the policy of King William I is how the north reacted to the royal language policy. Among

---

[3] We want William out—should William grow wiser—we want William back.

William's closest cabinet ministers and collaborators we count both adversaries and sympathizers. Two of the most ardent among the latter group were the cabinet ministers Van Maanen and Falck, who went out of their way to make William's policy succeed. As far as the bulk of the population is concerned, the scarce information we have seems to indicate that they were not really interested in anything William did or endeavored in the south. When William abdicated in 1840, the press as well as academic researchers published some retrospectives on his reign and policies. Not one of them even mentions his language policy although, from the point of view of the Dutch language at large, there can be no doubt that this was his main achievement. Later historians added little to that picture, but all agreed that in the matter of the Belgian secession language had hardly played a role at all (Rutten 2007). That corroborates the conclusions recent research has come to.

William's policy influenced not only the external situation of Dutch but also the internal evolution of the language. As mentioned in the previous chapter, it is the reunification into one United Kingdom of the Netherlands that put an end to the linguistic solo play of the south, as it was taking shape during the final decades of the Austrian regime. The reintroduction of the northern norm prevented Des Roches from becoming the Siegenbeek and Weiland of the South, as Rutten (2011) remarks.

In general, the reunion of the Netherlands, although short-lived, was of the utmost importance to the Flemings, who, for the first time in centuries, experienced that their language was not held in contempt anymore but was used in administration, politics, the judiciary, and education. A group of Flemish cultural leaders and intellectuals was very much influenced by both the Dutch standard language and the new linguistic opportunities (Vosters 2011). After 1830 they formed the hard-core nucleus of the Flemish movement. In this way, King William's relatively short reign was decisive even for how Belgium eventually evolved.

The North after 1830

LANGUAGE STANDARDIZATION

Societal Factors

After the dissolution of the United Kingdom of the Netherlands, the situation in the north did not change significantly. Being rid of the *muitzieke rot der Belgen* (mutinous bunch of the Belgians), as some northern newspapers put it, was not really felt as a decisive event, and the linguistic situation did not change either. In the field of standardization and language planning, nothing spectacular happened. Still, societal changes were taking place smoothly (nothing revolutionary) and would eventually and inevitably also affect the language.

During the whole 19th century, there is a continuing opposition between a slowly changing spoken language and a conservative written language. By the end of the century alongside and, increasingly, against the traditional grammarians, language reformers diligently tried to convince the population to adapt their writing to their speech, a completely novel idea that, even if accepted, would not be easy to implement.

Not the most spectacular but probably the most effective change was brought about by the gradual but steady decline of the dialects, mainly caused by external, extralinguistic factors. In the strongly centralized state the Netherlands had become, civil servants (and their families) changed their posts regularly, resulting in a mix of the population. Conscription, which was established simultaneously, had a similar effect. Industrialization resulted in people leaving the countryside to go and live in cities and in peasants becoming factory workers. All of this accounted for a mobility and a language contact never witnessed before and contributed to the spread of a more general language.

A major reorganization of the educational system was another supporting factor. New school types for primary and secondary instruction were created, such as Meer Uitgebreid Lager Onderwijs (MULO, or extended primary school) in 1857 and Hogere Burgerschool (HBS, a new type of secondary education) in 1863, which, among other things, introduced Dutch as a school subject. In 1876 the *gymnasium* system (high school) was established, and simultaneously Latin was abolished as the academic language of instruction, giving hitherto unknown opportunities for the vernacular as a language of academia and scientific research.

Dialect Loss

People do not lose or give up their dialects in the twinkling of an eye. Dialect loss is a complex and complicated phenomenon spanning over a long period of time. It is the consequence of a combined action of various factors, four of which are of paramount importance.

a) The social factor. Losing one's dialect and using another variety instead creates a diglossic situation in which various language varieties have a specific function. This occurs first of all in people in the more educated and upper social strata, who reduce dialect usage to very informal interactions and make sure that the standard language is seen as a characteristic par excellence of their class. In so doing, they are downgrading the linguistic behavior of all other groups. The dialect gradually becomes a characteristic of the lower social classes, who are also aware that upward social mobility is possible only through imitating the linguistic behavior of the higher classes.

b) The geographical factor. Since the educated and higher social classes are found more in urban than in rural environments and more in the economic and cultural center of gravity than in the periphery, dialect loss starts in urban centers, first of all in the Randstad (the large urban agglomerations in the western part of the country such as Amsterdam, Den Haag, Haarlem, Leiden, and Rotterdam).

c) The temporal aspect. Dialect loss starts in the younger generations, partly because of the school influence and partly because youngsters are more susceptible to social trends and the social prestige the standard language provides. The young upper classers are the trendsetters, and they determine the linguistic behavior of the upcoming generations. The influence of the peer group in this process has been clearly demonstrated.

d) The functional factor. Even within one single social class or urban community the dialect does not disappear at once. It is a slow-moving process, characterized by the fact that one dialect function after the other is lost. And it always starts in the formal domain. Someone speaking dialect at home may refrain from doing so at his workplace; one may address the butcher in dialect while using standard language with the physician or city official. This way, dialects lose prestige; in addition, gradually people tend to believe that dialects are unfit in many domains and that they cannot perform certain tasks that demand the use of the standard language. This acts as a self-fulfilling prophecy, and at the end of the process it becomes a reality: the less the dialect is used, the less usable it is. Also, the more dialect competence decreases, the more its communicative function diminishes, until it is completely replaced by another variety.

All of this takes a long time, and during the process of loss two (or more) varieties continue to coexist and compete, sharing the various communicative functions between them. This explains why, in spite of the progressing loss, the dialects remained, throughout the 19th century, the habitual medium at home, on the job, and even in many more formal gatherings such as city councils. It is mostly during the 20th century that the dramatic consequences of these processes are really experienced.

Preacher Dutch

As a result of the previous, a more general, formal variety gradually emerged, initially with a very restricted scope, performing a very limited amount of functions. It started out as a written language that, after some time, was also read aloud on official and solemn occasions (e.g., church preaching or other speeches). It is assumed that this preacher-Dutch, as it is often called, could be understood all over the country, although probably not by all social layers of the population. Gradually preacher-Dutch must have been used for more private interactions in a limited number of communicative settings. The pioneers presumably were those who also used it in its solemn functions: preachers, lawyers, and teachers. After some time they were imitated by other members of the upper and middle classes, turning preacher-Dutch into a variety cherished by the well-to-do.

But even so, as we know from metalinguistic comments in the 18th and 19th centuries, this precursor of a more general, more standardized variety was heavily accented and displayed an unmistakably regional coloration as far as pronunciation and probably also as far as the lexicon, the morphology, and the syntax are concerned. As to its further development, the influence of the social factor, already important in the 17th century, has constantly increased and has finally become the paramount characteristic. The example to follow was the language as it was used by the *gegoede stand* (the well-to-do classes). Since most of those were found in the Randstad, the emerging standard variety imbibed the local Randstad features. Gradually that variety was accepted and imitated elsewhere as well.

THE SOCIOLECT OF THE CULTIVATED AND WELL-TO-DO HOLLANDERS

Pronunciation

For obvious reasons, we know little about exact pronunciation in the 19th century. When, in 1796, the National Assembly of the Bataafsche Republiek met for the first time, the representatives coming from all over the country had a lot of trouble understanding each other's accents (Van der Sijs 2004, 208). This clearly indicates that a more or less generalized standard pronunciation did not yet exist. Grammarians and other language planners who addressed the item at all had already conveyed the same impression. Guidance as to normative pronunciation is almost never to be found. We may safely assume, therefore, that every region had its own pronunciation, even in the more formal register. On the other hand, we know that both private planners and the government tried to interfere to advance the elaboration (creation?) of a uniform language, as suited in a uniform Fatherland.

Although the importance of a general civilized pronunciation has continuously been stressed from the Renaissance onward, almost no pronunciation guides had ever been published. We had to wait until the 19th century for the first pronunciation guides finally to emerge. In 1844 a J. F. Bosman, from Zeeland, publishes his *Korte uitspraakleer der Nederlandsche taal* (Concise Pronunciation Guide of Dutch) in which he made a difference in pronunciation between *ei* and *ij, au* and *ou,* the *scherplange* and the *zachtlange* e. Obviously, such guides were not very successful, since they lacked the main requirement already mentioned: the flair of the well-to-do Randstad speakers, who had given up these differences a long time ago (Van der Sijs 2004, 207–208).

For lack of authoritative pronunciation manuals, the only practical advise people could be given was to use the written language as the model for pronunciation. "Speak as you write," as the influential language planner Siegenbeek put it, was all they had to offer. Speaking *op de letter,* as it is said in Dutch, characterized the pronunciation of future Algemeen Beschaafd Nederlands (ABN; see chapter 6) as well as its forerunners, and this also partly explains the commotion every time a new spelling was introduced or even proposed. In preacher-Dutch, Van der Sijs (2004) tells us, *mensch* used to be pronounced by many with an audible *ch* at the end, *wandeling* sounded as /wandelinch/, and *heerlijk* rhymed with *leerrijk,* or so we're told by the contemporaries. Also, *houwe, ik vin,* and *hij leit* may have been said by every Hollander in their everyday speech, but when speaking formal ABN it was *houden, ik vind,* and *hij ligt* that was uttered.

The government's main contribution to language planning was the endowment, for the first time ever, of a professorship for the study of the mother tongue. Its first incumbent at the State University of Leiden in 1797 was the *dominee* (Reverend) Matthijs Siegenbeek, for whom preacher-Dutch came easily and automatically. He was the author of the official spelling of Dutch, which appeared in 1804. A few years later the universities of Amsterdam, Utrecht, and Groningen followed suit.

Very soon "speak as you write" was amended to "speak as the cultivated people write," a tricky piece of advice. Still, by the end of the 19th century, we witness a growing agreement on a cultivated (or educated) way of pronouncing Dutch, that is, on the pronunciation used by the cultivated social and intellectual elite of the Randstad.

In the 17th century, Vondel had already argued (see chapter 4) that Dutch was spoken in the best possible way (*allervolmaeckst*) by the *betere standen* (upper classes) in Amsterdam and The Hague. That is the way it continued to be until far into the 20th century. It can safely be assumed that what Voortman (1994) discovered for the 20th century holds true more still for the preceding one, namely, that in spite of the *notabelentaal* (language of the dignitaries) differing geographically because of regional interference, it still had an identical social function everywhere: to set its speakers apart from the language use of the lower classes. By the end of the 19th century the general, cultivated language acquired a general, cultivated pronunciation as it was heard in church and schools and, eventually, on radio and television.

Although a normative pronunciation guide still did not emerge, we see how during the second part of the 19th century the cultivated and educated spoken language was continuously gaining in popularity among the well-to-do inhabitants of the Randstad. Shortly after, it started to penetrate the rest of the country as well.

Vocabulary

Words—and, more still, different words for the same thing—are what appeals greatly to the imagination of the general public. Of all language levels, the lexicon is indeed displaying the largest amount of variation (both regional and otherwise). Specific words are often regarded as symbols for the individuality of a region or a city. A standardization of vocabulary, therefore, takes a lot of persuasive power as well as extensive planning materials, mainly dictionaries.

The *Woordenboek der Nederlandsche Taal* (WNT) was a dictionary mainly meant for experts (philologists and linguists). But the intellectual part of the general public was in need of a dictionary as well, and the first one to professionally recognize that need was Johan van Dale, a schoolmaster from the small village of Sluis in Zeeland, 10 miles from Brugge but on the northern side of the state border. The first edition of what became the authoritative dictionary of Dutch appeared in 1872, or at least the first installments did. Van Dale unfortunately never saw the finished dictionary because he died a couple of months later at the age of 44 (Van Sterkenburg s.d. [1983]). A dictionary by Koenen was published in 1897, whereas in Flanders the *Modern woordenboek* by Jozef Verschueren appeared in 1930–1931. Although both of them are still regularly updated, they never even came close to the authority Van Dale has.

According to a malevolent definition, dictionaries are plagiarism in alphabetical order, since every one of them has at least one predecessor. This applies to the Van Dale as well. The point of departure for our Sluis schoolmaster was the *Nieuw Woordenboek der Nederlandsche taal*, a dictionary published by the Calisch brothers in 1864. Van Dale adapted the spelling and added many words, most of all in the field of the exact sciences. He added a total of 18,000 words, and after that his assistant and disciple Jan Manhave finished the dictionary and also took care of the subsequent edition in 1884.

Although actually less than half the dictionary was composed by Van Dale, it carries his name and always will, since he was the one who took the initiative and provided the Dutch-speaking world with a dictionary that has come to be accepted by all as the lexical codex of law of Dutch vocabulary. It also won him a statue in his hometown of Sluis. Up until today (the 14th edition in three thick volumes was published in 2005) all Van Dale's successors have denied, or at least weakened, the prescriptive authority of their dictionary. Kruyskamp, one of the most famous among them, used to say that a word is not right because you find it in Van Dale; you'll find it in Van Dale because it is right, a subtlety lost on the habitual user of the dictionary.

Anyway, since the authority of a dictionary (or a grammar for that matter) depends on its users, Van Dale's authority is unlimited: everyone in the Dutch language territory, north or south, will agree: a word is Dutch and correct Dutch when it is in Van Dale. Scientifically speaking this is nonsense, since every dictionary has to list a lot of words that are not (or not anymore) "correct", but that doesn't bother Van Dale's many buyers.

Grammar

In the late 19th century, the linguistic journal *Taal en Letteren* was very ardent in its attempts to change the norm of the language, and its editorial staff was very much aware of the fact that this could be done only through or by means of the schools. Two of them, Kollewijn (well-known as a spelling reformer) and the Fleming J. Vercoullie, each wrote a grammar for the Dutch and the Belgian schools, respectively, meant to reform simultaneously the language teaching practice and the norm of the language itself. They were part of the growing group of linguists and intellectuals who wanted to turn the early 19th-century slogan, "speak as you write," into its opposite, "write as you speak." That too was tricky advice not only in the north, where people still spoke differently according to the part of the country they lived in, but still more so in the south, where most people were not familiar at all with the way the northern Netherlanders (of whatever geographic origin) spoke. Vercouillie was an integrationist Fleming (see the following section), who not only prompted the Flemings to adhere to the northern norm but was also eager to help them to succeed in what was not a simple endeavor.

The most famous grammar in the genre, though, was written by the schoolmaster C. H. den Hertog and was published between 1892 and 1896 (*Nederlandsche spraakkunst: Handleiding ten dienste van aanstaande (taal)onderwijzers*). Apart from (or because of) the inherent merits of the book, it is famous because all subsequent school grammars, both in Belgium and in Holland, were based on Den Hertog's example. Although he set the standards (and the norm) for generations to come, his is no longer the authoritative grammar of Dutch, occupying the same place as Van Dale does in lexicography. That role was taken over by the ANS, which was written more than half a century later (see chapter 6).

LINGUISTICS

As already mentioned, the early 19th century has also seen the real beginning of Netherlandistics as a scientific, academic discipline; its two pioneers were Siegenbeek and Weiland, the authors of the official and authoritative spelling and grammar of Dutch respectively. Weiland's grammar consists of two volumes: phonetics and morphology; and syntax. Both works are the typical and probably also the best representatives of the normative tradition (De Bonth et al. 1997, 380). Naturally, the university chairs installed a few years earlier also added to the academic prestige of Netherlandistics.

In the mid-19th century, the normative tradition gives way to historical-comparative linguistics, which was going to dominate the European scene for the rest of that century (and a lot longer still). Although the everyday usage of the language continues to be affected by norms and rules, the standardization process is influenced by historical linguists as well, not only indirectly because of their specific views on language development but also directly through the dictionaries they published. One of its most prominent representatives, Matthias de Vries (1820–1892), a professor of Dutch philology at the University of Groningen and afterward Leiden, was one of the initiators and the first author of the *Woordenboek der Nederlandsche Taal* (Dictionary of the Dutch Language).

The WNT, as it is commonly called, was one of the most important practical results of the first Dutch Congress organized in 1849 in Ghent for northern as well as southern participants (fig. 5-2) (box 5.2). From a political point of view 1849 was the right moment: by then the Belgian secession was two decades old, and in 1839 Holland and Belgium had signed a peace treaty that officially ended their state of war. Both countries, moreover, had come closer together since both their monarchs were frightened and shocked by the democratic movement and political uproar in neighboring France, Germany, and other European

BOX 5.1 } Hendrik Conscience (1812–1883)

In the 1830s and 1840s the *dominating* prose genre was the historical novel.[4] In the south the genre was represented by Hendrik Conscience. His novels—exactly 100 in all—are often clumsily put together, his characterization is mostly crude and superficial, and there is often a complete lack of historical authenticity. But he was the first novelist to emerge from the south in a period following almost two centuries of low Dutch cultural life. Also, his aim in writing was not solely literary. This son of a French immigrant, who had settled in Antwerp, was fiercely committed to the Flemish movement, and though he lacked sophistication and technique he did not lack enthusiasm or the power to transmit it. His influence, therefore, was immeasurably more profound than the purely literary value of his work would indicate. He wrote with the express purpose of waking up the Flemings and making them read again, and in that he certainly was successful. He therefore earned the epithet *"De man die zijn volk leerde lezen"* (The man who learned his people to read). His first book *In 't Wonderjaer 1566* (The Year of Wonders 1566), published in 1837) contains an introductory manifesto in which the Flemings' right to a literature in their own language was ardently defended.

His most popular novel *De Leeuw van Vlaanderen* (The Lion of Flanders; 1838) deals with the attempt of the French king to crush the heroic resistance of his Flemish feudal territories and ends with the victory of the Flemish armies over the French knights in the famous Guldensporenslag (Battle of the Golden Spurs) of 1302. It made him one of the most popular Belgian writers of all time, and the novel, hailed as a foundational document of the emerging Flemish movement, soon functioned as a true national epic. It became the most widely read 19th-century novel, and around 70 Dutch editions have been published so far. He was renowned across borders, from England and France to Germany, where books of his had been translated very soon after he wrote the first editions. During the second half of the 19th century, 75 volumes of Conscience's work appeared in German, 50 in French, and 34 in English. Many translations in other languages soon followed.

[4] The main (but not the only) sources of information in all the boxes on literature (in this and the other chapters) are Meijer (1971) and Hermans (2009).

643　　　TAAK (II).

Gecommitteerden ontfangende voor haar moeyte
... een taack wyns, *Utr. Placaatb.* 3, 575 *a* (a°.
1571). Een taak Rynsen wyns ; zynde taak een
oud woord, zoo veel beteekenende als een stoop,
v. ALKEMADE, *Displ.* 1, 284.

TAAKS. Zie TAKS.

TAAL (I) — TALE —, znw. vr., mv. *talen.* Mnl.
tale; ofri. *tale, tele* ; os. *tala,* mnd. *tale,* nnd. *tâl*; ohd.
zala, mhd. *zal,* nhd. *zahl* ; ags. *talu,* meng. *tayl(e)*
enz., neng. *tale* ; on. *tala* ; de. *tale.* Verwant met
Tal, Talen, Tellen enz. Van den oorsprong is
niets met zekerheid bekend. — De oude vorm *tale*
is nog in vast gebruik in de verbinding *tale Ka-
naäns.*

De verschillende toepassingen waarin *taal*
gebruikt wordt, zijn niet altijd scherp te scheiden ;
eenige willekeur was dan ook in het onderstaande
onvermijdelijk.

1) Het door de spraakorganen voortgebrachte
middel waarvan de mensch zich bedient om
zijn gedachten of gevoelens kenbaar te maken,
de spraak. Vervolgens ook toegepast op de aan-
duiding van dat middel door schrift of druk.

a) In toepassing op de menschelijke spraak
in 't algemeen, of althans zonder dat de gedachte
aan één bepaalde *taal* in onderscheiding van
andere (zie daarvoor onder *b*)) op den voorgrond
staat. || De tale is een vroedwyf der zinnen, een
tolck des herten ende een schildery der ghedachten,
die anders binnen den mensche verborghen ende
onzichtbaar zyn, COORNHERT, vóór *Kort Begr.*
1, IX. Die de subtijlste tale, en onghemeene woorden gebruycken, en zijn de welsprekenste niet,
maer die-ze best naer tijd en stoffe, konnen voe-
ghen, DE BRUNE, *Bank.* 1, 225. De kunstige Taal
... zal een zamenvoeging zijn van onderscheidene
en willekeurige klanken, welke geen ander ver-
band hebben met de denkbeelden die zij uitdruk-
ken, dan 't geen voortkomt uit het onderwijs,
en steunt op de gemaakte overeenkomst, CHOMEL
3587 *b.* Die zuiverheid van gekuischte taal (*t. w.
bij Cicero*) ; die keus van juiste en schilderachtige
woorden, V. D. PALM, *Red.* 2, 8. Ik dacht in gemeenzame taal : want wie is er deftig, wanneer
hij denkt ? GEEL 77. De figuurlijke taal, 185.
Die rede zong, gelijk men beweert, in de kinder-
jaren van het menschdom. ... Hare uitdrukking
geleek nog niet naar de volkomene taal der be-
schaving, 268. ,,En is 't van Tollens niet — het is
hem nagezongen", schreef Messchert. ... Mij
heugt de tijd, dat men geen glas hippocras kon
drinken ... bij het aanteekenen, — geen kar-
deelstok roeren in den kraamkamer *enz.* ...,
of men moest er een vers bij slikken, in den trant
... van den man, wien studie de kunst leerde
met de taal te tooveren, POTGIETER 1, 280. In de
geheimen van taal en stijl ... niet ingewijd, en
daardoor tot het recht genieten van een aantal
schoonheden onvermogend, BEETS, *Versch.* 4, 44.
Hunne taal is even onvolmaakt als zij (*de men-
schen*) zelf zijn, maar het grootsche is juist de
rustelooze opeenvolging van al die verschillende
phasen, KLUYVER, *Eenh. en Verscheidenh. in de
Taal* 25.
— *Wel* (enz.) *ter tale zijn,* welbespraakt zijn. ||
W e l ter t a l e n z ij n. *Estre bien enlangagé,*
PLANT. — Een Boerinne worde van een Courti-
saen gevrijt, Die sich liet beduncken dat hy wel ter
tael was ..., Na sijn sprake wanende dat hy een
Wael was, Dacht, ick wil niet hebben ... Een
krom-tongh *enz.,* VISSCHER, *Brabb.* 58. Doe wierd
daer sterck gescheld, midts quamen in de kamer

TAAL (1), 1, *a*).　　644

Twee mannen, braef ter tael ; ick hoorde noyt
bequamer, STARTER 225. Want ick ben gantsch
niet ter tael, en met woorden moet mese (*t. w.
de vrijsters*) voên, 424. Dien die kloeck ter tale is,
Jes. 3, 3. Waarlijk, meester, gij zijt goed ter tale ;
ik heb lang gedacht, dat er meer in u stak, dan
gij wilt laten blijken, CONSC. 2, 356 *a.* Een knap
man ..., die flink ter tale was, KNEPPELH. 8, 72.
Gij zijt niet slecht ter tale ? SLEECKX 8, 383.

b) In toepassing op het middel van geestelijk
verkeer tusschen de leden van een bepaalde men-
schengemeenschap, t. w. een volk, een natie enz.,
in onderscheiding van hetgeen andere dergelijke
gemeenschappen voor hetzelfde doel gebruiken.
Zonder nadere bepaling wordt die *taal* bedoeld,
welke door de gemeenschap of in het land waar-
van sprake is, gebezigd wordt. || Dies hen luy
(*t. w. de rederijkerskamers*) het zuyveren, verryken
ende vercieren des taals (ende niet het rymen
alleen) eyghentlyck betaamt, *Kort Begr.* 1, III.
Deur dien sy met veel vreemde natien handelen
ende omgaen, soo connen sy veel talen spreken,
als Spaens, Engels, Francoys ende Duyts, *O.-I. e.
W.-I. Voyag.* 5, 4 *a.* Benaminge (*van de jicht*)
in verscheyde Talen, V. BEVERW., *Schat d. Onges.*
2, 105 *a.* Het (zal) aan de cadets niet alleen ge-
permitteert zyn eenige inlandse talen ... aan te
leren, maar men zal dezelve ook daartoe moeten
houden, *N.-I. Placaatb.* 5, 82 (a°. 1743). Al
mijne hoop ligt nog alleen bij de geestelijkheid.
Deze moet bij onze bevolking den Duitschen geest
opwekken, taal en zeden herstellen, WILLEMS, *Br.*
166. Te rekenen van den eersten Januari 1823
zal in de opgenoemde provinciën Limburg, Oost-
Vlaanderen, West-Vlaanderen en Antwerpen
geene andere taal dan de taal des lands, voor de
behandeling van openbare zaken, erkend of
gewettigd zijn, *Besl. v.* 15 Sept. 1819 (*Stbl.* 48),
a. 5. Alle ... akten ... zullen voortaan, in het
geheele Rijk kunnen worden opgemaakt in de taal,
welke de belanghebbende partijen verkiezen,
Besl. v. 4 Juni 1830 (*Stbl.* 19), *a.* 1. Wie thans
een der in het Fransch door Amalia geschreven
brieven in handen neemt, herkent daarin de
beschaafde vrouw niet. Aan taal en spelling wordt
meer dan gewoon geweld aangedaan, VEEGENS,
Hist. Stud. 1, 236. Of zouden er misschien geene
meer zijn, die evenmin de taal van eenen Vlaming
verstaan als 't geknor van een ziek varken ?
DE VOS, *Vl. Jong.* 141. Die taal, die na vijftien
jaar lang de officiëele taal des lands geweest te
zijn nu tot een samenraapsel van ellendige tong-
vallen verklaard werd, ROOSES, *Schetsenb.* 67.
Van zijne aankomst (*te Gent*) af werd hij (*Willems*)
daar eerevoorzitter der maatschappij ,,de Taal
is gansch het Volk", 84. Te haten ook begon zij
den rauwen klank der taal (*t. w. het Engelsch*),
V. EEDEN, *Koele Meren* 405.
— *Een taal hanteeren,* zie HANTEEREN, III, 3) ;
—*spreken.* || Al waer 't dat ick de talen der men-
schen ende der Engelen sprake, 1 *Cor.* 13, 1.
— *Iemands taal* is in den regel de *taal* van hem
en zijn landgenooten, *onze taal* die van spreker en
zijn landgenooten; er kan echter ook de door hem
of ,,ons" gewoonlijk gesproken *taal* bedoeld zijn. ||
Ik doorwroet ons grondwoord-ryke taal, SPIEGHEL
7. Ick heb u volkomelick gekent, gelijck wy in
onse tale seggen, by name ende toename, *Jes.* 45,
Kantt. 15. Uwe Britsche en Hoogduitsche voor-
gangers hebben daar van, ten opzigt van hunne
taalen, de bespottelijkheid aangetoont, V. EFFEN,
Spect. 7, 133. Ook de meest bevooroordeelden

FIGURE 5.2　Page from the "WNT"

countries in 1848. Hence, it was now politically safe to advocate a closer cooperation between Belgians and Dutchmen.

During the first decades after the secession, young Belgian writers such as Hendrik Conscience (box 5.1) had started to write successful novels for a larger public. Also, a growing number of people had acquired experience with using Dutch in administrative writing, whereas philological edition and explanation of Middle Dutch texts and other studies in and on Dutch grew very popular among the men of letters. What we are witnessing here is the genesis of a young Belgian yet Dutch-speaking intellectual elite. They were the first to experience that it was necessary to unify and modernize the language, and this explains their interest in standardization. Politically speaking, most of them were progressive sympathizers of the liberal party and, at the same time, part of the integrationist faction that came up with the idea to organize a Nederlandsch Congres (Dutch Congress) in 1849.

This first north–south reunion after the Belgian defection served a dual purpose: establishing contact with men of letters from the northern Netherlands would not only favor "the advancement of the Dutch language and literature" but also strengthen the Flemish movement, or so they hoped. In fact, these were but two aspects of one and the same ambition. Success, though, was not to be predicted during the period immediately preceding the congress. In general, the Dutch were rather indifferent to the cause of the Flemish activists and did not want to interfere in what most labeled domestic Belgian policy. Consequently, only a handful of Dutch men of letters attended the Congress, determined moreover to restrict to scholarly issues and not to indulge in language political debate. On the domestic front the particularist faction did not attend.

BOX 5.2 } Ajuin

The WNT was published in *installments*; the first one appeared in 1864 and the complete first volume (A-AJUIN) in 1882. Van Vloten, an academic rival of De Vries, whom he called an *ijdel kathederboefje* (a professor steeped in vanity; literally, a vain lectern scoundrel), made the following satirical "poem" to celebrate the "early" appearance of the first volume of the WNT:

> O, luid weerklink de lofbazuin!
> Het Woordenboek kwam tot ajuin
> In dertig jaren al; dat heet
> Zijn tijd voorzeker welbesteed!
> 't Duurt nu geen dertig jaar gewis
> Eer 't tot azijn genaderd is;
> Stel voor elk verdre letter maar
> Tweederde van die dertig jaar,
> Dan staat al na een eeuw of vier
> 't Geheel gedrukt reeds op papier!

The Congress opened on August 26, 1849, in the University of Ghent and started a tradition of congresses that continued through 1912. In retrospect, the Nederlandsche Taal- en Letterkundige Congressen (Dutch Congress on Language and Literature) neither profoundly determined the course of the Flemish movement nor directly influenced the situation and status of Dutch in Belgium. Nevertheless, the first congress was a pioneering event, and subsequent ones positively contributed to one of the permanent goals (or at least strategies) of the Flemish movement, viz. intensifying contact with fellow Dutch speakers of the north and gaining sympathy and support in the Netherlands for the Flemish cause (Willemyns 1993).

One of the most important practical results of the congress was the acceptance and subsequent implementation of the northern participant Gerth van Wijk's suggestion to commission an extensive dictionary "for our common tongue" (Handelingen, 85–90).[5] It was an old dream: from the beginning of the 18th century onward regular negotiations between northern and southern scholars on how to accomplish a comprehensive dictionary of Dutch had taken place. It took until 1849 to make it come true. Matthijs de Vries was nominated as the author of this dictionary, which was written in the tradition of the *Deutsches Wörterbuch* (German Dictionary) of the Grimm brothers. De Vries got his final instructions from the second congress in Amsterdam in 1850 and started effective work shortly after that. He regularly reported on the progress made on many subsequent congresses. The first volume of his dictionary was published in 1882, and it turned out to be a very long-lasting lexicographic enterprise: it was brought to a successful end in 1998 when the 40th and final volume was published, making the WNT the largest dictionary in the world. Still, it didn't take the four centuries predicted by De Vries's fierce opponent Van Vloten in a satirical poem (box 5.1). From the very beginning financial support was provided by both the Dutch and the Belgian governments. Later it was carried on by the binational Instituut voor Nederlandse Lexicografie (Institute for Dutch Lexicography) in Leiden, which is still coordinating the official lexicographic efforts of the Low Countries, under the auspices of the Nederlandse Taalunie (see chapter 6). Apart from its scientific value in the field of lexicography and lexicology, it should be born in mind that the *Woordenboek der Nederlandsche Taal* was also a major instrument in both the elaboration and the implementation of the integrationist norm in Flanders.

De Vries and his coauthor, Lammert Allard te Winkel (1809–1868), thought that their huge enterprise necessitated a new and uniform orthography of Dutch. Its main designer was Te Winkel, but the new spelling is called the De Vries–Te Winkel system. It was made compulsory by the Belgian government in

---

[5] Handelingen (Proceedings) used to be published after every conference. Until 1912 they were organized alternatively in a Flemish and a Dutch city.

BOX 5.3 } The Largest Dictionary in the World

The WNT is a monolingual, alphabetical, historical-descriptive, and scientific dictionary written in the tradition of the *New English Dictionary* (James Murray) and the *Deutsches Wörterbuch* (Grimm *brothers*). It contains information on the period from 1500 to 1921. The first installment appeared in 1864 and the first complete volume (A-*AJUIN*) in 1882. In 1998 King Albert II of Belgium and Queen Beatrix of the Netherlands were presented with the officially finished dictionary.

In 147 years some 2.5 to 3 million quotations were considered, 1.6 million of which were incorporated into the dictionary. The largest dictionary of the world, it has 40 volumes and takes up 3 meters of bookshelf space. There are 90,000 columns on more than 45,000 pages. In 2001 three volume *aanvullingen* (supplements) were published, bringing the dictionary up to date till 1976. In 2007 the whole dictionary, including the supplements, were put online (http://wnt.inl.nl).

1864 and officially accepted by the government of the Netherlands shortly after. It was this system, the general guidelines of which are still at the basis of the present orthography of Dutch, that definitively established orthographic unity in both parts of the Low Countries.

Two of De Vries's former students, Jacob Verdam and Eelco Verwijs, are the authors of the 10-volume *Middelnederlandsch Woordenboek* (Middle Dutch Dictionary), the first volume of which appeared in 1885. *Verdam,* as it is commonly called (Verwijs died not long after the start of the enterprise), also represents a formidable achievement in the field of historical linguistics and lexicography. The combination of both dictionaries—Verdam's *terminus ad quem* being around 1500, the year the WNT took as its *terminus a quo*—provided an extensive overview of the vocabulary of Dutch and its evolution from early Middle Dutch times onward.

The South after 1830

BELGIUM

After the 1830 secession, Belgium was constituted as an independent constitutional monarchy with a parliamentary system dominated by the bourgeois elite, which secured its position by adopting a poll-tax system: out of 3.5 million people, initially only 46,000 had the right to vote (Ruys 1981, 47). Both the voters and the elected were rich, powerful, and French speaking. For this bourgeoisie, French was a natural choice as the language of the state and, therefore, the only language used in the administration and indeed in public life in general, both in the French- and the Dutch-speaking parts of the country. All over Belgium the government appointed only French-speaking civil servants and started a generalized and very deliberate discrimination of Dutch, which continued throughout the 19th century (Witte, Craebeckx, & Meynen 2009; Witte & Van Velthoven 2010). Although the majority of the population was Dutch-speaking (2.3 million Dutch speakers and 1.2 million French speakers; Ruys 1981, 47), no legal means were provided for their language.

From the point of view of the Dutch language, therefore, the creation of the Kingdom of Belgium was not a happy occurrence. For one it meant the traumatic end of the first official endeavor in centuries to enhance the prestige, the image, and the usability of the language. Furthermore, the fact that now the Belgians were in charge was anything but reassuring. Previous foreign rulers may have favored the use of French, but the domestic French speakers (be they Walloons or Gallicized upper-class Flemings) were ultimately responsible for the systematic disfavoring and discrimination of Dutch. "The prestige factor associated with French led to what has been called a 'double language boundary,'" Baetens Beardsmore (1981, 10) says, since on top of the geographic division between Flanders and Wallonia "there was a socio-economically determined language boundary within the Dutch area in which upward social mobility went hand in hand with language switch from Dutch to French. The result produced an elite estranged from the masses" (ibid.).

The language struggle that would dominate Belgian political life started as soon as Belgium was created. Although the new constitution (1831) provided for linguistic freedom,[6] it was obvious that this freedom was profitable only for the rich and the powerful, that is, the bourgeoisie from Wallonia and Flanders, all of whom were French speakers. It was a freedom permitting the judge not to understand the language of those brought before his court; a freedom making it possible to appoint civil servants in Flanders, having no command whatsoever of the language of the people they were supposed to serve; a freedom letting pupils be taught in a language they didn't understand; a freedom making sure that in the army no other language than French was used.

IUS LOQUENDI: THE FLEMISH MOVEMENT

A so-called Flemish movement fought a long and acrimonious battle for cultural, linguistic, and economic rights for the discriminated Flemings. The movement has four distinct periods, the decisive criterion of each being what was achieved linguistically.

What eventually became a mass movement appeared, in the first period, to be of interest only to a handful of *taalminnaars* (mother tongue enthusiasts), men of letters, artists, and philologists who were trying, floating on the waves of the romantic ideas of their time and without much popular support, to create goodwill for the Flemings' right to use their mother tongue in dealings with

---

[6] *"L'emploi des langues usitées en Belgique est facultatif,"* the official French text of the constitution read (Bouveroux 2011, 12).

BOX 5.4 } Jan Frans Willems (1793–1846), the Father of the Flemish Movement

Born a citizen of the French Republic in the Flemish city of Boechout, Willems acquired Dutch citizenship in 1815 and died as a Belgian in 1846, without ever leaving his native land.

He adhered to the political liberal movement, which agreed well with his romantic love for freedom and his Dutch mother tongue and with his free-thinking, nonreligeous philosophy. In his younger years he wrote plays and poetry and made a great impression with his poem *Aen de Belgen* (To the Belgians), published in 1818. It is a poem in which the author urged the Flemings not to neglect their language and culture.

He enthusiastically welcomed the reunification of the Low Countries, and he wholeheartedly supported King William's policy to revitalize Dutch language and literature. He published a number of spirited and eloquent writings in support of the native tongue of the Netherlands.

During and after the Belgian sessesion of 1830 his political sympathies stayed with the so-called Orangist faction, and he continued his efforts for the cultural integration of the northern and the southern Netherlands. One of the highlights was when he succeeded in creating a new orthography for Dutch. The *Willems spelling*, also known as the *committee spelling* (made official in Belgium in 1844) mirrored the Siegenbeek spelling in Holland and in so doing practically reintroduced the orthographic unity between the north and the south. In November 1864 the De Vries–Te Winkel system established orthographic uniformity between Holland and Belgium once and for all. Due to his premature death, Willems didn't live to acclaim what he would have considered his most important triumph.

He published several learned critical editions of Middle Dutch texts, and he was the first to translate *Van den vos Reynaerde* into modern Dutch. In 1851 a number of free-thinking liberal Flemish activists founded the Willemsfonds named after him. It was to be an important player in the cultural and political Flemish movement.

---

the authorities and to wheedle respect for it. Their natural leader was Jan Frans Willems, a lower-rank civil servant, famous as a man of letters, who was later hailed as the father of the Flemish movement (box 5.4). What the *taalminnaars* expected the government to do was formulated by one of Willems's followers, Blommaert, as early as 1832: "the language of the people . . . is the basis of nationality, so that a national government has a duty to uphold [it] with special care."[7]

The government, though, didn't in the least intend to uphold the language of the people, and, consequently, during the second period of the Flemish movement the central theme was the struggle for language laws that would introduce a system of bilingualism in Flanders by allowing Dutch alongside French for official use.

---

[7] Translation by Paul Vincent in Brachin (1985, 36).

As soon as the Flemish movement achieved more political impact, some members of parliament started legislative work to legally enforce some of the (very modest) claims of the Flemings. The first achievement was a law passed in parliament in 1873, giving the people in Flanders the right to demand a Dutch procedure in courts and other legal proceedings. In 1878 language use in the civil service was regulated in the same sense. A law passed in 1883 made Dutch the language of instruction in state secondary schools, and in 1898 the Gelijkheidswet (Law of Equality) finally officially declared Dutch and French texts of laws to be equally legal. In 1893 the *meervoudig algemeen stemrecht* (plural universal suffrage) was introduced, and from then on all (male) Flemings had the right to vote (although some had two or three votes, according to the amount of taxes they paid), which increased the number of voters 10-fold. That made their vote and their voice important; they were the majority after all. Suddenly, the Dutch-speaking majority of the country was a political factor that could no longer be neglected (Bouveroux 2011, 21).

In each and every case it took years of struggle and political debating to get those basic rights granted and, almost always, more problems still to implement them. Although the majority of the representatives were elected in Flanders, many of them, part of the Francophone upper-class elite, joined the Walloons in opposing Flemish demands. Very often the bills introduced by Flemish representatives were amended in such a way that the final approved law was no more than a feeble, watered-down version of the bill that had been proposed. Yet in spite of how unsatisfactory this may have been for the protagonists of Flemish rights, these laws are what created a climate that allowed for enforcement of more radical changes later on. From that time on, the large group of monolingual Dutch speakers was given the opportunity to use the sole language in which they were proficient with civil servants, in their schools, and in court, at the same time making it imperative for magistrates, lawyers, civil servants, and teachers to be proficient in it.

A growing number of middle-class Flemings and intellectuals came to understand that the Dutchification of public life would guarantee not only more respect but also better career opportunities and upward social mobility; thus, the number of supporters of the Flemish movement increased massively. During the third period, therefore, linking social to linguistic factors created the conditions for a growing popular following. Instead of bilingualism, the leaders of the Flemish movement now advocated an officially monolingual Flanders with a new, proud Flemish elite. Dutch in Flanders and French in Wallonia were now the aim. During that third period the whole makeup of the country was finally changed. It started in 1930 when, after a century of struggle, the Flemings finally achieved the Dutchification of the University of Ghent, meaning that now at last, after 100 years of Belgian independence, Dutch-speaking university students were taught in their own language. Prior to this, the one man, one vote system (1921) and an increasing Flemish representation in parliament had already led to a period of rearguard actions by Francophones. Afterward, things developed considerably faster: two sets of laws in 1932 and 1963 guaranteed what had been the ultimate goal of the Flemish movement: since the Walloons were opposed to widespread bilingualism throughout the country, Belgium gradually turned to the territoriality principle (McRae 1975; see box 1.2) to accommodate its various linguistic groups. It linguistically homogenized the language groups and regions.

During the fourth period, revisions of the constitution in 1970 and 1980 provided for cultural autonomy and a considerable amount of self-determination for the linguistically divided parts of the country. Subsequent changes in 1988 (Coudenberg 1989; Witte & Van Velthoven 2010) and 1993 (Alen & Suetens 1993) finally turned Belgium into the federal country it is now. The third and fourth periods have already brought us into the 20th century and will be discussed further in the following chapter.

NORMA LOQUENDI: THE INTERNAL LANGUAGE BATTLE OF INTEGRATIONISTS VERSUS PARTICULARISTS

Very soon the first leaders of the Flemish movement realized that linguistic rights for Dutch speakers could be obtained, if at all, only by the means of a linguistic legislation that in its turn could be brought about only after enhancing the prestige of the language. It was a vicious circle that was very hard to break. Consequently, in 1830 several problems emerged simultaneously, the first of which was that the new rulers were very determined to establish French as the sole official language of the young, new country.

Seven years of functioning under King William I as the official language had revealed that southern Dutch needed some remodeling as well as some adjustment in the direction of the northern model. The latter was the conviction of the *integrationists*, one of the two factions in the debate on the ongoing standardization of southern Dutch. Their opponents, those advocating a domestic standardization based on the local and regional varieties, were the *particularists*.

After a few decades, the integrationist solution had prevailed, and their victory was never seriously challenged afterward. One of the reasons for this victory was undoubtedly political: the only possibility of keeping French from dominating was to support and spread a language that is also used in the Netherlands, thus profiting domestically from the prestige it had acquired there. The strategy used to convince the relevant part of the population was the same as the one used to beat the particularist adversaries: if you want rights for your language (and for those who speak it), you should use the prestige variety, which for centuries has been preserved only in Holland. To adopt it now means only to gain repossession of the heritage that has always been there for you to collect, Jan Frans Willems and his followers incessantly repeated. It is obvious that this action was essentially ideological, appealing to political feelings that, as years went on, grew more and more intense in large portions of the population. The results of this first period of language planning in modern Belgium are therefore essentially of an attitudinal nature.

The struggle for the *ius loquendi* (the right to use a language) has significantly influenced the *norma loquendi* (the way a language should be used). Recent (and ongoing) investigations (De Groof 2004; Vanhecke 2007) have established that 19th-century linguists such as De Vreese (1899, 38) and Peeters (1930) who maintained that real Frenchification in Flanders started mostly from 1830 onward (i.e., after the Belgian state was founded) were basically right. Until not so long ago, the tendency prevailed to underestimate the perversity of the purposeful official discrimination of Dutch by the first Belgian rulers. One single quotation may suffice as an indication. In 1830 the provisional government issued a decree to justify why only French could function as the official administrative language of Belgium and why the majority language apparently could not: "since both Dutch and German, languages used by the inhabitants of certain places, may vary from province to province and even from county to county, it is impossible to draft the text of laws and decrees in either Dutch or German,"[8] they sneered (Peeters 1930, xiv).

In spite of the obvious malevolence (laws and decrees had been drafted exclusively in Dutch and in German for centuries) as well as the downright offense of calling the majority language a "language used by the inhabitants of certain places," Flemish activists took to heart the opinions expressed in such texts. This helps us to understand why the Flemings were so obsessed with wanting to convince everybody (and Belgium's French speakers in the first place) that their language was not a mere bunch of dialects but was a real standard language instead. And they would be successful only if the language was perceived by all to be the same one as the standard language used in Holland.

French may not have been the language of the majority of the Belgians; however, it surely was the country's prestigious language, and its societal superiority was held responsible not only for the discrimination of Dutch but also for its corruption. It was a general feeling in the second part of the 19th century—although not corroborated entirely by recent research—that the quality of Dutch in Belgium was constantly deteriorating. Language reformers, the most famous of which were Willem de Vreese and Hippoliet Meert, have constantly repeated that the language of even the best-educated Flemings had been corrupted by interference of French, which lead to numerous calques and gallicisms (De Vreese 1899; Meert 1899). Meert, for one, complains, "How

---

[8] In the original: "Considérant d'autre part que les langues flamande et allemande, en usage parmi les habitans de certaines localités, varient de province à province, et quelquefois de district à district, de sorte qu'il serait impossible de publier un texte officiel des lois et arrêtés en langues flamande et allemande."

could you expect the Fleming, who received insufficient instruction in his mother tongue...to be perfectly fluent in the Dutch standard? Every day we are influenced by the French texts we have to read and a lot of French expressions are locked in our head, the correct Dutch equivalent of which we are not familiar with and which, therefore, we simply translate" (21). In *Nederlandsch Museum* (1890, 286), his colleague De Vreese combines a similar complaint with a theoretical justification of the integrationist views: "it cannot be denied that we, people of the Southern Netherlands, because of all kinds of deplorable circumstances not remedied so far, have lost our language flair almost completely. I am convinced, therefore, that our only option is to learn our language again from those who never lost its command, viz. the Hollanders." De Vreese was an academically trained linguist and could therefore afford to let language political arguments overshadow purely linguistic ones: "the only possible solution I see is to rely as much as possible on Hollands. I prefer Hollands over French and that is my way of being a Flemish activist."[9]

Therefore, before Dutch had been made the language of instruction at the University of Ghent (as late as 1930), conscious attempts could not be made to bring actual language performance in line with the convictions and attitudes discussed later; it was from then onward only that Dutch in Belgium had become a language used also in and for science.

THE HALF-HEATHEN, HALF-JEWISH LANGUAGE OF THE HOLLANDERS

The province of West Flanders was historically a stronghold of religiously motivated aversion for the language variety of the protestant north. In Brugge the guild of *Sinte Lutgaarde,* mostly composed of Roman Catholic priests, united people who are often (but erroneously) called the second-generation particularists. Mainly during the final quarter of the 19th century they vehemently attacked the standard language as it was used in Flanders, under the pretext that it was the "half-heathen, half-Jewish" language of the Hollanders, as Gezelle called it (quote in Gezelle 1918, 200–201). However, for them the language aspect was only a by-product of a religious fundamentalist movement, and their main purpose was to safeguard the ultramontane, catholic character of (West) Flanders. They were convinced that promoting the West Flemish dialect to the detriment of any kind of supraregional Dutch (be it northerly or southerly flavored) was a necessary weapon in that religious battle (Willemyns 1997b) (box 5.5).

Since using a language's formal variety may sometimes be unavoidable, the Sinte Lutgaarde guild advocated the use of French rather than standard Dutch (Gezelle 1885). "French is what we prefer a thousand times to this kind of

---

[9] In *Verslagen en Meededelingen van de Koninklijke Vlaamsche Academie van Taal- en Letterkunde* (1899, 108–109).

BOX 5.5 } Full of Wind and Rhetoric

L. de Bo, famous as the author of a scholarly acclaimed dialect dictionary of West Flemish (De Bo 1873), states the following during the second annual meeting of the Guild of Sinte Luitgaarde: "In Holland, as in Germany, Protestantism has been introduced and spread mostly by the way of preaching. Yet, Protestantism is a false doctrine and not the Truth and, consequently, the preaching of Protestantism could not…be simple, natural and open-hearted. The consequence had to be—as indeed it has been—that this language was stiff and twisted, that it became far-fetched, artificial, bombastic, full of wind and rhetoric. And isn't it revealing, that those who would like to introduce this language in Belgium, are indeed all people who don't think much of the truth themselves; instinctively they sensed that this language was theirs, this language of falseness and arrogant ignorance" (SLG II, 19–27).

One of the presenters at the third meeting of the Guild of Sinte Luitgaarde, called De Carne, a professor at a priests' seminar, appears to be well introduced in the historical grammar of the Germanic languages. His presentation, "*Over den invloed van het duitsch op de nederlandsche tale*" (On the Influence of German on Dutch; SLG III, 77–86), shows that he is acquainted with the contemporary research (he quotes Franz Bopp and Moritz Heyne). Yet to what avail is no less than appalling: among other things he claims that the diphthongization of the long vowels in German is a devilish contraption because Luther, the "German antichrist," is responsible for it. Before he wrote his bible, De Carne says, the Germans pronounced [wien]; Luther's Saxon changed that into [wain]: "From Luther's times onward we see how the old, pure, full Swabian sounds of the *Minnesänger* and *Heldendichter* are replaced by the new-fashioned Saxon sounds: Middle High German long *î, û* and *iu* were diphthongized (SLG III, 78–79)."

The heathen character of a diphthong and the Roman Catholic character of a monophthong, he assures his audience, is also apparent in the Low Countries where we see that the heathen Hollanders have introduced diphthongization: "Step by step the Hollanders have followed their neighbors on the other Rhine bank, and our old sounds underwent the same fate as the old High German ones: they were swept away by triumphant Saxon" (o.c.p.80). From then on, De Carne says: "the language was no longer a ray of sun coming out of the heart but an artificially shaped doll's head" (SLG III, 85).

Flemish or whatever one likes to call it," the canon and historian Duclos, the guild's chairman, declared (Allossery 1930, 133). Consequently, they wanted to perpetuate the use of French as the prestige language of culture, education, and administration and at the same time to bar an eventual usage of Dutch in formal functions forever. A yearbook (SLG) was published containing not only very precise minutes of the gatherings but also stating without any restraint the religious-ideological foundations of their involvement with language. The famous priest-poet Gezelle himself put it very clear and very bluntly: "Our whole movement has been, from the very beginning, a catholic one, an ultramontane one even ... yet, it is of the utmost importance that we conceal our real purposes and priestly considerations from the bulk of the population" (Westerlinck 1977, 476).

LANGUAGE IN CITY ADMINISTRATIONS

As part of a larger project on the linguistic development of 19th-century southern Dutch, the interplay between political change and language usage in city administrations has recently been thoroughly investigated (Vanhecke 2007). A huge corpus of texts that had never been used for (socio)linguistic research before was collected and analyzed, and in-depth investigations were made of all relevant primary sources collected in the city administrations of some larger cities as well as some smaller towns. On top of that, purposeful inquiries into the archives of some 190 supplementary communes were carried out (Vanhecke 2007). For one of every five communes (21 percent), it has now been established which languages were used by the city administrators. At the same time, orthographic choice and general language proficiency of the scribes throughout the 19th century were examined. This brought (in a nutshell) the following insights:

a) Language choice in the chancelleries of smaller cities is completely different from what could be expected on the basis of the received opinion. That so many of them had always and in all circumstances stuck to Dutch was unknown before and came as quite a surprise.

b) In spite of the rapid succession of spelling systems, the scribes appear to have had no problems coping with them. Obviously they also must have made some kind of an agreement among them as to which spelling system to use where and when.

c) The amount of spelling "variation" does not even remotely match the amount found in the nonprofessional lower- and lower-middle-class corpus (Vandenbussche 2002).

d) It is very plausible that switching to another orthography at the onset of a new political regime was an expression of political allegiance.

e) Even when, for whatever reason, the use of the language changes, official texts continue to be written by the same scribes. Bilingual competence, therefore, was largely present among Flemish chancellery clerks.

f) Corpus planning appears to have been quite successful, at least in the professional scribes examined so far.

g) It is obvious that, as mentioned before, King William's language policy did not fail but was a much greater success than could ever have been expected.

Since we cannot detail all these intriguing results, only one of them will be elaborated upon here: how the town hall administrations used to cope with the often contradictory language regulations of three consecutive political regimes (fig. 5.3):

a) Language choice in 1819, five years after the end of the annexation by France and before any new specific language regulations had been made, reveals that Dutch had been ruled out almost completely (Dutch: 14.7 percent; French: 85.3 percent).

b) In1823, it is startling to observe how well William's language decree was carried out. French has disappeared almost completely from the official documents, even in those areas where formerly only French had been used (Dutch: 95.8 percent; French: 4.2 percent). Results like these were possible only because in most chancelleries the switch to Dutch had taken place even before it was required.

c) In September 1830, after King William had loosened the linguistic rigor, virtually none of the city administrations involved seized the opportunity to switch back to French (Dutch: 92.6 percent; French: 7.4 percent). How soon changes could occur is demonstrated by the situation in November 1830, and this time in a Belgian context (Dutch: 68 percent; French: 32 percent).

d) It was indeed only after Belgium was created that the picture changed radically, as we see on the basis of data for 1831 (Dutch: 60 percent; French: 40 percent). Here again we may well be amazed by the pace of change. The young Belgian state had no official linguistic regulations whatsoever as far as the communes were concerned. Still, a lot of city administrations immediately followed the French inclination of their government—first of all in larger cities like Brugge and Antwerp and shortly after that in some smaller ones. All of this happened in spite (or maybe because) of the fact that in the meantime language usage had constitutionally been declared optional.

e) In 1840 the use of French has reached its climax, but even then, Dutch was still used in many administrations. The year 1840 is the only time (in the entire 19th century) in which French was used in a majority of Flemish city administrations (Dutch: 43 percent; French: 57 percent).

f) The situation 40 years later reveals that new attitudes reigned in Flanders, due to the actions of the Flemish movement and early linguistic legislation passed by the Belgian Parliament. In 1880 Dutch enjoyed a rather strong position already (Dutch: 60 percent; French: 40 percent), and it would get stronger and stronger until, by the end of the 19th century, French disappeared completely from Flanders' town halls.

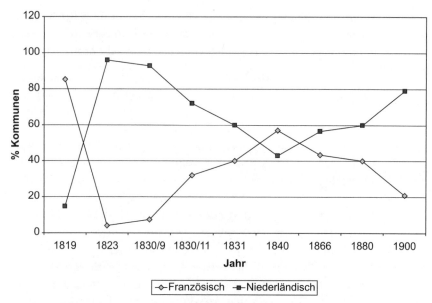

FIGURE 5.3 Chancellery language choice in Flanders (19th century) Legend: "Französisch" = French; "Niederländisch" = Dutch; "Jahr" = year

Maybe the most important conclusion is that until recently the received opinion was that the situation was almost completely the opposite of what it really was (Willemyns, Vanhecke, & Vandenbussche 2005).

SOCIALLY DETERMINED LANGUAGE USE

Another persistent myth regarding the 19th-century language situation is that the Flemish upper classes used French and the lower classes used the local Flemish dialect and that almost nobody used Standard Dutch. This too has now been proven untrue. An examination of a corpus of original handwritten documents of one of the most prestigious upper-class archers' guilds, the *Guild of Saint Sebastian* in Brugge, allows for a much subtler and more differentiated picture. Instead of the cliché dichotomy between formal French and informal dialect with little or no room for Standard Dutch, the upper classes were found to display a highly varied variety choice, governed by social, political, and pragmatic considerations (Vandenbussche 2004). Contrary to received opinion (as in Deneckere 1954), real Frenchification of the Flemish upper classes did not take place so much during the 17th and 18th century but rather after Belgian independence. Together with the outcome of other investigations, this indicates once more that in fact 1830 was the annus horribilis and that the summit of real Frenchification in Flanders was reached in the period between 1830 and 1850 (De Groof & Vanhecke 2004).

There is no doubt that Standard Dutch was used next to French for highly formal purposes by writers from the most prestigious social elite groups in 19th-century Flanders. This implies that their command of the Dutch language enabled them to use it for all purposes, another fact ignored until very recently. Members of the upper class appear to have used or avoided specific languages or varieties, depending on whether they wanted to include or exclude certain interlocutors in a specific sociopolitical context (Vandenbussche 2004).

Spelling

The year 1777 saw the first ever governmentally decreed spelling system in the Netherlands at large, viz. Jan des Roches's *Nederduytsche spraek-konst* (Dutch Grammar), devised for the Austrian Netherlands. In the north, Siegenbeek's spelling, commissioned by the government, was the compulsory guideline from 1804 onward.

The written language of the majority of the population remained largely unaffected by language planning activities, and most of them did not conform to any official or unofficial spelling norm at all. Only toward the end of the 19th century did standardized spelling finally spread, gradually going down from the higher to the lower social classes (Vandenbussche 2001). An analysis of corpora of craftsmen, upper-class archers, particularist intellectuals, and others made clear that personal school training and a profession involving a lot of writing are the paramount factors determining the quality of the linguistic and orthographic output.

However, as far as official language use is concerned, political decisions did certainly play a part, and this is all the more interesting since the19th century is a period covering many different political regimes.

From 1795 through 1814, during the time when France annexed the southern Netherlands, the use of French is obligatory in all official documents. An official spelling for Dutch, consequently, does not exist. The northern Netherlands was not annexed but transformed into a Napoleonic vassal state in which Dutch was not prohibited, and Siegenbeek's spelling remained in use.

In the southern part of the reunited Kingdom of the Netherlands (1814–1830) the use of Dutch as an official language is compulsory from 1824 onward. The Siegenbeek spelling, obligatory in the north, was very much encouraged in the south as well. Its official usage was soon generalized and is considered a sign of political allegiance (De Groof & Vanhecke 2004).

After 1830, French is the sole administrative language of the newly created Belgium. Even so, documents were written in Dutch in all Flemish city halls. The way city administrators did or did not comply with language regulations and spelling norm changes is fascinating as already discussed.

The dissolution of the United Kingdom of the Netherlands in 1830 had given way to a renewed feeling of uncertainty and insecurity as far as the norm of the spelling was concerned. To remedy this situation the Belgian government, strongly lobbied by integrationist organizations, organized a contest and installed a committee to judge the entries. This jury unanimously rejected all 12 entries and, in 1839, published a system of its own, known as the *commissie-spelling*. With only a few exceptions (*y* instead of *ij, ue* instead of *uu*, and *ae* instead of *aa* in closed syllables) the committee spelling mirrored the Siegenbeek spelling in use in Holland, and in so doing the committee practically reintroduced the orthographic unity between the north and the south (De Groof 2001). In spite of the fierce opposition of particularists, supported by French-speaking Belgians, the Belgian government made the committee spelling official by Royal Decree. To fully grasp the impact of this decision, one has to realize that at that moment orthography was considered an integrated part of the language or, even more to the point, the spelling *was* the language. Taking over the northern spelling system consequently was felt as taking over the northern language variety. The symbolic value of that decision was enormous. It explains why the particularist opponents experienced it as a harsh defeat, whereas its integrationist supporters cheered it as a decisive victory. The latter celebrated its acceptance with a thundering victory party in Ghent in the presence of the Dutch ambassador (box 5.6).

From that moment on, the particularist tendency never again succeeded in really influencing the views of the mainstream Flemish cultural elite. Finally, in November 1864 the De Vries–Te Winkel system, devised for the WNT, which was equally official in the North, was made compulsory by Royal Decree (De Groof 2003).

BOX 5.6 } Spelling Norm and Practice during the 19th Century

---

a) In the north
- - Prior to 1804: intuitive orthography
- - From 1804 through 1864: the Siegenbeek system
- - From 1864 onward: the De Vries–Te Winkel system

b) In the south
- - Prior to 1814: intuitive orthography or Des Roches's system
- - From 1815 through 1830: Siegenbeek or intuitive orthography
- - From 1830 through 1840/1844: back to the situation prior to 1814
- - From 1840/1844 through 1864: the committee spelling
- - From 1864 onward: the De Vries–Te Winkel system

CHARACTERISTIC FEATURES

The basic principles of the De Vries–Te Winkel spelling still govern today's orthography, albeit with some changes. Its main rule had already been formulated by Lambert ten Kate in the 18th century: the spelling was to be based on "civilized pronunciation" (*stel in uw schrift de beschaafde uitspraak voor*). None of those who formulated this rule have ever tried to make clear how exactly it ought to be implemented.

There were a few exceptions to this general rule:

- We write *kaart* with *t* and *paard* with *d*, although the pronunciation is the same, because of the principles of analogy and uniformity saying that, whenever possible, the same word should always be written the same way. The fact that in the plural form *kaarten* (maps) and *paarden* (horses) we hear a *t* and a *d*, respectively, accounts for their singular forms being written differently as well. Strangely enough, the principle of uniformity does not apply as far as *v–f* and *z–s* oppositions are concerned: *hoeven–hoef* (hoof) and *wezen–wees* (orphan).
- The previous point still does not explain why *ik lijd* (I suffer) and *rouw* (mourning) are written with *ij* and *ou*, whereas the homophonous *ik leid* (I lead) and *rauw* (raw) are written with *ei* and *au*. The rule here is the principle of etymology (both *ei*'s and *ou*'s are historically different), which, as De Schutter (2002, 452) correctly observes, leads to "phonetically unmotivated oppositions." This has caused tremendous problems (and still does) to all language users who are not that well grounded in Old Germanic (De Vries, Willemyns, & Burger 2003, 156–164).

HOLLANDSCHE BEENEN OR *HOLLANDSE BENEN*?

In the late 19th century, a great deal of criticism emerged. From various sides, the slogan *schrijf zoals je spreekt* (write as you speak) was heard. This principle was the basis of a language planning action, mainly supported by writers and linguists to, as its main protagonist Kollewijn put it in his famous article, *Onze lastige spelling* (Our tricky spelling), in 1891, "simplify the written language." The main literary impulse came from famous poets like Kloos, Gorter, and Van Deyssel, all belonging to the Tachtigers (a name referring to the decade in which they gained prominence) as well as the novelist Multatuli (see box 5.7). The journals *De nieuwe Gids* and *Taal en Letteren* (succeeded in 1907 by *De nieuwe taalgids*) propagated those views vehemently.

Kollewijn's main objection to the spelling in use was directed toward the backbone of De Vries–Te Winkel's system: the principle of etymology. Together with many teachers and linguists he pointed out that the use of cases and the single or double writing of *e* and *o* were responsible for a huge amount of mis-

BOX 5.7 } Multatuli (Eduard Douwes Dekker) (1820–1887)

The magnum opus, *Max Havelaar,* of the free thinker and free mason Eduard Douwes Dekker was, and still is, the most discussed novel in Dutch literature. His nom de plume Multatuli (Latin for "I have suffered a lot") illustrates how he viewed his own life. At the age of 18 Dekker went to the Dutch Indies. In a romantic-quixotic way he thought he was the chosen protector of the oppressed and that swift action was expected of him. So he began investigating the abuses of power in the district. After a few weeks in office, he brought a charge against the Indonesian prince who held the position of regent. The charge was considered hasty and insufficiently documented, and Dekker was advised to withdraw it. He refused and handed in his resignation. Finally he went back to Europe and settled down in Brussels, where in 1859 he wrote his novel about what had happened in Lebak.

When the first edition of *Max Havelaar* appeared in May 1860 it was an immediate and enormous success, which has lasted to the present day. It has become an undisputed classic of Dutch literature and, what is more, a classic that is still alive and kicking and still capable of arousing emotions. The center of the book is an account of the events in the Indies that led to Dekker's resignation. In spite of its chaotic appearance, *Max Havelaar* is an extraordinarily well-controlled and coherent novel in which all characters and all situations are closely linked and arranged in such a way as to put one another in perspective.

The stir caused by *Max Havelaar* was greater than any previous commotion in the history of Dutch literature. The book was discussed in Parliament in The Hague, and one of the speakers remarked that it had sent a shiver through the country. But also in the literary field and in how to handle the language, the influence of *Max Havelaar* as well as Multatuli's later work was immense, and few of his contemporaries and successors escaped the impact of his pungent style.

Abroad, too, *Max Havelaar* made a great impression. In 1868 was the first complete translation in English, in 1875 into German, and in 1876 into French. No less than five different German translations appeared between the two World Wars, and new translations in English and French were published in 1967 and 1968, respectively. The German translations and anthologies of Wilhelm Spohr made Multatuli one of the most widely read authors in Germany in the last years of the 19th century.

One of Multatuli's other famous works was called *Ideën* (Ideas). He numbered his ideas from 1 to 1282 and eventually collected them in seven volumes (1862–1877). These *Ideën* are the most complete expression of a writer's personality to come out of the 19th century. No other writer has so freely and independently recorded what he thought of the society in which he was living. Some of the *Ideën* are only short aphorisms and some are longer essays, but the book also contains a five-act play and, scattered through the seven volumes, a long novel titled *Woutertje Pieterse.* It is a novel of childhood and is to a certain extent autobiographical.

FIGURE 5.4 Multatuli (courtesy of Ons Erfdeel vzw, Flanders, Belgium)

takes in children and grown-ups alike. Kollewijn wanted to change that in the first place. He also suggested changing the suffixes *-isch* (as in *Belgisch* or *practisch*), into *-ies*, *-lijk* (as in *wenselijk* or *mogelijk*) into *-lik*, as they were pronounced. By the same token the *-sch* suffix in for example Hollandsch or Vlaamsch had to be simplified as well to Hollands and Vlaams.

Most of those changes were finally accepted and made official in 1934. Therefore, they will be discussed, together with other propositions and changes, in chapter 6 on the 20th century.

Conclusions

In the words of Brachin (1985, 31), "a Dutch text from the middle of the 19th century often strikes us as very old-fashioned." Still, if we eliminate the use of the genitive *des* (of the), *mijns* (of my), and *eener* (of a), the pronouns *welke* (who, which) and *gij* (you), which were used even in very informal writing, and, most of all perhaps, the extremely frequently used pronoun *dezelve*, which as Brachin rightly observes "seemed to have no other purpose than to differentiate the written from the spoken language," the antiquated character of such texts largely dissipates. And that is exactly what happened during the second half of the 19th century. It was an evolution that progressed very gradually and very slowly. Mainly thanks to influential writers, language planners, and other men of words, language "went on changing along with society. More slowly than their powerful neighbours, and yet irreversibly, the Netherlands became modernised" (Brachin 1985, 34).

Multatuli strongly supported changes in spelling and language, and he too wanted the written language to be as near to the spoken one as possible (fig. 5-4) (box 5.7). He knew, though, that this was not always very easy, something he expressed in his very own aphoristic way as follows: "*Ik leg me toe op 't schrijven van levend Hollands. Maar ik heb schoolgegaan*" (I strive to write living Dutch, but I have been to school). Anyway, in the later editions of his *Max Havelaar*, Multatuli replaced *gij* with *je, zeide* and *weder* with *zei* and *weer*, and *eener* with *van een. Gehuwd* gives way to the more familiar *getrouwd* (married), and *wijl* becomes *omdat* (Brachin 1985, 33). It is obvious that nowadays nobody would even consider using the first element of those pairs. Under the influence of authors but also grammarians as De Hertog, at the onset of the 20th century Dutch evolved more and more into a living language, even in its written form. Not only the way of writing but also the way of speaking gradually changed: "from approximately 1900 onward a moderate Hollands or Randstad-accent was accepted as the standard pronunciation in The Netherlands" (Van der Sijs 2004, 209).

In Flanders, people were less preoccupied with how to use the language than with being allowed to use it at all. During the 19th century the fate of Dutch in the south constantly oscillated between exasperation and hope. Proscription of Dutch during the French annexation was followed by its complete restoration in the United Kingdom of the Netherlands. Immediately after, rock bottom was reached during the initial decades following Belgian independence. And from then on, the Flemish movement performed a gradual but absolutely remarkable case of reversing language shift (RLS) as Fishman (1991) calls it. This not only has been decisive for the future of Belgium and the cohabitation of its various language groups but has also been one of the most important events in the language territory at large. Both the internal and the external development of Dutch would have been completely different if not for Willems and his contemporary and later supporters, who prevented one-third of the Dutch language community from being lost forever.

6}

The 20th Century: The Age of the Standard Language

Rise and Fall of ABN

ABN

The late 19th century in Holland has been labeled by Hulshof (1997, 455) as an *"overgangsperiode van onnatuurlijke schrijftaal naar ABN (de beschaafde spreektaal)"* (a period of transition from an unnatural written language to a civilized spoken language). For the concept of a civilized spoken language, he uses the acronym ABN, which, during approximately the first three-quarters of the 20th century, used to be very popular in Holland and Flanders alike. It stands for *Algemeen Beschaafd Nederlands,* which, although it is hard to translate, might be rendered in English as General Cultivated Dutch."[1]

ABN is used for the first time in the magazine *Taal en Letteren* between 1895 and 1900. This way, it emerged, for the first time, as a "separate spoken variety of the standard language," Van der Sijs (2004, 209) says. Whereas in her view "ABN and Standard Dutch are synonyms" (Van der Sijs 204, 619), and in spite of the fact that the concept certainly refers to Standard Dutch, it is obvious to me that both terms are not synonymous. This became fully apparent when, during the last quarter of the 20th century and mainly at the instigation of sociolinguists, the *B* in ABN (standing for *Beschaafd,* i.e., cultivated) was gradually dropped. Since then the standard language is usually referred to as AN (General Dutch). Apart from solving our translation problem, both the usage and the subsequent dropping of *Beschaafd* may be significant as to the nature of the language standardization process in the Low Countries.

---

[1] Other translations have been used as well, such as civilized. Paul Vincent, in his translation of Brachin's French book, prefers General Educated Dutch (Brachin 1985, 5).

Thanks to the first comparative-historical linguist in Europe, Lambert ten Kate (in his *Aenleiding tot de Kennisse van het verhevene deel der Nederduitsche Sprake*, Amsterdam 1723), we know that in the early 18th century a more or less "general" spoken Dutch did not yet exist (see chapter 4). In fact, the cultivated (aka civilized) standard variety of Dutch was hardly a medium for oral communication until the early 20th century, and even then, as the famous Leiden professor of linguistics G. G. Kloeke (1951) complained, the number of people who were able to communicate in ABN was no more than 3 percent of the population of the (northern) Netherlands. This is merely an estimate, but the low number indicates either that language standardization in the Netherlands has not been very successful or that the B in ABN signals that ABN is indeed something else than a language variety permitting speakers of differing dialects to communicate with each other. It is hardly conceivable that in 1951 no more than 3 percent of the Dutch would have been able to do so. According to Van der Horst & Van der Horst (1999, 374), in the early 20th century ABN ("chic ABN") was spoken exclusively by the upper layers of society. By mid-century the social middle class found its way to ABN as well, since it was seen as a means of upward social mobility. This was the era of middle-class ABN. In the1970s a democratization of ABN and of society at large occurred (Van der Sijs 2004, 618).

It is clear, therefore, that the *B* in ABN indicates the involvement of a social component (as in *received pronunciation* or *King's English* in Britain). ABN is not simply general Dutch; it is the general Dutch (the sociolect) of the educated and the cultivated, that is, of a particular class of the population of the Low Countries.[2] When in the late 19th century a spelling reform was propagated with the apparently democratic slogan "write as you speak," we observe once again, as was already the case from Vondel's time (the 17th century) onward, how the social variable is what determines the norm. "Write as you speak" was democratic only at the surface: in reality and par-adoxically it was a rather elitist affair, since the only spoken language deemed fit to be the guideline in writing was the *beschaafde taal* (cultivated or civilized language) of the social and intellectual elite, a "small upper layer of society" (Hulshof 1997, 458). Obviously, propagating this variety was also seen as a way of perpetuating social distinctions by way of language.

Even without the B, though, it is hard to define what Standard Dutch is (or any standard language for that matter). What lives in the general public and is found in grammars, dictionaries, and style manuals addressing the topic at all is that Standard Dutch is the language variety used by "educated and cultivated

---

[2]Although the term ABN was equally popular in both the northern and the southern Netherlands, I am reasonably sure that it refers to two more or less different concepts, in that the "B" was very important in Holland, while not being equally relevant in Flanders.

people." *Keurig* is the Dutch adjective mostly used in this respect.[3] Often a regional criterion is added to this: it is the language variety used by the educated and cultivated people "in the western part of the Netherlands."

A substantial and different definition is given in the first edition (1984) of the ultimate normative grammar of Dutch, the *Algemene Nederlandse Spraakkunst* (General Grammar of Dutch; ANS). Its introduction states that the ANS was written to enable language users to "judge the grammaticality and acceptability of the present-day usage of Dutch" (10). It then explains what the present-day usage of Dutch is and in so doing almost officially defines the norm of Standard Dutch: "We consider standard language to be the language which can be used in all parts of the Dutch language territory in so-called secondary relations, i.e. in contact with strangers. The standard language is a supra-regional variety which is usable in all kinds of circumstances and interactions, which is not restricted to a specific style..., a specific region...or a specific group....In sum, Standard Dutch is the language which guarantees contact in secondary relations in the Dutch language territory always and everywhere" (12). Strangely enough, in the second edition of 1997, this definition disappeared and was replaced by a more extensive description of language variability, which the authors probably thought was more scientific. The definition that remains in the second edition is that Standard Dutch is "a language variety containing no elements or structures which definitely strike as being 'non-general'" (16)—a vicious circle indeed.

Attempts in other grammars or dictionaries to define what Standard Dutch is or to locate its norm are equally vague, but then it is probably not possible to be more precise. For the most part, the amount of variation allowed within the confines of the norm is not theoretically specified either, presumably once again because there is no way of describing or delineating it.

It took longer in Belgium than in Holland for ABN to be used regularly in oral communication. Remember that, after Belgium's secession from the United Kingdom of the Netherlands in 1830, the new rulers were very determined to establish French as the only official language of the new country. Another problem was that the Dutch language had lost some of its functions during the preceding centuries and seemed to be in need of remodeling and modernization. On how to achieve this, two factions may be discerned: particularists and integrationists. The integrationists, who insisted that basically the Flemings should take over as much as possible the standard language as it already existed in the Netherlands, prevailed (see chapter 5). The results of this first period of language planning in modern Belgium were therefore essentially attitudinal.

---

[3] From the alternatives offered by the dictionaries for "keurig," "nicely" and "properly" are probably catching the best the connotation of this typically Dutch word, which cannot really be translated without loosing some of its gist.

The underlying reasoning was permanently ingrained, however, and has determined language planning and policy in Flanders up to the present day. The 20th-century evolution can be understood only with this historical development in mind. One of the most important changes during the 20th century undoubtedly is that after more than two centuries Flanders finally managed to regain a voice regarding the standardization of Dutch.

During the 19th and part of the 20th century the lack of direct and frequent contact with the Netherlands made implementing the northern norm in Belgium a precarious and difficult task. The practical obstacles were so huge that only after World War II did substantial success occur. The popularization of radio and later television was undoubtedly the biggest help in overcoming these issues. It also helped that in the 1960s and 1970s at least 25 percent of all Flemings switched to Dutch television for their daily entertainment programs (Schramme 2006).

The most important contribution was the massive involvement of the core of Flemish linguists. Especially in the 1960s and 1970s the Flemish media also contributed actively by giving linguists the opportunity to address their audience and spread their views. Radio and television channels had prime time programs and almost every newspaper in Flanders had a daily column to help Flemings gain proficiency in the northern-flavored standard language, which was, as was constantly repeated, their own. Most of these programs were of the "do not say...but say..." kind and were meant to help eliminate dialect interference and gallicisms (French calques). Following the column title of one of the prestigious newspapers, the umbrella term for all of these activities was *language gardening*, and the gardeners were mostly established linguists and university professors. The results of this combined effort were quite amazing, since the very tough and unusual task of providing an almost entire population with a more or less new variety of their language in just a couple of decades was carried out successfully. Although in Flanders, as opposed to Holland the focus was on eliminating regional accents rather than stressing the social aspect, in Flanders too, the cultivated component of ABN used to be heavily stressed, mainly in order to get rid of the traditional cliché that being civilized, successful and culturally sophisticated automatically implied speaking French.

Another unusual factor should be emphasized: the massive language status planning effort was performed with almost no official government involvement. Although without a doubt the ABN policy enjoyed the moral support of almost the entire cultural and political establishment, there was very little official governmental backing, and the main effort was performed through private initiatives. Even so, the movement succeeded in gaining large popular support. In many places *ABN kernen* (ABN clubs) were created, mainly in schools. They resembled youth or scouts clubs, and their main "good deed" was to rather fanatically propagate the use of ABN always and everywhere. Unfortunately, this mostly implied simultaneously suppressing the dialect. These youngsters, after becoming parents, started to socialize their children in ABN and thus paved the way for the massive wave of dialect loss that was soon noticed.

The ABN movement had become part of the Flemish movement, and from then onward fighting for the linguistic rights of the Flemings had to be done in and through ABN. This certainly is one of the paramount motives explaining the popular success of a rather unique movement that, at the surface, was merely advocating the use of a particular language variety.

ABN AND THE LEXICON

Not many standard language words (except for official terminology) exist only in Holland or in Flanders. The main difference is in the field of frequency or domains of use, that is, whether a word is often or only seldom used. All Flemings are familiar with and occasionally use the words *zoenen* and *kuil* (to kiss, pit), but they mostly replace them with *kussen* and *put*, words the Dutch use as well but less frequently. A Dutchman drives too *hard* (fast) and a Fleming too *snel*, but in both cases they know what is meant. Even the *snel*-driving Fleming is called a *hardrijder*, since *snelrijders* do not exist. Sometimes a word may seem too formal or old-fashioned in the north but is considered normal in the south. The following word pairs are examples of that: *reeds–al* (already); *gans–heel* (whole); *verwittigen–waarschuwen* (to warn); and *vermits–omdat* (because).

In recent decades words have crossed the border at an increasing pace, mostly in that both new and older northern words have reached the south and are now commonly used. *Leuk* (funny, pretty, nice), which used to be a very typical northern word, is now constantly on everybody's lips, and the number of examples of such words is vast. Traditional wisdom has it that this occurs only as a north–south movement, and, although it is indeed stronger than the opposite, many southern words are imported in the north as well. Everybody knows about sports terminology (mostly cycling). *Afzien* for *lijden* (to suffer), *klassieker* (a major cycling competition), *lossen* (not being able to follow), *op kop rijden* (take the lead), *vals plat* (a seemingly flat part of the road), or *vlammen* (to go very hard) are all southern words initially used only by northern sport journalists but very common now even outside the sports domain. Among everyday terminology, southern words as *eindejaarsuitkering* (New Year's bonus), *gezapig* (languid, mild), *living* (for living room), *peperkoek* (ginger cake), *prietpraat* (nonsense), *stilaan* (gradually), *uitbater* (person who runs a business), *vertrekpunt* (point of departure), and *op voorhand* (beforehand) have been adopted in the north.

Still, many southern words are not used by northerners or are even unknown to them; They are part of the *peripheral vocabulary* and how to label these words in dictionaries has always been a problem, even more in a dictionary like

Van Dale because of its authoritative status. All editions since 1992 take a stratificational stand, meaning that their point of departure is that language is composed of various layers or levels, which are labeled accordingly. For the north a distinction is made between, for example, regional words (labeled *gewestelijk*) or words used in informal language (*omgangstaal*), compared with unmarked words that are supposed to pertain to the normal (i.e., the standard) language.

Van Dale has always had a lot of trouble figuring out what to do with words mostly or exclusively in use in Flanders. As a consequence of the new stratificational procedure, words generally used in Flanders should be differentiated from those that are not and and therefore deserve a special label. Words that are supposed to be part of the southern standard are marked as Belgisch Nederlands (Belgian Dutch). Examples are *arbeidsgeneesheer* (N. *bedrijfsarts*; company doctor), *onderzoeksrechter* (N. *rechter van instructie*; magistrate), or even *eenzaat* (loner; no equivalent in northern Dutch). Informal southern words are labeled Belgisch Nederlandse spreektaal (Belgian–Dutch spoken language): *autostop* (N. liften; hitchhike) and *pateeke* (N. gebakje; cake) are two examples from that category. Dialect words are regional and are therefore labeled *gewestelijk*; examples include *teljoor* (N. *bord*; plate) and *tas* (N. *kopje*; cup). The latter examples show how tricky this labeling business is, since there is absolutely no conceivable reason *teljoor* would be Belgisch Nederlands as opposed to *pateeke,* which is labeled *gewestelijk*. There can be no doubt that their stratificational status is the same.

Although the stratificational Van Dale obviously is an improvement, it didn't change the underlying view that what is used (only) in the North is the norm, whereas everything else deviates from the norm and is considered "abnormal". Van Dale has no label to mark words used only in the north. Since *onderzoeksrechter* (magistrate) is used only in the south, it is obvious that *rechter van instructie* is exclusively used in the north. There is no label to convey the latter information. The first dictionary to introduce the label *northern Dutch* is the third edition (2009) of the *Prisma Handwoordenboek Nederlands*.

As opposed to what is often thought, peripheral vocabulary is not an unsystematic and hopelessly confused amount of lexicological material. It generally originates from the following sources:

a. Institutional terminology (words designating institutions and customs specific to the extra peripheral country), such as *schepen*[4]/*wethouder* (alderman) and *aanhoudingsmandaat*/*arrestatiebevel* (arrest warrant)

---

[4] In all these word pairs, the first one is southern and the second one is northern (and standard language).

   b. Archaisms (words seldom used in the center yet still common in the periphery), such as *wenen/huilen* (to cry) and *nagel/spijker* (nail)

   c. Dialect interference (words existing in geographical dialects of the periphery and often used in peripheral standard language), such as *beenhouwer/slager* (butcher) and *hesp/ham* (ham)

   d. Loanwords from other languages not used in the center of gravity, such as *mazout/stookolie* (fuel oil) and *frigo/koelkast* (fridge)

   e. Calques, such as *dagorde/agenda* (agenda of a meeting) and *rondpunt/ verkeersplein* (roundabout)

   f. Hypercorrections, such as *regenscherm/paraplu* (umbrella) and *wisselstukken/reserveonderdelen* (spare parts)

   g. Neologisms (of the periphery, not (yet?) having made their way to the center), such as *brugpensioen/VUT* (early retirement) and *langspeelfilm/avondvullende* film (feature film)

   h. Southern terminology without a northern equivalent, such as *vluchtmisdrijf* (hit-and-run), *hongermaal* (a frugal meal), and *aprilse grillen* (fickle weather in April) (none of these words are even in the dictionaries)

Still, according to Geeraerts (2000), the editor of the electronic Van Dale, less than 2 percent of all its words are labeled as peripheral vocabulary. On the other hand, as we have seen, many of them are not even mentioned and therefore obviously cannot be labeled. The main reasons for the omission may be:

   a. A lack of awareness of the problem at hand in lexicographers mainly preoccupied with the standard language as used in the center of gravity

   b. A lack of awareness of or a lack of an appropriate methodology to deal with problems of language standardization, norm, codification, and style levels

   c. A lack of information about lexical variation in the language territory lexicographers are supposed to cover

Variation in Dutch

GEOGRAPHICAL VARIATION AT THE MICROLEVEL: DIALECTS

From the preceding chapters we know that a standard language is rather new; that is, it is a young phenomenon. It gradually grew from the renaissance period onward, starting out as a more general (i.e., supraregional) variety, first of all in writing and only considerably later also in speech. From then on we are in the presence of some kind of competition between this more general variety and the habitual spoken language, the dialect that previously was the exclusive means of oral communication of the people. Today, many places and regions still use both dialect and standard language as well as some intermediate varieties that have gradually grown in between; this puts a rather diverse supply of language varieties at the disposal of many speakers. In recent times, however, that supply has been diminishing again, as a consequence of what is called dialect loss, a phenomenon occurring everywhere in different ways and with a different pace. In the present chapter, both language diversity and dialect loss as they occur in the 20th century in the Low Countries will be discussed.

Variation is oscillating between two poles: formal and informal. In general one can say that, the more people are paying attention to what they say and how they are saying it (*monitoring* is the technical term used here) the more language use gets formal. Furthermore, variation is a function of age and gender, birthplace, social status, education and many other things and all of that can mostly be heard in people's speech.

In the present chapter many kinds of variation will be discussed: first dialects and sociolects and then an overview of the many ways to vary the standard language both in the north and in the south.

Dialect Areas

The dialect landscape of the Low Countries displays a wide range of variety, and speakers of peripheral dialects (e.g., Gronings, West Flemish, and Limburgs) are convinced they can hardly understand each other. It is hard to verify this assumption since the notion of "intelligibility" has relatively limited value.

It is a fact, though, that on both sides of the state border the some 200 kilometers separating east from west display the whole pallet of east–west oppositions present in the language territory at large. Although the dialects of Sittard and Breskens or Maaseik and Koksijde have a lot in common (they're all Dutch dialects after all), they also display the largest amount of oppositions that can objectively be established within the Dutch language territory.

The chapter on Middle Dutch demonstrated that the east–west oppositions are the oldest and most discriminating ones. This is still the case in today's dialects. In the south they are commonly divided into three main groups—Flemish, Brabants, and Limburgs—with transitional zones in between. Starting from West over East Flemish, going over Brabants the dialects are gradually coloring more easterly until the heart of Limburgs is reached.

The same east–west antagonism obviously exists in the Netherlands as well, where it is supplemented with a south–north opposition. Someone walking from Vaals in southern Limburg to Middelburg in Zeeland will notice, if he is a keen observer, a lot of changes. In Vaals he will hear people say *machen;* a little bit farther on it will be *maken*. In Limburg he will savor *ies* and more to the west *ijs*: the monophthong changes into a diphthong [ei] (as in English ice). As soon as *ies* changes to *ijs,* the observer will notice that *baum* gives way to *boom* and *schwimmen* or *schwemmen* to *zwemmen*.

Going farther west, the umlaut disappears, and a *beumke* (little tree) becomes a *boomke* in the same way as *vuuten* (feet) turns into *voeten*. The pronoun *ich-* is replaced with *ik-*. In the heart of Brabant *geleuven* (to believe) is *geloven*. Near Antwerp *zoeken* replaces *zuuken*. Having finally reached Zeeland, the valiant walker will once again be able to buy *ies* instead of *ijs*. It is only when he has traveled a long way and looks back that he will be able to clearly understand that the language (dialect) of his starting point differs considerably from what people are speaking where he is now. Where exactly the borders between the various dialects are located has been impossible to establish en route: neighboring dialects are merging almost imperceptibly. In the late 19th century, linguists therefore tended to believe that separate dialects do not really exist. Although we now realize that this conclusion was premature, even today's dialectologists are still struggling with the grouping of dialects into dialect areas.

If our walker is taking the *smokkelroute* (smugglers' path), he will also notice that the dialect characteristics he observes are independent from the state border. Brabants is spoken not only in Eindhoven but also in Turnhout; Limburgs is spoken both in Maaseik and Maastricht. And crossing the border between Knokke and Sluis he will hear that not only West Flemings but also Zeeuwen (as the inhabitants of Zeeland are called in Dutch) speak West Flemish. The state border between the Netherlands and Belgium is nowhere a dialect border (fig. 6.1).

Drawing borderlines between dialect features (e.g., the borderline between *ich* and *ik*) reveals that many of them run parallel. The technical term for such lines is isoglosses, and bundles of such isoglosses usually are the confines of so-called dialect areas, i.e. areas displaying a number of identical features (sounds, words, grammar) setting it apart from other dialect areas. Tracing isoglosses is the technique used to divide a territory into dialect areas.

To define dialect and how it should be distinguished from other language varieties, the first observation is that one of the most visible characteristics of a dialect is that it is a linguistic system used, in that specific form, in one regionally restricted area only. Moreover, there are structural differences among the dialects as well as between a dialect and the standard language. Those differences are the most spectacular in the lexicon (for a word like ladybug, for example, a couple of dozen various dialect words exist in the Dutch territory),[5] and they are the most striking as far as pronunciation is concerned (*hoes, huus, us, eus, (h)uis, ooes, oois*[6] are but some of the possible pronunciations of *huis* (house)). Furthermore, there are important differences in the fields of morphology and syntax.

Following a different approach, we see how there are also differences in function and prestige: a dialect is not used in formal domains. It is, for example,

---

[5] *Piempampoentje* is one of them. In the standard language it is *lieveheerbeestje*; some other examples are *kukeluusjen, piepauwtje, pietemelletje, hemellammetje,* and *meulentendje.*
[6] [huːs], [hyːs], [ys], [œːs], [(h) œ.ys], [oᵊs], [oᵊis].

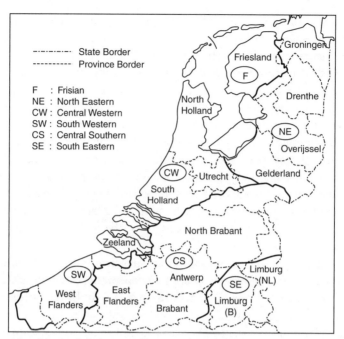

FIGURE 6.1 Map of the Dutch dialect areas (Courtesy of G. de Schutter)

not an administrative or school language, it is not the language of the media, it is used almost exclusively orally, and it mostly has a lower prestige than other varieties and certainly than the standard language.

In summary, a dialect is a local variety, varying from area to area, which, compared with the standard language, displays important differences in structure and function and enjoys only limited prestige. It is hardly ever used outside its own territory. Still, it is a complete linguistic system of its own.

Dutch dialects are defined here as genetically related dialects used in a territory where the Dutch standard language is the official one. This sociolinguistic definition excludes both the genetically related dialects spoken in Germany (those are German dialects) as well as the Frisian dialects, which are more related to Frisian than to Dutch.[7]

Using the isogloss method, Weijnen (1966), the authoritative treatise on Dutch dialectology, divided the Dutch language territory into six main groups of dialects (NL, Netherlands; B, Belgium):

1. The northern-central dialects, comprising the largest part of the province of Utrecht (NL) as well as the provinces of Noord- and Zuid-Holland (NL)

---

[7] An exception is made for the dwindling Flemish dialects in France (French Flanders). They are Dutch dialects used in an area where Dutch is not an official language (anymore).

2. The northwestern dialects, in use in Noord-Holland north of the IJ (NL), the non-Frisian Wadden islands (NL), and most of the Zuid-Holland isles (NL)
3. The southern-central dialects, as spoken in the provinces of Vlaams-Brabant and Brussels (B), Antwerpen (B), part of Oost-Vlaanderen (B), Noord-Brabant (NL), and southern Gelderland (NL)
4. The southwestern dialects of the provinces of West-Vlaanderen (B) and Zeeland (NL), part of Oost-Vlaanderen (B), together with French Flanders (France)
5. The northeastern dialects spoken in the provinces of Groningen (NL) and Overijssel (NL) as well as eastern Gelderland (NL) and some northern stripes of Friesland (NL)
6. The southeastern dialects, at home in both the Belgian and the Dutch provinces of Limburg as well as some villages in Noord-Brabant (NL). There is no clear-cut border between those dialects and the ones used in Germany, east of the Dutch–German state border

No dialect isoglosses run parallel to the Dutch–Belgian border: all important language isoglosses divide the Dutch language territory into western and eastern language zones, as the large folding map in Weijnen (1966) shows. Consequently, the West and (part of the) East Flemish dialects constitute a continuum with those spoken in the Dutch province of Zeeland, as do the dialects of the Belgian provinces Antwerpen, Vlaams-Brabant, and Limburg with those of the Dutch provinces of Noord-Brabant and Limburg, respectively. Still, dialect loss is disrupting linguistic ties of old, but since these dialects are under the umbrella of the same standard language, nothing as dramatic is happening as on the Dutch–German border.

It has indeed never been possible to cut a clear border line between the dialects spoken on both sides of the Dutch–German border, which share the following important features (not existing in the Dutch standard language or in the more western dialects): the Saxon common plural (all three persons of the plural having the same ending); morphological umlaut alternations in the building of the diminutive (*boem* > *buumke*) or of the plural (*voet* > *vuuten*) (Sloos & Van Oostendorp 2010); or the tone opposition between *stoottoon* and *sleeptoon* (checking and drawling accent) shared by Limburg and the bordering German Rhineland. However, due to dialect decline and the ever-increasing penetration of the respective standard languages on both sides, what used to be a dialect continuum is rapidly falling apart into two different language areas. When dialect speakers on both sides of the border read a book or write a letter, the Dutch one will read and write standard Dutch, whereas his German counterpart will read and write standard German. Were they to exchange books or letters, they could not easily understand the other's language, yet in practice they speak the same dialect (Donaldson 1983, 11). Studies edited by Bister-Broosen (1998) detail all aspects of this evolution and demonstrate how nowadays the differing standard languages even affect the dialects themselves.

Dialect Loss

The aspect that has influenced language evolution and language change the most during the whole 20th century (and the small part of the 21st we know so far) is dialect loss, also discussed in chapter 5. The fact that almost half of the population of the Netherlands lives in the Randstad (the large urban agglomerations in the western part of the country such as Amsterdam, Den Haag, Haarlem, Leiden, and Rotterdam) is very revealing, not only for the demographic and social but also for the linguistic makeup of the country (Van Bree & De Vries 1996). From the Randstad, where the modern Dutch standard language gradually took shape from the 17th century onward, it spread geographically as well as socially over the rest of the territory, at first only within the Netherlands and afterward also in Belgium. A map shown in Hagen (1989) illustrates how dialect competence and use increase the further one moves away from the Randstad. Hagen's map is drawn on the basis of intuitive knowledge. More recent studies (discussed in Willemyns 1997) show that very often matters are much less straightforward. Both the acceptance of and the attitudes toward linguistic varieties are determined by the fact that the western standard language is not only the supraregional means of communication but also the sociolect of the better-situated classes in the country at large. Occasional negative attitudes mainly derive from social resentment against this particular sociolect function of the standard language. Interestingly, socially determined linguistic attitudes are the strongest in the Randstad: the *stadsdialecten* (urban dialects) of the popular classes in this highly urbanized region mostly provoke negative attitudes. Despite the fact that, from a purely linguistic point of view, the peripheral *regiolecten*[8] (regiolects) differ more widely from the standard than the urban dialects do, the attitudes toward them are generally more favorable, mainly because they mostly (still) lack the social stigma.

Dialects lose ground rapidly everywhere, but the movement is not a straightforward one. A discrepancy has indeed been observed between positive attitudes toward the dialects on one hand and a rapid decrease of those dialects on the other. Also, dialect proficiency and dialect usage don't go hand in hand anymore: even in places where proficiency is still high, a dramatic and rapid decrease in dialect usage has been observed. The intermediate age group in Bree is an example of this. In the north a few examples of what might be called contradic-

---

[8] As opposed to the dialect of one single place, regiolect has been used for some time now to refer to the regional speech of a larger area in the periphery, i.e. outside of the *Randstad* (Hoppenbrouwers, 1990).

tory tendencies are the following. In Maastricht a tendency to a more rapid dialect loss in the higher classes is combined with a "remarkable vitality of the dialect," Münstermann says. He also notices a "discrepancy between the rapidly decreasing dialect proficiency" and the amazingly "positive attitudes" toward the dialect. Schumans noticed the same in Sittard, another Limburg town. The opposite seems to be the case in Landgraaf (in the province of Limburg) and Hengelo (province of Overijssel), where Roncken and Roncken-Wieffer found that the most important dialect loss occurs where the attitudes are the most negative. In Vorden (in the province of Gelderland), on the contrary, we see the same pattern as in Maastricht and Sittard: very positive attitudes combined with a rapid dialect loss (Boers). As all the studies mentioned (more detailed information on all of them in Willemyns 1997) emphasize, the direct relationship between dialect proficiency and dialect usage seems to have disappeared almost everywhere.

As soon as the earliest figures on dialect loss in the Dutch language territory in Belgium were published (some 30 years ago), it appeared that the situation in both West Flanders and Limburg deviated from the remaining part of Dutch-speaking Belgium in that dialect resistance there was stronger. This was attributed mainly to the peripheral location of both provinces. A real-time investigation stretching over 23 years has confirmed dialect resistance in West Flanders but also revealed dialect loss with distinctive differences in both pace and intensity (Willemyns & Vandenbussche 2008).

A comparison between the present-day situation in Limburg (based on a recent survey in the small town of Bree) and West Flanders shows that, as opposed to 30 years ago, the situation is completely different now. In Limburg, the younger generation has abandoned the dialect altogether. The middle generation, although still competent in the local vernacular, deems it unfit for usage

BOX 6.1 } Diglossia

In sociolinguistics this term, coined by Ferguson (1959), describes any stable linguistic situation in which there exists a functional differentiation between a (socially) L(ow) and a H(igh) variety, meaning that both varieties are used in different communicative circumstances and situations. Classical examples are Switzerland with High German as the H and *Schwyzerduutsch* as the L variety or Haiti with French as H and Creole as L.

Nowadays the definition is extended to all linguistic societies with two distinct varieties with different functions. One of the characteristics of diglossia is the notion that differing communicative situations require the use of different language varieties, such as dialect in an informal and the standard language in a formal situation.

Willemyns and Bister (1989) give a detailed overview of the change in meaning and use of the term diglossia.

in most of the (not only formal) communicative situations. Only the older generation masters and effectively uses the dialect frequently (Willemyns, Vandenbussche, & Drees 2010). Peripheral location therefore does not seem to be a useful explanation for dialect resistance anymore.

The Scientific Apparatus of Dutch Dialectology

Information on Dutch dialects in general is provided in dialect atlases and dialect dictionaries. Since the 1930s, an ever-increasing number of recorded sound samples has been at our disposal.

Dialect atlases are compilations of maps and other materials displaying regional diversity. Three of them cover the Dutch language territory at large. In the *Reeks Nederlandse Dialectatlassen,* each atlas has a volume of maps and one with the dialect material written out in the International Phonetic Alphabet (IPA). They are based on surveys that started in the 1920s. In an impressive amount of places the surveyors asked two or three dialect speakers to "translate" a list of 140 sentences. This is a very reliable procedure, generating valuable dialect information. For some of the features, maps were designed. The *Taalatlas van Noord- en Zuid-Nederland,* on the other hand, is a word atlas: from the whole language territory the dialect names for various things or concepts were collected by means of written surveys. Afterward the information gathered was mapped. A written survey is always less reliable than an oral one.

In 1998, the first issue was published of a completely new *Fonetische Atlas van de Nederlandse Dialecten* (FAND), founded on very recently gathered materials. The FAND has maps illustrating the evolution of the West Germanic sound system in the Dutch dialects, supplemented with dialectological and language historical comments. Next, two other publications founded on the same principles and using the same procedures appeared: the *Morfologische Atlas van de Nederlandse Dialecten* (MAND); and the *Syntactische Atlas van de Nederlandse Dialecten* (SAND).

The *Sprachatlas des Nördlichen Rheinlands und des Südöstlichen Niederlands Fränkischer Sprachatlas* (Speech Atlas of the Northern Rhineland and Southeastern Netherlands) by Jan Goossens (1988 ff) and the *Taalatlas van Noord en Oost Nederland en aangrenzende gebieden* (Linguistic Atlas of the Northern and Eastern Netherlands and adjacent regions) (1957) are regional atlases.

Dialect dictionaries display the lexicon of the dialects of a particular place or region. Not only professional dialectologists but also many amateurs are fascinated by this line of work; consequently, there is not only an enormous amount of such dictionaries but most of all an enormous discrepancy in procedures and quality between them. The most important and useful ones, therefore, are the dialect dictionaries made at the Universities of Nijmegen and Ghent. Some of them are finished; others are still being published in installments: the *Woordenboek der Brabantse dialecten* and the *Woordenboek der Limburgse dialecten* (both in Nijmegen) and the *Woordenboek der Vlaamse dialecten* (in Ghent).

All three provide information on the dialects on both sides of the state border. The materials they're based on have been most carefully collected from different sources, including many new inquiries. The dictionaries are not alphabetically but systematically ordered (i.e., covering word fields) and include dialect maps, etymological explanations, photographs and drawings, and a lot of other very useful information.

GEOGRAPHICAL AND SOCIAL VARIATION AT THE MACROLEVEL: NORTH–SOUTH

Internal Standard Language Variation in the Low Countries

THE NETHERLANDS

At the beginning of the 20th century, the activities of language purists, teachers, and linguists alike continued along the same lines as in the late 19th century and were concentrated on prescribing how the language ought to be standardized and used. The Netherlands prior to World War II, as Van den Toorn (1997, 479) points out, was a conservative country, and "that applies to the Dutch language as well: there were no substantial changes until long after 1940."

As already mentioned, the main language planning focus between 1920 and 1940 was on the pursuit of ABN, the language used by the better-situated classes in the Randstad. This variety was implemented through the educational system as well as through the media. Its acceptance and usage became "a characteristic of civilization and a product of disciplining" (Van den Toorn 1997, 480). In 1935, in her Troonrede (opening speech to parliament) and with the authority of her government, Queen Wilhelmina made an appeal "for the correct pronunciation of the language to become an issue of government concern" (Van der Sijs 2004, 210). As a consequence, in schools special attention was given to correcting pronunciation. To establish which kind of pronunciation was to be regarded as correct and to agree on the proper procedure, a *Commissie ter bevordering van een meer verzorgd mondeling taalgebruik* (Commission for the promotion of more careful use of spoken language), known as the Commission Bolkestein, was created. In 1939 it produced a report for the *Commissie van Leraren in Levende Talen* (Commission of teachers of modern languages; ibid.).

Furthermore, Van den Toorn (1997) continues, the western flavor gradually grew more important than the fact of being general. In addition, whereas in the first half of the 20th century the traditional definition of an ABN speaker, in imitation of Jespersen's famous words, still was somebody whose speech did not betray his geographic origins, in the century's second half "somebody whose speech does betray his western origin" was the more adequate description.

As far as variety choice is concerned, we see how Netherlanders with dialect proficiency use it less often and in fewer communicative interactions still than the Flemings. In Holland and Utrecht, dialects hardly survived at all.

Regiolects are found outside the Randstad, in the internal periphery. Interference is responsible for a provincial touch or accent in the standard language realization of many peripheral Netherlanders, and small deviations are mostly tolerated. Speakers from Groningen, Drenthe, Overijssel, or Eastern Gelderland often pronounce the final *n*, saying *stoelen* instead of *stoele*. Dropping the final *e* (*stoeln*), though, which occurs often as well, gets less social acceptance.

In Drenthe, Overijssel, Gelderland, and Zeeland, Noord-Brabant and Limburg *ee, eu,* and *oo* are pronounced as pure vowels (as in Flanders) instead of the corresponding diphthong typical of Hollands pronunciation. The *zachte g* (i.e., a voiced velar [ɣ], as opposed to Hollands voiceless guttural fricative [χ]) can be heard in Arnhem and Nijmegen, in the Betuwe, as well as in Zeeland, Noord-Brabant, and Limburg (and, of course, in Flanders).

The west as well, of course, has its own provincialisms: even Western Dutch is regional Dutch, although the inhabitants of the Randstad do not realize this or are unwilling to see it that way. As mentioned, *ee, eu*, and *oo* are pronounced more like *ei, ui*, and *ou;* the *zachte g* has been replaced by the *harde ch.* Consequently, *geven* (to give) and *goochelen* (to conjure) are pronounced more or less like *cheeive* [xeʲv ə] and *choouchele* [χouχələ], and this has become the generally accepted norm in the west and actually also in the rest of the country even by those who do not use this pronunciation themselves.

In the 1960s, things evolve more rapidly, and we see how, for the first time, most of the barriers between the written and the spoken language were gradually leveled. This had often been recommended before but had never actually been reached. Now the younger generation turned against the careful, somewhat artificial speech of the older generations. In the Netherlands (but not in Belgium) some striking changes in pronunciation occurred. The Poldernederlandse vowels and diphthongs (see previous) are part of it, Van der Sijs (2004, 210) says. Also, *v, z,* and *g* were pronounced voiceless, almost like *f, s,* and *ch,* and with some people they coincided (the tendency was already noticed in the 16th century). This was also the cause of hypercorrections like *zoep* or *veitelijk* instead of *soep* (soup) and *feitelijk* (actually). Also a lot of variation occurred as the pronunciation of the *r* is concerned; one of them, the *Gooise r* is a vowellike *r*, almost like the *r* in English. The dialectologist P. J. Meertens signaled its existence for the first time in 1938 (Van der Sijs 2004, 211).

FLANDERS

Today's language situation in Flanders is characterized by the use of various codes that build a linguistic continuum reaching from dialect to standard Dutch. Also, since French has lost all the functions it used to have at the beginning of the 20th century, standard Dutch is the only variety that can be used in formal situations. Dialect loss and dialect leveling are responsible for the disappearance of the former diglossic situation in the larger part of Flanders (box 6.1).

We see a dramatic decrease of the mastery and the use of dialects and, at the same time, a considerable increase of the use and the proficiency in the standard variety (cf. also chapter 9). Most youngsters and most inhabitants of the central regions of Flanders have shifted away from the dialects.

Although a continuum is characterized by a smooth overlap, the language continuum in Flanders can, for practical purposes, be said to be composed of the following varieties. First of all, there is the dialect, which until two or three decades ago was omnipresent. In younger generations the mastery of a dialect has dwindled, whereas in older generations dialect competence is mostly still there; however, people restrict its usage very often to informal situations or even the family. The geographical accent, which is the most prominent remnant of the dialect, very often colors the other varieties as well.

Vernacular is used here to refer to a variety situated between dialect and the standard language. Linguistically it is based mainly on the structure of the dialect system with some changes in the direction of the standard, especially with respect to pronunciation and vocabulary. For the less educated and many elderly people, this code constitutes the most formal variety they have at their disposal.

Tussentaal (intermediate variety) lies between regional dialect and the standard language as well, although its function is quite different. It is used by many as a substitute for the standard language, although it lacks the main characteristics of a standard language: there is no real codification; and there is no real authority to turn to in case of doubt, since there are neither authoritative dictionaries nor grammars. It started out as a complementary variety alongside others (dialect, standard) but now has a growing amount of native speakers, socialized in this variety. Its center of gravity is the Brabant region (roughly the provinces of Vlaams-Brabant, Brussels, Antwerpen, and part of East Flanders). Therefore, it may probably best be characterized as a supraregional variety displaying a huge amount of Brabantic interference. *Verkavelingsvlaams* and *Schoon Vlaams* are other names often used for this variety.

Standard Dutch is situated on the right-hand side of the continuum. It is the common national language based on the same linguistic norms in both the Netherlands and Belgium. Since all polycentric languages show some variation, it is obvious that in Flanders the common standard language takes its own southern form. A synonymous expression is VRT-Dutch, named after the public television station.

Dutch as a Pluricentric Language: Oscillating between Convergence and Divergence

The integrational doctrine has always held that the south has to adapt to the north and that all language planning efforts have always been directed at the linguistic integration of Flanders with Holland. But even so, language standardization in Flanders could not proceed along exactly the same lines as in the Randstad.

Although the decision to adapt to the northern norm was made in the 19th century, the real implementation could start only from the moment when Flemings were in a position to really listen to the northern realization of the language on a regular basis. The integrational effort demanded from the Flemings that they come to grips with pronunciation, lexical aspects, and morphological and syntactic issues. This has succeeded only because most Flemings, for various reasons, were indeed more than willing to make the effort.

PRONUNCIATION

Pronunciation is the aspect that has caused the least amount of trouble, and convergence toward the northern norm was reached very soon. Recent research (e.g., Van de Velde 1997) has established that in southern Standard Dutch pronunciation has not significantly changed over the past 60 to 70 years. The norm remained the pronunciation standard as it had been laid down in 1934 already by Blancquaert, whose aim it was to follow the northern example and who had readily been accepted as the authoritative guide in pronunciation matters. Deviation is seen only where the northern standard showed variation itself or has been changed afterward. Some examples of the former are that the southern [ɣ] is velar and shows no signs of rasping (*zachte g*); the /r/ is mostly alveolar, with the uvular /r/ increasingly as a valuable alternative. The /w/ is usually bilabial.

Examples of the latter are that mostly southern *ee* (/e./) and *oo* (/o./) are pure monophthongs and that word initial /v/ and /z/ are voiced (Van de Velde 1997, 56). The same used to be the case in what Van de Velde (1997) calls "Older Northern Standard Dutch," that is, the variety used in Holland between 1935 and 1950. In "Present-day Northern Standard Dutch (i.e., after 1950), however, a number of characteristic novelties appear: a very distinct devoicing of /v/ and /z/ in word initial position, a strong uvular vibration of the *g* ([χ]; the *harde g*) and diphthongization of /e./ and /o./. The vocalic realization of /r/ is rapidly gaining field and trilled realizations of postvocalic /r/ have disappeared almost completely. In a dissertation devoted completely to *r* variation, Tops (2009) establishes that there is a large amount of ongoing change regarding the pronunciation of that particular semivowel and that the so-called uvular (*huig-*) *r* is rapidly winning ground in the south. The vocalic realization of /r/, on the other hand, also known as *the Gooise r,* remains an almost exclusive northern affair although even there it is heard only in a particular region or a particular (jet-set) sociolect.

One of Van de Velde's (1997) most interesting conclusions is that over the past 60 years variation in pronunciation has not really become more extensive either in the Netherlands or in Flanders. There is no evidence that the norm has been abandoned; it just, in his words, "shifted a bit." Around 1935, the time when in Flanders the norm for the standard pronunciation was firmly determined and accepted, the Dutch, on the other hand, started to slowly shift away from the norm that also used to be theirs. This shift has gained momentum over the past decades. The north–south diversion must therefore, says Van de Velde (1997, 60–61) be interpreted as a conversion that has not yet been carried to an end, since increasingly the Dutch will be moving away from the official norm of pronunciation, whereas most Flemings will stick to it.

Furthermore, it has to be noted that many speakers in the southern part of the Kingdom of the Netherlands *onder de grote rivieren* (south of the rivers Maas, Rhine, and Waal), as the expression in Dutch goes (i.e., the internal periphery), are in some respects nearer to the Belgian than to the Hollands pronunciation. In the Netherlands the *zachte g* is seen as a shibboleth, even a stigma for the southern Dutch provinces of Noord-Brabant and Limburg, where, as in Flanders, *ee* (/e./) and *oo* (/o./) mostly are pure monophthongs and the voiced pronunciation of word initial /v/ and /z/ is the habitual one.

Still, as De Schutter (2002, 445) observes, "As far as systemic aspects of Standard Dutch phonology are concerned there is little or no variation in the whole language area, including Belgium."

VOCABULARY

In the lexical field the picture is different. Vocabulary is undoubtedly what appeals most of all to the imagination of the public, and lexical change hardly ever passes unnoticed.

Recent investigations reveal that north–south leveling in the lexical field is a still continuing process (fig. 6-2). Between 1950 and 1990, as Geeraerts, Grondelaers, and Speelman (1999) established, lexical convergence between Flanders and the Netherlands has constantly increased. As to the direction of this convergence, Deygers and Van den Heede (2000) demonstrate that, at least in written texts, in most cases the south adapted to the north rather than the other way around. As to the procedures, both theoretically possible mechanisms do occur: taking over typically northern items as well as gradually dropping typically southern expressions. The latter mechanism, though, appears to be more frequent than the former one. As the same researchers noticed, well-known deviations from the northern norm (i.e., those constantly mentioned in manuals on proper language use) are been given up to a much larger amount than those of which the southern status is not known; this reveals that the Fleming is actually very much prepared to follow the northern standard, even in the lexical field. The part of well-known "suspicious Belgian Dutch words," as Deygers and Van den Heede call it, in the corpus of the 1990s "is only approximately 17 percent (which means that the authors have preferred a standard Dutch term in more than 80 percent of the cases); the part of the 'unsuspicious Belgian words' is much stronger with approximately 76 percent" (Deygers & Van den Heede 2000, 308). They conclude that "Belgian Dutch words are disappearing in favour of standard Dutch words" and that there is, in other words, "a strong converging tendency" (ibid.).

FIGURE 6.2 Cartoon (by Kim Duchateau) on lexical variation

An analysis of the language used in the Belgian media reveals that journalists too have massively switched to typically northern words and expressions over the past few decades (Theissen 2003).

MORPHOLOGY AND SYNTAX

North–south convergence in the field of morphology and syntax has been less investigated, and variation therefore often passes unnoticed. A notorious exception, though, is the discussion on the pronominal system with respect to the forms of address. Most southern dialects have, as English does, a one-pronoun system of address, *gij*, as opposed to a dual system with an informal (Dutch *jij*, German *Du*) and a formal (Dutch *u*, German *Sie*) pronoun in Standard Dutch. For a long time and in spite of language planning efforts, this one-pronoun system remained characteristic of the standard language of many southerners. The advocates of the northern norm succeeded in weakening this stronghold considerably. Still, replacing a one-pronoun system by a dual system not only is a matter of attitude and goodwill but also may lead to practical problems even for those who made the theoretical decision to adopt it. Switching from one system to another and especially mixing both systems in inappropriate conditions are some of the characteristics of a pronominal chaos, a frequent sign of linguistic insecurity in a transitional period.

Recently, and as a consequence of the destandardization wave discussed in chapter 9, there seems to be a revival of the one-pronoun southern (Brabantic) system. Interestingly, the plural dual-system *jullie–u* (cf. German *Ihr–Sie*) seems to be less giving way to the Brabantic *gij* than the singular one-pronoun system.

In one of the first inquiries meant to produce quantifiable data, Vandekerckhove (2004, 2005) investigates the role of geographical conditioning and the age variable in this matter (for more ample information, see chapter 9). Vandekerckhove reveals that West Flanders is the only province where the use of standard language *je* supersedes the use of Brabants *ge* and is also the only province where younger subjects use *je* more often than older subjects. Her charts also indicate that West Flanders is the only province where *jou* is the most frequently used pronoun, and *u* is used only half as often as elsewhere. Finally, she demonstrates that, once again, West Flanders is the only province where the diminutive -*je* (instead of Brabants -*ke*) is used more often by her younger than by her older subjects.

ATTITUDES

People going to a physician in Maastricht or Ghent don't have to reflect whether they are going to speak Dutch or French; in Brussels, though, they have to. Such a decision is made not only on the basis of the linguistic competence of the doctor or patient but also on which judgments or prejudices come with the choice for one or the other language and how the physician might react to that choice. Furthermore, what applies to different languages may also be impor-tant if there is a choice between varieties of the same language: the patient in Maastricht may consider whether he is going to address the doctor in standard language or in Mestreechs, the local dialect of which most of its inhabitants are proud (even if they do not always use it).[9] The patient's dilemma, of course, raises the question of what the appreciation of the local varieties is and who accommodates linguistically to whom.

In the largest part of the Dutch language territory, the solidarity value of dialects is very high. The outcome of most surveys is that dialect speakers are perceived to be nice, commendable, and straightforward—in other words, nice guys. Speaking the dialect is also praised as a sign of loyalty to the region. The standard language, on the other hand, scores points on the status scale. Those using it are considered to be self-confident, ambitious, intelli-gent, and competent, and that is how the variety they use, Standard Dutch (AN) is also perceived.

Since Standard Dutch (AN) is used in the south as well as in the north, other surveys have tried to find out whether the appreciation just mentioned still holds true when the Standard Dutch (AN) of the other part of the territory is concerned. In other words, what are the attitudes of the Dutchmen toward the standard language of the Flemings and vice versa? Are those speaking it also perceived as self-confident, ambitious, intelligent, and competent? Until recently

---

[9] The famous international bandleader André Rieu is a native of Maastricht. On TV coverage of his performances in the United States or Australia, he can be heard talking to some of his musicians in the dialect of his hometown. He also has recorded a song in which he conveys his love for his birthplace in five different languages, one of them being his *mestreecher* dialect in which he invites his international audience to *kom mit misch mit no Mestreech* (come with me to Maastricht).

the Dutch used to have a rather paternalistic attitude as far as the southern Dutch Standard was concerned. A majority seldom reacts very positively to the speech of the minority. Also, they're mostly not familiar enough with the Flemish situation to be able to put things into perspective and to distinguish whether their Flemish interlocutors are using a dialect, a regiolect, or the standard language.

In Flanders the northern variety of the standard language used to score high on the status scale. Still, the "Hollander" was given both the positive and negative characteristics that came with his language usage, meaning they are often perceived as arrogant and displaying a feeling of superiority. The same feelings accidentally often pop up in surveys where Netherlanders from outside Holland, that is, from the internal periphery are asked for their opinion; they too stress the negative characteristics of the Hollanders. Anyway, in most cases the Flemings appear to prefer and to appreciate the southern standard over the northern one and vice versa.

Still, in recent years attitudes seem to be shifting. In a 1999 survey, students reading Dutch at both Dutch and Flemish universities were asked to evaluate the speech of TV news journalists. All subjects agreed that news journalists are supposed to use the ideal form of the standard language. Flemish students think that the speech of the northern journalists is less careful than that of the southern journalists. Surprisingly, and for the first time in similar surveys, the Dutch students credited both southern and northern journalists with an equally careful language and had less negative feelings toward the southern speech than the Flemish students had toward the northern language usage. The conclusion of the authors of the survey therefore was that the Dutch are getting more respect for the realization of the standard language by southern journalists than the Flemings have for the northern journalists (Van de Velde & Houtermans 1999). The prestige of northern standard Dutch appears to suffer mostly, they add, from what Flemings perceive to be careless pronunciation on the part of the Dutch.

Language Struggle and Federalization in Belgium

ON THE THRESHOLD OF THE 20TH CENTURY: THE GELIJKHEIDSWET

In the course of the 20th century, what had started out as the less prestigious and hardly respected language of Belgium ends up as the proud language of a monolingual Flanders, the autonomous and economically, politically and culturally leading part of the country. Dutch has finally reached the status it ought to have had from the outset, namely, the prestige language of the country, mother tongue to the large majority of its inhabitants. For the history of the language at large, this is one of the most important changes ever. If it hadn't been for the Flemish movement, which has been active in enhancing the status of Dutch and fighting what Kloss (1966, 12) calls the francophone arrogance, this outcome would never have been reached.

During the final quarter of the 19th century a number of laws on language use and language rights had been approved in parliament (see chapter 5). All of them were relevant only for Flanders, and the language rights were meant to give Flemings more possibilities to use their own language in their own territory. All those legislative efforts until ca. 1930 made Flanders a more bilingual region and didn't affect the rest of the country at all.

The very first (and most important) language law concerning Belgium at large was the Gelijkheidswet, voted in 1898, on the threshold of the 20th century. This law of equality officially declared that Dutch and French official texts had the same force in law. The large group of monolingual Dutch speakers was given the opportunity to use the sole language they were proficient in with civil servants and in their schools and in court, at the same time making it imperative for magistrates, lawyers, civil servants, and teachers to have a sufficient command of that language. Moreover, a climate making it possible to enforce more radical changes later on was created.

A few minor changes, hardly significant in itself, paved the way and were the signs that more radical changes were to be expected. Between 1885 and 1888 bonds, coins, and banknotes were made bilingual. Stamps followed, and in 1895 the *Government Gazette*—until then known only as *Moniteur Belge*—became *Belgisch Staatsblad* as well. In 1887 the king held his first speech in Dutch ever, and a year later the first intervention in parliament in that language was to be heard. In that same year civil servants were allowed to take the oath of office in Dutch—and all of that in a country where Dutch speakers constitute the majority of the population.

Still, these meager successes, however hard it may have been to obtain them, did not bring real change; instead, what made the most impact was the social and political changes such as a plural universal suffrage (1893), obtained through the continuing efforts of the socialist and liberal parties and the workers unions. All (male) Flemings now had the right to vote (although some had two or three votes, according to the amount of taxes they paid), which increased the number of voters 10-fold. That made their vote and their voice important; they were the majority after all.

World War I caused a serious backlash and divided the Flemish movement. To some (called activists) the emancipation of the Flemings was more important than anything else, and the activists did not object to accepting the help of the German occupants, who had cleverly devised a very attractive *Flamenpolitik* (policy for Flanders).

Immediately after the war, universal suffrage (for all Belgian men) was instated. As a result the socialist party won a huge victory, and it was within that party that Flemings and Walloons agreed on the *Compromis des Belges*, implying that both peoples could decide for themselves on language policy in their own territory. This compromise served as the model for the solution that would eventually solve Belgium's language problems, namely, by means of the so-called territoriality principle.

Still, the better part of the first decade postwar was lost with heated discussions inside and outside of parliament on the demand that Dutch be the medium of instruction in the University of Ghent. The alliance of the French-speaking Flemish bourgeoisie with most of the Walloon members of Parliament could postpone this Dutchification for some more years. One of the Francophone professors called university teaching in Dutch a crime against civilization, and in 1906 the primate of Belgium, Cardinal Mercier, had publicly declared that Dutch could never be a language of science. Thus, in 1930 Flanders finally got its own university in its own language. For the first time ever,[10] Flemish youngsters were able to study from kindergarten through university without having to use a foreign language.

The fact that many Flemings knowing little or no French could now increasingly use the only language they mastered was exciting and made them want more. More and more, the Flemish petty bourgeoisie and intellectuals understood (and experienced) that the Dutchification of public life enhanced their chances for jobs and upward social mobility significantly. Alongside the rich and mostly French-speaking grande bourgeoisie of old, a new middle class emerged that spoke Dutch and could attend university and occupy jobs previously unattainable. It was from their midst that more and new adherents of the Flemish movement were recruited.

THE TERRITORIALITY PRINCIPLE

After that, it was time for the next stage: replacing the personality principle, which had existed from the very beginning of Belgium, with the territoriality principle (see box 1.2).

The language laws of the 1930s marked the start of a completely new era since they prepared the country for subsequent federalism because they were founded on a different language policy altogether. Since the Walloons were vehemently opposed to a system of generalized bilingualism in the country at large, territorial monolingualism was the only possible solution. For the first time ever, the language laws regulated their use not only in Flanders, as had previously been the case, but also now in Belgium at large.

On June 28, 1932, the new *wet op het taalgebruik in bestuurszaken* (Law on Official Language Use) became effective. Basically it stipulated that the Flemish and the Walloon part of the country had to be governed in Dutch and

---

[10] Up to 1830 the medium of instruction at universities in the Low Countries was Latin.

French, respectively, and had to be addressed by the central government in those languages as well. The political decision to pass this law and a few consecutive ones has had the most far-reaching and the most long-lasting consequences ever. The language laws of the 1960s (see following) were its logical complement.

Still, although this was a serious step toward the territoriality principle, the final piece was still lacking: to determine the language border between both parts of the country. Why is that important? In 1846, Belgium started conducting censuses including a question on language usage that provided statistical information until 1947 (De Metsenaere 1998). For various reasons, information gathered this way is often inaccurate: the exact wording of the questions was changed from one census to another, and, more important still, two basic requirements for reliable information gathering—honest intentions and scientific support—were hardly ever met (Gubin 1978). The most important insight yielded by the first census (1846) is that the administrative division of the country into provinces, *arrondissementen* (counties), and even communes did not take into account language and had never intended to provide for more or less linguistically homogeneous administrative entities. On the other hand, the information allowed for a borderline to be drawn, neatly separating the French-speaking (i.e., Walloon dialect) and the Dutch-speaking (i.e., Flemish dialect) communities. For almost one century (and in spite of the deficient methodology), there were no significant differences from one census to another, a fact demonstrating the remarkable stability of Belgium's linguistic communities.

A dramatic change occurred beginning in 1932, the year in which the language border became a political issue. To implement the de facto acceptance of the territoriality principle, a precise legal description of the delimitation of the Dutch- and French-speaking territories, in other words of the language border, was needed. The 1932 laws did not provide such a description but held a provision that communes with a linguistic minority of at least 30 percent should be governed bilingually and that, should a minority become the majority, the linguistic status of the commune must change accordingly. This seems fair enough, except that the only means of acquiring the necessary information was the census that thus, unfortunately, acquired important political significance.

The first census with these political implications was scheduled for 1940 but was postponed because of the war, and when in 1947 it was finally carried out it resulted in an outburst of political commotion. Contrasting heavily with the stability the returns had shown for more than a century, this time notorious shifts were not only registered but all went in the same direction: many Dutch-speaking villages appeared to harbor so many French speakers that they turned into either bilingual or even French-speaking communes (Martens 1975). Since fraudulent maneuvering by (local or national) authorities was very apparent, the Flemish reaction was extremely vigorous, and the government was finally forced to skip language questions from future census questionnaires altogether and to look for a political solution that might, once and for all, determine the language border between the communities. A law to this effect came into being on September 1, 1963, and since its underlying philosophy was to produce linguistically homogeneous administrative entities, several adjustments had to be made (Verhulst, De Metsenaere, & Deweerdt 1998; Witte & Van Velthoven 2010).

Even after the comprehensive and far-reaching linguistic legislation of the early 1960s, the situation continued to be explosive, mostly because of some unsolved odds and ends. One of those, with a huge symbolic value, would not only make it explode but also change the country forever. The proximate cause is known as the Leuven question.

In spite of the fact that, according to linguistic legislation, the medium of instruction in all schools has to be the official language of the region, the French-speaking part of the University of Leuven had remained in that Flemish town. In 1968, a revolutionary year all over Europe, students urged them to move to Wallonia. Not only did the bishops (Leuven was and is a Catholic university) want the francophones to be accommodated in French in monolingual Dutch-speaking Leuven, but they also announced plans to spread over the rest of the Dutch-speaking province of Brabant. Soon things were getting totally out of hand. The government collapsed, and it also appeared that within the traditional political parties the Flemish and Walloon factions could no longer accept sharing one party and split up. First of all the (then) powerful Christ-democrat party was split in two, and soon the socialist and liberal parties followed suit. From that moment on, no political parties in Belgium are left to represent the whole country. Gradually they even became political antagonists, with—in spite of their ideological nearness—completely different programs and agendas. As to the proximate cause of all this, a new government made the French-speaking part of the university move south of the language border. The new campus was baptized Louvain-la-Neuve. Simultaneously, the bilingual university of Brussels was split into a Dutch-speaking (VUB) and a French-speaking (ULB) university.

At the same time a considerable change in the nature of the language struggle can be discerned from the early 1960s on. Language problems were replaced with community problems, as they are called, and the border between Wallonia and Flanders moved from a merely linguistic to a social one as well. This can be accounted for by major economic changes.

From the mid-century on, the economic center of gravity shifted toward Flanders, entailing major shifts in the political, social, cultural, and linguistic fields.[11] A dramatic industrial development in Flanders turned this formerly

---

[11] The amount of daily newspapers sold in Belgium may shed some light: during the second quarter of 2009, 68 percent of them were in Dutch (917,584 copies), whereas 32 percent (431,683) were in French (*De Standaard*, September 8, 2009, 2).

agricultural territory into a highly industrialized region, largely dominating the political, social, and economic scene. At the same time the outdated industrial structure of Wallonia was slowly breaking down, giving way to a serious and continuing economic recession.[12] This influenced the cultural and linguistic balance of power and enabled Flemings to achieve more in recent decades than during the entire preceding century. The economic shift that made Flanders the forerunner in industrial development and general prosperity contributed most to shifting the linguistic prestige in the direction of Dutch. Also, because of the territoriality principle, the practical consequences of the economic shift were felt earlier and more intensively. This combination of linguistic legislation (or language planning) and economic evolution also influenced the situation in Brussels, although the territoriality principle was not effective there. Still, the political world regrets to this very day that a definitive solution for the problem of Brussels was not incorporated in these regulations.

THE FEDERAL STATE: A PERMANENT DIPLOMATIC CONFERENCE BETWEEN TWO COUNTRIES

Subsequent revisions of the constitution in 1970, 1980, 1988, and 1993 finally turned Belgium into the federal country it is now (Witte & Van Velthoven 2010). The latest constitutional change in 1993 ushered in a new country. Article 1 stipulates that Belgium is a federal country, albeit a very complicated one. It consists of three *gemeenschappen* (communities), a Dutch-, a French-, and a German-speaking one; three *gewesten* (regions), a Flemish, a Walloon, and a Brussels one; and four language territories, Dutch, French, German, and bilingual, the latter being Brussels. The fact that some of them overlap surely doesn't make living together any easier.

Consequently, not all problems have been solved. In summer 2001, the Lambermont accords transferred additional competences as well as tax money from the federal to the state governments. This was a mainly Flemish claim, which was only partially fulfilled. Federal elections in 2007 and 2010 exposed that more competences for the states was a claim all Flemish parties and not a single Walloon party supported. Because of this difficult situation, the country has become quasi-ungovernable, and it was only after 540 days of negotiations that finally a six-party government was built—the government program of which includes a new substantial change of the constitution (FS & TC 2011, 7).

Still, one may tentatively conclude that after more than a century the Flemish movement's desire for a federal Belgium has finally been fulfilled. Although language as such has, for a long time already ceased to be a problem, it is important to realize that we started out in 1830 with a country governed

---

[12] Unemployment figures from January 2011: Flanders, 7 percent; Wallonia, 14.1 percent; Brussels, 20.7 percent (*De Standaard*, April 2, 2011, 33).

almost exclusively in French. It was very clear, though, that it would take more than only linguistic legislation to make sure that both larger communities of the country would enjoy the same rights and duties.

Thee Tastes Better than *Tee*[13]: The Spelling of Dutch

In 1972 the mayor of Antwerp, Lode Craeybeckx, edited a book entitled *Sluipmoord op de Spelling* (Assassination of the Spelling), in which a large number of famous and influential writers, journalists, politicians, and other "very important" people of Holland and Belgium protested all in their own way against propositions to change the spelling of Dutch.

In the Low Countries, there is this popular belief that in Dutch one spelling reform chases the other. Actually, this is a myth; the number of official spelling reforms in all the years between 1864 and today is—two[14]. On the other hand, a great number of committees, commissions, official instances, and private associations have produced a steady stream of propositions, creating the impression that the spelling of Dutch is in constant turmoil.

At the beginning of the 20th century, the valid spelling was the one devised by De Vries and Te Winkel in 1864. Its main principles and characteristics were discussed in chapter 5. Kollewijn devised a new spelling system and created a *Vereniging tot vereenvouding van onze schrijftaal* (Association for the simplification of our written language). His system was (partly) implemented in the 1930s. In South Africa, Kollewijn's spelling rules were taken as the basis for the official orthography of Afrikaans in 1917 (discussed in chapter 5; see also chapter 8).

Changes were finally agreed upon in 1934 when Marchant, the Dutch minister of education, devised the Marchant spelling, in which almost all of Kollewijn's suggestions were incorporated (with the exception of -*lik* (*mogelik*) and -*ies* (*krities*), which remained unchanged). The minister made the new system compulsory, but only in education. The Marchant spelling was popular in Flanders as well. However, because of the troubles brought about by the prewar situation and the war itself, it took until 1946 to make the Marchant spelling compulsory in Belgium. The Netherlands followed suit in 1947. After 80 years, the first spelling change was now accomplished.

The main changes have to do with the principle of etymology. Not only were historical forms as *mensch* changed into *mens* (i.e., written the way they were

---

[13] Said, almost a century ago, the popular author Carry van Bruggen, who admitted that her point of view was not reasonable. But she added, "Do we always have to be reasonable?" (De Vries, Willemyns, & Burger 2003, 153). Not being reasonable in spelling debates was (and is) indeed the rule rather than the exception.

[14] The Marchant spelling and the Taalunie spelling.

pronounced anyway), but also the difference between *eele* and *oolo* in open syllables was given up. The fact that *beenen* (legs) used to be written with a double *ee* and *breken* (break) with only a single *e* was accounted for by the fact that the *ee* in *beenen* was a *scherplange ê* (from the Old Germanic diphthong *ai*), whereas the forebear of the *e* in *breken* was the short Old Germanic vowel (the *zachtlange*). The same applies to the *oolo*: *koolen* (cabbages) and *kolen* (coal) were now both spelled as *kolen* (Rutten 2009c).

It took until 1954 before the official spelling guide, the *Woordenlijst van de Nederlandse taal* (popularly known as the *Groene Boekje* [Green booklet]), was finally published "on behalf of the Belgian and Dutch governments." From that point on the language user was finally provided with official guidelines (legal and compulsory in both countries) on how to use the new spelling.

No one had anticipated the huge emotional reactions the publication of the *Woordenlijst* would provoke or that the new spelling system would be so often and so heavily attacked. Although the main changes outlined here met with large public approval, others created an unexpected commotion. To understand this, a short theoretical reflection on what spelling is may be in order.

From a purely linguistic point of view, spelling is not a real linguistic issue: orthographic rules enabling us to make spoken language visible are pure convention, and, in principle, which system is used is linguistically completely irrelevant. On top of that, a spelling can be inconsistent, "illogical," incomprehensible, based on nontransparent principles (or no principles at all), hard to learn, different from one part of the language territory to the other, and still be used to write the largest lingua franca of the world: English.

One of the reasons many linguists are involved all the same is that discussions on spelling often include nonorthographic aspects as well. The question of whether a spelling system should be phonetically or phonologically consistent or be founded on the principle of etymology is important and obviously falls within the field of the linguists even when the public at large often disagrees with what they have to say on the matter.

In the Dutch territory a notorious example of a nonorthographical aspect involved in the spelling debate is gender. The historical difference between masculine and feminine nouns has gradually been lost in part of the language territory (mostly the north), whereas it has been kept in most of the southern dialects, including the Brabant and Limburg dialects as spoken in the Netherlands.

With the loss of gender, obviously a problem arises with the pronominal agreement. In Holland one would both say and write *de zon, hij schijnt* (the sun, he is shining), *de deur, hij is open* (the door, he is open), whereas in Brabant (both in the Netherlands and in Belgium) it would be *de zon, zij schijnt* (the sun, she is shining), *de deur, zij is open* (the door, she is open). In Brabant people know that *sun* is a feminine word; in Holland one doesn't (anymore). This became a spelling issue because the *Woordenlijst* of Dutch also provides the gender of the nouns listed and would have had to designate whether *zon* and *deur* would be labeled *m* (masculine) or *v* (feminine). Finally, an agreement was reached: the relevant nouns were labeled as *v. (m.)*, that is, feminine but (between brackets) also masculine. In other words, from a historical perspective, the word is feminine; therefore, one can say, talking about the *zon,* that *she* shines. On the basis of language change having occurred in the north, it was also acceptable to say that *he* shines. In other words, the decision was left with the language user. In the north this freedom generated a great deal of uncertainty and many mistakes, in that many masculine words were referred to with *zij* and *haar* as well; this was called the *haar-ziekte* (i.e., literally, the her-sickness), and it spread epidemically.

In another issue as well, the 1954 *Woordenlijst* left the final decision with the language user, and, here too, the result was uncertainty and sometimes even chaos. I am referring here to what is called in Dutch *bastaardwoorden*, that is, loanwords that are completely integrated within the system of the Dutch language. The source of trouble was the double standard, meaning that loanwords were allowed to be spelled in either a *voorkeurspelling* (preferred spelling) or a *progressieve spelling* (progressive spelling). Consequently, *contact* was allowed as well as *kontakt, analyseren,* and *apotheker* and *analyzeren* and *apoteker*. In each case the former (conservative) spelling was the preferred, or official, one. This system was often and heavily attacked.

FIGURE 6.3 Cartoon (by Stefan Verwey) on spelling

Apart from the trouble with the double standard, people were also confronted with the unpredictability of the decisions made. In most cases the spelling labeled as preferred was the conservative one (*cultuur* instead of *kultuur*), but in some cases it was the progressive one (*kopie* instead of *copie*); alongside *enthousiasme* three variants: *entousiasme, entoesiasme,* and *enthoesiasme* were allowed albeit not preferred). If you wanted to avoid consulting the *Woordenlijst* at every instance, you had to learn by heart a whole list of preferred spellings, the more so since their use was compulsory in the classroom. But even then, your problems were not over. Having memorized that *kopie* was preferred over *copie*, you then had the unpleasant surprise of finding out that *fotocopie* was preferred over *fotokopie* (fig. 6-3).

The hope of the *Woordenlijst* committee was that time would bring the solution. It didn't. It brought a lot of mistakes and spelling insecurity instead. It has taken 40 years to finally get rid of it. Still, the reproach of planning to assassinate the spelling was not directed at the instigators of the mess just mentioned but at a subsequent committee created to remedy the situation.

The governments of Belgium and the Netherlands, conscious that something had to be done, installed a new committee in 1963 called the Pée/Wesselings committee after its two chairmen. Their *Eindvoorstellen* (Final Suggestions) were published after six years and caused a storm of indignation and social commotion in which Antwerp's mayor was not the only one to take part. What had they done to earn this absolute contempt that finally led to their suggestions being buried forever?

First of all, they decided not to choose between the preferred and the progressive alternatives but to suggest other spellings that were even more progressive than the former progressive ones. Instead of *curiositeit* or *kuriositeit*, they came up with *kurioziteit*; *clavecimbel* was replaced not with *klavecimbel* but with *klavesimbel* instead. All of this was ridiculed at the extreme in the press on both sides of the border, along with other examples as *sitroen* for *citroen* (lemon) or *sjofeur* for *chauffeur* (driver), two words for which no change at all had been suggested in 1954. The absolute killer, though, was *odeklonje*, which was suggested as a replacement for *eau de cologne.* The Pée/Wesseling Committee did not survive this, the more so since, as so many previous committees, they decided not to stick to the task they were given but to enlarge it into also changing the spelling of verb forms. In Dutch the 3 persons of the singular of, for example, *vinden* (to find) are spelled *ik vind, jij vindt, hij vindt,* all pronounced identically. The committee suggested dropping the *t* in the latter forms. In the same line of thought they suggested to change the existing difference between present and past tense of, for example, *antwoorden* (to reply), *wij antwoorden* (present)—*wij antwoordden* (past) by dropping one *d* in the latter case, thus writing *wij antwoorden* in both cases. Here, as well as with the *bastaardwoorden*, they tried to turn the devise "write as you speak" more or less into reality. Although there is a sound grammatical foundation for the verb rule they wanted to skip, there is a reasonable chance that the changes in the spelling of verb forms might have gotten large popular approval, since everybody remembers how they have struggled with those rules in primary school. *Hij vind* and *ant-woorden* in the past tense, though, went down with *odeklonje*, all never to be heard of again.

For several reasons, not in the least the public being fed up, the governments were not eager to start a new experiment very soon. Another important reason was that the Netherlands and Flanders were negotiating to create the Nederlandse Taalunie, an international body to which they wanted to transfer their prerogatives in all matters concerning language and literature of both countries. One of the competences the governments were thankfully transferring to the new body was spelling.

The Taalunie was very much aware of the importance but also of the risks of the enterprise and proceeded extremely cautiously. They too, of course, started with a committee, and after a first one had given up a second one was created in 1990. It was given a very open-ended list of tasks, but the main challenge was to suggest a consistent spelling. Linguistic professors of Dutch and Flemish universities immediately went to work and delivered a very consistent list, founding the spelling of Dutch on clearly defined and as consistent as possible rules.[15] On the other hand, they had to solve the *bastaardwoorden* problem and the double standard as well, and here choices had to be made for which linguists are not better prepared than anyone else. Most of all, the public and the media were hostile and suspicious, and very soon some rather bold solutions were leaked to the press: *adolessent, faze, feutus, ginekoloog, klakson, mite, sitroen* instead of *adolescent, fase, foetus, gynecoloog, claxon, mythe, citroen* (adolescent, phase, fetus, gynecologist, horn, myth, lemon) were not received very well, and the Committee of Ministers (two Dutch, two Flemish), the ultimate decision makers at the Taalunie, dismissed the spelling committee, even before their proposals had been discussed in the parliament, as the normal procedure would have been. The fear of the politicians of the possible verdict of the voters made them dismiss a very consistent set of rules on the basis of the (rather irrelevant) suggestions for the spelling of a handful of words.

Shortly thereafter, the Committee of Ministers asked the *Taaladviescommissie* (Committee for language advise), one of the standing committees of the Taalunie, to suggest a solution without experiments to get rid of the double standard. In an astonishing short period of three months the Taaladviescommissie did what they had been asked for, and the ministers readily accepted. Nobody else was asked.

In 1995 the new (and present) system (Taalunie spelling) came into force. It has, once again, been visualized in a new official *Woordenlijst* (Word list). Some

---

[15] The spelling of compound words being one of the more important ones.

small changes concern the use of hyphens and some other diacritical signs (e.g., *Zuid-Afrikaans* instead of *Zuidafrikaans*; *zee-egel* instead of *zeeëgel*). It abolished the double standard (mostly in a conservative direction) and got rid of most inconsistencies (along with *kopie,* now *fotokopie* got a *k* as well) and also made some changes in the spelling of compound words (*pannenkoeken* instead of *pannekoeken*). The latter change (actually the opposite of "write as you speak") was not received favorably by the public and the media, but apparently nobody had the energy to start a new spelling war.

It has been agreed that forthwith the Taalunie will have a new Groene boekje published every 10 years, not to add new rules or change existing ones but to actualize the lexicon. An interesting example is that, since Suriname had become an associated member of the Taalunie, some specifically Surinam words have been included in the *Woordenlijst*. An introduction to the characteristic features of the Dutch spelling is provided in *Leidraad Woordenlijst Nederlandse taal* (2005).[16] Finally, it must be stressed that since the authority to change the spelling was passed from the Belgian and Dutch governments to the Nederlandse Taalunie, the spelling unity in existence since 1864 can never be challenged or lost again.

The disproportional commotion over orthographic issues during more than a century probably has to do with the former equation (in the head of the public) of spelling and language. Orthography was considered an integrated part of the language, or, even more to the point, the spelling was the language; therefore, a spelling change was (and very often is) felt as an assault on the language. The former may be the main reason many linguists are involved in spelling issues. Spelling may not be a purely linguistic issue, but the vehemence by which the public mostly reacts surely turns it very much into a sociolinguistic issue. On top of that, in 19th-century Flanders, spelling used to be a passionately debated political issue and a weapon in the struggle of the Flemish movement.

Still, I think that in sum we can agree with the American professor of Dutch William Shetter that "apart from some minor exceptions and irregularities, Dutch spelling can be said to be almost entirely consistent"(quoted in Brachin 1985, 46).

Language Planning

INSTITUTIONS

De Nederlandse Taalunie (NTU)

Since Dutch is the mother tongue and vehicular language of at least 60 percent of the Belgian population, it seems altogether natural for the Belgian

---

[16] The Officiële spellingregels van het Nederlands (2009) (Official spelling rules of Dutch) can also be downloaded from the Instituut voor Nederlandse Lexicologie website.

government to be concerned with promoting the language and to be anxious to remain in permanent contact with the government of the Netherlands. As history reveals, the Belgian government has for a long time been hostile to the language of the majority of its subjects, which has limited such contacts until after World War II, when the so-called Cultural Agreement (officially the Convention on the Cultural and Intellectual Relations) between both countries was ratified. It has always been the ultimate goal of the Flemings to convince the Dutch to stimulate such contacts as well, and this has often proven to be a tough job. The conclusion of the Cultural Agreement has been acclaimed as an important step in the desire for integration,[17] but undoubtedly the Taalunieverdrag is felt to be the real consecration of these efforts. The Nederlandse Taalunie (Dutch Language Union) was created with a treaty passed by the Dutch and Belgian governments in 1980, which transferred to this international body their prerogatives in all matters concerning language and literature.

The Nederlandse Taalunie was established as a consequence of the Treaty between the Kingdom of Belgium and the Kingdom of the Netherlands concerning the Dutch Language Union on September 9, 1980; the instruments of ratification were exchanged in The Hague on January 27, 1982. The text begins as follows: "His Majesty the King of the Belgians and Her Majesty the Queen of the Netherlands... have decided the creation of a union in the field of the Dutch language."

The Taalunie (the seat of which is in The Hague) is composed of four institutions: a Committee of Ministers, comprising ministers of both countries[18]; an Interparliamentary Commission, comprising MP's of both countries; a secretary general; and a Council for Dutch Language and Literature (Willemyns 1984).

Aiming at "integrating as far as possible the Netherlands and the Dutch-speaking Community of Belgium in the field of the Dutch language and literature in the broadest sense" (Article 2), the Nederlandse Taalunie is undoubtedly a remarkable piece of work and a very unusual occurrence in international linguistic relations, since no national government had so far conceded to a supranational institution what is generally considered to be its own prerogative: to decide autonomously on linguistic and cultural affairs. The activities of the Nederlandse Taalunie lie both in the fields of corpus and of status planning.

On December 12, 2003, Suriname adhered to the *Nederlandse Taalunie.*

---

[17] In January 1995 this Cultural Treaty was replaced with a new one, this time concluded between the Government of the Netherlands and the Government of Flanders, to which the constitutional reform had granted the right to conclude treaties with foreign nations. Both the Dutch and the Flemish governments have also passed cultural agreements with all their neighboring states.

[18] Almost immediately after the treaty was ratified, the Flemish government replaced the Belgian government, which was no longer competent for cultural affairs.

Instituut voor Nederlandse Lexicologie

The Instituut voor Nederlandse Lexicologie (INL) is a Dutch–Flemish funded lexicological institution working under the supervision of the Nederlandse Taalunie. For a very long time its main job has been to edit the *Woordenboek der Nederlandsche Taal* (WNT). As of today its scope is much broader. On the INL website (http://www.inl.nl) information can be found on all the dictionaries the INL is, or has been, working on. Most of them can be accessed electronically (and for free).

Apart from the WNT and the *Middelnederlandsch Woordenboek* (Middle Dutch Dictionary; MNW), which are mentioned in chapter 5, the following may be of interest:

- *Algemeen Nederlands Woordenboek* (General Dictionary of Dutch) is a corpus-based electronic dictionary of contemporary Dutch.
- *Etymologisch Woordenboek* (EWN) is a scientific etymological dictionary of modern supraregional Dutch, in four volumes published on paper.[19]
- *Oudnederlands Woordenboek* (Old Dutch Dictionary; ONW) is a corpus-based scientific dictionary of the oldest Dutch.
- *Vroegmiddelnederlands Woordenboek* (Early Middle Dutch dictionary; VMNW) is a scientific, alphabetical dictionary of the lexicon of more than 2,200 administrative documents dating from the 13th century as they appear in the *Corpus van Middelnederlandse teksten* (Corpus of Middle Dutch Texts; Gysseling 1977–1988); published electronically.

The INL has a longstanding tradition as an institute where lexicographers and linguists are working on the description of the Dutch language. This has resulted among other things in an extended lexicographical description of 15 centuries of Dutch language, to be found in the online historical dictionaries of INL and the description of recent Dutch language (see INL website). The dictionaries form the basis of a computational lexicon (GiGaNT), to be used to enrich new corpus material not only as an efficient way to extend the inventory of the Dutch language, but also to enable a better retrieval on the texts. The lexicon is attestation based and contains all quotations from the different dictionaries."[20]

The INL also has various corpora available that can be accessed via the Internet. Apart from the five million word *Corpus* 1994 and the 27 million word *Krantencorpus* (Newspaper Corpus 1995), the 38 million words *Corpus* 1996 consists of three main components: a miscellaneous one (documents from 1970–1989); a newspaper one (*Meppeler Courant*, 1992–1995); and a legal one (documents from 1814 to 1989). *The* PAROLE *Corpus* 2004 is a collection of

---

[19] On the site *Etymologiebank* (by the Meertensinstituut) (http://www.etymologiebank.nl) some 20 etymological dictionaries are online.
[20] Katrien Depuydt in a presentation at the INL on November 24, 2011.

modern Dutch texts (amounting to about 20 million tokens), for the greater part originating from newspaper or magazine articles. The texts are annotated for typographical and text-structural features. The PAROLE corpus is accessible free of charge. For the Early Middle Dutch period there is also the Gysseling Corpus (1977–1985), available in both book and CD-ROM format. The corpus of neologisms can be consulted via the INL website.

The *Spoken Dutch Corpus* 2004 (CGN) is a database of contemporary Dutch as spoken by adults in the Netherlands and Flanders. It contains some 9 million words, two-thirds from the Netherlands and one-third from Flanders. The corpus displays a large variety of speech types: 800 hours of speech recordings of spontaneous face-to-face conversations, telephone dialogues, interviews, debates, meetings, reports, lectures, and seminars. Since all participants were asked to use Standard Dutch exclusively, the CGN can also be used as a kind of catalogue of variation in the standard language.

The HLT Agency (Centrale voor Taal- en Spraaktechnologie), founded in 2004, is a Dutch–Flemish agency responsible for the "management, maintenance, and distribution of Dutch-language digital language resources." The HLT Agency maintains these language resources and makes them available for education, research, and development. The HLT Agency is funded by the Nederlandse Taalunie and is carried out by the INL on a project basis.

P.J. Meertens Instituut

The P.J. Meertens Institute, established in 1926, is a research institute of the Royal Netherlands Academy of Arts and Sciences (http://www.meertens-knaw.nl). It investigates "the diversity in language and culture in the Netherlands." Its research group on variational linguistics describes and investigates linguistic variation in Dutch, that is, geographically (dialects), socially, and culturally determined variation. Their main goal is "to gain insight into the nature of linguistic variation, the linguistic factors playing a part in this, and the language-external factors (like age, gender, ethnicity, etc.) that cause or influence variation in Dutch." The materials of the Goeman-Taeldeman-Van Reenen project, which are the basis of the FAND, MAND, and SAND atlases, are filed here and are at the disposal of scholars.

The most interesting database, Soundbites, files tape recordings of Dutch dialects (hundreds of hours of sound material) collected in past decades by the Meertens Institute (formally called Dialectenbureau). It gives a splendid overview of the Dutch dialects spoken around the middle of the past century. All materials are freely available for research and displayed on a *Sprekende Kaart* (speaking map).

Koninklijke Academie voor Nederlandse Taal- en Letterkunde

The Koninklijke Academie voor Nederlands Taal- en letterkunde (Royal Academy of Dutch Language and Literature; KANTL) in Ghent (http://www.kantl.be) was created by the Belgian government in 1886 and was given the task of stimulating culture and literature in Flanders. It was the first official institution in the Kingdom of Belgium to work on behalf of the Dutch language and in Dutch. Its area of expertise is language and literature, and in both functions it acted and acts as an official advisory board of the government. At present the support and enhancement function is supplemented by scientific research in the fields of Dutch linguistics and literature. The latter aspect is coordinated by the Centrum voor Teksteditie en Bronnenstudie (Center for Text Edition; CTB).

One of the important corpora kept at the KANTL is the Materiaal Willems, which has recently been digitalized. It contains data from a 19th-century dialect survey carried out by Pieter Willems, who had the famous *Wenker Sätze*—the sentences that form the basis of the Deutscher Sprachatlas, or German dialect atlas—translated into various dialects of the Dutch language territory, totaling 35,000 pages. They had never been published before and are now electronically at the disposal of all researchers. The digital version contains 19,000 pictures and four million items from dialects in Flanders, the Netherlands, and French Flanders (see KANTL website).

NORM INSTRUMENTS

Because Dutch is a pluricentric language, it is normal not only that the actual realization of the norm may vary slightly according to region but also that the very notion of the norm itself is not necessarily identical in all parts of the language territory. Nowadays the consensus on the norm is much larger than it ever used to be. As far as the norm instruments are concerned, there is a general consensus on where they can be found: Van Dale's dictionary and the *Algemene Nederlandse Spraakkunst* (ANS) are undoubtedly the generally accepted referees in norm discussions and function as prescriptive instruments on vocabulary and grammar, respectively.

Van Dale contains approximately 140,000 headwords, describes modern Dutch, and also provides a retrospective of the development of the Dutch vocabulary from approximately 1850 to 2005. The 14th edition appeared in 2005. It is a descriptive dictionary, but since it is limited to the standard language it is also implicitly normative.

The *Groene Boekje* (officially *Woordenlijst der Nederlandse Taal*) is the official spelling norm and is published under the authority of the Nederlandse Taalunie.

Finally, there is the ANS, the second edition of which was published in 1997. It is concerned with "what is important in language use" and has the ambition to be accessible to nonspecialists. It is not prescriptive but simply notes and discusses the forms and constructions that occur in the Dutch language. Still, with the general public it is considered to be the instrument par excellence as far as the norm of the Dutch grammar is concerned.

As far as pronunciation is concerned it is less easy to pinpoint a norm source. None of the few existing pronunciation dictionaries has ever succeeded in acquiring the norm status of the publications mentioned above for other aspects of the language. The most recent one is Heemskerk and Zonneveld (2000). On the CD-ROM accompanying the Van Dale in 2000, all words listed have their pronunciation recorded. In some cases two variable possibilities are mentioned, one common in Belgium and the other in the Netherlands. This is the case in only 1 percent of the items (Van der Sijs 2004, 213).

7 }

Colonial Dutch

Mi be fraj: Pidgins, Creoles, and Dutch Overseas

Most native speakers of Dutch will be able to effortlessly understand the following utterance: "*as die tan sal pin mi weeran, dan mi sal loop fo trek die*" (Dutch: "*als die tand weer pijn gaat doen, dan zal ik hem gaan laten trekken*"; should my tooth hurt again, I shall go and have it pulled). However, the language is not Dutch but a Dutch-based pidgin called Negerhollands (Negro Dutch). In another sentence—"*Dank, mi be fraj*"—Dutch speakers will probably recognize all the words but not necessarily capture the meaning: "*Dank je, met mij gaat het goed*" (thank you, I'm fine).

Pidgins, even if they're said to be Dutch-based, can be (or have become) quite different from the language of origin, the more so since a pidgin is mostly a mixture of two or, often, more languages still. An explanation of pidgins and Creoles is given in box 7.1.

One of the questions dealt with in this chapter is how Dutch became the basis of pidgin and Creole languages so far away from home and how the Dutch language fared in the many colonial possessions the Dutch acquired over the centuries in the Caribbean, North and South America, Asia, and Africa.

During the last third of the 16th century, in the mainland, the Low Countries tried to get rid of their Spanish occupants. Although the rebellion started in Flanders, it was eventually only the north that gained its independence (see chapter 4). Long before the official end of the Eighty Years' War in 1648, the commercial fleet of the young northern republic cruised the world oceans, where it ran into the same enemy it was also facing at home: the Spaniards. In the battle for colonies, the Dutch succeeded in getting their share, at the detriment not only of Spain but also of the other main seafaring rivals of the moment: the British, the French, and the Portuguese. In many colonies, therefore, one occupant chased the other until more or less stable conditions were established.

A pidgin is a simplified system of communication that has developed between groups not having a language in common but that need to communicate with one another for specific reasons, such as trade. It is not the native language of any speech community but is learned as a second language instead. It is based on two or more so-called European "parent languages" and usually enjoys a rather low prestige. Pidgins typically have a limited vocabulary and a simplified grammatical structure. Since they have been mainly (short-lived) oral languages, few records remain.

Most documented pidgins evolved in the last 500 years as a result of the voyages of discovery and the expansion of European maritime power, which led to an intense slave trade.

Pidgins may become Creole languages when a generation whose parents speak pidgin to each other hand it down to their children as their first language. Creoles can then become the native language of a community (such as Tok Pisin in Papua New Guinea). Creoles have generally been regarded as degenerate variants or dialects of their parent languages. Still, they tend to be more complex in grammar and have a larger vocabulary (e.g., French-based Creoles in the Caribbean) than pidgins.

Many of the creoles that arose in the European colonies have become extinct. Based on Baker and Prys Jones (1998, 142 ff).

In 1667 Admiral Abraham Crijnssen took possession of Suriname by ousting the English, who had been establishing sugar plantations there from 1650. In 1667 the Dutch and the English concluded the Treaty of Breda, in which it was agreed that both countries could keep the possessions they had taken from one another. As a consequence, the Dutch were to maintain their possession of Suriname in exchange for New Netherland and its capital New Amsterdam (New York), which had been taken over by the British. At that moment the Dutch shareholders of the West India Company believed they had made the better deal, in view of the profits they expected the slave trade in Suriname to bring. If they only had known!

The Europeans first learned of Aruba when Amerigo Vespucci and Alonso de Ojeda happened upon this Caribbean island in August 1499. Aruba was colonized by Spain for over a century. It has been under Dutch administration since 1636, initially under Peter Stuyvesant. In the same year they also "discovered" Curaçao and the neighboring island of Bonaire. The first settlement in Sint Eustatius was established in 1636, and the land changed hands 22 times in its history, between the Dutch, the French, and the Spanish. Columbus was the first to sight Saba, but it was the Dutch who colonized the island in 1640. The Dutch were also the first to colonize Sint Maarten in 1631, but within two years the Spanish invaded and evacuated the settlers. After a scattered history, in 1817, the current partition line between the Dutch and the French was established.

The Portuguese were the first Europeans to arrive in Indonesia (in 1512). At the beginning of the 17th century the Dutch took over. In 1602, the Dutch Staten Generaal had awarded the Verenigde Oost-Indische Compagnie (East India Company; VOC) a monopoly on trade and colonial activities in the region, and they opened their first permanent trading post in 1603. In 1619, the VOC conquered the West Javan city of Jayakarta, where they founded the city of Batavia (present-day Jakarta). They established a permanent foothold in Java, from which grew a land-based colonial empire that became one of the world's richest colonial possessions.

In September 1609 the Dutch language sailed into North America on board *De halve Maen*, steered by the English captain Henry Hudson. It was called *Nieuw Nederland* (New Netherland). In 1625 the Dutch settled in Manhattan, which was to become their capital *Nieuw Amsterdam*. In 1664 it was attacked by the British and governor Peter Stuyvesant had to surrender the province to them.

In 1627 the Dutch merchant Abraham van Peere founded the colony Berbice in what is now Guyana. As so very often is the case, a pidgin called Berbice-Dutch (Kouwenberg 1991) developed as a mixture with three components: (1) Dutch, in the form of its Zeeland regional variety, which was Van Peere's mother tongue; (2) the local language of the Indians; and (3) the language slaves from Nigeria had brought with them. According to the international language data-bank Ethnologue, its last native speaker died in 2005. Consequently, the language is officially extinct now. Another Dutch-based pidgin–Creole that used to exist in Guyana, Skepi, has been extinct longer than Berbice-Dutch. Apparently both languages, though Dutch based, were mutually unintelligible (Van der Sijs 2010). Negerhollands (Negro Dutch) has had the same fate: dying out of the last speakers. It was spoken until the early 20th century on the Danish Antilles, now part of the American Virgin Islands (Den Besten 1986; Van der Voort 2006).

The rest of this chapter is devoted to the fate of Dutch in Suriname, the Dutch Antilles, Indonesia, and the United States. Other places where there was less Dutch influence or where it did not last as long (such as Taiwan, Sri Lanka, Congo, and Japan) are treated briefly at the end of the chapter. The history and fate of Afrikaans, the only surviving daughter language of Dutch, is discussed in the next chapter.

Suriname for New York: Quite a Deal

A DUTCH-SPEAKING CREOLE COMMUNITY

In 1855, the black Surinamer Hendrik Focke published his *Neger-Engelsch woordenboek* (Negro–English dictionary); *Neger–Engelsch* was the denigrating name used to refer to Sranan Tongo, Suriname's lingua franca. It is difficult to imagine that something of the kind might have been accomplished by a "native" in the East Indies, which demonstrates how very different the influence of the Dutch language has been in their various colonies.

As mentioned before, Admiral Abraham Crijnssen took possession of Suriname in the name of the republic, and in 1667, as part of the Treaty of Breda, it was agreed that the Dutch would maintain their possession of Suriname in exchange for New Amsterdam (New York), which was ceded to the English.

Thus, Suriname officially became a Dutch colony, and ever since Dutch has not only been in use in Suriname but also has been its official language. However, throughout its history, several other languages have been used in Suriname alongside Dutch, most of all Sranan (Tongo), the English-based Creole language developed among the earliest slaves on the plantations, which still is today's lingua franca. After the English left, the number of whites did not really increase, but since a total number of 300,000 Africans has been deported as slaves to Suriname, this brought the ratio up to 1:12 in the initial period of Dutch rule.

As far as the past use of Dutch in Suriname is concerned,[1] it is generally assumed that the core of the Dutch-speaking community consisted of a group of locally born speakers of mixed European and African ancestry who emerged in the course of the 18th century. This group soon began to form a new middle class in the capital city of Paramaribo, and, in an eager attempt to assimilate into the Dutch community, they also took over the language of the Dutch.

The group of colonists in the early years was by no means exclusively Dutch but had a distinctly international character, which it continued to have until well into the 20th century. There was a significant Jewish population of both Portuguese and German descent. By 1694 their total number is estimated at 600. In 1684 a total of 579 non-Jewish whites lived in Suriname as well, but it remains unclear how many of those were Dutch. So during this period the Dutch were outnumbered by non-Dutch colonists, and in 1688 the colony's governor deemed it necessary to publish an ordinance stating that documents in languages other than *Nederduytsch* (Dutch) would no longer be accepted.

Communication with and among the slave population of African descent, which by the end of the 17th century had grown to around 7,500, was in Sranan. This habit continued in the 18th century. In 1736 the white population numbered 1,288, but it still remains unclear how many of these were Dutch. In 1787, there were some 1,000 non-Dutch Jews and some 2,000 other whites, half of which lived in the countryside and the other half of which lived in the capital city of Paramaribo. By that time the city also harbored some 650 free mulattos and blacks. From the approximately 60,000 slaves, only about 10,000 lived in Paramaribo.

The colony continued to have a highly international character throughout the 18th century, including remarkably few Dutch. Given the multilingual

---

[1] The most important source in this account of the linguistic situation in Suriname has been De Kleine (2007), supplemented by other sources.

character of the European community, it is quite plausible that most of the white population resorted to Sranan. School regulations in 1726 officially stated that it was forbidden for children to use Sranan in class, which indeed illustrates the general use of Sranan among the white colonists. Throughout the 18th century Dutch functioned merely as the official language of government and, for the Dutch-born population, as the language of education and religion.

Surinamese society experienced a number of significant changes during the 19th century. A census in 1811 reported a total population of 5,104 free persons, most of whom lived in Paramaribo and 3,075 of whom were free nonwhites. By 1830 free nonwhites had begun to outnumber the white population in Paramaribo, a trend that persisted throughout the remainder of the century.

Also, the Dutch remained a minority among the Europeans, representing less than a quarter in 1830, and, consequently, the European community in Suriname lacked cultural as well as linguistic coherence. By the end of that century, though, a Dutch-speaking community had started to emerge from within the nonwhite population of Paramaribo. As early as 1760, the first school for nonwhites had opened its doors, presumably using Dutch as the medium of instruction. In the early 19th century a class of nonwhite Surinamese intellectuals emerged, most of whom received at least part of their education in Holland. Hendrik Focke, the author of the Negro–English dictionary, is a striking example of how this group managed to function bilingually. Members of this elite group held high social status, and, unlike the transient white community, they resided permanently in Suriname and were thus able to develop a stable Dutch-speaking community.

As a result of a lack of governmental regulation, up to the first decades of the 19th century, the quality of the schools and their teachers had left much to be desired. This situation changed after 1817 when the government began regulating elementary and secondary education, setting clear standards for teachers and subject matters to be taught and thereby improving quality significantly. As mentioned in chapter 5, William I was the king of the United Kingdom of the Netherlands, the new country that emerged in Europe from the reunification of the northern and the southern Netherlands (1814–1830). His language policy in the European motherland gives testimony of the same interest in the Dutch language as a unifying factor in his entire kingdom and of his conviction that education was the main tool to achieve that aim. Both in Holland and Flanders he founded *normaalscholen* (or *kweekscholen*; teacher training academies) to improve the quality of both the elementary schools and their teachers. In Suriname, the schools were instructed to use Dutch as the medium of instruction.[2] The slave population, on the other hand, was officially forbidden

---

[2] William had done the same in Flanders, where he succeeded in turning French-medium secondary schools into perfectly well-functioning Dutch-medium schools in only six years' time.

to receive education until 1844, when the slave children were taught in Sranan, though the number of slaves receiving an education remained very small.

This situation changed dramatically when in 1876, following the abolition of slavery and the manumission of more than 30,000 slaves, the Dutch government introduced compulsory education for every child aged 7 to 12. Simultaneously, they now started to pursue an active policy of assimilation, with the intention of transforming Suriname into a Dutch province. Dutch was made the only medium of instruction, both in public and in religious schools. In so doing, after 200 years of reserving the Dutch language for a small elite, the authorities then went to the other extreme by forcing a Dutch-only policy onto the Surinamese and actively suppressing the use of Sranan in education.

Still, the large majority of pupils entering the school system had a language background that did not include Dutch, resulting in its massive second-language learning. This policy may well have found strong support among parents, who were very much aware that Dutch was now more than ever the paramount vehicle for upward social mobility. It took another 25 years, though, for Dutch to take hold in social life as well.

On the other hand, the introduction of Dutch on a large scale through education was delayed by the arrival of many new Asian immigrants, new agricultural laborers, in a deliberate attempt to create a labor surplus to keep (future) wages low after slavery was abolished. Chinese contract laborers were recruited from China and the then Dutch East Indies, followed by larger-scale immigration from then British India as well as Java. Between 1873 and 1917, more than 30,000 people were recruited in India, while an equal amount of Javanese arrived in Suriname between 1891 and 1938.

At first, the Asian immigrants mostly settled in the countryside. Although theoretically they were subject to the new laws regarding compulsory education in Dutch, an exception was made for them in 1890, as they were expected to reside in Suriname only temporarily. As a compromise, the *koeliescholen* (coolie schools) were established, where education was provided by Indian teachers in Hindi and Urdu. As a result, the East Indians were largely unaffected by the Dutch assimilation policy, and the Dutch language did not penetrate into these Asian immigrant communities until much later. It was therefore mostly the population of African descent, the Creoles, who, by the end of the 19th century was receiving instruction in Dutch. Also, as early as 1877, a teacher training academy was founded and thus, from then onward, some of the teachers were recruited locally instead of being recruited in Holland.

As a consequence of all this, in the early 20th century an elite group existed within the Creole population in Paramaribo. It was bilingual in Dutch and Sranan, and their children acquired Dutch as a first language. In addition, Creoles of a middle-class background favored Dutch language socialization as well, since they (rightly) viewed Dutch as the vehicle for social advancement. Often children from middle- and upper-class families were forbidden to speak

Sranan altogether. Numerically this group, like the European-born population in general, shrank to insignificance during the first half of the 20th century when compared with the number of slave descendants, who relocated in the city and remained predominantly Sranan-speaking after abolition. They mostly acquired Dutch as a second language in the classroom, which created a linguistic gap between the higher and lower social classes. An even sharper distinction developed with respect to the city versus the countryside variable, and along with this, a distinction between ethnic groups. From the late 19th century onward and until the middle of the 20th century, a disproportionate number of Creoles lived in the city, while the majority of the Asians remained in the countryside and experienced little exposure to Dutch.

In short, although a number of speakers acquired Dutch as a first language, for a much larger part of the population it was a second language. In the educational system this caused serious problems for many Surinamese children, who often failed to acquire a proper command of Dutch. After the Second World War, the East Indian population began to move to the city as well, and an increasing number of them switched to Dutch at home.

When Suriname gained independence in 1975, Dutch presence virtually came to an end, and Suriname Dutch, although generally perceived to be rather nonstandard, was increasingly heard in public communication and specifically in the media. However, simultaneously, independence has also resulted in increased exposure to European Dutch, among other things as a result of the vivid contact between the many Surinamers having emigrated to the Netherlands and those having remained at home. For the same reason, and despite ever weakening political relations between Suriname and the Netherlands, the influence of European Dutch persists up to the present day (fig. 7-1).

THE CURRENT SOCIOLINGUISTIC SITUATION IN SURINAME

In multilingual Suriname,[3] language usage is partly organized along ethnic lines (Charry, Koefoed, & Muysken 1983). Many ethnic groups are using their own ethnic language at home and at some specific informal occasions. Some of those languages are:

- The language particular to the East Indians (Dutch: *Hindostanen*) is Surinamese Hindustani, today commonly referred to as Sarnami. Along with Sarnami, the East Indian community also employs (standard) Hindi and Urdu, mainly for religious purposes, in the media and education.

[3] Since in the Netherlands Frisian has official status as have French and German in Belgium, the only country where Dutch is the sole official language is Suriname, notwithstanding the fact that some 20 more languages are spoken there.

FIGURE 7.1 Map of Suriname (courtesy of Ons Erfdeel vzw, Flanders, Belgium)

- Chinese born in China have brought Mandarin Chinese to Suriname.
- Javanese (Dutch: *Javanen*) have, like all other Asian groups, maintained the use of their original language.
- Maroons (Dutch formerly *bosnegers*, now *Boslandcreolen*) have their own English-or Portuguese-based Creole languages, such as Saramaccan or Mataway (Eersel 1971).
- Some Amerindians may still use Carib or Arawack or one of the many other Indian languages.

Both Sranan and Dutch are the languages spoken across ethnic boundaries by the majority of the population. Sranan functions as the lingua franca in informal settings, while Dutch, the country's official language, is typically employed in more formal settings, including in the media, in government, and in education. On top of that it is, obviously, the language of government, legislation, and jurisdiction. Consequently, what we actually see is some kind of double diglossia, meaning that in most of the formal settings Dutch is used, whereas in informal settings the kind of L-variety used is variable. A difference has to be made between interethnic and extraethnic communication. In the former case the normal choice is the ethnic language of the group in question (e.g., Sarnami); in the latter case the appropriate variety is Sranan, the only L-variety spoken across ethnic boundaries.

Also, since Sranan is no longer looked down upon, its usage among higher social strata has increased, and in more recent times it has even become more acceptable in some formal situations in which it was once avoided, such as in professional settings, resulting in Dutch experiencing increased competition from Sranan.

Of the utmost importance for the linguistic future of Suriname are the linguistic habits and attitudes of the population of Asian extract (i.e., East Indians as well as Javanese and Chinese), who together make up more than half the country's population. The Suriname-born Chinese, for example, typically prefer Dutch over Sranan for intergroup communication. Unfortunately, the information on the linguistic attitudes and intentions as well as actual linguistic behavior is rather thrifty.

Deprez and De Bies (1985), as part of a project that investigated the knowledge and use of Dutch, Sranan, and Sarnami as well as attitudes toward these languages among Creoles and East Indians, produced one of the few inquiries yielding quantifiable information. As far as the speakers' self-reported knowledge of Dutch is concerned, we learn that 35 percent of the high-status Creoles boast a "perfect to very good" command of Dutch and 65 percent a "fair" command. With low-status Creoles the figures are 6 percent and 94 percent, respectively. All (100 percent) of the East Indian group members estimate their command of Dutch to be "fair." The inquiry results also allow for an interesting comparison between the language the informants spoke at their childhood home and the language they use (or used) later on with their own children. The overall result is that a vast majority of Creoles employ Dutch when addressing their children; the main difference between Creoles and East Indians is an ethnic rather than a social issue.

The main problem with the Deprez and De Bies (1985) investigation is that the number of informants was desperately low: a total of 61 informants was used, 34 of whom were of Creole and 27 of East Indian origin. Consequently, it may be rather dangerous to extrapolate the figures gathered from so small a group. Also, what we have here is "reported behavior" containing the danger that respondents may very well "overreport" Dutch language use, as it is the language with high prestige, associated with sophistication in general and education specifically. One conclusion, though, is nevertheless justified: the majority of Creoles in Paramaribo are exposed to a significant amount of Dutch in the home and thus can be said to acquire Dutch natively. At the same time it is undisputed that Sranan is also used extensively within the Creole community.

In multilingual settings, variety choice can often be tricky, because by opting for one or the other language or code a speaker is giving away a lot about himself. Nevertheless, in Suriname, as De Kleine (2007) establishes, most people appear to have an unerring instinct for making the right choice in every situation.

Domain usage has been fixed for some time ago already and is not depending on individual choice or preference. One example is that Dutch is the only language used in science, education, government, and jurisdiction. At home, on the contrary, either only Dutch or a combination of Dutch with an ethnic mother tongue or even solely the latter is normally used. In the domains of culture and the media, Dutch is used alongside the formal variant of an ethnic mother tongue (e.g., Hindi). In a situation like this, language function is extremely important as well, since the functions performed by various languages and varieties may vary according to many variables. Here again, the Surinamer feels pretty secure: in general he is not led by language political or ideological motives as is so often the case in language contact situations, which mostly turn into language conflict. It is practicality that decides who is speaking which language to whom and when. At the same time, most Surinamers are also aware of other language functions. Everyone is aware that language is also a symbol of group adherence and functions as a medium for handing down cultural and ethnic values to the next generations. It also determines linguistic accommodation. Since Dutch is Suriname's prestige language, proving competence in that language is very important; therefore, the general rule is to use Dutch as a means of upward accommodation: youngsters addressing their elders or lower social strata speaking to higher ones will almost always begin the conversation in Dutch before (possibly) switching to another variety.

As far as the linguistic behavior of the various layers of the Surinam population is concerned, no fundamental change is expected in the near future.

The Surinam variety of Dutch (Gobardhan-Rambocus 1993) does, of course, differ from the so-called European Dutch (by which Surinamers mean Dutch as spoken in the Netherlands) in the lexicon, pronunciation, and some grammatical features. We are in the presence of a continuum, the two poles of which are a very locally colored Surinam Dutch and the pure European Dutch. Individual speakers as well as, for example, geographical and social groups of them can be situated somewhere on that continuum both for their general competence and for each single instance of communication. Many speakers have a competence in more than one of the varieties of the continuum.

Sometimes more important than factual differences are attitudes. In the periphery of every language territory there are always—often heated—discussions as to the amount and extent of deviations of the standard language that are allowed or acceptable. Attitudes toward the peripheral variety as well as toward the standard language and their speakers are mostly the decisive factor. The same goes for the question of whether peripheral speakers should or should not try to enhance their competence in the standard variety to produce (or imitate) it as close as possible. In German-speaking Switzerland, for example—the latitude is extreme, and the Swiss seem to be proud of their provincialisms to the extent that dialects are used much more often than Swiss-colored and -accented standard German, even in very formal situations. In Québec, on the contrary, the pressure to prefer European French over the Canadian variety is huge, and the reason can be found in domestic language political motives: it is believed that European French may be a weapon in the struggle against linguistic domination by English-speaking North Americans.

Although in Suriname the situation is totally different, the fact that European Standard Dutch is the prestige variety explains why, here too, the same discussion has a long history. Local pride may be one reason for allowing the use of Surinam Dutch in particular situations; another may be the conviction that a peripheral speaker can never match the level of competence of the native speaker of the European variety. This has brought more and more people to concede the right of existence or even the desirability of a Surinamese variety of standard Dutch. It is obvious that its sheer existence certainly cannot be denied: the second edition of J. van Donselaar's (1989) *Woordenboek van het Surinaams-Nederlands* (Dictionary of Surinam Dutch) contains some 6,600 words differing in form or meaning from European Dutch. De Bies (2009) is a more recent dictionary.

On the other hand, the fact that Suriname became an associate member of the Nederlandse Taalunie (Dutch Language Union; see chapter 6) alongside Holland and Flanders speaks for its determination to remain part of the Dutch language community. Both Van Dale (the authoritative dictionary of Dutch) and the *Groene Boekje* (the official spelling guide) honored that by including some 500 words from the Surinam variety of Dutch.

Their determination to have their "Dutchness" recognized and accepted by all was made utterly clear when Suriname forced Unasur, the Union of South American States, to accept Dutch as one of its official languages, alongside English, Spanish, and Portuguese.

Above and under the Wind: Dutch in the Caribbean

Six Caribbean islands have a Dutch past, and the Dutch language is present in some way in all of them (Mijts & Rutgers 2010). Since 1986 Aruba has had a status aparte; the other five used to be part of the Netherlands Antilles, divided geographically into the (northern) Bovenwindse eilanden (Windward Islands) Saba, Sint Eustatius, and Sint Maarten; and the (southern) *Benedenwindse eilanden* (Leeward Islands) Bonaire and Curaçao. Aruba, too, is a Leeward island. As to the number of inhabitants, Curaçao has 141,766, Sint Maarten 40,917, and Bonaire 12,877. Sint Eustatius and Saba are the least populated, with 2,768 and 1,601 inhabitants, respectively. The new state of affairs as of October 10, 2010, is explained in the following section (fig. 7-2).

SHORT HISTORY

The first settlement in Sint Eustatius was established in 1636, and the island changed hands 22 times in its history among the Dutch, French, and Spanish. In the 18th century the island became a duty-free port, which propelled it into a major port with rapid population growth that lost momentum after the American–British peace treaty in 1783.

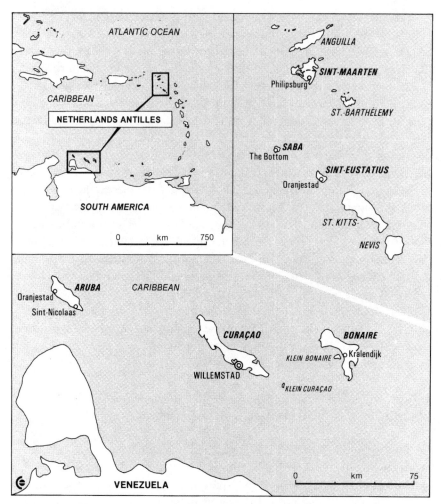

FIGURE 7.2 Map of the Caribbean with the 6 formally Dutch Islands

Columbus was the first to sight Saba, but it was the Dutch who colonized the island in 1640 with a party from Sint Eustatius. Because of its difficult terrain, the island's growth progressed only slowly, and it is still the least populated island of them all.

The Dutch were the first to colonize Sint Maarten in 1631, but within two years the Spanish invaded and evacuated the settlers. After a scattered history, in 1817 the current partition line between the Dutch and the French was established. The island flourished through the exportation of salt under a slave-based economy, until the abolition of slavery in 1863.

Europeans first learned of Aruba when Amerigo Vespucci and Alonso de Ojeda happened upon it in August 1499. Aruba was colonized by Spain for over a century. It has been under Dutch administration since 1636, initially under Peter Stuyvesant. In the same year they also discovered Curaçao and the neighboring island of Bonaire. The capital of Curaçao, Willemstad, used to be the capital of all the Dutch Antilles. Curaçao is the largest and most populous of the three ABC islands: it has a land area of 444 square kilometers (171 square miles) and as of January 2009 it had a population of some 142,000.

From 1568 to 1648 the Dutch and the Spanish fought the Eighty Years' War in Europe. Between 1633 and 1639 the islands of Curaçao, Bonaire, and Aruba were occupied (and kept) by the Netherlands. The Dutch West India Company, founded in 1621, had its ships stop in Bonaire to obtain meat, water, and wood and turned it into a plantation. The natural harbor of Willemstad, Curaçao quickly proved to be an ideal spot for trade. Commerce and shipping—and piracy—became Curaçao's most important economic activities. In addition, the Dutch West India Company made Curaçao a center for the Atlantic slave trade in 1662.

In 1845 the Windward islands were united with Curaçao, Bonaire, and Aruba in a political unit. As of 1954, the federation of the Netherlands Antilles (Curacao, Bonaire, Saba, Sint Eustatius, and Sint Maarten) was semiautonomous in most internal affairs. The Kingdom retained authority over foreign affairs, defense, final judicial review, and Kingdom matters including human rights and good governance. Aruba was part of this federation until January 1, 1986, when it gained its status aparte. Citizens of all the islands hold Dutch passports. Changes in the situation of the islands among each other, but mostly as far as their relationship with the Netherlands is concerned, have been envisaged for decades already but had—so far—always been postponed. They finally took effect on October 10, 2010, and are discussed in the following section.

LANGUAGE

In all the islands, Dutch used to be the official language. Recently Papiamento and English acquired the status of official languages as well. Papiamento is a Creole language that has been evolving through the centuries and has been influenced by indigenous and other languages, most importantly Portuguese and Spanish.

In practice, English is used only seldom for official purposes, but it is widely spoken on the islands; the same holds true for Spanish. English has historical local connections and is known by many. Most inhabitants of the polyglot ABC islands are fluent in Papiamento, and many of them even master all four languages. Throughout colonial history, Dutch was never as widely spoken as English or Spanish and remained exclusively a language for administration and legal matters; popular use of Dutch increased toward the end of the 19th century and the early 20th century, but it has never been the language of the people.

EDUCATION

Until the late 19th century, education on Curaçao, Aruba, and Bonaire had been predominantly in Spanish, while simultaneously efforts were made to introduce bilingual popular education in Dutch and Papiamento. Dutch was made the sole language of instruction in the early 20th century. In recent years, the authorities have shown an increased interest in acknowledging the cultural and historical importance of their native language. It is only since 2002 that Papiamento has been introduced as a language of instruction in the primary schools of the ABC islands. Until far in the 20th century, most teachers considered it not to be a "real" language since it lacked a grammar. This prejudice seems to be superseded now.

Inclining to the other extreme, recent political debate has centered on the issue of Papiamento becoming the sole language of instruction. Proponents argue that it will help to preserve the language and will improve the quality of primary and secondary school education. Proponents of Dutch language instruction argue that students who study in Dutch will be better prepared for the free university education offered to them in the Netherlands. Finally, in 2008 Curaçao reintroduced Dutch as a language of instruction in primary schools. On the other hand, the Curaçao minister of education announced in December 2011 that, beginning in the 2012–2013 school year, a Papiamento-speaking school will provide *havo/vwo* (secondary) instruction in Papiamento, which is, as he stressed, the national language of Curaçao.

Higher education in the ABC islands is reputedly good relative to regional standards. The main institute of higher learning is the University of the Netherlands Antilles (UNA). Dutch derives its status as prestige language partly from the fact that it is the language of higher education.

To strengthen the competence in Dutch, which has decreased as a result of the influence of Papiamento, the education ministers of the three ABC islands have agreed that new measures are in order. One of them is that in 2006 a request has been filed to apply the Treatise of the Dutch Language Union (Nederlandse Taalunie), which now applies only to Flanders, the Netherlands, and Suriname, to the Antilles as well. An agreement was signed in 2007, and in 2008 the Foundation for Language Planning of Curaçao (its official name in Papiamento is Fundashon pa Planifikashon di Idioma) has worked out a list of specific steps to be taken in the near future.

The linguistic situation on the remaining three islands is more transparent. Although the Windward Islands Sint Maarten, Saba, and Sint Eustatius are polyglot societies as well, the everyday practice is that English is their habitual language. Still, in 2007 Dutch, Papiamento, and English were recognized as the official languages in spite of the fact that Papiamento is hardly used here and Dutch performs only the most formal and official functions yet is completely absent on all other levels except in secondary schools where it is the language of instruction.

According to the 2001 census, the average usage (in percentage) of the various languages on the five islands of the Dutch Antilles is approximately as seen in table 7.1.

Census figures, of course, do not diversify according to domain, functions, and similar sociolinguistic variables, and their usefulness is therefore rather limited.

TABLE 7.1 } Average Use (In Percentage) of the Various Languages on the Dutch Antilles

	Papiamento	English	Dutch	Spanish	Other
Aruba[a]	77.2	7.3	7.3	7	1.1
Bonaire	75	3	9	12	1
Curaçao	81	3	8	6	2
Saba	1	88	2	5	4
St. Eust	2	83	4	6	5
St. Maarten	2	68	4	13	13

[a]The Aruba figures date from 1994.

FORTHCOMING CHANGE

As of October 10, 2010, the political, and probably the linguistic, situation of five of the six Caribbean islands, which together used to build the Netherlands Antilles, has changed dramatically. Curaçao and Sint-Maarten both gained independency of some sort, with a status comparable to the *status aparte* Aruba has had since 1986. The smaller islands Bonaire, Sint-Eustatius, and Saba (also called the BES islands) are now special municipalities (communes) within the Netherlands; that is, they are part of the continental Dutch territory that, therefore now suddenly stretches to the Caribbean. Since all of them remain part of what is officially called "the Kingdom of the Netherlands," the latter political construct now consists of four countries: the Netherlands (proper); Aruba; Curaçao; and Sint-Maarten. The Netherlands proper also includes the three BES islands. A strange and paradoxical consequence of this change may be that the contact between the islands and their inhabitants with Holland may well intensify. Since the Antillean administrative level disappears, they will from now on conduct their business with The Hague directly, without the intermediary of the administration of the Netherlands Antilles. Such a construct harbors many other paradoxical consequences as well. Some of the most interesting ones are that in the three BES islands, now part of Holland, Dutch law only partly applies, since large parts of the old Antillean law still remain in effect. One would also expect them to be part of the European Union, but that is not the case. "The new structure of the Kingdom implies huge legislative and administrative transformations within the new 'states' and within the new municipalities of the Netherlands" (Mijts & Van Bogaert 2011, 297).

It is highly probable that this political change will have consequences as far as the position of Dutch in this multilingual and multicultural construct is concerned, and it is a fair bet that the use and influence of Dutch will decrease further, which is paradoxical since never before has there been so large a portion of the Antillean population having received higher education in Dutch.

Nevertheless, it appears that only a small minority of them regularly uses Dutch outside the school. Mijts and Rutgers (2010, 38) predict that "even if the use of Papiamento in the educational system does not increase, because it is too costly, it cannot be excluded that preference will be given to English or Spanish rather than to Dutch." But even so, they add, "As long as the Antillean youth continues to go to Holland for their university education, this intellectual elite will remain under Dutch influence."

Too Little, Too Late: Dutch in Indonesia

During Holland's Golden (17th) Age, its commercial fleet conquered territories in all continents[4] (fig. 7-3). Both the VOC and the Dutch West India (VWC) companies set sail to Asia, Africa, and the Americas and planted the flag of the young republic either on territories already previously "discovered" by others or on "new" land. Although their goals were purely commercial, they still brought things Dutch over the oceans, and with it also came—to a certain extent—the language. The fact that the Dutch language almost never stayed in these countries is partly attributed to the fact that the company leaders never felt responsible for the expansion of the Dutch language and culture. In the few cases where a permanent place for Dutch was nevertheless secured, it was mostly in spite of the company (and, subsequently, the Dutch government), whose language policy was, as Groeneboer (1998, 1) quite rightly observes, "marked above all by pragmatism", a policy that hindered rather than promoted the spread of Dutch.

Even so, in the beginning, the VOC occasionally used language as a weapon or a tool against previous conquerors whose influence they wanted to diminish or rule out completely. In territories previously occupied by the Portuguese, for example, Dutch was intended to be a weapon against both the commercial rivals and their Roman Catholic religion. Still, even as the Dutch had ousted the Portuguese from what would later become Indonesia, the language remained omnipresent as can be deduced from the words by Joan Maetsuyker, Governor-General of the East Indies, in 1674 complaining that "corrupted Portuguese is on the up and threatens to oust Dutch completely." Although similar complaints were often heard in VOC times, no real attempts were made to change the situation by strengthening the position of Dutch (fig. 7-4).

It is indeed more than striking that the languages of other colonial powers, be they Portuguese, Spaniards, French, or British, have deeply impregnated their former colonies forever, whereas the Netherlands failed to do. Apart from Suriname, where Dutch is the official language, and South Africa, where

[4] My main source in this account of the history of Dutch in Indonesia has been Groeneboer (1998), supplemented by other sources.

FIGURE 7.3 Map of Indonesia

Afrikaans, the only daughter language of Dutch, played and plays an important role, the remnants of Dutch in all other colonies are definitely less than impressive.

If we want to understand the reasons for this, the example of *Oost-Indië* (the East Indies), as present-day Indonesia used to be called, is very revealing, the more so since it is obviously the largest Dutch colony and the one where their stay and tenure was the longest.

From the beginning to the end we see how the Dutch, be it the VOC leaders or the government, were torn between two ideas. On one hand they felt that (part of) the indigenous population could be bound to the motherland by means of the Dutch language. On the other hand, knowledge of Dutch by the bulk of the population or by the "heathens" was considered a threat to the state. Even in times when the former consideration was preponderant, it has never ever been the aim to encourage competence in Dutch for the masses.

Occasionally we see how knowledge of Dutch could bring certain privileges: in 1641 Governor-General Van Diemen ordained that only slaves with a fair command of Dutch could wear a hat. Without a hat they could never be manumitted. Native women were allowed to marry a European man only if they could communicate in Dutch. Whatever that accomplished, it certainly did not contribute very much to Dutchify the colony or to change the

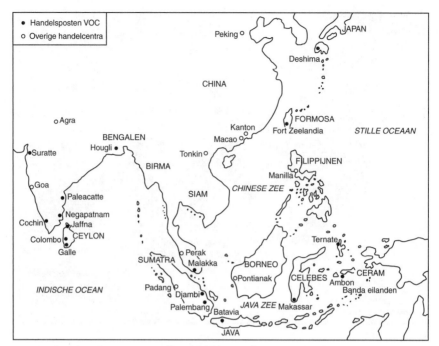

FIGURE 7.4 VOC Trade posts Legend: "Handelposten VOC" = VOC Trade posts; "Overige handelscentra" = other trade posts"

conclusion that, as far as the VOC time is concerned, the language policy aiming at strengthening the position of Dutch was a failure, even with the European population. By the end of the 18th century Dutch had all but died out in the East Indies, and both Portuguese and Malay turned out to be the winners.

These two languages were even used by the Dutch colonists themselves in certain communicative situations. The strongest rival of Dutch in the initial days was Portuguese, which, larded with many Malay words, had become the lingua franca of East Africa and from Madagascar to the Philippines before the Dutch even set foot in the East Indies. The VOC itself used this language to communicate with the Eurasians of mixed Portuguese and Asian descent, most of whom were Christians. In many households in Batavia, the capital of the East Indies, Portuguese was the home language, since it was the tongue of the slaves who brought up the children. Even in the churches of Batavia Portuguese was used, alongside Dutch and Malay.

After the Napoleonic wars, the Netherlands took repossession of their colony, which had been ruled by the British in the meantime. In the course of the 19th century, mainstream ideas on education and instruction changed drastically, even in Holland and even with the colonial authorities in the East Indies. Education for all was the new common ideal, and that was what made the authorities announce in 1818 that schools for the natives would now be created. As in Suriname we recognize here as well the hand of King William I. However, this was easier said than done, since neither money nor qualified personnel were available. We can judge how scarce personnel was by the fact that the 12 million inhabitants of Java were governed by only 175 Dutch civil servants. Since the first aim of language political endeavors remained to strengthen the position of Dutch within the group of Europeans, the only schools effectively created were for them, which led to a slightly broader diffusion of Dutch amid the European community in Indonesia. Even so, it took more than 50 years to see the tide turning, since it took that long for the new European educational system to reach its full effect. In 1870 no more than 20–30 percent of the Europeans spoke Dutch; by the turn of the century that number had increased to a mere 40 percent. Apart from the improved quality of education, the main factor securing this "success" was the faster means of communication and transportation, bringing a larger number of "fresh" Netherlanders to the East.

A negative factor undoubtedly was that the Dutch still were not convinced among themselves on which aims to pursue and—most importantly—how (or whether) to finance the Dutchification process. Shortly after the middle of the 19th century, there was a fierce debate in the motherland not so much on how but more on whether the Dutch language was also to be propagated among the indigenous population. As opposed to the language policy of the British in British India, the Dutch authorities were not in favor of a pronounced Western orientation in education. It was felt that "an uncontrolled spread of Western knowledge by means of a European language would only endanger the existence of the colony" (Groeneboer 1998, 297). In 1865 5 different indigenous languages were used as a medium of instruction; in 1900 there were 13; and by 1940 no less than 30 indigenous languages were used for that purpose. A more convincing example of linguistic *divide et impera* carried to the extreme is probably nowhere to be found. The bonus for linguists was that the indigenous languages were investigated thoroughly to be able to put dictionaries, grammars, and other schoolbooks at the disposal of the students.

Some of the arguments put forward by those opposing the introduction of Dutch in schools for the indigenous population were as follows:

- Dutch might degenerate to the point that some kind of
  Indisch-Nederlandsch (Indo-Dutch) could function as a
  lingua franca, something that had to be prevented by all means.

- It would turn the natives *hoogmoedig* (arrogant), causing a lot of problems for the administration.
- It was a known fact that proficiency in Dutch was very hard to acquire *speciaal voor den oosterling* (especially for the Oriental).

Consequently, in 1864 the idea of supporting Dutch as the general medium of communication and of replacing Malay with Dutch as the lingua franca was abandoned for good. Still, it was simultaneously felt that promoting the proficiency of Dutch in a small indigenous elite could be advantageous for the administration of the colony and might strengthen the ties with the motherland. Also, and not in the least, it was hoped that in the long-term it would be cheaper to employ indigenous speakers of Dutch in a multitude of functions. This opening *de Poort tot het Westen* (the gateway to the West), as it was called, resulted among other things in a change of the educational system.

Rather abruptly, Holland had become aware that it had a debt of honor to redeem vis-à-vis its Asian subjects. The native was suddenly turning into a younger brother whom should be denied nothing of what had made Holland (the older brother) prosperous. From then on, Dutch was introduced as the language of instruction in all schools where native teachers and civil servants were trained. Moreover, schools that were supposed to be on par with the European schools were put at the disposal of native East Indians and Chinese. On top of that, a system of vocational schools was developed. Generosity on the part of the Dutch certainly wasn't the only and probably not even the main reason for this change in policy. It may have occurred to them that training and employing a certain amount of indigenous civil servants, teachers, lawyers, and physicians would help to keep a lid on the cost of the colonial administration. But even so, the estimated number of indigenous speakers of Dutch in 1900 was no more than 5000, plus some 600 Chinese. Therefore, in 1907 the Hollandsch-Indische School (HIS; Dutch–Indian school) was introduced, followed in 1908 by the Hollandsch-Chinese School (HCS; Dutch–Chinese School). In both systems Dutch was the language of instruction. They were meant exclusively for a small native elite. Since a much larger number of them were eager to learn Dutch and to embrace the civilization of their colonial masters, it is only fair to admit that the poor results of the language policy just mentioned are to be attributed in the first place to the unwillingness of many Dutch officials, both in the East and in the motherland.

After WWI the demand for Dutch language education from the indigenous side grew more pressing still. Debates among educational specialists, Dutch and East Indians alike, gave way to a consensus that Dutch should be the language of instruction and that the indigenous languages should be developed to better function as language of instruction as well. Still, the government not only considered it practically and financially impossible to meet the demands for more Dutch language education but also continued to believe it "unwise" to do so. In

1931, the governmental Hollandsch-Indische Onderwijs-Commissie (Dutch–Indian Education Committee) recommended—contrary to all the wishes expressed by the indigenous people—to refrain from any further expansion of the HIS system. At the same time drastic cutbacks in educational cost were carried through. The spread of HIS and HCS schools was stopped completely, and the number of enrolled students remained at the level of some 60,000 for the whole country. Consequently, the so-called wild schools (a form of private instruction) that had started in the 1920s became more numerous and popular still, and the explosive increase, as Groeneboer (1998) calls it, of Dutch learners in the 1930s is mainly attributed to wild education. Although in 1942 the number of indigenous Dutch speakers had increased to 860,000, a number considerably larger than the amount of Indonesia's European Dutch speakers, it still represented a mere 1.2 percent of the Indonesian population.

On the eve of WWII the government yet again devised a new language educational policy in that both Dutch and Malay were to be added to school curricula on a larger scale than before, but it never had a chance to prove itself. The Japanese occupation in 1942 brought a ban on the Dutch language, and after the war there was hardly any time left.

Still, for decades to come the new leaders of the independent Republic of Indonesia were fluent in Dutch. In 1965 President Sukarno notes in his memoirs, "Dutch is the language in which I do my thinking and even nowadays, when I am cursing, I am cursing in Dutch. When I pray to God, I pray in Dutch" (Sukarno 1965, 81–82).

The fact that this proficiency in Dutch of the Indonesian leading politicians was not matched by their subjects can only be blamed on the reluctance of the Dutch, both in VOC times and afterward, to make it possible for them to learn a language that many of them craved to acquire, since it was the only possibility to improve their socioeconomic position. By 1940 not even 2 percent of the indigenous population had acquired fluency in Dutch because of the failing language policy of the Dutch, often characterized as a *kruidenierspolitiek* (narrow-minded policy), which, as Salverda (1989) observes, has always been too little, too late.

In 1928, the Indonesian nationalist movement proclaimed Malay to be the only standard language of the East Indies and subsequently (by the name of Bahasa Indonesia) of the independent Republic of Indonesia. The simple explanation for that is that Malay was indeed the only working lingua franca for the whole Indonesian Archipelago, a role Dutch could never claim or acquire because the Dutch authorities made sure that it could never function as such. Yet an important way Bahasa Indonesia differs from Malay as spoken in Singapore, Malaysia, and Brunei is the enormous amount of Dutch loanwords it contains (Van der Sijs & Willemyns 2009, 111–113). On December 27, 1949, sovereignty was transferred to the Indonesians, and almost immediately Dutch was banned from both the administration and the educational system.

Nevertheless, even as of today, being able to read Dutch is indispensable in scientific research in the fields of history, anthropology, sociology, linguistics, agriculture, and many others, since most of the necessary sources are in Dutch. But most important, the jurists and lawyers need a thorough competence in Dutch. Even when, after some time, all the legal codes have been translated in Indonesian (which will not be achieved for a very long time), they will need Dutch to consult the jurisprudence. Consequently, Dutch is still taught in present-day Indonesia, and specific courses in Dutch are offered for the tens of thousands of students who need to know the language (Sunjayadi, Suprihatin, & Groeneboer 2011).

A Cookie from Santa Claus: Dutch in the United States

As opposed to the cases discussed so far, the United States[5] is a country where Dutch has been the official language only for a short period and only in a small part of this huge land. Yet there is reason enough to have a closer look into it and try to determine exactly what has been the impression made on American society by Hollanders and Flemings.

In September 1609 the Dutch language sailed into North America aboard *De Halve Maen,* steered by the English captain Henry Hudson. In 1614 the land was claimed for the Dutch by Adriaen Block. He called it Nieuw-Nederland (New Netherland). In 1624, the Dutch officially acknowledged their colony, and Nieuw-Nederland became a Dutch province with Dutch as its official language. In 1625, the Dutch settled in Manhattan, which would become their capital. They called it Nieuw Amsterdam (New Amsterdam).

This was the first wave of Dutch speakers to arrive in the United States. The second wave arrived well into the 18th and 19th centuries. As opposed to the first wavers, who were mostly traders, the latter ones emigrated from the motherland for economic as well as religious reasons. Both their form of settlement and their linguistic and cultural impact were completely different, as were the conditions of the land they settled in.

THE PIONEERS

In 1626 Nieuw-Nederland's governor, Peter Minuit, bought the island Manhattan from the local Indians, in exchange for goods valued at 60 guilders. "*Hebben t'Eylant Manhattes van de wilde gekoght voor de waerde van 60 gulden, is groot* 11,000 *morgens*" (Have bought the island Manhattes from the natives at

---

[5] An important source in this account of the linguistic situation in the United States has been Van der Sijs (2009), supplemented by other sources.

the value of 60 guilders; is 11,000 morgens [a morgen is about 2 acres] large), he reported to the Staten Generaal back in Den Haag.

Although the Dutch colony was not long-lived, it left an impressive mark on American society. In spite of occasional quarrels with *de wilden,* as they called the Native Americans, the Dutch had much more to fear from other European powers in North America. In 1664, the English sailed into New Amsterdam, and Governor Peter Stuyvesant had to surrender the province to them. This was one of the causes of the Second English–Dutch War. During the peace negotiations in 1667, it was agreed that the English and the Dutch could keep the American colonies they had taken from each other. This meant that the Netherlands could keep Suriname and surrounding territories in South America and that the British could continue their dominion of Nieuw Nederland. Apparently, the shareholders of the West Indian Company welcomed this situation in view of the profits they expected the slave trade in Suriname to bring.

The English renamed Nieuw Amsterdam as New York, and the rest is history.

The period of Dutch supremacy of the American East Coast lasted from 1624 to 1664. During that time it was a province of the Netherlands, and Dutch was its official language.

Varieties of Dutch in the United States

New Netherland was a huge territory, comprising most of the present-day states of Connecticut, New York, New Jersey, Pennsylvania, and Delaware. It was many times larger than Holland and Belgium together. As in other former Dutch colonies, a large number of other Europeans were already there or followed in the wake of the Dutch. In the province at large, the Dutch and the Dutch language constituted a large minority, yet in New Amsterdam proper they were a significant majority. Most of the new colonists came from North Holland and Utrecht, which colored the variant of Dutch as it developed in the new world. It acquired the name of Leeg Duits (Low Dutch).

Leeg Duits, the foundations of which, according to Buccini (1995), were laid between 1640 and 1690, was not the only variant of Dutch used by the settlers and their offspring. Another one was the language of the church, the rather formal and archaic official Dutch (Nederduits) as it was written down in the *Statenbijbel* and other significant worship texts. Jersey and Mohawk Dutch were another important variety still, and the lesser-known Negro Dutch closes the list.

There is no doubt that Leeg Duits was the variety through which Dutch made its long-lasting impression on the American English language. It was the language used in New York, even a long time after it was taken over by the British. Most of the originally non-Dutch-speaking European colonists learned the language and eventually took it over (Bachman 1982, 1983).

The presence of the English and the pressure they exerted to replace Dutch with their language was an important reason many of the Dutch settlers decided

to leave Manhattan and Lange Eylandt (Long Island). They found new territories in Albany and New Jersey. What George Washington called the Dutch
Belt reached from the north along the Hudson through New York to the Raritan
River in the south in New Jersey. Homogeneous communities developed here
and stuck to their Dutch language, to their church, and to Dutch traditions and
customs. In the second half of the 18th century, the Dutch inhabitants of big
cities like Albany and Kingston formed a large majority, and they controlled
the local administration. And new Dutch speakers kept arriving as well.

In addition to the Low Dutch spoken language, the Nederduits of the
Nederduits Reformed Church, an archaic, highly formal language, was used in
the churches and taught in the Dutch schools, since all the preachers (Dutch:
dominees) came from the Netherlands or had received their training there. The
fact that the Dutch language and the Church remained so closely linked
together for more than a century supported the preservation of Dutch in the
United States for a long time. On the other hand, as the discrepancy between
the Dutch used in the church and the language spoken by the people grew
larger and larger, the clerical Nederduits was no longer in a position to continue this preserving function. Most of the time its role was taken over by
English right away.

The other varieties of settler's Dutch include what has been called Jersey
Dutch and Mohawk Dutch (box 7.2). They are the descendants of Low Dutch
transported to other locations, namely, two regions that had no contact with
each other: Bergen and Passaic County in North New Jersey; and the Mohawk

BOX 7.2 } An Example of Jersey Dutch

En kääd'l had twî jongers; de êne blêv täus;
de andere xong vôrt f'n häus f'r en stat.
Hai waz nît tevrêde täus en dârkîs tû râkni arm.
Hai dogti ôm dat täus en z'n vâders pläk.
Tû zaide: äk zal na häus xâne. Main vâder hät plänti.
In standard modern Dutch:
Een man had twee jongens; de ene bleef thuis;
de andere ging voort van huis voor een vermogen.
Hij was niet tevreden thuis en hij werd daardoor arm.
Hij dacht aan thuis en zijn vaders plaats.
Toen zei hij: ik zal naar huis gaan. Mijn vader heeft voldoende.
In English:
A man had two sons. The one stayed at home;
the other went abroad from home to make his fortune.
He was not content at home and therefore then he became poor.
He thought about home and his father's place.
Then said: I shall go home. My father has plenty.
Source: Prince (1910)

Valley, west of Albany in upstate New York. Dutch was spoken there until well into the 20th century. The last native speakers may have been born between 1860 and 1880, and up until the 1960s there were a few elderly people who still managed to speak the language.

According to the wife of the Dutch ambassador in New York, in a letter dated 1866, "one in ten people will understand you when you speak Dutch to them," although they do not exactly speak "our civilized Dutch," she added, but rather a farmer's dialect (Van der Sijs 2009, 37). A Dutch preacher who visited New Jersey in the 1820s had already described the Dutch language spoken there as *"zeer slecht, lomp en plat, en met vele verkeerde uitdrukkingen besmet"* (very bad, uncouth, and coarse and infested with many wrong expressions) (ibid.). To speak in denigrating terms of other varieties of Dutch than their own is typical for Hollanders, an unpleasant habit many continue to exhibit up to the present day.

The American linguist J. D. Prince (1910), who wrote an essay on New Jersey Dutch, reported that there is a small colony of old negroes living on the mountain back of Suffern, N.Y. [the Ramapo Mountains] who still use their own dialect of Jersey Dutch. A white informant of his called this variety Negro Dutch, and apart from the fact that it has existed and used to be spoken by black people, many of whom had a Dutch name like De Freese (De Vries) or De Groat (De Groot), hardly anything specific is known about this particular variety of the language.

A very interesting aspect of all varieties of New Netherland Dutch is, as Buccini (1996, 37) remarks, that it is "the dialect of the only major colonial settlement of Dutch-speakers outside of Southern Africa" and it is amazing, he adds, that "the dialect has received remarkably little attention" (ibid.)

Loss of Function and Territory

After the transfer of power to the British, the position of Dutch in official matters was taken over by English. There were exceptions, though: on Long Island, municipal archives were kept up in Dutch until the American War of Independence in 1776. Regardless, the impact of the language, culture, and costumes of the first settlers on the American East Coast was there to stay for a long time. In the last quarter of the 18th century, the number of Dutch speakers was probably at its peak. According to some calculations it is estimated that in the states of New York and New Jersey, about 100,000 people spoke Dutch in 1790.

At the time of the American Revolution, probably a third of the population of New York could still speak Dutch. On top of that, the social prestige of Dutch and Dutchness equaled and sometimes even exceeded the number of its speakers. Gradually, the Dutch inhabitants of New York joined the other Americans to build the new nation, disregarding their private interests and their own language and culture.

In rural areas outside New York City, on the other hand, Dutch lasted longer still, but as a result of fundamental social changes an increasing number of people exchanged Dutch for English in the course of the 19th century. The compulsory education law, introduced in 1910, proved to be the fatal blow to the last vestiges of rural Dutch.

As to the question what remains of 17th-century Dutch, Van Hinte (1985, 73) estimates that in the early 20th century about two million Americans were descended from the original Dutch colonists. This is a lot, in view of the fact that there were no more than 10,000 colonists in New Netherland when the English took over in 1664, and of those probably only 6,000 came from the Low Countries. Three American presidents were of Dutch descent: Martin van Buren, Theodore Roosevelt, and Franklin D. Roosevelt. Martin van Buren's mother tongue was Dutch, and his command of English was reported to be rather deficient. From 1837 through 1841, he was the eighth president of the United States.

The Dutch colonists formed the aristocracy of New York for a long time, and the Dutch families maintained all kinds of Dutch customs even after they had given up the Dutch language. The most visible remnants of Dutch in New York are the toponyms. A number of street names in the city of New York remind us of the presence of Dutch settlers. Some street names deriving from Dutch are, for example, Bowery Lane (Dutch: *boerderij*), Broadway (Dutch: *Breede Weg*), and Wall Street (Dutch: *Walstraat*; this was where the wall was built that protected the city against attacks from Englishmen and Native Americans). New York's Bronx as well as the suburb Yonkers are Dutch names. Others had been named by the colonists after a town or village in the Low Countries, for instance, Brooklyn (named after *Breukelen*), Flushing (named after *Vlissingen*), Gravesend (probably named after *Gravensande*), Harlem (named after *Haarlem*), and New Utrecht (named after *Utrecht*). Coney Island (after Dutch *Conyne Eylandt*, or rabbits' island), Long Island (translation of *Lange Eylandt*), and Staten Island (*Staaten Eylandt*, so called in honor of the Dutch Staten Generaal) were originally named by the Dutch.

A HEALTHY AND FRUGAL RACE: THE SECOND-WAVE IMMIGRANTS

"Our Streets Have Been Taken by the Dutch": Emigrants in the 19th and 20th Centuries

In the second half of the 19th century, colonists from the Netherlands and Belgium went en masse to America (United States and Canada). Not only did they arrive in a completely different country than the first wavers had, but also their own background was very different. Many of them came because poverty and famine had driven them out of Europe (as was the case with innumerable people from other European countries). A large part of the Hollanders, though, were religiously motivated. Since the 17th century, Dutch Calvinists have displayed a tendency to split up in numerous different churches and sects, and almost every secession entailed another one. In spite of Holland's reputation for tolerance, they did not seem very inclined to apply that to their co-religionists who differed in what, to outsiders, looks like insignificant details. Secessionists (*Afgescheidenen* in Dutch), came to the new world beginning in 1845 and were, in the best Dutch tradition, religious fundamentalists very much convinced that only they were right and always trying to be purer in the faith than other religious fundamentalists.

In 1845, a first group of secessionists left for Illinois. The largest groups, though, came, together with members of the Reformed Church, to Michigan and Iowa. There, Holland became their main settlement, surrounded by smaller daughter settlements with names like Graafschap, Overisel, Drenthe, Zeeland, and Groningen. Another group of secessionists founded the well-known town of Pella in Iowa. Their arrival didn't pass unnoticed, as illustrated in a Grand Rapids newspaper in 1849: "During the past week our streets have been taken by the Dutch. The Hollanders have resorted here in uncommon numbers and their ox teams have made quite a caravan.... They are a very stout, apparently healthy and frugal race" (Van der Sijs 2009, 61).

At about the same time, groups of Roman Catholic Flemings settled in a number of places, including Moline and Chicago (Illinois), Kansas City and St. Louis (Missouri), South Bend (Indiana), Detroit and Rochester (Michigan), Paterson (New Jersey), and Victor (Iowa). Toward the end of the 19th century, a group of Frisians came to Whitinsville in Massachusetts, where Frisian was spoken until after World War II. The group of Dutchmen and Flemings who, after World War II, came to North America trying to secure a better future for themselves primarily went to California and Washington State. Although over the years their amount totaled some 130,000, they hardly played a role as far as the presence of the Dutch language in the United States is concerned.

Language Loyalty and Language Loss

Historians have calculated that, of the 60,000 to 70,000 Dutch immigrants who had arrived in their new country in 1870, more than 90 percent lived in only 18 counties in seven states. In Pella, nearly two of every three migrants came from an area measuring only 60 by 90 kilometers, where closely related dialects were originally spoken (Webber 1988; Smits 1996). Apparently it was rather uncharacteristic for groups of immigrants to have settled so closely together. The reason the Dutch immigrants chose to live near each other has to be sought in their religious convictions. As other groups of religious fundamentalists had demonstrated before, this was the surest way to preserve, at the same time, their faith and their Dutch character.

Yet, in spite of their tendency to stick together, the new immigrants were forced to adapt more quickly than the Old Dutch branch. In their new homeland, English was by now the general daily language as well as the language of official documents and the schools. Among themselves, though, they managed to fully preserve the language, and thus, after 150 years, Dutch was still spoken to a limited degree by descendants of the original colonists. The fact that Dutch, for a very long time, remained the language of the pulpit in the Calvinist churches helped a lot as well.

After the foundation of Dutch settlements in the 1840s, the first three generations of children that were born there had a Dutch dialect as their mother tongue. However, it was inevitable that, gradually, Dutch would decline in domains, functions, and numbers. Dutch first lost ground in the schools, a change that started almost immediately upon arrival in the United States. Even the new immigrant churches slowly but surely became anglicized since the competence in Dutch with the youngsters was diminishing by the year.

Only the Christian Reformed Church, an orthodox secession of the Reformed Church, postponed worship in English until 1887. This Midwestern church, based mainly in Michigan, also persisted in using Dutch in education since, contrary to the Reformed Church, they opposed public schools. Calvin College in Grand Rapids was founded by members of the Christian Reformed Church. In this college, where since the end of the 19th century innumerable Calvinist *dominees* (preachers) were trained, Dutch remained a required course until the 1960s.

While the Protestants were pondering the question as to which language to use in their services, this was not much of a problem for the Roman Catholics. The language of the liturgy was Latin until 1962, which led the Catholics to abandon Dutch as a church language very quickly and shift easily to English. Moreover, the Dutch and Flemish Roman Catholics in the United States lived scattered all over the country and had no problem adhering to congregations of other Catholic nations, such as the Irish or the Poles.

From the beginning, the press played an important part in immigrant life and, consequently, this was a domain where Dutch survived a long time. The first newspaper, the *Sheboygan Nieuwsbode*, appeared as early as 1849, and the large numbers of Dutch papers and magazines published in the United States show that there was a large enough market for them. When the First World War started, 25 Dutch-language papers and periodicals still existed. During that war, the U.S. administration discouraged the use of foreign languages. By the 1930s and 1940s, the amount and the circulation were reduced drastically.

Although a commercially self-supporting Dutch language press has not survived up till the present day, some titles have, although the number of Dutch articles they contain is mostly considerably lower than those written in English. Often they can survive only because they are financed by the governments of Holland or Flanders. The *Gazette van Detroit* (founded in 1914), which used to be the news medium of the Flemish auto industry workers in Michigan, is now a bilingual paper. In the beginning it appeared as a daily newspaper and later became biweekly. The current subtitle reads, "The only Belgian newspaper

serving the Belgian communities around the world." In 2006, thanks to a dona-
tion by the Flemish Government and a large-scale publicity campaign, the
Gazette van Detroit ensured the continuation of its operations (http://www.
gazettevandetroit.com).

As mentioned already, the last stronghold of Dutch was the home and the
family. It took the First World War for most Dutch and Flemish immigrants
and their children to once and for all switch to English at home. Public opinion
was against the use of a foreign language, especially German, and many
Americans lumped Dutch and German together. The Dutch and the Flemings
did not want to be associated with the enemy and gave in to social pressure by
abandoning Dutch as their home language. Before the start of the Second
World War, all Dutchmen and Flemings were securely entrenched in American
society. Nevertheless, pockets of speakers of Yankee Dutch subsided scattered
all over the immigrant region. Pella Dutch can still be heard today, though the
number of speakers is steadily decreasing.

Joshua Fishman (1966), in "Language Loyalty in the United States," reports
that in 1940 nearly 290,000 Americans claimed to have Dutch as their mother
tongue, and in 1960 this number had risen to 322,000 thanks to a new wave of
immigrants. Of these, 124,000 were first-generation speakers of Dutch, and the
same number were second-generation speakers—they had learned Dutch from
their parents in America. Some 74,000 claimed they were third-generation
speakers of Dutch.

According to the U.S. Census from 2000, only 150,000 people stated that
they spoke Dutch at home. Five years later, in 2005, this number had decreased
to around 130,000, a very low number, especially if compared to the 5 million
Americans who claim Dutch ancestry. From the census, moreover, it seems that
most Dutch speakers reside in California (over 27,000, yet only .07 percent of
the population), Pennsylvania (the so-called Pennsylvania Dutch is, in spite of
its name, a variety of German not Dutch), Florida, New York, and Ohio (with
a good 10,000 each). Dutch is also spoken, albeit to a lesser extent, in (listed in
decreasing order of speakers) Michigan, Indiana, Texas, New Jersey, Washington,
Illinois, and Wisconsin.

The interest in everything Dutch and Flemish diminished in the United
States after 1920. Dutch and Flemish immigrants became invisible in American
society, and the number of loanwords the Americans borrowed from the 19th-
and 20th-century immigrants was relatively limited.

CONCLUSION

In spite of everything, the contributions of the Dutch language to American
English over the past four centuries are substantial and are explained in
detail in Van der Sijs's (2009) book *Cookies, Coleslaw and Stoops,* mentioning
three of the important borrowings from Dutch. Although only 246 Dutch

loanwords are attested (i.e., in American English; the approximately 500 Dutch loanwords that used to be part of the British variety of English long before that are not counted here), the Dutch language has left its ineradicable mark on everyday American life, the more so since the Dutch formed a very small minority among the inhabitants of America; even in New Netherland there were many other Europeans, making it a multinational and multilingual province. According to the American linguist Charlton Laird (1972), "More words per capita have been borrowed into American English from [the] early Hollanders than from any other sort of non-English speakers. (quoted in Van der Sijs 2009, 14)". Among them are high-frequency words as *Yankee, dollar*, and *boss*. In Van der Sijs (2009) all 246 of them are discussed in detail.

Other

OCEANIA

After the independence of Indonesia, Western New Guinea remained a Dutch colony until 1962, known as Netherlands New Guinea. Despite prolonged Dutch presence, the Dutch language is not spoken by many Papuans because it was donated to Indonesia in 1963.

Immigrant communities can be found in Australia and New Zealand. The 2006 Australian census showed 36,179 people speaking Dutch at home. According to the 2006 census in New Zealand, 16,347 people claim sufficient fluency in Dutch to hold an everyday conversation.

AFRICA

Belgium held a colonial empire from1885 to 1960, consisting of the Belgian Congo and the protectorates Ruanda and Urundi. From 1885 through 1908 the Congo was a "personal possession" of the Belgian King Leopold II. From 1908 to 1960, it was a Belgian colony. Contrary to Belgium, the colonies had no official language policy although, in principle, Belgian legislation—including the language regulations—was applicable to the colonies as well. In spite of the fact that a majority of Belgians living in the colonies spoke Dutch, French was de facto the sole language used in administration, jurisdiction, and secondary education. For the children of the Belgian colonists both French- and Dutch-language education was provided, and in the course of the 1950s a bilingual (French and Dutch) university was founded in Elisabethstad (today's Lumumbashi).

The colonial authorities regularly used Lingala, Kongo, Swahili, and Tshiluba in communication with the local population and in education. Kirundi was used in Ruanda-Urundi. Knowledge of French—or, to an even lesser extent, Dutch—was hardly passed on to the "natives," of whom only a small number were taught French to work in local public services. After independence in 1960, French would become an official language of the Congo, Rwanda, and Burundi. Of these, Congo is the most francophone country. Knowledge of Dutch in former Belgian Africa is virtually nonexistent.

ASIA

Ceylon (Sri Lanka)

The presence of the VOC on Ceylon (now Sri Lanka) from 1656 through 1796 has left some traces in the vocabulary of Singhalese, the majority language on the island. They were imported in the language through the Burghers—Dutch, Portuguese, and Eurasian colonists and their often mixed-blood descendants. Even during the period of British rule, after 1796, the Burghers continued to enjoy a privileged position in society, although they were not on equal footing with the white British. Most of them had jobs as lower civil servants. After Sri Lanka's independence, though, they were treated disparagingly by both the Singhalese and the Tamils.

The Dutch loanwords in Singhalese date from the pre-British period, that is, before English became the island's official language. Even during the 17th and 18th centuries—during the Dutch VOC times—Dutch was used only by the government and the church, the Nederduitsch Gereformeerde Kerk. In less formal circumstances, Portuguese was, as in so many other Dutch possessions, the usual means of communication, also for the Dutch officials.

A few examples of the few hundred Dutch loanwords in Singhalese are *kalabere* (Dutch *klaveren* in a game of carts; clubs), *kerekoppu* (Dutch *kerkhof*; cemetery), *tarappe* (Dutch *trap;* stairs), *lakke* (Dutch *laken*; sheets), and *sukiri* (Dutch *suiker,* sugar).

Formosa (Taiwan)

The Dutch colonial government on Formosa (now Taiwan) lasted from 1624 to 1662. In the context of the Age of Discovery the Dutch East India Company (VOC) established its presence on Taiwan to trade with China and Japan and also to obstruct Portuguese and Spanish trade and colonial activities in East Asia.

Although in this particular case the Dutch were not confronted with a European rival language or pidgin, their period of rule was too short to exert any kind of lasting influence. The colonial period was brought to an end by the invasion of a rebel army after only 37 years.

Japan

In 1609 the VOC established a trade post on the Japanese island Hirado. In 1641 it was transferred to the artificial island Deshima in the bay of Nagasaki.

This small island, measuring 120 by 75 meters, for two centuries has been Japan's window on the outside world, and it was populated exclusively by Dutchmen. The reason is simple: Japan had ousted the Portuguese and the Spaniards, a ban that lasted until 1854. Following the device "my enemy's enemies are my friends," the Dutch were the only foreigners admitted and in so doing got a trade monopoly with Japan. The amount of Dutch VOC people admitted on Deshima never exceeded 10 at the same time, and 1 or 2 of them were always physicians.

They transmitted Dutch books—and hence Dutch loanwords—in the fields of medicine, astronomy, physical science, geography, and military strategy to the Japanese, along with lancets, globes, telescopes, quadrants, maps, and other scientific objects. Since all they knew from the West came through the Dutch, western science and technology were referred to in Japanese as *rangaku*, which literally means "knowledge of the Netherlands."

After the Dutch left, almost no more Dutch loanwords passed into Japanese. Nagasaki continues to have a Dutch open-air museum where the canals and step roofs are reproduced to scale. Some examples of Dutch loanwords in Japanese are *biiru* (Dutch *bier;* beer), *bisuketto* (Dutch *beschuit*; biscuit), *buriki* (Dutch *blik*; can), *mesu* (Dutch *mes*; knife), *koroku* (Dutch *kurk;* cork), and *tarappu* (Dutch *trap*; stairs).

In Hindsight

In 1939 the French professor G. H. Bousquet expressed his astonishment for what he called "the bewildering apathy of the Dutch as far as their own language and culture are concerned. Dutch colonial policy" he says, "has never for a moment considered that the Dutch language could play a part in the culture and civilization to be given to the native. On the contrary, by opposing him with a language intended to mark the distance which sets him apart from the European, the Dutch have striven and still strive, though vainly, to deprive their ward of contact with the outside world" (Bousquet 1940, 89).

All who study the colonial language policy of the Dutch share Bousquet's bewilderment. Our perplexity only increases if we add to this the following pertinent observation, made by Kees Groeneboer (1998, 2), the specialist as far as language policy in Asia is concerned: "Of all the colonial European languages in Asia (Portuguese, Spanish, Dutch, English and French) four now belong to the group of twelve great supranational languages of the world. Dutch colonial language policy helped to boost not Dutch but Malay into that group."

To try to explain, two aspects have to be taken into account:

a) Why did Dutch fare differently from the others?
b) Did they ever want their language to play a role on the world scene?

Dutch is not part of the previously mentioned world languages for various reasons, all of which relate to Indonesia:

- The (language) policy of the VOC and, subsequently, the Dutch government was marked above all by pragmatism, which hindered rather than promoted the spread of Dutch.
- When the Dutch set foot on Indonesian soil, other languages of culture as well as a Portuguese–Malay-colored Creole were already there, and functioned as an established lingua franca in all of the region.
- As opposed to other colonial superpowers, the Dutch thought that educating the natives, let alone letting them benefit from a mastery of their language, would make them arrogant and threaten the power of their masters.
- In the best of cases, the language policy devised by the authorities both in the Dutch East Indies and in the motherland from 1596 onward until the transfer of sovereignty in 1949 has been half-hearted, but most of the time it was counterproductive to the dissemination of the Dutch language and culture in Asia.
- The country's dimensions were gigantic, and only an infinitesimal small number of civil servants ever sent to the East Indies.
- The avarice and greed of the Dutch who didn't really want to invest in a policy of language and culture.

Even with all of this, the question remains as to how other colonial powers in Asia, mainly the British and the French, succeeded in generating a completely different outcome:

- Both the French and the English were convinced that it was in their proper interest to impose their own language and culture on their new subjects.
- In British India the outcome of extensive discussions during the 1830s about how much Western-style education to establish with English as the language of instruction was the decision to introduce extensive English language education. This policy underwent no substantial changes up to independency in 1947. It was directed mainly at the urbanized upper classes.
- The French, for their part, were convinced that the teaching of French was *une mission civilisatrice,* which would simultaneously strengthen the political role of France in the world. By spreading French over the whole of Indochina, they also had the intention of eventually realizing their ideal of a *France asiatique.*
- Compared with the Dutch, proportionally two or three times as much money was spent on education in British India and French Indochina.

The Dutch, moreover, spent the most attention (and money) on codifying and modernizing the indigenous languages.

In conclusion, the following may be summarized:

- In all Asian colonies the Western powers attempted first of all to assimilate a small elite and to train a middle class. Only the Netherlands decided not to introduce Dutch generally into the Dutch East Indies, a language policy that underwent no significant change up to the independence of Indonesia.
- Everywhere this resulted in the creation of a social elite educated in a European language. In Indonesia this group remained smaller than anywhere else.
- The Dutch linguistic policy was a *divide et impera* policy, aimed at preserving the structures of colonial society.

Much of this theoretically also applied to the Dutch colonies in the West Indies. The main difference, though, was that in the West the relatively large numbers of Creoles (compared with Asia) and the relatively smaller population sizes made the colonial language the obvious choice for the national language. Even so, it was more thanks to the determination of the Creoles than of the Dutch, that today Dutch is the official as well as the habitual language of Suriname.

8 }

Afrikaans

History

EAST INDIA COMPANY PERIOD

When in the year 1652 Jan van Riebeeck officially took possession of the Cape of Good Hope on behalf of the *Vereenigde Oost-Indische Compagnie* (East India Company; VOC), the foundations were laid for what was to become "the only language of Germanic origin which is spoken exclusively outside Europe" (Brachin 1985, 129) and the only still extant daughter language of Dutch (fig. 8-1).

Van Riebeeck's mission was merely to create a self-sufficient refreshment station with a small number of rotating company employees. The relations with the surrounding Hottentots (as they were then called) were to be restricted to trading, and there was no question of directly submitting them to VOC rule. The evolution into a permanent settlement started in 1657 when the European presence became more expansive and Van Riebeeck discharged a small number of company servants who were to become the Cape's first free burghers and full-time agriculturalists at the service of the company. According to Stell (2008, 5) a distinct class of free blacks (*vrijezwarten*) was simultaneously starting to take shape. Slavery was formally introduced in 1658, a slave trade route was opened, and slaves from other parts of Africa and from Asia were brought in. In this way, what was originally nicknamed a "Vitamin C post," eventually evolved into a complex colonial society whose demographic and linguistic features made it stand out as unique among all VOC possessions (ibid.).

Jargonized forms of Dutch emerged among the indigenous Khoikhoi (formally Hottentots; Raper 2011) and served as their medium of communication with the Europeans (Roberge 2003, 17). The slaves, who came from many geographical and cultural origins, constituted the most diverse population of any recorded slave society. And since there is always a need for communication

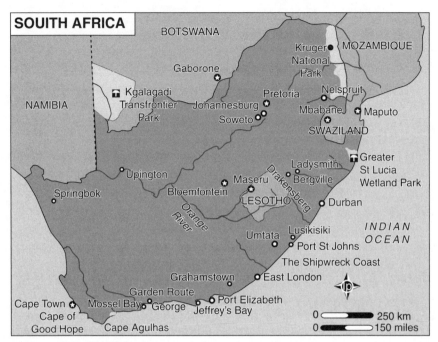

FIGURE 8.1 Map of South Africa

between the various segments of a polyglot society, this "led to the creation of a stable Cape Dutch Pidgin within the Afro-Asian substratum between 1658 and 1711 (the year in which the slave population surpassed the slave-owning European population)" (ibid.).

As in many VOC possessions, the Dutch were not the only, and very often not even the majority, group. The proportions of the main groups in the free-burgher male population over the period 1657–1707 were approximately as follows: 44 percent from Holland; 36 percent from Germany; 7 percent from the southern Netherlands; and 12 percent from France. The latter were mainly Huguenot refugees who emigrated after the Revocation of the Edict of Nantes, which guaranteed protection to French Protestants until 1685. The Huguenots did not come directly from France but from the Netherlands, where they had already spent three years. The Dutch element was able to linguistically assimi-late the other European groups at the Cape despite some persistence of French and the steady arrival of Germans (Ponelis 1993, 17–26). Up to the early 18th century, Europeans were more numerous than slaves but were vastly outnum-bered by the native population. Until the British conquest of the Cape (1806), its official language was Dutch, the language of the VOC and of the Calvinist church. In this multiethnic colonial society, the Khoikhoi quickly assimilated to the European lifestyle and to Western economic values, and the ensuing process of detribalization favored the acquisition of Dutch by the Khoikhoi population. At subsequent stages, at least part of the Bantu speakers and Indians (for many

slaves arrived in the Cape from the subcontinent too) also adopted Cape Dutch as a prestige or native language (Stell 2008, 45). More details on 18th-century varieties of Dutch at the Cape are given in Ponelis (1996).

In the subsequent evolution of what was to become Afrikaans, several stages can be discerned (Ponelis 1994, 107). In the 17th century, the most prominent variety of Dutch was an urban Hollands koine, which appeared very early and in a short time was subject to profound changes due to language contact. Borrowing from other languages was important—consider high-frequency words as *nooi* (girl), *dalk* (perhaps), and *baie* (very much)—but more decisive still was the fact that Dutch was also used by nonnative speakers. The first attestations of Dutch as spoken by slaves date from as early as 1671. They had been forced to acquire Dutch very quickly and in unfavorable conditions. As a result, a process of Creolization was started. Some of its major characteristics were the loss of gender (Dutch: *de man, het huis;* Afrikaans: *die man, die huis*), subject–verb agreement (Dutch: *ik vind—wij vinden;* Afrikaans: *ek vind, ons vind*), the imperfect tense (Dutch: *ik werkte;* Afrikaans: *ek het gewerk*), and the distinction between strong and weak verbs (Dutch: *gebroken, gezeten;* Afrikaans: *gebreek, gesit*). Whether the so-called double negation such as "*die tweede tradisie is **nie** veel jonger as die eerste **nie**"* (the second tradition is not much younger than the first one) is a result of the Creolization process as well, is generally accepted, though not by all. In Van Rensburg (1996) we find an innovating overview of "Koi-influence" in Afrikaans.

In a second stage of development, we see how the Afrikaans vernacular[1] develops regional variation. There are three main dialect areas: Southwestern Afrikaans (aka Western Cape Afrikaans); Northwestern Afrikaans (aka Orange River Afrikaans); and Eastern Cape Afrikaans.

Finally, the third and fourth stages in the evolution of Afrikaans are those characterized by the influence of English (from the early 19th century) and Standaardafrikaans (from the early 20th century onward), respectively (fig. 8.2). Another and most interesting development in Afrikaans is the coming into being of a variety called *Flaaitaal* during the 1930s. *Flaaitaal* is a kind of secret, private language, used by urban blacks for whom Afrikaans is not their mother tongue and who belong to several different language communities such as Zulu, Tswana, Xhosa, and Tsonga. *Flaaitaal* obviously has no native speakers.

BRITISH CONQUEST

When the British took possession of South Africa, their first settlement was at the Cape. Eventually, their rule forced a number of originally Dutch settlers (Boers as they have traditionally been referred to in English, although these days the term Afrikaners enjoys greater frequency) to leave the Cape for the

---

[1] The Afrikaanse omgangstaal is what Ponelis (1994, 107) calls it, as opposed to the Afrikaanse Kultuurtaal.

interior of the country, where they would found republics of their own. In the present chapter both the fate of Dutch and Afrikaans at the Cape and in the Boer republics will be briefly related.

The Cape

In 1806 the Cape was permanently occupied by British troops (the Low Countries at that time were occupied by Napoleon; see chapter 4). This occupation was marked by a series of slow yet determined measures aimed at preparing the territory for incorporation into the British Empire, officially effected in 1814. To take effect, a minimal number of English-speaking subjects was obviously required but by 1818, the British population was still limited, totaling little more than 10 percent of the Colony's Europeans; the number doubled in 1820, with the massive arrival of settlers, mainly in the Eastern Cape around Port Elizabeth and Grahamstown. By the mid-19th century, the Cape already had become a socio-economically diverse part of the colony's population: besides the British administrative personnel, there was a distinguishable lower social class composed of Irish, Scots, and Northern Englishmen (Stell 2008, 25). This was a deliberate measure by Lord Somerset, the English High Commissioner of the Cape Colony, to water down the non-British component of the population. Despite measures taken in the 19th century by the British to anglicize the Cape, the British never managed to make South Africa a predominantly English-speaking country. Nowhere else in the British Empire—other than in Canada, where English has managed to dominate over French—did the British ever occupy a territory previously occupied by another European power without their descendants soon outnumbering those of that other European colonial power.

In 1822 Somerset announced in a proclamation the government's design to turn the Cape into an officially monolingual Crown possession (Stell 2008, 26). Education was the first means by which anglicization was hoped to be achieved. In 1821, the first English and Scottish teachers had arrived at the Cape, and the first single-medium government schools were established. By 1830, all administrative and judicial proceedings were conducted in English, and the knowledge thereof had been made a prerequisite for public office. Even the Dutch hegemony in the Dutch Reformed Church was weakened by the appointment of a growing number of Scottish ministers. But even this attempt to convert the Dutch to English from the pulpit failed because the Scots were often anti-English and the Scottish ministers were absorbed into Dutch society.

Nevertheless, as a consequence of all this, a significant portion of the Dutch urban elite had been linguistically assimilated by 1840. In the countryside, on the other hand, anglicization had achieved little. Political lobbying finally resulted in the reinstatement of Dutch as a co-official language in the Cape Colony in 1882. Meanwhile, an active knowledge of English among the Dutch had become firmly established in the urban areas. There were also symptoms of a process of language shift among younger generations of the Dutch population.

On the other hand, the mass of the Colored population[2] of the Cape remained Dutch speaking during the 19th century. Signs of English linguistic influence were nonetheless eventually seen among Cape Town's Coloreds, and by the late 19th century English was commonly perceived as the privileged linguistic means of social advancement among their elite. Dutch maintained itself in religious life and informal settings. It achieved increased visibility toward the end of the 19th century under pressure from the rising pro-Afrikaner lobby groups.

The Boer Republics

Around 1834 a large number of the mostly rural Dutch population (the Boers) started the Groot Trek (the Great Trek) in an eastern and northern direction, which eventually led to the creation of three new countries: Natal; the Oranje Vrijstaat (OVS); and the Zuid-Afrikaansche Republiek (ZAR). Natal's independence was cut short by the British, who took possession of it in 1843, while the other two eventually developed, at least for some time, into independent republics. The British annexed Natal as they wanted to deny the Boers access to a seaport, and thus to possible contact with Britain's potential enemies. The other two republics, being landlocked, were not seen as a threat to British interests—diamonds followed by gold eventually changed that. On February 23, 1854, with the signing of the Orange River Convention, the country between the Orange and Vaal rivers officially became independent as the Oranje-Vrijstaat. Its official language was Dutch. Although the Orange Free State developed into a politically and economically successful republic, it experienced a chronic conflict with the British, who wanted to end its independent status. After the two resulting wars (the Boer Wars; Afrikaans: Vryheidsoorlog)[3] the land was finally annexed as the Orange River Colony in 1900. It ceased to exist as an independent republic on May 31, 1902, with the signing of the Treaty of Vereeniging at the conclusion of the Second Anglo-Boer War. Finally, in 1910, it was incorporated in the Union of South Africa, a British dominion.

The other Boer state, ZAR, often informally known as the Transvaal Republic, occupied the area later known as the South African province of Transvaal. ZAR was established in 1852 and was independent until 1877 and then again from 1881 after the First Boer War, in which the Boers regained their independence from the British Empire. The ZAR's official language was Dutch. In 1900 ZAR was also annexed by the United Kingdom as a result of the Boers' defeat in the Second Boer War, although the official surrender of the

---

[2] Traditionally, in South Africa, a differentiation is made between the black population (Swartes or Swartmense) and the racially mixed population called Kleurlinge or Bruinmense (Colored in English).

[3] The First Anglo-Boer War (1880–1881) was a relatively brief conflict in which Boers successfully rebelled against British rule in the Transvaal, and reestablished their independence. The Second War (1899–1902) was a lengthy one, involving large numbers of troops, which ended with the conversion of the Boer republics into British colonies. The British fought directly against the Transvaal and the Orange Free State, defeating their forces first in open warfare and then in a long and bitter guerrilla campaign.

territory took place only later. By May 31, 1902, the last of the Boer troops surrendered, mourning the deaths of 26,000 mainly women and children who died in British concentration camps. In 1910 it became the Transvaal Province of the Union of South Africa.

When the Boers founded their two independent republics, they did not want to adopt their everyday vernacular (Afrikaans) as their official language but reserved that role for Dutch (or Hollands, as they called it). During the 18th and 19th centuries the language used was called by various names, including Cape Dutch and the disparaging *kombuistaaltje* (kitchen Dutch). Hooghollands, on the contrary, was a name indicating high prestige, and High Dutch was exactly what the Boers felt they were speaking. All of this explains why only Dutch was considered as the official language of the Boer Republics. In both republics, Dutch immediately faced strong competition from English in commercial and educational domains. Even before industrialization British subjects were already forming the majority of the OVS and ZAR urban populations. In ZAR, the gold rush had brought an influx of non-Dutch European settlers (called *uit-landers*, outlanders by the Boers), leading to a destabilization of the republic.

In education, English had been allowed to coexist as a medium of instruction with Dutch and even to supplant it at a number of institutions in both republics. The sprawling city of Johannesburg as well as the satellite mining towns soon came to form English-speaking islands in the middle of an overwhelmingly rural Dutch-speaking society (Stell 2008, 28). For the Boers, Dutch was a symbol of their independence. The growing linguistic awareness was reflected in President Francis William Reitz's 1895 statement that "if we neglect our language, then we must also expect our identity to gradually fade away, and ultimately disappear" (quoted in Stell 2008, 28).

In ZAR, measures aimed at protecting Dutch were most determined under Paul Kruger's presidency (1883–1902). One of the most remarkable of them was that, at his invitation, a stream of 6,500 Dutch speakers from Belgium and Holland arrived in the republic, where a large proportion of them were used to staff the public service or the educational sector (Stell 2008, 28). On the other hand, there was no government policy for nonwhite education whatsoever and no support offered to it.

The discovery of diamonds and gold in the Boer Republics was not the least of the reasons that, after two wars, the two republics were eventually incorporated into the Union of South Africa.

Taalstryd (Language Struggle)

The attempted anglicization of the Cape provoked a *taalstryd* (language struggle) that was long in coming and that is traditionally divided into two phases. Traditional Afrikaans historiography regards the founding of the *Genootskap van Regte Afrikaners* (GRA; Society of True Afrikaners) in 1875 as the commencement of the *Eerste Afrikaanse Taalbeweging* (First Afrikaans Language Movement). The end of that movement is also traditionally located in the last years of the 19th century. The GRA was succeeded in 1880 by the *Afrikanerbond* (League of Afrikaners), determined to unite all (white) Afrikaners under the banner of the *volkstaal* (language of the people).

A period of renewed promotion coincided with the *Vryheidsoorlog* in 1899–1902 (Second Anglo-Boer War) and the institution of a reactionary anglicization policy in its aftermath by Lord Alfred Milner, British High Commissioner for South Africa (1897-1905). This time saw the emergence of Afrikaans as a powerful symbol of pan-Afrikaner unity and inspired a fledgling literature of genuine merit (Roberge 2003, 29). This is usually called the *Tweede Afrikaanse Taalbeweging* (Second Afrikaans Language Movement).

In 1875, in Paarl a group under the leadership of the conservative Dutch Reformed minister S. J. du Toit (1847–1911) founded the *Genootskap van Regte Afrikaners.* "The aim of our movement," the statutes declared, "is to defend our language, our nation and our country." This first language movement set itself the task of promoting the use of Afrikaans (a term its advocates preferred over

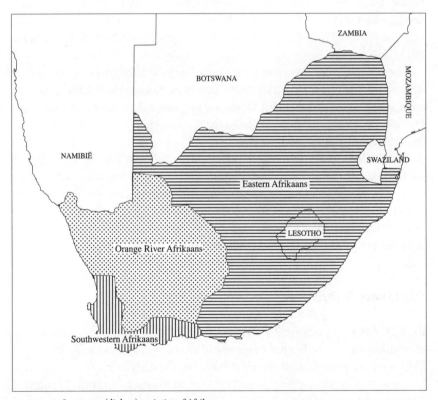

FIGURE 8.2 Language (dialect) varieties of Afrikaans

all others) as a written medium and its use in public domains hitherto reserved for English or Dutch and also of advancing Afrikaner political interests. "The GRA marketed Afrikaans as a God-given emblem of the Afrikaner people," Roberge (2003, 25) observes. The religious argument was indeed used from the very beginning as the ultimate argument in favor of both Dutch and Afrikaans. According to the GRA, Afrikaans had been given to the white Afrikaners by God himself: *"Onse Liewe Heer het op die aarde verskillende Naties gestel en an ider Natie syn Taal gege.... Onse Lieuwe Heer het ver ons in Afrika geplaats en ver ons die Afrikaanse taal gege"* (The Good Lord has made various nations on earth and has given a language of its own to everyone of them. The Good Lord has put us in Africa and has given the Afrikaans language to us) (Maartense et al. 1981, 141). Nevertheless, part of the GRA motivation for advocating Afrikaans over Dutch was that Dutch had become inaccessible to Coloreds for whom the gap between it and Dutch was even wider than for white Afrikaners.

After the Boer War, the British renewed their anglicization efforts. The 1902 treaty did establish a degree of bilingualism in schools and courtrooms, but the concession was a conditional one and in any case did not take any account of Afrikaans. It was at this moment that the second language movement was organized. Its supporters were concerned with fighting English by means not of Dutch but of Afrikaans. Therefore, they had to Africanize religious life, scholarship, and literature. Their motto was *"Afrikaans schrijven en spreken, Hollands lezen, albei leeren"* (Speak and write Afrikaans, read Dutch, learn both) (Brachin 1985, 130).

The second language movement, from roughly 1903 to 1919, formed an *Afrikaanse Taalgenootskap* (Afrikaans Language Society) in the Transvaal and an *Afrikaanse Taalvereniging* (Afrikaans Language Association) in the Cape Province. Both organizations agitated for the recognition of Afrikaans in education, administration, and the church.

In 1909 the *Zuid-Afrikaanse Akademie voor Taal, Letteren en Kunst* (South African Academy for Language, Letters, and Art) was founded as "a united front between the pro-Dutch and pro-Afrikaans camps" (Ponelis 1993, 53). The founders, according to Roberge (2003, 30), "explicitly construed *Hollands* to mean either Dutch or Afrikaans, thereby finessing a contentious language issue until the time was right to choose between them."

From Dutch to Afrikaans

In 1925, Afrikaans was legally recognized as an official language of the Union of South Africa and effectively superseded Dutch. Dutch has maintained some legal position, though, as there are still old laws written in it.

There is a persisting and often heated debate among historiographers of Afrikaans as to when and how (less as to why) the vernacular language in South

Africa managed to become a language in its own right, that is, Afrikaans and not Dutch any longer. Although some sources are available, they are always less numerous than one would wish, and, most of all, the information is but rarely unequivocal and has to be interpreted. A permanent source of problems is that, for a long time still, Dutch was used by many people in writing even when it was not used orally anymore. And finally, we cannot overlook the fact that South African racial philosophy and policies have also influenced the debate on the origins of Afrikaans: some people did not like to be reminded that nonwhites have played an important part in the development of what they liked to consider a white language.

The received opinion in Afrikaans linguistics is that "by 1750 and certainly no later than 1775, a vernacular separate from Dutch had crystallized and had become the spoken language of the colony. . . . However, the standard view does not claim that *all* defining features were fully diffuse by ca. 1750–1775 but rather that this period saw the greatest convergence of variants into a discrete linguistic code" (Roberge 2003, 20, italics in original). As opposed to that standard view, Roberge is more inclined to support Deumert's (1999, 2001) thesis "that there was no popular recognition of the Cape Dutch Vernacular as 'separate' from Dutch before the last quarter of the nineteenth century" (ibid.).

The arrival of the British and the expansion of their dominion brought profound social changes, which obviously also influenced language loyalty and usage. Increasingly, Stell (2008, 45) argues, "High Dutch found itself confined to ritual or iconic functions whereas English was functioning as an H-language endowed with not only social prestige but also a practical value in economic life." Still, for all the efforts of the British, anglicization was far from complete by the late 19th century and in fact was never achieved.

The same "British imperial factor," as Roberge (2003, 24) calls it, influenced not only the use of Afrikaans but also its internal evolution since part of the impetus for language standardization was the reaction of the white Cape Dutch population to British dominance. One of the events that brought this about was the Boer Wars, "which aroused sympathy among white Dutch-speaking South Africans in the Cape for their brethren in the north" (ibid.). Awareness of a common language, homeland, history, and origin "fostered not only group solidarity against British hegemony but an inchoate sense of ethnic identity, whereby the term Afrikaner came to acquire a political meaning" (ibid.). It can be concluded, therefore, that the struggle for survival in the face of English hegemony is both at the root of the Afrikaans taalstryd, in favor of a distinct Afrikaans language and of "its form, radically breaking away from High Dutch" (Stell 2008, 45).

Anyway, there is a general agreement that the first conscious attempts to write Afrikaans instead of Dutch date from the 19th century and that various subsequent (and sometimes simultaneous) Afrikaans "writing traditions" (Ponelis 1994, 110) can be recognized. A very early one is Meurant's

Zamenspraak (see below), which is based on the orthography of Dutch and the main principles of which still govern present-day Afrikaans spelling. There is also, the Arabic–Afrikaans writing tradition developed in the first half of the 19th century in the Muslim schools of the Cape, using the Arabic alphabet, which survived into the 1950s. At the same time, we have the Patriot tradition (named after the journal, founded by S. J. du Toit) of the *Genootskap van Regte Afrikaners* which disassociated itself from Dutch writing practice. The ultimate writing system is that of the South African Akademie, which was published in 1917 and is still being used today, albeit in a slightly adapted form. As to its linguistic form, the basis of Standard Afrikaans is the eastern dialect: "*Standaardafrikaans is gevorm uit die oostelike dialek*" (Ponelis 1994, 112). This dialect was not only the oldest but, as a consequence of the continuing urbanization, also ended up the majority dialect, since it is the variant that prevailed in both the old Boer republics, brought there from the Eastern Cape by those who undertook the Great Trek.

It is obviously impossible to decide when exactly Dutch was definitively succeeded by Afrikaans. They must have coexisted for a long time, but also the genesis of Afrikaans has been a continuous evolution, with both varieties serving as points in a continuum. Both simultaneously and afterward for a long time there was a sort of diglossic situation in which Afrikaans was the everyday, spoken L-language, whereas Dutch was used as an the H-language in formal situations and in writing. According to Buccini (1996, 36–37), a closer look at New Netherland Dutch could be very rewarding, since "the dialect of New Netherland is relevant to the story of Afrikaans." There is some disagreement as to which book is the first to be printed in Afrikaans. For a long time it was thought that *Zamenspraak tusschen Klaas Waarzegger en Jan Twijfelaar,* by L. H. Meurant, was the first Afrikaans book. Meurant's book (1861) is a collection of popular sketches that he had previously published in *The Cradock News/Het Cradocksche Nieuwsblad* in 1860–1861. Later it was thought that the first book was *Betroubare woord*, presumably printed in 1856, which would then precede the *Zamenspraak* by six years. It is written in a Dutch-based literary variant referred to as Arabic Afrikaans, using the Arabic alphabet. Subsequent scholarship has given reason to think that *Betroubare woord* is from the early 20th century. If so, the oldest extant Arabic–Afrikaans book would have been published in 1877 (though written a few years before).[4]

The (white) Boere-taal, as opposed to Hottentots-Afrikaans, was the medium explicitly used by Du Toit in the works he published himself and later on in the magazines *Patriot* and *Ons Klyntjie*. They would be the carriers of that new language, whose orthographic principles the author laid down in his

---

[4] Many thanks to Paul Roberge for this additional information as well as for much other information throughout the text. Personally, of course, I am not in a position to take a stand in this debate.

Eerste beginsels fan di Afrikaanse taal (1875), later on complemented by an outline of the grammar (1897). Obviously and, as opposed to earlier times, there was no longer any question of including the Colored population in the beneficiaries of the programs of cultural uplifting.

The first Afrikaans grammars and dictionaries were published in 1875 by that same *Genootskap van Regte Afrikaners* in Cape Town. The main guideline for Afrikaans literary production was *skryf soos jy praat* (write as you speak), a slogan used during that same period in Holland as well. Although that guideline was mainly concerned with spelling, it was as tricky a piece of advice, as was the analogous slogan in the Netherlands (see chapter 6).

The public targeted by the second Afrikaans language movement proved much more receptive than before to the idea of a new linguistic symbol. The political and cultural context in the years after World War I was propitious since the British hegemony was bitterly resented, the more so since the recognition of Afrikaans as a co-official language in 1925 did not bring about an immediate change in language practice. The postwar years had seen the rise of white Afrikaner nationalism and intense campaigning in favor of their *volkstaal*. All through that campaigning, the nonwhite population, once again, played at most a marginal role, disregarding the fact that Afrikaans was the mother tongue of almost the entire Colored population.

Norm codification, as an essential part of standardization, could only really commence in the post-WWI years when enough receptivity could be found to experiment with Afrikaans in High functions. By then indeed, the demand for a full-fledged H-language had to be dealt with urgently. To that challenge, the most immediate and practical response was a massive recourse to Dutch norms. The earlier opposition between the advocates of Afrikaans and Hollands thus became transfigured into an opposition between a radically local Afrikaans form of purism and a Dutch-oriented form of purism. Ultimately, those two extremes would rather tend to be merged than be kept distinct in Afrikaans prescriptive literature on language.

Once that debate had been concluded, the way was free to amend the constitution. Article 137 of the constitution of the Union of South Africa (1909) stated, "Both the English and Dutch languages shall be official languages of the Union, and shall be treated on a footing of equality, and possess and enjoy equal freedom, rights and privileges." In 1925, the Union government bestowed constitutional recognition on Afrikaans in an amendment to Article 137 that thenceforth stipulated that "Afrikaans is included under Hollands as one of the official languages of the Union" (Stell 2008, 47). Afrikaans was to replace Dutch in all written proceedings from 1926 onward. Print media were crossing over to Afrikaans in the 1920s, and the "ultimate triumph" of Afrikaans was consecrated when in 1933 the official Afrikaans version of the Bible was published (Ponelis 1993, 54). The role of the Statenbijbel in the Dutch Reformed churches was the last bastion of Dutch in South Africa that Afrikaans had to conquer.

Linguistic Development in the 20th Century

The Standard Afrikaans that we know today probably developed between roughly 1900 and 1930 (Roberge 2003, 31). In 1917 the Academy brought out the first edition of the *Afrikaanse woordelys en spelreëls* (Afrikaans Wordlist and Spelling Rules), based on the propositions Kollewijn had published in Holland in 1891 in his attempt to simplify the spelling of Dutch (see chapters 5 and 6). The 10th edition of the *Woordelys* (Wordlist) appeared in 2010.

The existence of government agencies, such as the Vaktaalburo (Terminology Bureau), created in 1950, has played an important role in the standardization of Afrikaans. A most notable achievement is the monumental *Woordeboek van die Afrikaanse taal* (Dictionary of the Afrikaans Language), initiated by J. J. Smith in 1926 and continued at the University of Stellenbosch. A total of 13 volumes have appeared so far (until 2011), up to the letter R.

In 1965 the first edition of the *Verklarende handwoordeboek van die Afrikaanse taal* (Explanatory Dictionary of the Afrikaans Language; HAT) appeared and has continually been updated ever since. A CD-ROM of the 5th edition appeared in 2009. This lexical handbook is regarded as particularly authoritative (box 8.1).

The seeds for change, even in this particular field, were sown from the moment the National Party (*Nasionale Party;* NP) came to power. Segregation laws in South Africa already existed before the advent of the apartheid regulations in the 1950s. Education, residential areas, and the workplace were segregated. The

---

BOX 8.1} Prisma Groot Woordenboek Afrikaans en Nederlands—Het Spectrum

---

In April 2011 Amsterdam saw the launch of a new kind of Dutch–Afrikaans dictionary. The editor-in-chief, the Amsterdam lexicography professor Willy Martin (2010), explains how a completely new technique has been used to produce a dictionary of two languages so closely related as Dutch and Afrikaans. He calls it the amalgamated dictionary, meaning that an Afrikaans–Dutch and a Dutch–Afrikaans word list were telescoped. This should, among other things, make it possible to call attention to the many false friends existing between closely related languages. Very often you're convinced you capture the meaning of a particular word or phrase, but then it appears that you didn't really understand at all. A convincing example is a word like *amper.* In Dutch it means hardly, and in Afrikaans almost. Although *robot* may indeed mean robot in both languages, in Afrikaans its primary and most common meaning is "traffic lights"!

Although a place has also been given to the famous and even notorious purisms of Afrikaans (*tuisrekenaar* for pc; Dutch *pc, skootrekenaar* for laptop, Dutch *laptop*), the main intention, Martin says, is to give language enthusiasts the opportunity to just browse and read. "It's not only a bilingual dictionary, it's a reading dictionary as well."

Source: NOS 23. April 2011.

---

victory of the NP in the 1948 elections paved the way for a policy of complete segregation called apartheid (literally separateness), a word that was eventually taken over as a loanword in almost all the languages of the world.

Nevertheless, as far as language was concerned, apartheid led to a dilemma. The nonwhite population offered a huge potential for Afrikaans, which the NP continued to consider as its very own *volkstaal,* the property of the white Afrikaner. On one hand, the educational policies of the new NP government contributed to a larger diffusion of Afrikaans among blacks, Coloreds, and Indians; on the other hand, the ideology behind the imposition of Afrikaans and the cultural and political stigma associated with that language in nonwhite perceptions had been stirring resentment that ultimately proved utterly damaging to the Afrikaans cause (Stell 2008, 76).

During the presidency of Nobel Peace prize winner Frederik Willem de Klerk[5], originating from the former Boer republic of the Transvaal, equal constitutional rights for everyone were granted in less than four years. From 1991 on nobody could claim preferential rights or treatment on the basis of racial descent anymore. The first general election under the new system was won by the ANC in 1994, and Nelson Mandela was elected state president.

In 1976, a slogan of the high school students in Soweto had been "Afrikaans stinks." To safeguard the future of Afrikaans in the post-apartheid era and to render cross-ethnic cooperation possible around the common heritage of Afrikaans, its negative exclusively white connotations had to be shed. This meant the downfall of *Algemeen Beskaafde Afrikaans,* a name that mimicked *Algemeen Beschaafd Nederlands* (ABN; General Cultivated Dutch), which at that time was very popular in the Low Countries (see chapter 6). It was observed that Standaardafrikaans as a prescriptive set of language rules was perceived as alien by the nonwhite speakers of Afrikaans. Therefore, the inherent ethnic and geographic diversity of Afrikaans had to be given a place of honor in standard norms (Stell 2008, 80). The new rhetoric on Afrikaans had a number of effects. The notion of *Algemeen Beskaafde Afrikaans* with its exclusive social and formal connotations was undermined by Coetzee (1982), who put Standaardafrikaans on a par with *algemeen gebruikte of bruikbare Afrikaans* (generally used or useable Afrikaans).

The Colored intelligentsia of the Cape found a new voice in what it called *Alternatiewe Afrikaans,* as opposed to establishment Afrikaans, and many other intellectuals agreed to take the same path. According to Ponelis (1994, 120), "the movement for *Swart Afrikaans* (Black Afrikaans) or *Alternatiewe Afrikaans* (Alternative Afrikaans) among Colored Afrikaans speakers (of mainly the southwestern dialect area) is a reaction against the ideological links between Standaardafrikaans and Afrikaans nationalism and an attempt to add a new value to Afrikaans" (my translation) (fig. 8-3).

---

[5] He shared his prize (1993) with Nelson Mandela.

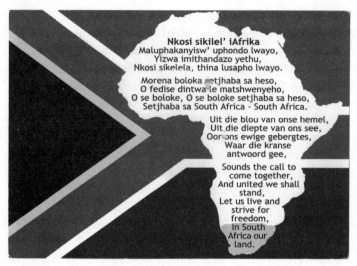

FIGURE 8.3 Picture post card with the national anthem of South Africa in four different languages

The Future of Afrikaans: A Fight for Survival

The new political situation in South Africa after the transition to majority rule in 1994 made the future of Afrikaans very uncertain. Under the previous system there had been two national languages: Afrikaans and English. Now, there are 11; in the still provisional constitution 9 "black" languages were added (Deumert 2010), which account for the home language of almost 78 percent of South Africa's inhabitants. Nevertheless, by South African standards, Afrikaans is a comparatively strong home language. In 2001 it was the home language[6] of roughly six millions South Africans (i.e., 13.3 percent of the country's population). These numbers place Afrikaans in third national position behind Zulu and Xhosa, respectively. The absolute numbers of L1-speakers of Afrikaans show an increase against the 1996 figures, but their share in the nation's totals has been steadily diminishing from 15.1 percent in 1991 and 14.4 percent in 1996. This relative demographic retreat, also found among the English-speaking community (8.9 percent in 1996 versus 8 percent in 2001), is attributable to decreasing fertility rates and is taking place against a background of a faster growing Bantu-speaking population (altogether 76.5 percent in 1996 versus 77.9 percent in 2001). In both South Africa and Namibia, the majority of the population with Afrikaans as home language is formed by nonwhites (Stell 2008, 87).

---

[6] SA statistics uses the term home language in their questionnaires. Home language is defined as "the language most spoken at home, which is not necessarily the person's mother tongue." Here "home language" is used synonymously with "L1/first language" (Stell 2008).

Approximately one third of all Afrikaans speakers live in the Western Cape province, the historical center of the language, the homeland of the Cape Coloreds who form the largest population group in the Western Cape and the majority of Afrikaans speakers in South Africa. From the early 20th century onward, the majority of Afrikaans speakers moved into urban environments, where the rivalry with English is the fiercest. The Afrikaans language community is extremely diversified and is spread over all traditional groups of the population. They are also found in every political party and in most religious groups.

The all-powerful position of the Nasionale Party after 1948 helped Afrikaans to become entrenched across domains where previously only English had held sway. It also allowed Afrikaans to further spread into or regain previously lost ground across ethnic groups. But the Nasionale Party also introduced apartheid, which in itself carried the seeds of the 1975 language revolt: besides shattering the myth of white hegemony, the Soweto riots brought the realization that Afrikaans was threatened with being swamped by a remonstrant nonwhite community for which English embodied integration and empowerment and Afrikaans represented repression and prevented access to a wider world.

In anticipation of the end of Afrikaner political power, Standard Afrikaans was redefined in the interest of its survival in a multiracial society, where the white establishment was expected to lose some of its cultural influence. *Beskaafdheid* as a socially and racially exclusive qualifier of correct Afrikaans was abolished, theoretically opening the door to a process of language reform, in which both whites and nonwhites could have a say (Stell 2008, 82).

Stell (2008) also establishes how after a movement of destandardization we do now witness a restandardization process; this will probably lead to an Afrikaans that is rather different from the former one and that incorporates linguistic and cultural values of the whole Afrikaans-speaking community.

The problems Afrikaans had to face shortly after the end of the apartheid regime were (and are) enormous and multifaceted. I summarize Ponelis (1994, 115–116):

- The economic foundation is rather weak: keeping up a standard language is a costly affair, and most Afrikaans speakers, being often rural Coloreds, are poor.
- Afrikaans has not succeeded in playing an important role as a language of instruction outside of the Afrikaans-speaking community, as the striking example of the Soweto uprising demonstrates. This is one of the most decisive factors working to the detriment of Afrikaans.
- Although terminology bureaus did a tremendous job of creating and popularizing specific terminology in Afrikaans, we may doubt whether it is or will be extensively used by scholars, technicians, and artisans (for whom the effort was made in the first place) both in their daily practice and in their respective publications.

- The Calvinist churches have always been one of the pillars of the Afrikaans language and culture. Since the societal influence of religion is rapidly decreasing, their support for Afrikaans is less decisive now. As to the Muslim community, we see how the Arabic Afrikaans tradition has finally died out and most of its role has been taken over by both English and Arabic.
- The position of Afrikaans in radio and TV is constantly getting weaker.
- The question may be asked whether institutions typically meant to be the propagators of Afrikaans such as universities, cultural organizations, the still *lelieblanke* (lily white) *Suid-Afrikaanse Akademie*, schools, newspapers, and magazines aim to reach out to the whole Afrikaans language community and, in so doing, serve the South African society at large.

Post-apartheid South Africa has indeed seen a loss of preferential treatment by the government of Afrikaans in terms of education, social events, media (TV and radio), and general status throughout the country, in other words a significant decline in public domains. The country's five originally purely Afrikaans-medium universities have seen a gradual drift in the direction of dual or parallel medium instruction. A number of university degree programs in Afrikaans have been consolidated with other subjects or eliminated altogether; those that remain have seen dwindling enrollments. Afrikaans remains more or less coequal with English as a major language of the law, but it is losing ground to English in commerce, finance, science, and technology (Webb 2002, 95). The international standing of English virtually assures it a prominent role in official and other public spheres. The extent to which Afrikaans will maintain its public role over the long haul remains to be seen.

Despite all the problems of depreciation and emigration that Afrikaans faces today, the language still competes well in some domains such as Afrikaans pay TV channels and high newspaper and CD sales as well as popular internet sites. A resurgence of Afrikaans in popular music (from the late 1990s) has added new momentum to the language, especially among the younger generations. Even the Afrikaans language cinema is starting to experience some revival. Since 2009 Afrikaans also seems to be returning on radio and television, especially Afrikaans advertising seems to be selling very well in the current South African TV market. In April 2009 SABC3 started showing several Afrikaans language programs. In all these cases the audience is composed not just of white Afrikaners but of the whole Afrikaans-speaking community including even speakers of other languages who are competent in Afrikaans as a second, third, or foreign language.

Further latent support for the language comes from the depoliticized view of South Africans of younger generations: Afrikaans is less and less viewed as "the language of the oppressor," and the direct ties between Afrikaans and apartheid are being felt less, making lighter the ideological burden weighing on Afrikaans.

Afrikaans will almost certainly maintain its position as a home language. Whether it will also succeed in keeping its role as an important societal language will probably depend on whether the paths of white and Colored Afrikaans will further separate or, on the contrary, come closer together. One single Afrikaans, accepted by both the Kleurlinge and the Whites as their own language and part of their identity, has a reasonable chance of continuing to function as a language of culture and societal exchange.

Afrikaans in Namibia

Namibia (population of approximately 2.1 million; capital and largest city Windhoek) became a German imperial protectorate in 1884 and remained a German colony (Deutsch-Südwestafrika) until the end of World War I. In 1920, the League of Nations mandated the country to South Africa, which imposed its laws and, eventually, its apartheid policy. South-West had significant numbers of Afrikaans-speaking inhabitants long before it was mandated to South Africa—there had been important 19th-century migrations from South Africa into the territory. Actually, Nambia is an even more Afrikaans-speaking country than South Africa.[7] Although the South African government intended to incorporate southwest Africa into its territory, it never officially did so. In 1966, uprisings and demands by African leaders led the United Nations to assume direct responsibility over the territory. During all this time, however, Namibia remained under South African administration; it obtained full independence from South Africa in 1990.

In the pre-German period, Dutch was already enjoying so much prestige that it had become established as an oral and written lingua franca in the more sparsely populated southern and central parts of the territory. Germany's language policy in her dominions was generally to promote German at the expense of local vernaculars; in Südwestafrika this included Dutch. Nevertheless, in practice provision had to be made for (Cape) Dutch in official dealings, since it was then the most widely spoken language in the territory. Compulsory school attendance for natives eventually led to the adoption of that language among them too. According to Stell (2008, 32), "The competition between Dutch and German in *Südwestafrika* does in many respects resemble that which had been opposing Dutch and English in the Cape Colony. German, just as English, was entrenched as a prestige language associated with government and trade."

---

[7] Many thanks to Bruce Donaldson for this additional information as well as for much other information throughout the text.

The South West African People's Organisation (SWAPO) was the leading force in Namibia's armed struggle for independence. It took until 1988 for South Africa to agree to end its occupation of Namibia as part of a United Nations peace plan for the entire region. Namibia's first-ever one-person, one-vote election for a constituent assembly was held in October 1989 and was won by SWAPO, although it did not gain the two-thirds majority it had hoped for.

As of today, the mother tongue of half of all Namibians is Oshiwambo, a language spoken in the north of the country. The most widely understood language and lingua franca, however, is still Afrikaans. Despite this, for political reasons SWAPO decided to make English the sole official language of the new country. SWAPO spent its decades of exile in Zambia where it became an English-speaking organization with little affinity for Afrikaans. This also influenced the organization's attitude to Afrikaans on gaining independence. Afrikaans was given constitutional recognition as a national but not as an official language. Prior to independence, Afrikaans used to have equal status with German as an official language. Both Afrikaans and English are used primarily as a second language reserved for public communication, but small groups with Afrikaans as their first language, both white and particularly nonwhite, occur throughout the country.

Most of the white population speaks either German or Afrikaans, despite the fact that the official language is English. Even today, 90 years after the end of the German colonial era, the German language plays a leading role as a commercial language. Afrikaans is spoken by 60 percent of the white community, German is spoken by 32 percent, English by 7 percent, and Portuguese by 1 percent.

Concluding Reflections

The history of Afrikaans is one of language contact and language conflict. All in all, there have been various language movements and an almost perpetual language conflict in what was to become South Africa. Overall and continuously, of course, there was the struggle against English from the occupation by the British onward. It occurred on all levels and in the various parts of the Union of South Africa. This competition has, as used to be the case in 19th-century Belgium, an external as well as an internal linguistic dimension, that is, a struggle against anglicization as well as the endeavors to purify Dutch/Afrikaans from English influence.

Another conflict has been present from the earliest times as well: the competition between a specific South African variety of Dutch versus Standard Dutch, or the Standard Dutch as it was used in South Africa.

Finally, we are now witnessing a conflict that may, to the same extent as the preceding ones, be crucial for the survival of Afrikaans, namely, that of multiracial Afrikaans versus Standaard white Afrikaans or *Alternatiewe Afrikaans* as opposed to establishment Afrikaans. In all those cases we are basically in the presence of the opposition of new versus old, change versus conservatism, and partly also informal versus formal.

Finally, it has to be stressed that the internal linguistic influence of English on Afrikaans is overwhelming. In Donaldson's (1988, 287) opinion "the influence English has had so far on Afrikaans" is now "integral to the very nature of the language." There is no point in indiscriminatingly fighting "anglicisms," he maintains, since "the speech community has already unequivocally decided on many of the examples given in my corpus. It is time for prescriptive bodies and works to take note of this and accept these de facto decisions, even if they mean that standard Afrikaans will now deviate even more from Dutch and come closer to English" (ibid.). A change of attitude is urgent, he believes, since English influence is "apparently the inevitable product of the unique bilingual situation that exists today in the Republic of South Africa" (Donaldson 1988, 288). Although this was written a quarter of a century ago, there is no reason to think today's situation would be decisively different. There is every reason to expect that multiracial Afrikaans or *Alternatiewe Afrikaans* may be more susceptible still to English influence than white *Standaard Afrikaans* used to be.

9 }

Progress or Decay? The Future Development of Dutch

Predicting, as they say, is very precarious, the more so when it is about the future. Even so, the question we have to address in this final chapter is how Dutch might fare in the future: which factors will be decisive and how the linguistic varieties in the Dutch language community are going to interact. To thus enter the realm of linguistic futurology is possible only because the results of some current research are a sound basis to reflect on the possible (or likely) future development.

Progress or Decay

"Language Change: Progress or Decay?" is what an atrocious beast is asking on the cover of Jean Aitchison's (1985) book with the same title. It's a popular question known to cause heated debate both in bars and pubs and in the "Letters to the Editor" section of many newspapers.

Linguists are very much aware of the fact that language change is neither progress nor decay but simply change, yet they mostly find it hard to convince the layman. Change in language is normal and occurs always and everywhere; still it seems to make people nervous and uncertain as can be seen from the numerous letters to the editor every time spelling changes or attempts in that direction are announced. *Taalverloedering* (language decay) is a very popular word in such letters (it often seems that everybody's language is decaying but one's own). Since decay means that something is getting worse than it used to be, we cannot but conclude that the situation of, let's say 50 years ago, must have been considerably better than the present one. Although there is no doubt that 50 years ago the state of the language was different from today, that does not mean it was better. The best proof undoubtedly is that 50 years ago similar complaints of language decay were found in the papers and elsewhere, stating how much better language was 50 years previously. Even 400 years ago, when there were no newspaper editors to write to, people complained about language decay (see chapter 4). Consequently, language decay may be an issue but is certainly not a problem as far as the existence and the future of Dutch are concerned.

There may be other threats to the future of the language, and one of the most popular ones (throughout the centuries) is the threat apparently posed by competing languages. In the middle of the 16th century, the Antwerp-based musician and printer Thielman Susato assured his compatriots that songs in their Dutch mother tongue displayed the same amount of *konst ende soeticheyt* (art and sweetness) as those in the popular languages of the day, Italian and French. Today's most popular language of songs is English, not only in the Low countries but also in almost all other Western countries. So why should that be a problem? The only reasonable explanation seems to be that many people believe that song lyrics is not the only but rather one more domain Dutch has yielded to English. Since English is already the lingua franca of the scientific, economic, and political world, any more domain lost seems to be one too many and might eventually result in Dutch losing importance through attrition. Is it true that danger is looming up when one sees that some university curricula in Holland are partly or even completely taught in English and some people fear that it might soon supplant Dutch in high schools as well? Is it possible that the Dutch language no longer exists 50 or 100 years from now?

External Factors

Doomsayers predict that Dutch will disappear within the next few decades, swallowed up by English, Chinese, or some other language. Others fear that soon the language will have changed so profoundly under the influence of other languages (e.g., those spoken by immigrants) that it will cease to be real Dutch, whatever that is. How real are those fears, or, put the other way around, how strong is the position of Dutch at this very moment?

In Europe Dutch is the official language of the majority of the Belgians (over 6 millions) and of more than 16 million Dutch. These almost 23 million Dutch speakers occupy the 10th position in the 76-strong league of European languages. Among the approximately 6,000 languages of the world, Dutch is ranked 42nd. That means that approximately 5,950 languages lag behind Dutch, which makes it in the top 1 percent of languages in the world.[1] It is hard to perceive this situation as threatening.

---

[1] *Geheimen van het Nederlands*, supplement of the newspaper *De Standaard* (October 29, 2010).

It is true, of course, that English is rapidly and increasingly becoming a rival for Dutch in scientific publications written by native speakers of Dutch. Also, as a direct consequence of globalization, the international lingua franca English influences Dutch in many ways. In some domains English even plays a role as a medium of communication alongside Dutch (e.g., in international business) or as a language of instruction (in a small part of the curriculum in higher education). Obviously, this means a functional loss for Dutch, but there is no other way not to lose contact with international development. In the past Dutch has successfully survived massive borrowing from and even dominance by other languages, and therefore this evolution is also hard to perceive as a real threat (box 9.1).

As far as Europe and the institutions of the European Union are concerned, a paradoxical evolution can be observed in that there is, simultaneously, an increasing unification as well as a constantly growing regionalization. The policies and actions of Basks, Catalans, Northern Italians, German-speaking Belgians, Walloons, Flemings, Frisians, Greenlanders, Scotts, Welshmen, and many others are responsible for the fact that centrifugal tendencies in their countries contrast heavily with centripetal tendencies in the European Union at large. Which tendency will prevail is hard to predict, and eventually they may even prove to be complementary instead of conflicting. The future language policy in and of the European Union will depend on that outcome but will not endanger the position of Dutch. The official language policy of the EU is aimed at stimulating bilingual or trilingual competence in all Europeans, who are supposed to combine proficiency in their mother tongue with that in English and, preferably, another

BOX 9.1} Loanwords in and from Dutch

The fact that Dutch has borrowed many words from other languages has often been, from the Middle Ages through this very day, a source of irritation and indignation, as has been mentioned in many chapters in this book. In Van der Sijs and Willemyns (2009, 86–95) we find a top 10 list of languages Dutch borrowed from. Not surprisingly, the top four (in absolute numbers) are the neighbor languages French, Latin, German, and English. Their influence, though, has changed considerably in the course of the centuries. On numbers five and six we find Italian and Spanish, while Indonesian words are seventh, followed by words from Yiddish in eighth place. The list ends with Japanese and Russian, respectively.

In the top 10 languages that have borrowed from Dutch (Van der Sijs & Willemyns 2009, 105–121), the vernaculars of former colonies—Indonesian (Bahasa Indonesia), Sranan Tongo (Suriname), and Papiamento (Antilles)—are at the top. Numbers four to six are occupied by Scandinavian languages: Danish, Norwegian, and Swedish, respectively. Seventh and eighth are English and French, respectively, and Russian and German close the list.

European language as well. The prospect of a European Union where every citizen is proficient in English might, so pessimists say, enhance the prestige of English to such an extent that a substantial functional loss for the mother tongues would be inevitable. Such an outcome is more than improbable. Also, and not in the least, we still are (and unfortunately will remain so for a long time still) in a situation in which the vast majority of Europeans is monolingual. A persisting effort to provide a considerable part of them with a certain competence of the European lingua franca is certainly not superfluous, and all of us will profit from it.

A poll conducted by the newspaper *De Standaard* between February 23 and March 2, 2009, reveals how Flemings react to the prospected role of English. A total of 1,047 of them were confronted with the question of whether they would or would not agree with the EU having English as its sole working language. 47 percent of the subjects agreed, 46 percent did not, while 7 percent have no opinion on the matter. In other words, 54 percent of Flemings don't oppose the idea![2] Unfortunately, similar figures on the opinion of the Dutch do not exist.

Both in Holland and in Belgium there have never been so many speakers of the Dutch standard language. Never have there been so many foreign citizens using Dutch as their second language. Never have there been more French-speaking Belgians trying to gain an as good as possible competence in Dutch. Never have there been more foreign students reading Dutch in Dutch departments all over the world. Consequently, both status and function of Dutch have never been as strong as they are right now.

Also, the public interest in Dutch has never been so vivid as it is now, as can be seen from the great many "Letters to the Editor" in daily newspapers and magazines and in language-oriented magazines as *Onze Taal* or *Nederlands van Nu,* even when many of them are complaining about the decay of the language. The large circulation of language manuals, the amount of people registered for Dutch courses, and the ever increasing number of help questions asked from the language advisory boards (both official and private) are more than proof of how interested people are in correct language usage as well as the norm of their language.

One thing is for sure: the future of Dutch (and of any language for that matter) lies in the hands of its speakers. In our case, their confidence in their language is very large. When in 2008, the popular language society Genootschap Onze Taal celebrated its 75th anniversary, a book was published in which readers were invited to elaborate on the future of Dutch. And their confidence, as well as that of linguists and authors who participated as well, appears to be huge. A total of 99 percent of the participants in this large internet survey definitely excluded the idea that Dutch could disappear within the next 75 years. I completely agree, and frankly I can see no reason whatsoever that Dutch should stop growing and thriving even after that.

---

[2] *De Standaard*, March 9, 2009, 2–3.

Internal Factors

What about internal factors that might jeopardize the position of the Dutch standard language?

In both parts of the Low Countries, centrifugal tendencies (i.e., increasing variation away from the conventional norm of Standard Dutch) seem to have been detected. As far as the northern Netherlands are concerned, there is what Stroop (1998) calls *Poldernederlands*. An equally centrifugal evolution seems to be occurring in the south, where we witness the development of a linguistic variety often referred to as *Verkavelingsvlaams* (Van Istendael 1993) also called, more recently, *Schoon Vlaams* or *Tussentaal* (intermediate language variety).

The impact of both developments increases because they coincide with still another factor: the process of dialect loss and leveling, which in Flanders has started considerably later than in the Netherlands but is now gaining momentum everywhere. Many people are trading in their dialect in an increasing number of settings and functions for another variety of the language, which very often has a decidedly regional (southern or northern, respectively) flavor. For a constantly growing part of the population, both in the north and in the south, the conventional norm of the standard language appears to be no longer the target in an increasing amount of settings.

The fact that both centrifugal developments, although unrelated, occur simultaneously may influence the evolution of Dutch as a pluricentric language in the 21st century. This is the real theme to be addressed here, together with the question of whether or to what extent language planning strategies might or should be devised to influence or reverse this process.

This chapter contains comments on data, observations, and predictions from mainly three sources. One is Hans van de Velde's (1996) dissertation on variation and change in spoken Standard Dutch between 1935 and 1993. His point of departure is the observation that the pronunciation of Standard Dutch is changing and that the discrepancies between the southern and the northern pronunciation are increasing (Van de Velde 1997, 49).

A second source includes publications on Poldernederlands, the first and most important of which is Jan Stroop's (1998) book *Poldernederlands: Waardoor het ABN verdwijnt*. The second part of the title is an extreme example of the predicting ambition of some linguists, an ambition that decidedly culminates in the very last sentence of Stroop's book *Het Poldernederlands gaat een glorieuze toekomst tegemoet en wordt het Algemeen Nederlands van de eenentwintigste eeuw*. (There is a glorious future for *Poldernederlands*, which will become the Standard Dutch of the 21st century).

Finally there are a great many articles published over the last couple of decades on what the author Geert van Istendael has called Verkavelingsvlaams. Examples include Cajot (2010), De Caluwe (2002, 2009), Geeraerts, Penne, and Vanswegenhoven (2000), Goossens (2000), Jaspers (2001), Jaspers and Brisard

(2006), Taeldeman (1993), Vandekerckhove (2005), and Willemyns (2005b, 2007). Most of them try to do what Grondelaers and Van Hout (2011, 199) confess to in so many words: "outline scenarios for the further development of Belgian and Netherlandic Dutch."

THE CHANGING PRONUNCIATION

Van de Velde's (1997) research is concerned with pronunciation and is based on radio recordings from 1935 through 1993, both in Flanders and in the Netherlands, an excellent source for the diachronic study of variation in the standard pronunciation in real time (cf. chapter 6).

One of Van de Velde's most interesting conclusions is that over the past 60 years variation has not really become more extensive, either in the Netherlands or in Flanders. There is no evidence the norm has been abandoned, he declares; it "just shifted a bit." (Van de Velde 1997, 268). Around 1935, the time when in Flanders the norm for the standard pronunciation was firmly determined (mainly in Blancquaert 1934) and accepted, the Dutch, on the other hand, started to slowly shift away from that norm that used to be theirs. This shift has gained momentum over the past decades but has not been followed in the south. It is this point Van de Velde chooses to give his prediction. In Flanders, he argues, recent substandard varieties such as Verkavelingsvlaams will put growing pressure on the standard norm, causing increasing variation and eventually change. Most of those changes will be away from the northern pronunciation habits and be more Brabantic flavored instead (Van de Velde 1997, 60–61). Still, as mentioned before, on the level of the standard language, I believe that more and more the Dutch will move away from the official norm of pronunciation, whereas most Flemings will stick to it.

In Van de Velde et al. (2010, 385), the aforementioned research is compared and complemented with "a synchronic corpus of Belgian and Netherlandic standard Dutch from different regions at the turn of the millennium." According to the authors, we see that, after some 30 years, "The differences observed clearly mark the development of two divergent pronunciation standards, based on different linguistic (re)sources" (ibid.). Even so, they argue, "the relationships and the connectivity between both varieties will remain strong, based on their shared linguistic history and shared language policy, but also because they are neighbors, sharing infrastructure and economic links. As such, Dutch is not different from its two closest neighbors German and English" (ibid., 412).

POLDERNEDERLANDS

Another predictor, Jan Stroop, is detecting an equally centrifugal change in northern pronunciation habits. Poldernederlands, as he coined it, is responsible for radical "phonetic and phonological" changes. They have been initiated by the changes already acknowledged by Van de Velde (1996, 238–239) in what he calls Present-day Northern Standard Dutch.

The most prominent characteristic of Poldernederlands is the pronunciation *aai* for the diphthong [c.i]: *tijd* > *taaid, klein* > *klaain*. Yet a similar change appears to affect other diphthongs as well: [œ.y] turns into [au] (*buik* > *bauk, huis* > *haus*) en [ɔu] turns into [a.u] (getrouwd > getraauwd) (Stroop 1998, 25–26). The trigger for this lowering of diphthongs, Stroop argues, is the diph-thongization of the long vowels discussed in chapter 6 (*ee* > *ei; eu* > *ui* and *oo* > *ou: been* > *bein; neus* > *nuis; boon* > *boun*). This sets up a nice push chain (ibid., 32–33):

> *ee* > *ei*
>> *ei* > *aai* (*teken* > *teiken; kijken* > *kaaiken*)
> *eu* > *ui*
>> *ui* > *au* (*leuk* > *luik; buik* > *bauk*)
> *oo* > *ou*
>> *ou* > *aau* (*boot* > *bout; getrouwd* > *getraaud*)

In short vowels, Stroop detects the opposite movement—a heightening:

> *a* > *e*
>> *e* > *i* (*dak* > *dek; bellen* > *billen*)

In the perspective of this book, though, Stroop's sociolinguistic comments on the origin and spread of Poldernederlands are more interesting than the phonological ones. Stroop argues that the origin of this change, as opposed to what is often thought, is not found in the language variety of Holland or the Randstad. The real origin is socially and not geographically determined, that is, what they are and not where they come from. The group of speakers responsible for both the origin and the very fast spread of Poldernederlands are young, highly educated females. He estimates that three of four females under 40 discussing serious items on radio or TV are speakers of Poldernederlands (there has been no research yielding statistical evidence though), and he has not succeeded so far in finding one male speaker with the same kind of background and using this particular variety (Stroop 1998, 16–22). Many international as well as specifically Dutch dialecto-logical and sociolinguistic inquiries so far have revealed that females rather have a tendency to prefer standardized over less standardized varieties, and, therefore, it is amazing that in Poldernederlands it is females who initiated this evolution away from the standard language. At the same time it is interesting to notice that Van de Velde (1996, 266) declares not to have found any trace of this specific pronunciation is his recordings: "very wide diphthongs with a lowering of the first element (i.e. *aai*, RW) do not appear in our corpus."

Stroop (1998) blames the authorities and the kind of education they pro-vide (or fail to provide) for not having tried to stop the rapid spread of Poldernederlands. Is Stroop's reaction that of an angry schoolmaster (see also

Stroop 2011), shocked by people saying *maaid* instead of *meid*, or are we indeed witnessing a large-scale change threatening to overthrow the whole phonological system of the Dutch language? And if so, why is Stroop so upset by that perspective? Systematic phonological changes affecting whole (sub) systems are known to have happened in all kind of languages at all times in history. The Germanic and the High German sound shifts as well as the Great Vowel shift (in English), for example, have caused a lot of dramatic changes. The most obvious reason to be upset by this evolution would be the language political consideration that, since this change is not found in Flanders, it may threaten the unity of the language in the Dutch pluricentric language community. Substantial change originating in one part of that territory is potentially disruptive in nature indeed. This would be a very valuable argument (the only possible one even) for wanting to stop this evolution, and therefore it is utterly amazing that Stroop does not mention it himself. Although the change detected so far is restricted to pronunciation, there is reason enough to believe, Stroop maintains (without proof, though), that a brand new variety of Dutch is being created and that its spread and generalization will be fast and almost impossible to stop. The inevitability of this conclusion has yet to be demonstrated.

Poldernederlands is not the only variety disrupting the dialect–standard dichotomy of old. Hinskens (2007) reminds us that "the role of common medium for everyday oral communication was [as the dialects were gradually lost] not taken over by the standard language, but rather by two types of non-standard varieties, viz. 'regiolects' and regional varieties of the standard language, which developed in the linguistic space between the traditional dialects and the standard language" (284). Poldernederlands is the best-known regional standard variety but, as opposed to Stroop, he believes its use to be "confined largely to...the Randstad" (285), that is, geographically determined after all. Apart from the aforementioned, large-scale migration has led to the development of so-called ethnolects, or nonindigenous intermediate varieties, which have "developed among members of ethnic minorities" and which "typically are not the mother tongue of the first generation of speakers" (289). Many of these varieties, Hinskens says, "are not necessarily in every respect approximations of the standard," but do "contain features of the surrounding dialects" as well (ibid.). The Turkish and Moroccan ethnolects are the largest ones.

VERKAVELINGSVLAAMS/SCHOON VLAAMS/TUSSENTAAL

The southern centrifugal tendency is the development of a variety, based on essentially Brabantic characteristics often referred to as Verkavelingsvlaams or, more recently, as Schoon Vlaams or Tussentaal. According to De Caluwe (2009), *omgangstaal* is the sole appropriate term; colloquial speech seems to be his preferred English translation of that concept.

Examples of Tussentaal characteristics are found in, among others, Goossens (2000) and Geeraerts et al. (2000). The latter provide us with language samples taken from Flemish soaps:

- Pronunciation: *h* dropping (*ik eb* instead of ik heb), apocope and syncope in short function words (*da, goe* instead of *dat, goed*)
- Morphology: adjective declination (*ne kleinen bakker, nen boek*), diminutive suffix (*doekske*), use of pronouns (e.g., *gij, ekik*)
- Syntax: double negation (*ik hoor nie goe nie meer*)
- Lexicon: *klappen, bijkans, seffens*

De Caluwe (2009, 8) uses as an example sentence (unfortunately impossible to properly translate): "*Kunde gij mij ne keer zeggen waar dakik dienen bak moe zetten?*"

These (and similar) characteristics are not new: they have existed forever in all kinds of varieties on the scale between dialect and standard language. Previously, this used to be called dialect interference. The only thing new is that this variety (if variety it is) is now used in communicative settings where it was not (or less) used before. New is also the name, much more than the phenomenon itself. De Caluwe (2009) is right in assuming that the novelty doesn't lie in the formal characteristics but in its status and functions.

The most characteristic way this Schoon Vlaams differs from the norm is, according to Goossens (2000), not the pronunciation or even the lexicon but grammar. Its grammatical features, he says, have been directly taken over from the central, southern dialects (i.e., Brabants, RW). As a consequence, we are now in the presence of two "different languages" (i.e., Schoon Vlaams and Southern Standard Dutch), both of whom have their own specific linguistic structure. And he continues: "I don't think that Flanders needs two languages: one which is Dutch for use in official and formal situations, and one which isn't Dutch for every day usage" (11). Still, adapting one's linguistic behavior to the formality of the setting is a rather normal and natural thing to do and occurs spontaneously in almost any community. It is not different in nature from the diglossic communication patterns that used to exist not only in Flanders but also in many other places all over the world as well.

The reasons for Goossens's (2000) observations inspired by language policy are plausible, but what he calls a new kind of bilingualism is, in fact, a normal and even unavoidable evolution in cases of spontaneous dialect loss. Generally, the first substitute for the disappearing dialect is a vernacular, characterized by a large amount of regional interference. The next step (after a more or less long time) usually is the generalization of the Standard to the detriment of the regional standards, once those have served their purpose. Most people, including Goossens, would prefer to skip the intermediate stage and proceed to the generalization of the Standard right away. If at all, this would be possible only with extensive language planning measures but still would take a couple of generations.

The real danger, it is widely felt, is that this informal Schoon Vlaams threatens to flow over in situations where it is not deemed fit and thus becomes a rival of the standard language. Such an evolution might indeed be potentially disruptive for the unity of the language territory, and this probably explains Goossens's (2000) negative reaction. Stroop's rejection of Poldernederlands, on the other hand, has more to do with the fact that it might threaten Algemeen Beschaafd Nederlands (ABN), the "sociolect of the educated and the cultivated." That both are not on the same wave length is obvious when Goossens refers to Stroop and his followers as "the vulgarizing publications of a few rather noisy Dutch linguists on what they call *Poldernederlands* are dramatizing the differences in The Netherlands without reason" (13).

Schoon Vlaams is becoming increasingly popular on radio and TV. In the latter it is often used in series, both on public and commercial stations. In radio spots I noticed a long time ago already that there is a very specific and functional alternation between Standard Dutch and Tussentaal. In many spots where dialogue is followed by a comment, the dialogue (e.g., between a hairdresser and her costumer) is in Tussentaal, whereas the comment (inciting people to buy a hair product) is in very careful and normative Standard Dutch. In other words, the text writers are perfectly aware of the difference between both varieties and the ways to use them. Subsequent surveys by Saman (2003), Van Herreweghe and Slembrouck (2004), and Van Gysel, Geeraerts, and Speelman (2008) have confirmed my previous impressions.

Also, it is a common feeling that the media, in this way, are strengthening and popularizing this specific kind of diglossia. Geeraerts et al. (2000, 170) mention the very real danger that, by letting actors converse in Tussentaal, the authors of soaps and similar TV series not only contribute to its use but even leave the viewer in the illusion that it is perfectly acceptable or even preferable to use Tussentaal themselves in the situations depicted.

LANGUAGE PLANNING

Changing the course of a linguistic evolution takes deliberate and well-coordinated language planning. Stroop and Goossens, therefore, are urging official language planning measures; Van de Velde (as we have seen) is on the same wavelength, and others such as Cajot (2010) join them as well. Also, the Royal Academy for Dutch Language and Literature (KANTL) issued an official statement on September 25, 2011, at the occasion of its 125th anniversary, urging language users and language planners to strengthen the position of the standard language and its normative use.[3]

---

[3] "*We vragen daarom aandacht voor de standaardtaal—het Nederlands zoals dat in België wordt gesproken en geschreven—en voor de meer formele registers, die hun rechtmatige plaats in de openbare ruimte moeten blijven behouden. De overheid, het onderwijs en de media spelen hierin een cruciale rol. We geloven dat men een norm kan voorhouden zonder taalgebruikers te frustreren of te kleineren.*"

What kind of action do they have in mind? What kind could possibly be taken? From a purely scientific-linguistic point of view, there is no need to do anything at all. We can sit back and observe how things are developing. What is happening now does indeed allow for a privileged view on change in progress, a unique chance for every sociolinguist. But if we don't want to narrow our scope to (participant) observation, if we agree that language political concern for the status and function of Dutch and the unity of the language territory is legitimate, even for linguists, the present-day evolutions may, owing to circumstances, be rather disturbing indeed.

Developments that eventually succeed are mostly the results of compromises between *taalnatuur* and *taalcultuur*, that is, between natural evolution on one hand and language planning efforts to bring it under control on the other. Since in these particular cases *taalnatuur* has been allowed to proliferate, it is quite comprehensible that the call for remedying interventions is growing louder. Stroop and Goossens complain about what they call the language permissive climate in the schools, which tolerates or even favors this kind of excrescences. Both urge the authorities, specifically those responsible for school and education, to increase the number of language pedagogical efforts.

Van de Velde, for his part, proclaims that, as far as pronunciation is concerned, it would not be advisable that language planners try to intervene. But in general, he too agrees that some "counseling of the standardization process on the part of the authorities, the schools and the media might not be unwise" (Van de Velde 2000, 38). Cajot (2010, 24), who admits to deplore the previously mentioned evolution, is convinced that "the time for the authorities in The Netherlands and Flanders to start with an active policy of linguistic and cultural rapprochement has come," and he wants the Nederlandse Taalunie to take the lead and coordinate the initiative.

It is questionable, though, whether the time is ripe for new language planning initiatives and whether they will be able to generate a sufficient amount of sympathy and cooperation. Language planning on a private as well as on an institutional official level has essentially determined both the structure and the use of Dutch. During the 19th century, two waves of particularism failed to prevent the official Flemish cultural establishment from adopting an integrationist point of view. Consequently, the majority policy has always been that the standardization of Dutch in Belgium ought to proceed in accordance with the evolution in the northern Netherlands. The underlying motivation was a political one: to be able to use the prestige of Dutch as the official language of Holland in the domestic language struggle with French, the former prestige language in Belgium. But since the language question in Belgium has been settled for some time already, this particular purpose of integrationism has been fulfilled, and the relationship between the varieties of Dutch on both sides of the border is increasingly the habitual one between pluricentric language varieties. Attitudes and habits, built up in the past, will continue to play an important role, but they have ceased to be the sole decisive factors.

It is very hard to predict whether language planning efforts, equally strong on both sides, might eventually succeed in overcoming so many simultaneous problems, and it is even questionable whether such efforts may reasonably be expected, in Flanders for the reasons already explained, in the Netherlands because there has never been an integrationist tradition in the first place. One of the problems is that no language planning instance exists that might be responsible for this kind of initiatives. The Taalunie, explicitly named by Cajot and many others, has never been attributed a similar function, nor has it ever been eager to claim this kind of regulating role. Although the impact of linguistic diversity between parts of a pluricentric language community should not be dramatized, the problem at hand is one worth of our utmost attention. In view of the rather complicated situation, it is not surprising that Goossens's analysis stops short of offering or suggesting specific remedies. To find people willing to act now would presuppose a number of things. First of all, it should be clear that the tendencies mentioned should indeed continue in the way as feared by Van de Velde, Stroop, Cajot, and Goossens. Moreover, it would be necessary to find a lot of people willing and prepared to do something about it. And if so, an enormous language planning effort on a scale never witnessed before would have to be devised and implemented.

Destandardization?

According to Mattheier (2003, 239–240), an important characteristic of de-standardization is "a relativization of linguistic norms." The norms of the standard language, he observes, are "increasingly oriented towards the more variable spoken language" (ibid.). Consequently, there is a general decrease in linguistic uniformity and sense of norm. This sounds pretty familiar and seems to be a rather fitting description of the two developments just mentioned for the Low Countries. Still, destandardization does not necessarily imply the genesis of new language varieties, and vernaculars, regiolects, and substandards have always existed. The consequence of dialect loss and leveling is that many people are trading in their dialect in an increasing number of settings and functions for another variety that is not the standard language.

A DECAY OF NORMS?

Verkavelingsvlaams is not really new, and the same actually applies to Poldernederlands. I tend to agree with Hinskens (2007), who argues that the latter variety used to be a regional standard in Holland and Utrecht. Undisputed is that both varieties are used more often, in more situations, and in a larger number of domains than they used to be. This means that they are taking over functions from other varieties. Simultaneously, an important attitudinal change is upgrading the prestige of intermediate varieties: people seem to take them more seriously, and their use is more commendable. As a consequence, the standard language is pushed to the extreme formality side of the continuum. Together with dialect loss, these two developments are responsible for the creation of an enormous amount of space on the (theoretical) function continuum scale: fewer functions for the standard, fewer functions, and less proficiency for the dialect. That space is filled by the intermediate variety, which has the possibility to move either to the left or to the right according to the circumstances, thus alternatively taking the shape of a more regional or a more standard like variety.

In the past, the linguistic distance between dialect and standard language was huge, and both were looked upon as two really distinct varieties; this made the use of one instead of the other quasi-impossible. Today, the linguistic (and, most of all, attitudinal) distance is considerably smaller, and, as a result, many people see no inconvenience in using the intermediate varieties in situations where actually the use of the standard would be (or used to be) more appropriate.

A similar evolution occurs in larger parts of Western Europe: people are gradually restricting to one single variety, modified only slightly according to different communicative situations. This used to be the privilege of those who live in a region where the standard language was the habitual language of socialization and everyday speech (northern and western Germany, for example, or the Paris region). The loss of the dialects and their replacement with another informal variety creates the illusion that this particular variety might function in formal situations as well, even if, as Elspass (2005, 20) observes, "a characteristic feature of vernacular speech and colloquial standard usage...is the linguistic instability, which makes them susceptible for various forms of contact-induced language change."

In the Netherlands, the spoken Dutch of the upper classes, ABN, lost its status and prestige and could not hold onto its function as a linguistic model. From then onward it was felt that every kind of Dutch that was more or less intelligible would do. "The Dutchman sees his language as a tool, and he, but mostly she, turns to the easiest kind of Dutch that his/her environment, boss, teacher etc. is prepared to accept" (Stroop 1998, 102).

In Belgium, the astonishing pace of dialect loss, mainly in Brabant, has created a rather chaotic language situation. Dialect loss deprived people of the natural antipole of the standard language. By their sheer existence, dialects offered a sort of safeguard for the existence and the function of that standard language. De Caluwe (2009, 8) argues that "in the eyes of the young people the *tussentaal* is no less than their mother tongue, and perfectly fit for all types of supra-regional informal communication. If urged to use standard Dutch, as with the CGN recordings, they will make a few adjustments—lexical, phonological, morpho-syntactical—to their colloquial speech, but they will not switch to the standard code." For the large majority of Flemish youngsters (with the exception of the West Flemings), who cannot use the dialect anymore, *tussentaal* "is their language of daily conversation, also the language variety they use when text messaging and chatting" (ibid., 8).[4]

THE END OF DIGLOSSIA?

The aforementioned change put an end to the diglossic situation (see box 6.1) that used to exist almost everywhere in Flanders until a couple of decades ago. Diglossia requires the use of different language varieties in distinct communicative situations, for example, using dialect in an informal and standard language in a formal situation. There is ample evidence that where diglossia exists, the need for and the use of intermediate varieties are significantly lower than elsewhere.

Recent surveys and inquiries allow for plausible predictions regarding the future of Tussentaal in Flanders. The most significant ones are surveys of the situation in West Flanders, since that is the only province where the pace of dialect loss is still very low and where, in most parts of the province, the diglossic situation has persisted until the present day. Five consecutive surveys between 1979 and 2001[5] show that the number of West Flemings claiming dialect proficiency is always higher than 95 percent. Also, the informants are able to distinguish sharply between a [+ dialect] and a [– dialect] variety, which leaves hardly any room for an intermediate variety. As a consequence, in West Flanders a more or less standardized variety (H) is used in formal situations, that is, in situations where the dialect (L) is not deemed appropriate.

In one of the very first inquiries to produce quantifiable data, Vandekerckhove (2004, 2005) addresses two of the more interesting problems raised by Tussentaal, namely, where is it used most often and by which age groups. Using the huge database of present-day Standard Dutch (the *Corpus Gesproken Nederlands*), she examined two of the main characteristics of Tussentaal—the pronouns of the second person (the forms of address) and the diminutive suffix. In the former case, the subject and object form of the personal and possessive pronouns were examined comparing Tussentaal forms *ge, gij, u, uw* with Standard Dutch *je, jij, jou, jouw*. In the latter case *-ke* is the Tussentaal, and *-je* the standard form of the diminutive suffix. Vandekerckhove established that West Flanders is the only province where the use of *je* in subject function supersedes the use of *ge*. She also reveals that West Flanders is the only province where younger subjects use *je* more often than older subjects. Moreover, West Flanders is the only province where *jou* in object function is the most frequently used pronoun, and *u* is used only half as often as elsewhere. Finally, it

---

[4] As opposed to other quotes from De Caluwe, which I have translated, this one was taken from the English language abstract preceding his article.

[5] Willemyns (1979), Willemyns and Delacauw (1983), Van Keymeulen (1993), Willemyns and Dorchain (1997), and Vandekerckhove (2001). All necessary information is given in Willemyns (2000).

is demonstrated that West Flanders is the only province where the diminutive *-je* is used more often by younger than by older subjects.

Speakers from Brabant and Limburg do use Tussentaal forms considerably more often than West Flemings do, the latter also being the only group where in specific situations the younger speakers use the Tussentaal forms less often than the older ones. In Brabant and Limburg the opposite is the case in all situations. Vandekerckhove (2004, 990) concludes, "Quite ironically... the supraregional colloquial language of the region which is known to have the highest dialect vitality, approaches the standard language most closely." Actually, there is nothing ironic about is, since it is the normal and predictable outcome.

De Caluwe's (2009) figures are provided by the *Corpus Gesproken Nederlands* as well and refer to the spoken standard language usage of youngsters (between 18 and 24 years of age). Here too the diminutive suffix *(-je* vs. *-ke)* and the forms of address *(je* vs. *ge)* are examined, as well as two more features: the declination of the article *(een grote hond* vs. *ne groten (h)ond)* and the use of the redundant *dat* with conjunctions and pronouns (e.g., *ik weet niet of [dat] hij komt).* In the *Corpus Gesproken Nederlands* all subjects are urged to use only standard language. Still, all participants use nonstandard features as well, some occasionally and others very often. The lowest amount of Tussentaal features is, here again, found with West Flemings (16.4 percent), the largest with partic-ipants from the province of Antwerp (66.8 percent). In other words, there is an enormous gap between the West Flemish speakers and all the others. According to De Caluwe (2009, 20) the West Flemings use a bipolar model: dialect and standard language are two very distinct varieties. When explicitly asked not to use their dialect, West Flemings switch to standard language. As opposed to participants from other provinces, they don't consider Tussentaal to be an acceptable alternative. All of this confirms my previous hypothesis that Tussentaal is thriving precisely in those regions where dialect loss has occurred earlier and more intensely, whereas in regions where a diglossic situation con-tinues to exist, Tussentaal remains on a lower level (Willemyns 2005b).

As far as attitudes are concerned, we have Andries Geeraert's recent results of ongoing research, obtained through a matched guise inquiry.[6] In random order the respondents were presented with a text having the same content in Standard Northern Dutch, Standard Southern Dutch, Tussentaal, and a regio-lect of their respective province. After each sample, the respondents (all highly educated) were asked to indicate in how far they felt the variety in question might be suitable for use in a particular situation, from very informal through very formal. Respondents were subdivided into younger and older and also according to their geographic origin (province). Some of the most interesting results in a nutshell:

---

[6] As yet unpublished but available at the Dutch Department of the Vrije Universiteit in Brussels; a summary is available at http://www.standaard.be/artikel/detail.aspx?artikelid= HM2E8SIJ.

a) Age variable: Both older and younger subjects accept the use of the intermediate variety (Tussentaal) in informal settings; in the formal domain only the standard language is deemed appropriate.
b) Geographic variable: The appropriateness of Tussentaal in the informal domains is judged differently. The West Flemish situation is very explicit: their acceptance of Tussentaal is considerably lower than with the respondents from all other provinces.
c) The final two questions give an overview of the appropriateness of four different varieties (Northern Standard, Southern Standard, Tussentaal, and regiolect) subdivided for younger and older participants. The figures differ only slightly, and the tendencies in all groups run parallel. It is interesting to see that in formal circumstances the Northern Dutch Standard is considered to be more fitting than Tussentaal. One thing is utterly clear though: the Southern Standard beats them all!

Summarizing, we see how the most conclusive evidence in the Tussentaal debate comes from West Flanders. Not only are the attitudes of the West Flemings toward the intermediate variety significantly more negative than elsewhere, but they also use standard forms in situations in which others prefer Tussentaal. Also, there is ample evidence that younger speakers are more opposed to Tussentaal than older ones still.

A supplementary and interesting advantage of a diglossic situation is that people are used to always switching on their "monitor" when they're not speaking dialect and are, therefore, in a position to consciously choose which feature they are going to use. Diglossia increases the linguistic awareness of the language user considerably, which is one reason that West Flemings, when urged to use standard language (as was the case in the CGN recordings), can comply almost effortlessly and are able to consciously reduce interference from other varieties.

What about Tomorrow?

The present-day linguistic makeup of the Low Countries has been determined by, among others, the following recent sociolinguistically important factors or changes:

- The (language) politically motivated integrationism faded away.
- A new southern, local center of language prestige (Brabant) was born.
- Direct contacts between Flemings and Dutchmen gradually decreased.[7]

---

[7] Kloots's (2001) data based on a survey of teachers of Dutch in both countries are very relevant in this respect.

- A general process of democratization was put in motion that enabled all classes and layers of society to be involved in shaping the suprare-gional variety or varieties. The inevitable consequence is a more flexible norm for the standard language.
- Finally (and I am not sure whether this is a cause or rather a consequence), there is an increasing indifference as to how the Dutch language is used in other parts of the language territory. Something similar is happening in, for example, Switzerland and Luxembourg, that is, the external periphery withdrawing into one's own small cocoon while dropping the larger picture.

Maybe as a result of all this, it seems that during recent decades the influence of the major standardization factors—the social factor in Holland and the political one in Flanders—has been gradually fading away.

It is not sure at all that Poldernederlands is "the variety of the future," as Stroop fears it is. Probably we will witness an increasing influence of the so-called *Stadsdialecten* (urban dialects) of the Randstad, in other words an increasing Hollandization. Still, sooner or later the universal urge to distin-guish oneself through language, combined with the equally universal urge for upward social mobility, will restrengthen, and then things will probably change once more. There is not enough evidence yet to predict which direction it will take.

Tussentaal (or Verkavelingsvlaams or Schoon Vlaams) is a rather diffuse notion. It has become a generic term for all kinds of very heterogeneous tendencies that nobody knows for sure will continue to develop in the same direction. Therefore, it is equally hard to predict whether Tussentaal (Schoon Vlaams) is really going to become a new language variety or whether it will stay what it is today: a collection of features varying on the basis of age, gender, or region or maybe even from person to person.

We are actually in the presence of two simultaneous yet opposite phenomena. As opposed to the weakening of integration resulting in a destandardization of the spoken variety of Southern Dutch, there is ample proof of rapidly growing integration, that is, of increasing accommodation to the northern norm in all aspects of the written, formal language: in morphology, in syntax, and in the lexicon (see chapter 6).

As far as the language practice of youngsters is concerned, we will also have to discover in how far they are really aware of language variation on the microlevel. "Are they familiar with the varieties linguists have labeled dialect, tussentaal, standard language etc.," De Caluwe (2009, 23) pertinently asks, and are they able to determine what, in our jargon, is their stratificational status and function? I agree that many of them are using typically Tussentaal features without realizing that they are producing Tussentaal instead of standard language. "It is possible—and I think even probable—that the modal Fleming is not aware of a separate variety called *tussentaal*" (ibid., 16).

A potentially disruptive factor is that the north is witnessing innovations that are not adopted and very often even go unnoticed in the south. A general societal growing together or symbiosis as it used to exist in the 1970s and 1980s has been discontinued, and Flemings have become less familiar with what is going on in the north, linguistically or otherwise. Not only have they almost stopped watching Dutch television, but also the written media have become less popular: reading *Vrij Nederland* or the *Groene Amsterdammer* used to be indispensable for every Flemish intellectual, and even more popular magazines like the *Haagse Post* and *Elseviers* used to have a large circulation.

In both parts of the Low Countries the really decisive phenomenon may be that, as in larger parts of Western Europe, people are gradually restricting to one single variety, modified only slightly according to different communicative situations. The loss of dialects, and their replacement with an equally informal intermediate variety, creates the illusion that this particular variety might then function in formal situations as well. However, the fact that this "one variety speech" is usually strongly influenced by local, geographical features is potentially disruptive for language unity.

According to De Caluwe (2009, 22), the future of Dutch will mainly be determined by "the lexical, phonological and morpho-syntactic dynamics in the transitional zone between the colloquial speech and the standard language." We need more research, he adds, to see whether the colloquial speech is or will be gradually evolving into a more standardized way or whether a gradually more homogeneous, Brabant-based vernacular will take over the role and function that in other language communities is played by the informal register of the standard language.

Other language territories have learned to live with this kind of pluricentric variation (e.g., the United Kingdom versus the United States, Germany versus Austria), and maybe that is what the Dutch language territory will have to do as well. The problem is that, mainly in the northern Netherlands, tolerance toward accepting variability has no tradition at all, and even the prerequisite for tolerance, namely, familiarity with other variants, is lacking. In Germany, for example, (northern) people who would never use words like *Jenner* (for *Januar*; january), *Paradeiser* (for *Tomaten*; tomatoes), or *Marillen* (for *Abrikosen*; apricots) know perfectly well what they mean and find their use by southern Germans and Austrians perfectly normal.[8]

Viewed in a historical perspective, we are confronted with tendencies of change that have originated in some very specific groups of the population, in different parts of the language territory. Where and when short-term change switches into long-term (and durable) change depends on the well-known social

---

[8] According to Elspass (2005, 24) a recent survey indicates "a noticeable spread of 'southern' variants in northern Germany," and it is suggested that this development is the result of an increase in the covert prestige of southern German regionalisms.

variables as social class and profession, level of instruction, age, and gender as well as on domain-specific factors and language planning factors. As far as the Netherlands is concerned, Standard Dutch "seems to have started fragmenting...As a consequence, the standard norm may well be pushed back and become a norm for written standard language use only" (Hinskens 2007, 297). Grondelaers and Van Hout (2011, 199), who, as opposed to earlier researchers, are convinced that "it is not impossible to make reliable predictions about the future of Dutch," argue that "Belgian and Netherlandic Dutch are...developing towards a stratificational configuration without discrete intermediate strata between the base dialects and the standard. While the recent history of Netherlandic Dutch is characterized by downward norm relaxation (top to bottom), Belgian Dutch is characterized by bottom-up (re)standardization."

I want to end with a quotation from Vandenbussche (2010, 239), who concludes his comment on the findings of Van de Velde et al. (2010) on pronunciation with the reassuring prognosis that "there is no risk whatsoever of ending up with 'two divorced standard languages' any time soon."

As I mentioned earlier, the linguistic evolution of Dutch in the 21st century promises to be an exciting and thrilling affair, worth closely observing and participating in.

10 }

Chapter Main Sources and Further Reading

Every historiographer is indebted to many other people who have written on particular periods in history or on particular subjects in which they are not specialists. Consequently, they need to read a lot and synthesize this material and incorporate a large amount of facts, interpretations, and ideas others have found and published.

The bibliography should list them all, yet it does not reveal how each source has been used. Therefore, I compiled a list of what I call *main sources*. I list them by chapter and give an overview of publications I have used extensively. Although most of the quotations are indicated as such, the authors of these publications have inspired me much more than just by providing some useful quotations; these authors will often find their general lines of thinking woven throughout the chapters. I am very grateful for the extremely useful information these sources provided. In addition, the ideas presented in these main sources proved to be inspiring to my own thinking on the subjects in question, even in cases where I do not completely agree. The following list shows where my main sources of facts and inspiration can be found. In some cases I also provide references for further reading.

Histories of the Language

The number of histories of Dutch is rather limited. De Vries, Willemyns, and Burger (2003), Willemyns (2003), and Van der Sijs and Willemyns (2009) are three in which I have been involved. The work of my coauthors has, of course, been a great help for the present book as well. Van den Toorn et al. (1997) is the most recent scholarly overview of the history of Dutch.

Two books on the matter published in English, Donaldson (1983) and Brachin (1985) (in the English translation of Paul Vincent), were, among other things, also a great help in solving terminological problems. For further reading, see De Vooys (1952) and Van der Wal (2008²).

Histories of the Literature

In this book, anything having to do with literature (which is not my cup of tea) draws heavily on Meijer (1971) and the authors of various chapters in Hermans (2009). The supply of histories of the Dutch literature written in Dutch is not vast but covers the field really well. The authoritative *Geschiedenis van de Nederlandse literatuur* (Gelderblom & Musschoot 2006), commissioned by the Nederlandse Taalunie, began to be published in 2006. On translations into German of Middle Dutch literature, see Schlusemann (2010).

Chapter 1: Who Speaks Dutch and Where?

On language contact along the Dutch–German border from a language historical point of view, see Goossens (2008), which provides a great deal of interesting maps. On the more recent situation, see Bister-Broosen (1998) and *Taal en Tongval* 57(1) (2005). On the relation between Frisian and Dutch and the linguistic situation in Friesland, see Gorter (1996, 2001) and Ytsma (1995). Recent information on language proficiency and usage can be found in Provincie Fryslan (2007). The Wurdboek fan de Fryske taal/Woordenboek der Friese taal (WFT) was put online in 2010 (http://www.fryske-akademy.nl). Tiersma (1999) is a Frisian reference grammar. Oppewal et al. (2006) a history of Frisian literature.

A complete overview of language contact at the Germanic–Romance border all over Europe is in Treffers and Willemyns (2002). The situation in French Flanders, past and present, is analyzed in Ryckeboer (2002). The most recent overview of the language border in Belgium is Willemyns (2002). Historical data are provided in Martens (1975) and Verhulst, De Metsenaere, and Deweerdt (1998). On the Brussels suburban region, see De Witte (1975) and Detant (1998); on the six *faciliteiten* communes, see De Schrijver (1998) and Koppen, Distelmans, and Janssens (2002). On Brussels, see Witte (1993), De Metsenaere (1998), and Baetens Beardsmore (2000). A recent survey with up-to-date information on language and society is given in Janssens (2007).

Chapter 2: Old Dutch: Its Ancestors and Contemporaries

The evolution from Indo-European to Germanic is to be found in every book on the history of any Germanic language. My overview is mostly based on Van Coetsem (1970) and Gysseling (1978). More information on Ingvaeonic appears in Heeroma (1972) and Buccini (1992, 2010).

An overview of very recent research on Old Dutch is given in Schoonheim and Van der Sijs (2005). General information on Old Dutch is provided in Van Loey (1970), Van Coetsem (1970), Gysseling (1978), Quak (1997), and Quak and Van der Horst (2002).

All Old Dutch texts prior to 1300 are edited in Gysseling (1977–1987). For an extensive and annotated edition of the *Wachtendonckse psalmen*, see De Grauwe (1979); Cowan (1957) is more concise. Various opinions on *Hebban olla uogala*... are listed in Kettenis and Meijer (1980).

The website http://gtb.inl.nl/ gives free access to three scientific dictionaries: the Old Dutch one; the dictionary of Early Middle Dutch (1200–1300); and the *Woordenboek der Nederlandsche taal* (WNT) from 1500 onward. A link to Verwijs and Verdam's *Middelnederlandsch Woordenboek* (Middle Dutch Dictionary) can be found there as well.

Chapter 3: Middle Dutch: Language and Literature

The paramount Middle Dutch grammar is Van Loey (1980), now electronically available on the Digitale Bibliotheek voor de Nederlandse Letteren (DBNL) website (http://www.dbnl.org). More information on various aspects of the grammar of Middle Dutch is in, among others, Goossens (1974, 1980), Van Loey (1970), and Van Loon (1986). Both the internal and external history of Early Middle Dutch is given in Pijnenburg (1997) and of Late Middle Dutch in Willemyns (1997). The historical grammar of Dutch is another important source of information on Middle Dutch. The authoritative one is Van Loey (1971), popularly known as the Schönfeld.

The historical development of the Dutch phonological system is presented clearly and illustrated with a lot of dialect maps in the *FAND* (Goossens, Taeldeman, & Verleyen 1999); morphology and syntax are treated in the *MAND* (De Schutter et al. 2005) and the *SAND* (Barbiers et al. 2005), respectively. As to the lexicon of Middle Dutch, Verdam is the authoritative source; for the 13th-century Middle Dutch specifically, see the Vroegmiddelnederlands Woordenboek (http://www.inl.nl).

General information on the linguistic situation as well as language contact (and conflict) during the Burgundian period is in Armstrong (1965), Geyl (2001), and Willemyns (2003, ch. 5). Societal information for that period as well as demographic and financial data were taken from Blockmans and Prevenier (1997).

Chapter 4: Early New Dutch (1500–1800)

General information on the beginning of the Early New Dutch period is found in Van den Branden (1956), Hellinga (1938), and Weijnen (1974).

Van der Sijs (2004) gives an overview of spelling guides, dictionaries, grammars, and other linguistic treatises published in the 16th, 17th, and 18th centuries. A more specific and very detailed analysis of southern publications in that field is in Smeyers (1959); specifically on the 18th century, see Rutten (2011). On Becanus and similar protagonists of Dutch, see Hagen (1999).

De Bonth et al. (1997) provides an in-depth discussion of the internal and external history of Northern Dutch from 1650 through 1880.

The linguistic consequences of the political split of the language territory are discussed in Van Leuvensteijn (1997), Boyce Hendriks and Howell (2000), Van der Sijs (2004), and Taeldeman (2007). See also Howell (2002).

On the importance of the Statenbijbel, see Van Dalen-Oskam and Mooijaart (2000) and Van der Sijs (2005). Various bible translations from the 15th, 16th, and 17th centuries, including the Statenbijbel, have been digitalized and are available at http://www.inl.nl, www.dbnl.org and http://www.biblija.net.

Information on 18th-century *rederijkers* and grammarians is in Rutten (2011) and Smeyers (1959); the latter elaborates in great detail on Verhoeven and Verlooy.

The main source of information on language usage in administration and social life is Deneckere (1954). Smeyers (1959) and Lenders (1987) detail the linguistic policies of both the Austrian and the local administrations.

The new and innovative view on the 18th century as a less dull age (at least linguistically) is based on Rutten (2009c, 2011), Vosters (2011), Rutten and Vosters (2010, 2011), and Vosters, Rutten, and van der Wal (2010).

Information on how the northern Netherlands fared during the French period is mainly found in De Bonth et al. (1997) and Van der Sijs (2004). For the south see Vanhecke (2007) and De Groof (2004). The consequences of the French language policy for French Flanders are discussed in Duvoskeldt (1999) and Willemyns (2005). A comparison between the early revolutionary and the Napoleonic policies is in De Groof (2004). Language use of the various social classes in the late 18th and early 19th centuries is discussed in Vandenbussche (2002).

Chapter 5: Reunion and Secession: The 19th Century

The main source of information on the societal and linguistic situation in the United Kingdom of the Netherlands is provided in De Jonghe (1967); linguistic analyses are outlined in De Groof (2004) and Vanhecke (2007). Further evaluations of William's language policy are in De Groof (2004), François (1992), Vanhecke (2007), Van Goethem (1990), and Vosters (2011). On his policy for Wallonia see Janssens and Steyaert (2008).

The main sources on language evolution in the 19th-century Netherlands are in Hulshof (1997), Van den Toorn (1997), and Van der Sijs (2004, 2005).

Van der Sijs (2004) and Van der Wal (2008²) provide ample information on older Dutch grammars and dictionaries as well as the norms they intended to introduce.

Overall historical information on Belgium is given in Witte, Craeybeckx, and Meynen (2009). On Belgium from 1830 onward, see Bouveroux (2011). There is an enormous amount of literature on the Flemish movement. A treasure of information and details is provided in the *Encyclopedie van de Vlaamse Beweging* (*EVB*; 2 volumes 1973–1975) and, more recently, the *Nieuwe Encyclopedie van de Vlaamse Beweging* (*NEVB*; 3 volumes 1998). Language planning and policy are analyzed in De Groof (2004) and Ruys (1981) in German and Ruys (1973) in English.

On the territoriality principle and various models of multilingual countries consult McRae (1975). Language purism, particularism, and integrationism are in Suffeleers (1979).

All data on language in city administrations are taken from Vanhecke (2007) and supplemented by data published afterward (last overview to date is in Vanhecke, Vandenbussche, and Willemyns 2010).

Chapter 6: The 20th Century: The Age of the Standard Language

My main sources on the 20th-century evolution of Dutch and the rise and fall of Algemeen Beschaafd Nederlands are Hulshof (1997), Van den Toorn (1997), van der Horst and van der Horst (1999), Van der Sijs (2004, 2005), and Van der Wal (2008). On ABN planning in Flanders, more specifically the role of the language gardeners, see Willemyns (2003, 324).

A handy overview of the literature on spelling and spelling changes can be found in Molenwijk (1992). The official spelling rules of Dutch are in the *Woordenlijst* (*Groene Boekje*) and can also be downloaded from the INL website (http://www.inl.nl).

The main dialect groups and the most characteristic differences between them are discussed in the manuals of Weijnen (1966) and Goossens (1977); they also provide ample information on dialect atlases and lexica. Van der Sijs (2011) is a more popular display of dialect maps, illustrating lexical differences in the territory at large. The east–west antagonism is illustrated very clearly in Goossens (2008). Very recent atlases are the *FAND* on phonology (Goossens, Taeldeman, and Verleyen 1999), the *MAND* (De Schutter et al. 2005) on morphology, and the *SAND* on syntax (Barbiers et al. 2005).

The "soundbites" of the Meertens Instituut provide a huge selection of sound samples of Dutch dialects, displayed on a *Sprekende Kaart* (speaking map): www.meertens.knaw.nl/soundbites.

As far as dialect loss is concerned, Willemyns (1997a) summarizes all the relevant case studies in both the Netherlands and Flanders.

Many examples of southern words adopted in the north are discussed in Van der Sijs (2004). De Clerck (1981) is a dictionary of "South-Netherlandic words." More information on the labels in Van Dale are given in Geeraerts (2000), and labels in dictionaries in general are in Martin (2010).

An in-depth historical overview of the north–south debate is in Suffeleers (1979). On the Flemish movement, see the *Encyclopedie van de Vlaamse Beweging* (EVB 1973–1975) and, more recently, the *Nieuwe Encyclopedie van de Vlaamse Beweging* (NEVB 1998). A recent overview of the language question and community problems in Belgium between Walloons and Flemings is provided in Witte and Van Velthoven (2010). A very detailed account is also in Bouveroux (2011).

One of the very few English publications on the *Nederlandse Taalunie* is Willemyns (1984). The *Nederlandse Taalunie* website (http://taalunieversum.org) is also helpful.

Chapter 7: Colonial Dutch

Lexical influence of Dutch on other languages is listed in Van der Sijs (1998). What Dutch took from other languages is displayed in Van der Sijs (2006). A chronologic overview of loans per language is provided in Van der Sijs (2009).

My most important source for the history of Dutch in Indonesia is Groeneboer (1998); on the linguistic influence of Dutch in the United States see Van der Sijs (2009); for the linguistic situation in Suriname see De Kleine (2007). For more information on the Surinamese variety of Dutch, see Gobardhan-Rambocus (1993). Van Donselaar (1989) and De Bies (2009) are dictionaries of Surinamese Dutch. On the most recent changes in de Antilles, see Mijts and Van Bogaert (2011).

Chapter 8: Afrikaans

My main sources on Afrikaans are Ponelis (1993, 1994), Stell (2008), and Roberge (2003). On the influence of English on Afrikaans, see Donaldson (1988) and Deumert (2001).

Chapter 9: Progress or Decay? The Future Development of Dutch

On variation and change in spoken Standard Dutch between 1935 and 1993, see Van de Velde (1996).

On *Poldernederlands*, see Stroop (1998, 2011). My main sources on *Verkavelingsvlaams* are De Caluwe (2002, 2009), Geeraerts, Penne, and Vanswegenhoven

(2000), Goossens (2000), Vandekerckhove (2005), Willemyns (2005b, 2007), and Grondelaers and Van Hout (2011).

On de-standardization and other recent developments, see Van der Sijs (2004, ch. 10) and Willemyns (2007). On the most recent changes in pronunciation see Van de Velde et al. (2010).

On the website of the *Nederlandse Taalunie* (http://www.taalunieversum.nl) there is an annual newspaper entitled *Taalpeil* with updated information of the status and situation of Dutch at home and abroad.

BIBLIOGRAPHY

Aitchison, Jean (1985). *Language Change: Progress or Decay?* Cambridge: Cambridge University Press.

Alen, A. & L.P. Suetens (eds.) (1993). *Het federale België na de vierde staatshervorming.* Brugge: Die Keure.

Allossery, P. (1930). *Kan. Adolf Duclos (1841–1925). Met een kijk op den zoogenaamden taalparticularistenstrijd.* Brugge: Drukkerij Jos. De Plancke.

Algemene Nederlandse Spraakkunst (ANS) (1997²). Groningen: Wolters Plantyn.

Armstrong, C.A.J. (1965). The Language Question in the Low Countries: The Use of French and Dutch by the Dukes of Burgundy and Their Administration. In J.R. Hale, J. Highfield, & B. Smalley (eds.), *Europe in the Late Middle Ages.* London: Faber & Faber, 386–409.

Bachman, Van Cleaf. (1982). The Story of the Low Dutch Language. *De Halve Maen* 56: 3, 1–3, 21; 57: 1, 10–13.

Bachman, Van Cleaf (1983). What Is Low Dutch? *De Halve Maen* 57: 3, 14–17, 23–24.

Baetens Beardsmore, Hugo (1981). Linguistic Accommodation in Belgium. In Hugo Baetens Beardsmore & Roland Willemyns (eds.), *Linguistic Accommodation in Belgium.* Brussel: VUBPress. Brussels Pre-prints in Linguistics 5.

Baetens Beardsmore, Hugo (1990). The Evolution and Current Status of Brussels as a Bilingual City. In H. Baetens Beardsmore, *Bilingualism in Education: Theory and Practice.* Brussel: VUBPress. Brussels Pre-prints in Linguistics 11.

Baetens Beardsmore, Hugo (2000). Bruxelles. In W.F. Mackey (ed.), *Espaces urbains et coexistence des langues.* Terminogramme 93–94. Québec: Office de la langue française, 85–102.

Bakema, Peter, Patricia Dufour, Marianne Jacobs, Sabine Lefever, and Maurice Vandebroek (2003). *Vlaams-Nederlands woordenboek.* Antwerpen: Standaard Uitgeverij.

Barbiers, S., H. Bennis, G. De Vogelaer, M. Devos, & M. Van der Ham (2005 ff.). *Syntactische atlas van de Nederlandse dialecten.* Amsterdam: Meertens Instituut.

Barbour, Stephen & Patrick Stevenson (1990). *Variation in German: A Critical Approach to German Sociolinguistics.* Cambridge: Cambridge University Press.

Baugh, Albert C. & Thomas Cable (1978). *A History of the English Language.* Englewood Cliffs, NJ: Prentice Hall.

Bister-Broosen, Helga (ed.) (1998). *Niederländisch am Niederrhein.* Frankfurt: P. Lang.

Bister-Broosen, Helga (ed.) (1999). *Beiträge zur historischen Stadtsprachenforschung.* Wien: Edition Praesens Verlag.

Bister Broosen, Helga & Roland Willemyns (1988). Perifere woordenschat in woorden-boeken van het Duitse, Franse en Nederlandse taalgebied. *De nieuwe taalgids* 81: 417–29.

Blancquaert, Edgard (1934). *Praktische uitspraakleer van de Nederlandsche taal.* Antwerpen: De Sikkel.

Blockmans Wim & Walter Prevenier (1997). *De Bourgondiërs. De Nederlanden op weg naar eenheid 1384–1530*. Amsterdam: Meulenhoff.

Bousquet, G.H. (1940). *A French View of the Netherlands Indies*. London: Oxford University Press. (Translation of *La politique musulmane et coloniale des Pays-Bas*, Paris: Hartmann, 1939.)

Bouveroux, Jos (2011). *De barst in België*. Leuven: Van Halewyck.

Boyce Hendriks, Jennifer & Robert B. Howell (2000). On the Use and Abuse of Social History in the History of the Dutch Language. In Thomas F. Shannon & Johan P. Snapper (eds.), *The Berkeley Conference on Dutch Linguistics 1997*. Lanham, MD: University Press of America, 253–277.

Brachin, Pierre (1985). *The Dutch Language: A Survey*. Trans. Paul Vincent. Leiden: Brill Academic Pub.

Bremmer Rolf & Arend Quak (eds.) (1992). *Zur Phonologie und Morphologie des Altniederländischen*. Odense: University Press.

Brunot, F. (1905–1979). *Histoire de la langue Française des origines à 1900*. Paris: Colin.

Buccini, Anthony F. (1992). *The Development of Umlaut and the Dialectal Position of Dutch in Germanic*. Ann Arbor, MI: Microfilms International.

Buccini, Anthony F. (1995). The Dialectical Origins of New Netherland Dutch. In Thomas Shannon & Johan P. Snapper (eds.), *Dutch Linguistics in a Changing Europe. The Berkeley Conference on Dutch Linguistics 1993*. Lanham, MD: University Press of America, 211–263.

Buccini, Anthony F. (1996). New Netherland Dutch, Cape Dutch, Afrikaans. In Hans Den Besten, Jan Goossens, Fritz Ponelis, & Pieter van Reenen (eds.), *Afrikaans en variëteiten van het Nederlands*. Taal en Tongval special issue 9, 35–51.

Buccini, Anthony F. (2010). Between Pre-German and Pre-English: The Origin of Dutch. *Journal of Germanic Linguistics* 22(4): 301–314.

Cajot, José (2010). Van het Nederlands weg? De omgangstaal in Vlaanderen. *Ons Erfdeel* 53 (February): 14–25.

Chambers, W. Walker & John R. Wilkie (1981). *A Short History of the German Language*. New York: Methuen & Co.

Charry, Eddy, Geert Koefoed, & Pieter Muysken (eds.) (1983). *De talen van Suriname*. Muiderberg: Coutinho.

Claes, Frans & Peter Bakema (1995). *A Bibliography of Dutch Dictionaries*. Tübingen: Carl Winter Verlag.

Clyne, Michael (ed.) (1992). *Pluricentric Languages: Differing Norms in Differing Nations*. Berlin: Mouton de Gruyter.

Coetzee, Anna E. (1982). 'n Herorïentering van die begrip standaardtaal en'n voorstudie van die ontwikkeling van standard-Afrikaans gedurende die 20ᵉ eeu. *Tydschrif vir Geesteswetenskappe* 22(4): 271–289.

Coudenberg (1989). *The New Belgian Institutional Framework*. Brussels: Group Coudenberg.

Coutant, Yves (1994). *Middeleeuwse molentermen in het Graafschap Vlaanderen*. Tongeren: Michiels.

Couttenier, Piet (1998). Gilde van Sinte Luitgaarde. In *NEVB*. Tielt: Lannoo, 1320–1321.

Cowan, H.K.J. (1957). *De Oudnederlandse (Oudnederfrankische) Psalmenfragmenten*. Leiden: Brill.

Craeybeckx, Lode (ed.) (1972). *Sluipmoord op de spelling*. Amsterdam: Elsevier.

Darquennes, Jeroen (2005). *Sprachvitalisierung aus kontaktlinguistischer Sicht: Theorie und Praxis am Beispiel Altbelgien-Süd*. St. Augustin: Asgard-Verlag.

De Bies, Renata (2009). *Woordenboek Surinaams Nederlands*. Het Spectrum: Houten.

De Bo, Leonard (1873). *Westvlaamsch Idioticon*. Brugge: Gailliard.

De Bonth R.J.G. et al. (1997). Nieuwnederlands (circa 1650–1880). In M.C. van den Toorn, W.J.J. Pijnenburg, J.A. van Leuvensteijn, and J.M. van der Horst (eds.), *Geschiedenis van de Nederlandse Taal*. Amsterdam: Amsterdam University Press, 361–453.

De Caluwe, Johan (2002). Tien stellingen over functie en status van tussentaal in Vlaanderen. In J. de Caluwe et al. (eds.), *Taalvariatie en taalbeleid*. Antwerpen: Garant, 57–67.

De Caluwe, Johan (2009). Tussentaal wordt omgangstaal in Vlaanderen. *Nederlandse Taalkunde* 14: 8–25.

De Clerck, Walter (1981). *Zuid-Nederlands Woordenboek*. 's-Gravenhage: Martinus Nijhoff.

De Grauwe, Luc (1979). *De Wachtendonckse Psalmen en Glossen*. Gent: Koninklijke Academie voor Nederlandse Taal- en Letterkunde.

De Groof, Jetje (2003). Mit gezücktem Schwert die Sprache ausbauen? Die Rechtschreibereform in Belgien 1836–1844. *Sociolinguistica* 17: 71–87.

De Groof, Jetje (2004). Taalpolitiek en taalplanning in Vlaanderen in de lange negentiende eeuw: Een linguïstische analyse met speciale aandacht voor de wisselwerking tussen status- en corpusplanning. Ph.D. dissertation, Vrije Universiteit Brussel.

De Groof, Jetje & Eline Vanhecke (2004). 1830 als politiek keerpunt, de jure en de facto. *Verslagen en Mededelingen van de Koninklijke Academie voor Nederlandse Taal- en Letterkunde*, 55–70.

Degroote, Gilbert (1957). Taaltoestanden in de Bourgondische Nederlanden. *De nieuwe taalgids* 49: 303–309.

De Jonghe, A. (1967). *De taalpolitiek van Willem I*. Sint-Andries: Darthet.

De Kleine, Christina M. (2007). *A Morphosyntactic Analysis of Surinamese Dutch*. München: Lincom Europa.

De Metsenaere, Machteld (1998). Brussel. In *NEVB*. Tielt: Lannoo, 622–652.

De Metsenaere, Machteld & Els Witte (1990). Taalverlies en taalbehoud bij de Vlamingen te Brussel in de negentiende eeuw. *Bijdragen en Mededelingen betreffende de Geschiedenis der Nederlanden* 105: 1–38.

Den Besten, Hans (ed.) (1986). *Papers on Negerhollands, the Dutch Creole of the Virgin Islands*. Amsterdam: Publicaties van het Instituut voor Algemene Taalwetenschap, 51.

Den Besten, Hans, Jan Goossens, Fritz Ponelis, & Pieter van Reenen (eds.) (1996). *Afrikaans en variëteiten van het Nederlands*. Taal en Tongval, special issue 9.

Deneckere, Marcel (1954). *Histoire de la langue française dans les Flandres (1770–1823)*. Gent: Rijksuniversiteit.

Deprez, Kas & Renata De Bies (1985). Creolen en Hindustanen over Nederlands, Sarnami en Sranan: een onderzoek in Paramaribo. *OSO* 2: 191–211.

De Schrijver, Reginald (1987). Het vroege gebruik van "Vlaanderen" in zijn moderne betekenis. *Handelingen van de Koninklijke Zuidnederlandse Maatschappij voor Taal- en Letterkunde en Geschiedenis* 41: 45–54.

De Schrijver, Reginald (1998). Faciliteiten. In *NEVB*, 1105–1107.

De Schutter, Georges (2002). Dutch. In Ekkehard König & Johan Van der Auwera (eds.), *The Germanic Languages*. London: Routledge, 439–477.

De Schutter, Georges et al. (2005–). *Morfologische atlas van de Nederlandse dialecten.* Amsterdam: P.J. Meertensinstituut.

Detant, Anja (1998). Randgemeenten. In *NEVB.* Tielt: Lannoo, 2536–2547.

Deumert Ana (1999). Variation and standardization: The case of Afrikaans (1880–1922). Ph.D. dissertation, University of Cape Town.

Deumert Ana (2001). Language variation and standardization at the Cape (1880–1922): A contribution to Afrikaans sociohistorical linguistics. *Journal of Germanic Linguistics* 13: 301–352.

Deumert, Ana (2010). Imbodela zamakhumsha: Reflections on standardization and destandardization. In *Multilingua Special Issue: Changing Standards in Sociolinguistic Research: Celebrating the Work of Roland Willemyns* 29: 243–264.

Deumert, Ana & Vandenbussche, Wim (eds.) (2003). *Germanic Standardizations, Past to Present.* Amsterdam: Benjamins.

De Vooys, C.G.N. (1952). *Geschiedenis van de Nederlandse taal.* Groningen: Wolters-Noordhoff.

De Vreese, Willem (1890–1891). Zuidnederlandsche Taal- en Letterkundige Wetenschap. In *Nederlandsch Museum* 1890(1), 53–80; (2), 5–49, 73–106, 333–364; 1891(1), 102–123, 212–230, 329–349.

De Vreese, Willem (1899). *Gallicismen in het Zuidnederlandsch: proeve van taalzuivering.* Gent: Siffer.

De Vreese, Willem (1909). Over de benamingen onzer taal. *Verslagen en Mededeelingen van de Koninklijke Vlaamsche Academie voor Nederlandsche Taal- en Letterkunde,* 417–592.

De Vreese, Willem (1962). *Over handschriften en handschriftenkunde. Tien codicologische studiën bijeengebracht, ingeleid en toegelicht door P.J.H. Vermeeren.* Zwolle: Tjeenk Willink.

De Vries, Jan W., Roland Willemyns, & Peter Burger (2003). *Het verhaal van een taal,* 6th ed. Amsterdam: Prometheus.

De Witte, K. (1975). Randgemeenten. In *EVB.* Tielt: Lannoo, 1286–1299.

Deygers, K. & V. Van den Heede (2000). Belgisch-Nederlandse "klassiekers" als variabelen voor lexicaal variatieonderzoek: een evaluatie. *Taal en Tongval* 52: 308–328.

Donaldson, Bruce (1983). *Dutch: A Linguistic History of Holland and Belgium.* Leiden: Nijhoff.

Donaldson, Bruce (1988). *The Influence of English on Afrikaans.* Pretoria: Serva Publishers.

Dupont, Guy (2004). "Eene gheheeten Zwarte Mine biden Rooden Hond": Naamgeving en identificatie in het Brugse prostitutiemilieu tijdens de late Middeleeuwen. *Taal en Tongval* (Special Issue) 17: 30–63.

Duvoskeldt, E. (1999). Deux révolutionnaires néerlandophones et leur rapport à la langue: Bouchette et Andries. Paper presented at the Actes du Colloque 2me journée de la Coordination Universitaire pour l'Etude du Flamand, November 12, Lille-Dunkerque.

Eersel, Christian H. (1971). Varieties of Creole in Suriname: Prestige in choice of language and linguistic form. In Dell Hymes (ed.), *Pidginization and creolization of languages.* Cambridge: Cambridge University Press, 317–322.

Elspass, Stephan (2005). Zum Wandel im Gebrauch regionalsprachlicher Lexik. *Zeitschrift für Dialektologie und Linguistik* 72: 1–51.

EVB (1973–1975). Encyclopedie van de Vlaamse Beweging. 2 vols. Tielt: Lannoo.

February, Vernon (ed.) (1994). *Taal en Identiteit: Afrikaans en Nederlands*. Kaapstad: Tafelberg-Uitgewers.

Ferguson, Charles (1959). Diglossia. *Word* 15: 325–340.

Fishman, Joshua (1966). *Language Loyalty in the United States*. The Hague: Mouton.

Fishman, Joshua (1991). *Reversing Language Shift*. Clevedon: Multilingual Matters.

François, Luc (1992). De petitiebeweging in het Verenigd Koninkrijk der Nederlanden: balans van het onderzoek. In C.A. Tamse & E. Witte (eds.), *Staats- en natievorming in Willem I's koninkrijk (1815–1830)*. Brussels: Brussels University Press, 122–170.

FS & TC (2011). Van een unitaire staat naar een federaal België. Zes staatshervormingen op een rij. *ADVN-Mededelingen vierde trimester*, 4–8.

Geeraerts, Dirk (2000). Honderd jaar Belgisch in Van Dale. *Nederlands van Nu* 48: 19–23.

Geeraerts, Dirk, Stefan Grondelaers, & Dirk Speelman (1999). *Convergentie en divergentie in de Nederlandse woordenschat. Een onderzoek naar kleding- en voetbaltermen*. Amsterdam: P.J. Meertensinstituut.

Geeraerts, Dirk, A. Penne, & V. Vanswegenhoven (2000). *Thuis*-taal en *Familie*-taal: Taalgebruik in Vlaamse soaps. In S. Gillis, J. Nuyts, & J. Taeldeman (eds.), *Met taal om de tuin geleid: Een bundel opstellen voor Georges De Schutter*. Antwerpen: Universitaire Instelling, 161–170.

Gelderblom, A.J. & A.M. Musschoot (eds.) (2006–). *Geschiedenis van de Nederlandse literatuur*. Amsterdam: Bert Bakker.

Geyl, Pieter (1930a). *Geschiedenis van de Nederlandsche Stam. Eerste deel*. Antwerpen: Nederlandsche Bibliotheek.

Geyl, Pieter (1930b). *De Groot-Nederlandsche gedachte, deel II: Historische beschouwingen, kritieken en polemieken*. Antwerpen: Nederlandsche Bibliotheek.

Geyl, Pieter (2001). *History of the Dutch-Speaking Peoples, 1555–1648*. London: Phoenix Press.

Gezelle, Cesar (1918). *Guido Gezelle 1830–1899*. Amsterdam: Veen.

Gezelle, Guido (1885). Etudes de philologie néerlandaise. Les Flaminguistes. *Le Muséon* 4: 114–116.

Gilde van Sinte Luitgaarde (SLG 1). (1875). *Handelingen van de eerste vergadering (1874)*. Brugge: Beyaert-Defoort.

Gilde van Sinte Luitgaarde (SLG 2). (1876). *Handelingen van de tweede vergadering (1876)*. Brugge: Beyaert-Storie.

Gilde van Sinte Luitgaarde (SLG 3) (1877). *Handelingen van der derde vergadering (1877)*. Brugge: Boekdrukkerij A. De Zuttere.

Gilde van Sinte Luitgaarde (SLG 4) (1879). *Handelingen van de vierde vergadering (1878)*. Brugge: Boekdrukkerij A. De Zuttere.

Gobardhan-Rambocus, Lila. (1993). Het Surinaams Nederlands. In Lila Gobardhan-Rambocus & Maurits S. Hassankhan (eds.), *Immigratie en ontwikkeling. Emancipatie van contractanten*. Paramaribo: Anton de Kom Universiteit, 140–158.

Goebl, Hans, Peter Nelde, Stary Zdenek, & Wolfgang Wölck (eds.) (1996–1997). *Kontaktlinguistik. Ein internationales Handbuch zeitgenössischer Forschung*. Berlin: W. de Gruyter.

Goossens, Jan (1968). *Wat zijn Nederlandse dialecten?* Groningen: Wolters-Noordhoff.

Goossens, Jan (1974). *Historische Phonologie des Niederländischen*. Tübingen: Niemeyer.

Goossens, Jan (1977). *Inleiding tot de Nederlandse dialectologie*. Groningen: Wolters.

Goossens, Jan (1980). Middelnederlandse vocaalsystemen. *Verslagen en Mededelingen van de Koninklijke Academie voor Nederlandse Taal- en Letterkunde*, 161–251.

Goossens, Jan. (1989). Primaire en secundaire umlaut in het Nederlandse taalgebied. *Amsterdamer Beiträge zur älteren Germanistik* 29: 61–65.

Goossens, Jan (1998). Overmaas. In *NEVB*. Tielt: Lannoo, 2367–2368.

Goossens, Jan (1999). Over Tesi samanunga en zijn context. *Verslagen en Mededelingen van de Koninklijke Academie voor Nederlandse Taal- en Letterkunde*, 174–191.

Goossens, Jan (2000). De toekomst van het Nederlands in Vlaanderen. *Ons Erfdeel* 43: 3–13.

Goossens, Jan (2008). Dialectgeografische grondslagen van een Nederlandse taalgeschiedenis. *Handelingen van de Koninklijke Commissie voor Toponymie en Dialectologie* 80: 33–258.

Goossens, Jan, Johan Taeldeman, & G. Verleyen (1999). *Fonologische atlas van de Nederlandse dialecten*. Gent: Koninklijke Academie voor Nederlandse Taal- en Letterkunde.

Goossens, Jan, Rita Schlusemann, & Norbert Voorwinden (2008). *Heinric van Veldeken— Sente Servaes. Herausgegeben und übersetzt*. Münster: Verlag Münster, Bibliothek Mittelniederländischer Literatur.

Gorter, Durk (1996). Dutch-West Frisian. In Hans Goebl, Peter Nelde, Stary Zdenek, & Wolfgang Wölck (eds.), *Kontaktlinguistik. Ein internationales Handbuch zeitgenössischer Forschung*. Berlin: W. de Gruyter, 1152–1157.

Gorter, Durk (2001). A Frisian Update of Reversing Language Shift. In Joshua A. Fishman (ed.), *Can Threatened Languages Be Saved?* Clevedon: Multilingual Matters, 215–233.

Groeneboer, Kees (1998). *Gateway to the West: The Dutch Language in Colonial Indonesia 1600–1950: A History of Language Policy*. Amsterdam: Amsterdam University Press.

Grondelaers, Stefan & Roeland van Hout (2011). The Standard Language Situation in the Low Countries: Top-Down and Bottom-Up Variations on a Diaglossic Theme. *Journal of Germanic Linguistics* 23(3): 199–243.

Gubin, E. (1978). La situation des langues à Bruxelles au xixme siècle à la lumière d'un examen critique des statistiques. *Tijdschrift voor Sociale Integratie* 1: 33–79.

Gysseling, Maurits (1971). De invoering van het Nederlands in ambtelijke bescheiden in de 13de eeuw. *Verslagen en Mededelingen van de Koninklijke Vlaamse Academie voor Nederlandse Taal- en Letterkunde*, 27–35.

Gysseling, Maurits (1975). Vlaanderen. In *EVB*. Tielt: Lannoo, 1905–1912.

Gysseling, Maurits (1977–1987). *Corpus van Middelnederlandse teksten (tot en met het jaar 1300). M.m.v. en van woordindices voorzien door W. Pijnenburg. Reeks i: Ambtelijke bescheiden*, 9 vols. *Reeks ii: Literaire handschriften*, 6 vols. 's-Gravenhage: M. Nijhoff.

Gysseling, Maurits (1978). Zu einigen Grundlagen des Altniederländischen. *Niederdeutsches Wort* 18: 48–63.

Hagen, Anton (1989). The Netherlands. *Sociolinguistica* 3: 61–74.

Hagen, Anton (1999). *Schone moedertaal: Lofzangen op het Nederlands 1500–2000*. Amsterdam: Contact.

Handelingen van de *Nederlandsche Taal- en Letterkundige Congressen* (1849–1912); published after every conference.

Heemskerk, J. & W. Zonneveld (2000). *Uitspraakwoordenboek*. Utrecht: Spectrum.

Heeroma, Klaas (1965). Wat is Ingweoons? *Tijdschrift voor Nederlandse Taal- en Letterkunde* 81: 1–15.

Heeroma, Klaas (1972). Zur Raumgeschichte des Ingwäonischen. In *Zeitschrift für Dialektologie und Linguistik* 39: 267–83.

Hellinga, W.Gs. (1938). *De opbouw van de algemeen beschaafde uitspraak van het Nederlands.* Amsterdam: Noord-Hollandsche Uitgeversmaatschappij.

Héraud, Guy (1989). Deutsch als Umgangs- und Muttersprache in der Europäisches Gemeinschaft. Synthesebericht. In R. Kern (ed.), *Deutsch als Umgangs- und Muttersprache in der Europäischen Gemeinschaft.* Brüssel: Europäisches Büro für Sprachminderheiten— Belgisches Komitee, 31–49.

Hermans, Theo (ed.) (2009). *A Literary History of the Low Countries.* Rochester: Camden House.

Hinskens, Frans (2007). New Types of Non-Standard Dutch. In Christian Fandrych & Reinier Salverda (eds.), *Standard, Variation and Language Change in Germanic Languages.* Tübingen: Gunter Narr Verlag, 281–300.

Hoppenbrouwers, Cor (1990). *Het regiolect. Van dialect tot Algemeen Nederlands.* Muidenberg: Coutinho.

Howell, Robert B. (2002). The Low Countries: A Study in Sharply Contrasting Nationalisms. In S. Barbour & C. Carmichael (eds.), *Language and Nationalism in Europe.* Oxford: Oxford University Press.

Hulshof, H. (1997). Nieuwnederlands (circa 1880–1920). In M.C. van den Toorn, W.J.J. Pijnenburg, J.A. van Leuvensteijn, & J.M. van der Horst (eds.), *Geschiedenis van de Nederlandse Taal.* Amsterdam: Amsterdam University Press, 445–478.

Janssens, Guy & Kris Steyaert (2008). *Het onderwijs van het Nederlands in de Waalse provincies en Luxemburg onder Koning Willem I (1814–1830).* Brussel: VUBPress.

Janssens, Rudy (2007). *Over Brussel gesproken. Taalgebruik, taalverscheidenheid en taalidentiteit in het Brussels Hoofdstedelijk Gewest.* Brussel: VUBPress.

Jaspers, Jürgen (2001). Het Vlaamse stigma, over tussentaal en normativiteit. *Taal en Tongval* 53: 129–153.

Jaspers, Jürgen & F. Brisard (2006). Verklaringen van substandaardisering. Tussentaal als gesitueerd taalgebruik. *Leuvense Bijdragen* 95: 35–70.

Kettenis, G. & J. Meijer (1980). Veel trammelant om een klein zinnetje. In B. van Selm (ed.), *De letter doet de geest leven: Bundel opstellen voor Max de Haan,* 9. Leiden: Vakgroep Nederlandse Taal- en Letterkunde te Leiden, 9–25.

Kloeke, Gerard Gesinus (1951). *Gezag en norm bij het gebruik van verzorgd Nederlands.* Amsterdam: Noordhollandsche Uitgeversmaatschappij.

Kloots, Hanne (2001). Leerkrachten Nederlands en het andere deel van het taalgebied. *Taal en Tongval* 53: 175–196.

Kloss, Heinz (1966). Types of multilingual communities. In Stanley Liebersen (ed.), *Explorations in Sociolinguistics.* Bloomington: Indiana University Press, 7–17.

Kloss, Heinz (1976). Abstandsprachen und Ausbausprachen. In J. Göschel, N. Nail, & G. Van der Elst (eds.), *Zur Theorie des Dialekts.* Wiesbaden: Steiner, 301–322.

Kloss, Heinz (1978). *Die Entwicklung neuer germanischer Kultursprachen seit 1800,* 2d ed. Düsseldorf: Schwann.

Knowles, Gerry (1997). *A Cultural History of the English Language.* London: Arnold.

Koppen, Jimmy, Bart Distelmans, & Rudy Janssens (2002). *Taalfaciliteiten in de Rand.* Brussel: VUBPress, Brusselse Thema's, 9.

Kouwenberg, Sylvia (1991). Berbice Dutch Creole: Grammar, Texts, and Vocabulary. Ph.D. dissertation, University of Amsterdam.

Laird, Charlton (1972). *Language in America.* Englewood Cliffs, NJ: Prentice Hall.

Lenders, Piet (1987). Taaltoestanden in de Oostenrijkse Nederlanden in het bestuur van kerk en staat. *Wetenschappelijke Tijdingen* 46: 193–203.

Maartense, K. et al. (1981). *Zicht op Zuid-Afrika. Honderd jaar geschiedenis van Zuid-Afrika 1881–1981*. Amsterdam:Nederlands-Zuidafrikaanse Vereniging.

Martin, Willy (2010). Komt wie er het noorden bij verliest, in de bonen terecht? (en omgekeerd). Over het gebruik van de labels Belgisch-Nederlands en Nederlands-Nederlands in verklarende woordenboeken Nederlands. *Nederlands van Nu* 3: 32–35.

Martens, P. (1975). Taalgrens. In *EVB*. Tielt: Lannoo, 1552–1562.

Mattheier, Klaus J. (2003). German. In A. Deumert & W. Vandenbussche (eds.), *Germanic Standardizations, Past to Present*. Amsterdam: John Benjamins, 211–244.

McCrum, Robert, William Cran, & Robert MacNeil (1987). *The Story of English*. New York: Penguin Books.

McRae, Kenneth (1975). The principle of personality and the principle of territoriality in multilingual states. *International Journal of the Sociology of Language* 4: 35–54.

Meert, Hippoliet (1899). *Onkruid onder de Tarwe*. Gent: Siffer.

Meijer, Reinder P. (1971). *Literature of the Low Countries: A Short History of Dutch Literature in the Netherlands and Belgium*. Cheltenham: Stanley Thornes (2d ed., The Hague: Martinus Nijhoff, 1978).

Mettewie, Laurence (2007). Elèves non-néerlandophones dans l'enseignement néerlandophone à Bruxelles: analyse des répercussions éducatives de la traversée de la frontière linguistique. In Laurent Puren & Sophie Babault (eds.), *L'éducation au-delà des frontières*. Paris: L'Harmattan, 141–178.

Mettewie, Laurence & Luk van Mensel (2009). Multilingualism at All Costs: Language Use and Language Needs in Business in Brussels. *Sociolinguistica* 23: 131–149.

Mijts, Eric & Wim Rutgers (2010). Het bal ging niet door. De verzelfstandiging van de Nederlandse Antillen. *Ons Erfdeel* 53: 34–42.

Mijts, Eric & Viola van Bogaert (2011). Things Fall Apart: The New Kingdom of the Netherlands. *The Low Countries* 19: 296–97.

Milroy, James (1984). The History of English in the British Isles. In Peter Trudgill (ed.), *Language in the British Isles*. Cambridge: Cambridge University Press, 5–31.

Milroy, James (1999). The Consequences of Standardization in Descriptive Linguistics. In Tony Bex & Richard D. Watts (eds.), *Standard English: The Widening Debate*. London: Routledge, 16–39.

Molewijk, G.C. (1992). *Spellingverandering van zin naar onzin (1200-heden)*. 's-Gravenhage: SDU.

Moulton, William G. (1961). The Vowels of Dutch: Phonetic and Distributional Classes. *Lingua* 11: 294–312.

Muller, J.W. (1939). *De uitbreiding van het Nederlandsch taalgebied, vooral in de zeventiende eeuw*. 's-Gravenhage: Van Stockum.

Murphy, Alexander (1988). The Regional Dynamics of Language Differentiation in Belgium. Research paper no. 227, University of Chicago.

Nelde, Peter (1979). *Volkssprache und Kultursprache. Die gegenwärtige Lage des sprachlichen Übergangsgebietes im deutsch-belgisch-luxemburgischen Grenzraum*. Zeitschrift für Dialektologie und Linguistik, Beihefte 31. Wiesbaden: F. Steiner.

NEVB (1998). *Nieuwe Encyclopedie van de Vlaamse Beweging*. 3 vols. Tielt: Lannoo.

Oppewal, Teake et al. (2006). *Zolang de wind van de wolken waait. Geschiedenis van de Friese literatuur.* Amsterdam: Bert Bakker.

Pée, Willem (1957). *Anderhalve eeuw taalgrensverschuiving en taaltoestand in Frans-Vlaanderen.* Amsterdam: Bijdragen en Mededelingen van de dialectencommissie 17.

Peeters, Constant H. (1930). *Nederlandsche Taalgids, Woordenboek van Belgicismen met verklaring en opgave van de overeenkomstige woorden en uitdrukkingen in het algemeen Nederlandsch.* Antwerpen: De Sikkel.

Ponelis, Frits (1993). *The Development of Afrikaans.* Frankfurt: P. Lang.

Ponelis, Frits (1994). Standaardafrikaans in oorgang. In V. February (ed.), *Taal en Identiteit: Afrikaans en Nederlands.* Kaapstad: Tafelberg-Uitgewers, 106–128.

Ponelis, Fritz (1996). Variëteite van Nederlands in die agtiende eeu aan die Kaap. In Hans Den Besten, Jan Goossens, Fritz Ponelis, & Pieter van Reenen (eds.), *Afrikaans en variëteiten van het Nederlands.* Taal en Tongval, special issue 9, 86–111.

Pijnenburg, Willy (1997). Vroegmiddelnederlands. In M.C. van den Toorn, W.J.J. Pijnenburg, J.A. van Leuvensteijn, & J.M. van der Horst (eds.), *Geschiedenis van de Nederlandse Taal.* Amsterdam: Amsterdam University Press, 69–145.

Porteman, Karel & Mieke B. Smits-Veldt (2008). *Een nieuw vaderland voor de muzen. Geschiedenis van de Nederlandse literatuur 1560–1700.* Amsterdam: Bert Bakker.

Prince, J. Dyneley (1910). The Jersey Dutch Dialect. *Dialect Notes* 3: 459–484.

Provincie Fryslan (2007). *De Fryske taalatlas 2007. Friese taal in beeld.* Leeuwarden: Provincie Fryslan.

Quak, Aad (1997). Oudnederlands. In M.C. Van den Toorn, W.J.J. Pijnenburg, J.A. van Leuvensteijn, & J.M. van der Horst (eds.), *Geschiedenis van de Nederlandse taal.* Amsterdam: Amsterdam University Press, 37–68.

Quak, Aad & Jaap van der Horst (2002). *Inleiding Oudnederlands.* Leuven: Universitaire Pers Leuven.

Raper, Peter E. (2011). Another look at "Khoikhoi" and related ethnonyms. *Acta Academica* 43: 109–129.

Roberge, Paul (2003). Afrikaans. In Ana Deumert & Wim Vandenbussche (eds.), *Germanic Standardizations: Past to Present.* Amsterdam: John Benjamins, 15–40.

Robertson, Ian E. (1989). Berbice and Skepi Dutch. *Tijdschrift voor Nederlandse Taal- en Letterkunde* 105: 3–21.

Rutten, Gijsbert (2007). Taalgeschiedenis over de grenzen heen. De taalpolitiek van Willem I en het Noorden. *Verslagen en Mededelingen van de Koninklijke Academie voor Nederlandse Taal- en Letterkunde* 117: 103–118.

Rutten, Gijsbert (2009a). De bronnen van Jan Des Roches. *Tijdschrift voor Nederlandse Taal- en Letterkunde* 125: 362–384.

Rutten, Gijsbert (2009b). Over Andries Steven, wie het Voorschrift-boek schreef. In R. Boogaart, J. Lalleman, M. Mooijaart, & M. Van der Wal (eds.), *Woorden wisselen. Voor Ariane van Santen.* Leiden: Stichting Neerlandistiek, 301–312.

Rutten, Gijsbert (2009c). Uit de geschiedenis van de spelling. Over de scherp- en zachtlange [e:] en [o:]. *Verslagen en Mededelingen van de Koninklijke Academie voor Nederlandse Taal- en Letterkunde* 119: 85–140.

Rutten, Gijsbert (2011). *Een nieuwe Nederduitse spraakkunst. Taalnormen en schrijfpraktijken in de Zuidelijke Nederlanden in de achttiende eeuw.* Brussel: VUBPress.

Rutten, Gijsbert & Rik Vosters (2010). Chaos and Standards: Orthography in the Southern Netherlands (1720–1830). *Multilingua Special Issue: Changing Standards in Sociolinguistic Research: Celebrating the Work of Roland Willemyns* 29: 243–264.

Rutten, Gijsbert & Rik Vosters (2011). As Many Norms as There Were Scribes? Language History, Norms and Usage in the Southern Netherlands in the Nineteenth Century. In N. Langer, S. Davies, & W. Vandenbussche (eds.), *Language and History, Linguistics and Historiography*. Oxford: Peter Lang, 229–254.

Ruwet, J. & Y. Wellemans (1978). *L'analphabétisme en Belgique (XVIIIème—XIXème siècles)*. Louvain: Bibliothèque de l'universtité.

Ruys, Manu (1973). *The Flemings, a People on the Move, a Nation in Being*. Tielt: Lannoo.

Ruys, Manu (1981). *Die Flamen. Ein Volk in Bewegung, eine werdende Nation*. Tielt: Lannoo.

Ryckeboer, Hugo (2002). Dutch/Flemish in the North of France. In Jeanine Treffers & Roland Willemyns (eds.), *Language Contact at the Romance-Germanic Language Border*. Clevedon: Multilingual Matters, 22–35.

Salverda, Reinier (1989). Nederlands als wetenschappelijke bronnentaal voor Indonesische studiën in Indonesië. In K. Groeneboer (ed.), *Studi Belanda di Indonesia—Nederlandse studiën in Indonesië*. Jakarta: Djambatan, 401–409.

Saman, V. (2003). Studie van het taalgebruik in reclamespots op de radio in Vlaanderen van 1991 tot 2001. Tussentaal in opmars? Master's thesis, University of Gent.

Sanders, Ruth H. (2010). *German: Biography of a Language*. New York: Oxford University Press.

Sanders, Willy (1974). Der Leidener Williram. Untersuchungen zu Handschrift, Text und Sprachform. Habilitation thesis, University of Münster.

Schlusemann, Rita (2010). *Niederländische Literatur bis 1550*. Berlin: De Gruyter.

Schoonheim, Tanneke & Nicoline Van der Sijs (2005). Meer dan hebban olla vogala. Onderzoek naar Oudnederlands in stroomversnelling. *Onze Taal* 74(10): 266–269.

Schramme, Annick (2006). Language Variation in the Media of the Low Countries. In T. du Plessis & P. Cuvelier (eds.), *Multilingualism and the Media: Acta Academia* 2: 197–210.

Sieben, L. (1986). De talentelling van 1920. De waarde en betekenis van deze cijfers voor Brussel. *Taal en Sociale Integratie* 8: 461–481.

SLG (Gilde van Sinte Luitgaarde). *Handelingen I* (1874), Brugge: Beyaert-Defoort, 1875; *Handelingen II* (1876), Brugge: Beyaert-Storie, 1876; *Handelingen III* (1877), Brugge: Boekdrukkerij A. De Zuttere, 1877; *Handelingen IV* (1878), Brugge: Boekdrukkerij A. De Zuttere 1879.

Sloos, Marjolein & Marc van Oostendorp (2010). The relationship between phonological and geographical distance. Umlaut on diminutive in Dutch dialects. *Taal en Tongval* 62: 204–234.

Smeyers, Jozef (1959). *Vlaams taal- en volksbewustzijn in het Zuidnederlands Geestesleven van de 18de eeuw*. Gent: Koninklijke Vlaamse Academie voor Nederlandse Taal- en Letterkunde.

Smeyers, Jozef & J. Van den Broeck (1979). *J.B.C. Verlooy, Verhandeling op d'Onacht der moederlyke Tael in de Nederlanden, Tot Maestricht, MDCCLXXXVIII*. 's-Gravenhage: Martinus Nijhoff/Tjeenk Willink-Noorduijn.

Smits, Caroline (1996). *Disintegration of Inflection: The Case of Iowa Dutch*. The Hague: Holland Institute of Generative Linguistics.

Stell, Gerald (2008). Convergence towards and Divergence from Standard Norms: The Case of Morphosyntactic Variation and Code-Switching in Informal Spoken Afrikaans. Ph.D. dissertation, Vrije Universiteit Brussel.

Sternberg, Brigitte (1999). Frühe niederrheinische Urkunden am klevischen Hof. In Helga Bister-Broosen (ed.), *Niederländisch am Niederrhein*. Frankfurt: Peter Lang, 53–82.

Steven, Andries [¹1714] 1784. *Nieuwen Néderlandschen voorschrift-boek*. Ieper: J.F. Moerman.

Stroop, Jan (1998). *Poldernederlands. Waardoor het ABN verdwijnt*. Amsterdam: Bert Bakker.

Stroop, Jan (2011). *Hun hebben de taal verkwanseld. Over Poldernederlands, "fout" Nederlands en ABN*. Amsterdam: Athenaeum.

Strubell, Miquel (2001). Catalan a Decade Later. In Joshua A. Fishman (ed.), *Can Threatened Languages Be Saved?* Clevedon: Multilingual Matters, 260–283.

Suffeleers, Tony (1979). *Taalverzorging in Vlaanderen*. Brugge: Orion.

Sukarno (1965). *Sukarno, an Autobiography as Told to Cindy Adams*. Indianapolis: Bobbs-Merrill.

Sunjayadi Achmad, Christina Suprihatin, & Kees Groeneboer (eds.) (2011). *Veertig Jaar Studie Nederlands in Indonesië*. Depok: Fakultas Ilmu Pengetahuan Budaya Universitas Indonesia.

Taeldeman, Johan (1979). Het klankpatroon van de Vlaamse Dialecten. Een inventariserend overzicht. In *Woordenboek van de Vlaamse Dialecten. Inleiding*. Gent: Rijksuniversiteit, 48–120.

Taeldeman, Johan (1993). Welk Nederlands voor Vlamingen? In L. De Grauwe & J. De Vos (eds.), *Van sneeuwpoppen tot tasmuurtje, aspecten van de Nederlandse taal- en literatuurstudie, Spieghel Historiael* 33: 9–28.

Taeldeman, Johan (2007). De opbouw van het AN: meer zuidelijke dan oostelijke impulsen. *Tijdschrift voor Nederlandse taal- en letterkunde* 123: 97–107.

Theissen, Siegfried (2003). Elf jaar Belgisch Nederlands in Knack. De evolutie van 1991 tot 2001. *Verslagen en Mededelingen van de Koninklijke Academie voor Nederlandse Taal- en Letterkunde* 113: 243–59.

Tiersma, Pieter (1999²). *Frisian Reference Grammar*. Ljouwert: Fryske Akademy.

Tigg, E.R. (1939). Is *Elckerlyc* prior to *Everyman? Journal of English and Germanic Philology* 38: 568–596.

Tops, Evie (2009). *Variatie en verandering van de/r/in Vlaanderen*. Brussel: VUBPress.

Treffers, Jeanine & Roland Willemyns (eds.) (2002). *Language Contact at the Romance-Germanic Language Border*. Clevedon: Multilingual Matters.

Van Bree, Cor & Jan W. De Vries (1996). Netherlands. In Hans Goebl, Peter Nelde, Stary Zdenek, & Wolfgang Wölck (eds.), *Kontaktlinguistik. Ein internationales Handbuch zeitgenössischer Forschung*. Berlin: W. de Gruyter, 143–152.

Van Coetsem, Frans (1970). Zur Entwicklung der germanischen Grundsprache. In L.E. Schmitt (ed.). *Kurzer Grundriß der Germanischen Philologie bis 1500*. Berlin: W. de Gruyter, 1–93.

Van Coetsem, Frans (1988). *Loan Phonology and the Two Transfer Types in Language Contact*. Dordrecht: Foris.

Van Dalen-Oskam, Karina & Marijke Mooijaart (2000). *Bijbels Lexicon: Woorden en uitdrukkingen uit de bijbel in het Nederlands van nu*. Amsterdam: Prometheus.

Vandekerckhove, Reinhild (2004). Waar zijn je, jij en jou(w) gebleven? In J. de Caluwe, G. de Schutter, M. Devos, & J. Van Keymeulen (eds.), *Schatbewaarder van de taal Johan Taeldeman Liber Amicorum*. Gent: Academia Press, 981–993.

Vandekerckhove, Reinhild (2005). Belgian Dutch versus Netherlandic Dutch. New patterns of divergence? On pronouns of address and diminutives. *Multilingua* 24(4): 379–398.

Van den Branden, Lode (1956). *Het streven naar verheerlijking, zuivering en opbouw van het Nederlands in de 16de eeuw*. Gent: Koninklijke Vlaamse Academie voor Taal- en Letterkunde.

Vandenbussche, Wim (1999). "Arbeitersprache" in Bruges during the 19th Century. In Helga Bister-Broosen (ed.), *Beiträge zur historischen Stadtsprachenforschung*. Wien: Edition Praesens Verlag, 21–47.

Vandenbussche, Wim (2002). Dutch orthography in lower, middle and upper class texts in 19th century Flanders. In Andrew Linn & Nicola McLelland (eds.), *Standardization: Studies from the Germanic Languages*. Amsterdam: John Benjamins, 29–42.

Vandenbussche, Wim (2004). Triglossia and Pragmatic Variety Choice in 19th Century Bruges: A Case Study in Historical Sociolinguistics. *Journal of Historical Pragmatics* 5(1): 27–47.

Vandenbussche, Wim (ed.) (2010). *Multilingua Special Issue: Changing Standards in Sociolinguistic Research: Celebrating the Work of Roland Willemyns* 29: 235–438.

Van den Toorn, Maarten (1997). Nieuwnederlands (1920 tot nu). In M.C. van den Toorn, W.J.J. Pijnenburg, J.A. Van Leuvensteijn, & J.M. Van der Horst (eds.), *Geschiedenis van de Nederlandse Taal*. Amsterdam: Amsterdam University Press, 479–562.

Van der Horst, Joop (2004). Schreef J.B.C. Verlooy echt zo gebrekkig? Het 19de/20ste-eeuwse beeld van de 18de eeuw getoetst. In Wim Vandenbussche (ed.), *Terug naar de Bronnen*. Gent: Koninklijke Academie voor Nederlandse Taal- en Letterkunde, 71–82.

Van der Horst, Joop & Kees van der Horst (1999). *Geschiedenis van het Nederlands in de twintigste eeuw*. Den Haag: Sdu.

Vandermeeren, Sonja (1996). Language Attitudes on Either Side of the Linguistic Frontier: A Sociolinguistic Survey in the Voeren/Fourons-Area and in Old Belgium North. In Marlis Hellinger & Ulrich Ammon (eds.), *Contrastive Sociolinguistics*. Berlin: Mouton de Gruyter, 157–174.

Van der Sijs, Nicoline (1998). *Geleend en uitgeleend. Nederlandse woorden in andere talen en andersom*. Amsterdam: Contact.

Van der Sijs, Nicoline (2004). *Taal als mensenwerk: het ontstaan van het ABN*. Den Haag: Sdu.

Van der Sijs, Nicoline (2006). *Klein uitleenwoordenboek*. Den Haag: Sdu.

Van der Sijs, Nicoline (2009). *Cookies, Coleslaw and Stoops: The Influence of Dutch on the North American Languages*. Amsterdam: Amsterdam University Press.

Van der Sijs, Nicoline (2010). *Nederlandse woorden wereldwijd*. Den Haag: SDU.

Van der Sijs, Nicoline (ed.) (2005). *Leeg en ijdel. De invloed van de bijbel op het Nederlands*. Den Haag: SDU.

Van der Sijs, Nicoline (ed.) (2011). *Dialectatlas van het Nederlands*. Amsterdam: Prometheus.

Van der Sijs, Nicoline & Roland Willemyns (2009). *Het verhaal van het Nederlands. Een geschiedenis van twaalf eeuwen*. Amsterdam: Bert Bakker.

Van der Voort, Hein (2006). Het Negerhollands. Een uitgestorven Creooltaal van de Maagdeneilanden. *Tijdschrift voor Neerlandistiek in Scandinavië en Ommelanden*, November, 1–10.

Van der Wal, Marijke (2004). Simon Stevin: taalbeschouwer en taalgebruiker. In Jozef Devreese & Guido Vanden Berghe (eds.), *Simon Stevin 1548–1620. De geboorte van de nieuwe wetenschap,* Turnhout: Brepols, 170–177.

Van der Wal, Marijke (2008²). *Geschiedenis van het Nederlands. In samenwerking met Cor van Bree.* Utrecht: Het Spectrum.

Van de Velde, Hans (1996). Variatie en verandering in het gesproken Standaardnederlands (1935–1993). Ph.D. dissertation, University of Nijmegen.

Van de Velde, Hans (1997). Uitspraakdivergentie in klank en beeld. *Taal en Tongval, Special issue* 10: 49–62.

Van de Velde, Hans (2000). 100 Jaar uitspraak. *Nederlands van Nu* 48: 35–38.

Van de Velde, Hans & Muriel Houtermans (1999). Eén taal, twee uitspraaknormen. De voorbeeldfunctie van Vlaamse en Nederlandse nieuwslezers. *Onze Taal* 68: 148–150.

Van de Velde, Hans, Mikhael Kissine, Evie Tops, Sander van der Harst, & Roeland van Hout (2010). Will Dutch Become Flemish? Autonomous Developments in Belgian Dutch. *Multilingua Special Issue: Changing Standards in Sociolinguistic Research: Celebrating the Work of Roland Willemyns* 29: 385–416.

Van Donselaar, J. (1989). *Woordenboek van het Surinaams Nederlands,* 2d ed. Muiderberg: Coutinho.

Van Durme, Luc (2002). Genesis and Evolution of the Romance-Germanic Language Border in Europe. In Jeanine Treffers & Roland Willemyns (eds.), *Language Contact at the Romance-Germanic Language Border.* Clevedon: Multilingual Matters, 9–21.

Van Goethem, Herman (1990). *De taaltoestanden in het Vlaams-Belgische gerecht 1795– 1935.* Brussel: Academie voor Wetenschappen, Letteren en Schone Kunsten van België.

Van Gysel, S., D. Geeraerts, & D. Speelman (2008). Style Shifting in Commercials. *Journal of Pragmatics* 40: 205–226.

Vanhecke, Eline (2007). *Stedelijke kanselarijtaal in Vlaanderen in de negentiende eeuw.* Ph.D. dissertation, Vrije Universiteit Brussels.

Vanhecke, Eline & Jetje De Groof (2007). New Data on Language Policy and Language Choice in 19th-Century Flemish City Administrations. In S. Elspaß, N. Langer, J. Scharloth, & W. Vandenbussche (eds.), *Germanic Language Histories "from Below" (1700–2000).* Berlin: Walter de Gruyter, 449–469.

Vanhecke, Eline, Wim Vandenbussche, & Roland Willemyns (2010). Stadt-Land-Unterschiede in der Kanzleisprache Flanderns im 19. Jahrhundert. In C. Moulin, F. Ravida, & N. Ruge (eds.), *Sprache in der Stadt. Akten der 25. Tagung des Internationalen Arbeitskreises Historische Stadtsprachenforschung Luxemburg (2007).* Heidelberg: Universitätsverlag Winter, 75–96.

Van Herreweghe M. & S. Slembrouck (2004). Tekstondertiteling en tussentaal: de prag-matiek van het alledaagse. In J. de Caluwe, G. de Schutter, M. Devos, & J. van Keymeulen (eds.), *Schatbewaarder van de taal Johan Taeldeman Liber Amicorum.* Gent: Academia Press, 853–875.

Van Hinte, Jacob (1985). *Netherlanders in America: A Study of Emigration and Settlement in the 19th and 20th Centuries in the United States of America.* Grand Rapids, MI: Baker Book House.

Van Istendael, Geert (1993). *Het Belgisch labyrint. Wakker worden in een ander land.* Amsterdam: De Arbeiderspers.

Van Leuvensteijn, J. Arian (1997). Vroegnieuwnederlands (circa 1550–1650). In M.C. van denToorn, W.J.J. Pijnenburg, J.A. van Leuvensteijn, & J.M. van der Horst (eds.),

Geschiedenis van de Nederlandse Taal. Amsterdam: Amsterdam University Press, 227–360.

Van Loey, Adolf (1937). *Bijdrage tot de kennis van het Zuidwestbrabantsch in de 13de en 14de eeuw. Fonologie.* Tongeren: Michiels.

Van Loey, Adolf (1961). Palatalisatie Mnl. en Zuidned. uu, Mechelse a. *Handelingen van de Koninklijke Commissie voor Toponymie en Dialectologie* 35: 131–259.

Van Loey, Adolf (1970). Altniederländisch und Mittelniederländisch. In L.E. Schmitt (ed.), *Kurzer Grundriß der germanischen Philologie* (Band 1: Sprachgeschichte). Berlin: De Gruyter, 253–287.

Van Loey, Adolf (1971). *Schönfelds historische grammatica van het Nederlands.* Zutphen: Thieme.

Van Loey, Adolf (1980). *Middelnederlandse Spraakkunst,* 8th ed. 2 vols. Groningen: Wolters-Noordhoff.

Van Loon, Jozef (1986). *Historische fonologie van het Nederlands.* Leuven: Acco.

Van Loon, Jozef (2010). Neue Erkenntnisse und Hypothesen über die Germanenstellen bei Caesar und Tacitus. *Handelingen van de Koninklijke Commissie voor Toponymie en Dialectologie* 82: 325–362.

Van Rensburg, Christo (1996). Is koi-invloed op afrikaans werklik koi-invloed? In Hans Den Besten, Jan Goossens, Fritz Ponelis, & Pieter van Reenen (eds.), *Afrikaans en variëteiten van het Nederlands.* Taal en Tongval, special issue 9, 128–145.

Van Rossem, Stijn (ed.) (2007). *Portret van een woordenaar. Cornelis Kiliaan en het woorden-boek in de Nederlanden.* Antwerpen: Provincie Antwerpen, departement Cultuur.

Van Sterkenburg, P.G.J. (s.d. [1983]). *Johan Hendrik van Dale en zijn opvolgers.* Utrecht: Spectrum.

Van Sterkenburg, P.G.J. (2011). *Van woordenlijst tot woordenboek Een geschiedenis van woordenboeken van het Nederlands.* Schiedam: Scriptum.

Verhulst, Adriaan, Machteld de Metsenaere, & Marc Deweerdt (1998). Taalgrens. In *NEVB,* 2949–2962.

Vondel, Joost van den. 1654. Aenleiding ter Nederduitsche dichtkunste. In J.F.M. Sterck et al. (eds.), *De werken van Vondel. Vijfde deel 1645–1656.* Amsterdam: De Maatschappij voor goede en goedkoope lectuur, 484–491.

Voortman, Barbel (1994). *Regionale variatie in het taalgebruik van notabelen. Een sociolin-guïstisch onderzoek in Middelburg, Roermond en Zutphen.* Amsterdam: Universiteit van Amsterdam.

Vosters, Rik (2011). Taalgebruik, taalnormen en taalbeschouwing in Vlaanderen tijdens het Verenigd Koninkrijk der Nederlanden. Ph.D. dissertation, Vrije Universiteit Brussels.

Vosters, Rik & Gijsbert Rutten (2013). *Snoeijmes der Vlaemsche Tale. Een anonieme tekst over taalkunde uit de achttiende eeuw. Naar het handschrift uitgegeven en ingeleid door Rik Vosters & Gijsbert Rutten.* Gent: Koninklijke Academie voor Nederlandse Taal- en Letterkunde.

Vosters, Rik, Gijsbert Rutten, & Marijke van der Wal (2010). Mythes op de pijnbank. Naar een herwaardering van de taalsituatie in de Nederlanden in de achttiende en negen-tiende eeuw. *Verslagen en Mededelingen Koninklijke Academie voor Nederlandse Taal- en Letterkunde* 120: 93–112.

Webb, Vic (2002). *Language in South-Africa. The Role of Language in National Transformation, Reconstruction and Development. Studies in Language and Society.* Amsterdam: Benjamins.

Webber, P.E. (1988). *Pella Dutch: The Portrait of a Language and Its Use in One of Iowa's Ethnic Communities*. Ames: Iowa State Press.

Weijnen, Anton (1966). *Nederlandse dialectkunde*. Assen: Van Gorcum.

Weijnen, Anton (1974). *Het algemeen beschaafd Nederlands historisch beschouwd*. Assen: Van Gorcum.

Westerlinck, Albert (1977). *De innerlijke wereld van Guido Gezelle*. Nijmegen: Gottmer.

Willemyns, Roland (1971). *Bijdrage tot de studie van de klankleer van het Brugs op het einde van de Middeleeuwen*. Tongeren: Michiels.

Willemyns, Roland (1984). A Common Legal Framework for Language Unity in the Dutch Language Area: The Treaty of Linguistic Union. *Multilingua* 3(4): 215–223.

Willemyns, Roland (1990). A General Model for the Lexicographical Treatment of Peripheral Vocabulary. In M.A.K. Halliday, John Gibbons, & Howard Nicholas (eds.), *Learning, Keeping, and Using Language*. Amsterdam: John Benjamins, 25–39.

Willemyns, Roland (1993). Integration vs. Particularism. The Undeclared Issue at the first "Dutch Congress" in 1849. In Joshua Fishman (ed.), *The Earliest Stage of Language Planning*. Berlin: Mouton de Gruyter, 69–83.

Willemyns, Roland (1997a). Dialektverlust im niederländischen Sprachraum. *Zeitschrift für Dialektologie und Linguistik* 64: 129–154.

Willemyns, Roland (1997b). Laatmiddelnederlands (circa 1350–1550). In M.C. van den Toorn, W.J.J. Pijnenburg, J.A. van Leuvensteijn, & J.M. van der Horst (eds.), *Geschiedenis van de Nederlandse Taal*. Amsterdam: Amsterdam University Press, 147–226.

Willemyns, Roland (2000). Dialectverlies in West-Vlaanderen. In Gillis Steven, Jan Nuyts, & Johan Taeldeman (eds.), *Met taal om de tuin geleid. Een bundel opstellen voor Georges De Schutter*. Antwerpen: Universitaire Instelling Antwerpen, 483–491.

Willemyns, Roland (2002). The Dutch-French Language Border in Belgium. In Jeanine Treffers & Roland Willemyns (eds.), *Language Contact at the Romance-Germanic Language Border*. Clevedon: Multilingual Matters, 36–49.

Willemyns, Roland (2003). *Het verhaal van het Vlaams. De geschiedenis van het Nederlands in de Zuidelijke Nederlanden*. Antwerpen: Standaard Uitgeverij.

Willemyns, Roland (2003a). Dutch. In Ana Deumert & Wim Vandenbussche (eds.) *Germanic Standardizations: Past to Present*. Amsterdam: John Benjamins, 93–125.

Willemyns, Roland (2005a). Mieux vaut instruire que traduire. Taalcontact in Frans-Vlaanderen in de 19de eeuw. In Philippe Hiligsmann, Guy Janssens, & Jef Vromans (eds.), *Woord voor woord, zin voor zin. Liber Amicorum voor Siegfried Theissen*. Gent: Koninklijke Academie voor Nederlandse Taal- en Letterkunde, 445–456.

Willemyns, Roland (2005b). Verkavelingsbrabants. Werkt het integratiemodel ook voor tussentalen? *Neerlandica Extra Muros* 43: 27–40.

Willemyns, Roland (2005–2006). Dutch: One Language Divided by Two Countries. *Dutch Crossings* 29: 153–174.

Willemyns, Roland (2007). De-standardization in the Dutch Language Territory at Large. In Christian Fandrych & Reinier Salverda (eds.), *Standard, Variation and Language Change in Germanic Languages*. Tübingen: Gunter Narr Verlag, 267–279.

Willemyns, Roland & Helga Bister (1989). The Language Continuum as a Pluridimensional Concept. In Ulrich Ammon (ed.), *Status and Function of Languages and Language Varieties*. Berlin: W. de Gruyter, 541–551.

Willemyns, Roland & Jetje de Groof (2004). Is de taalpolitiek van Willem I werkelijk mislukt? In Saskia Daalder, Theo Janssen, & Jan Noordegraaf (eds.), *Taal in verandering. Festschrift A. van Leuvensteijn*. Amsterdam: Stichting Neerlandistiek VU, 185–191.

Willemyns, Roland & Wim Vandenbussche (2008). Diglossie versus Kontinuum? Der Einfluss von Dialektverlust. *Sociolinguistica* 22: 48–65.

Willemyns, Roland, Wim Vandenbussche, & Marie Drees (2010). Dialectgebruik en Periferie. In Johan de Caluwe & Jacques van Keymeulen (eds.), *Voor Magda. Artikelen voor Magda Devos bij haar afscheid van de Universiteit Gent*. Gent: Academie Press, 801–816.

Willemyns, Roland & Eline Vanhecke (2003). Corpus Planning in 19th Century Flanders and Its Consequences on Public Language Usage in the Administration. *Interdisciplinary Journal for Germanic Linguistics and Semiotic Analysis* 8: 83–96.

Willemyns Roland, Eline Vanhecke, & Wim Vandenbussche (2005). Politische Loyalität und Sprachwahl. Eine Fallstudie aus dem Flandern des frühen 19. Jahrhunderts. In E. Berner, M. Böhm, & A. Voeste (eds.), *Ein groß vnnd narhafft haffen. Festschrift für Joachim Gessinger*. Universität Potsdam: Institut für Germanistik, 197–208.

Wils, Lode (1956). Vlaams en Hollands in het Verenigd Koninkrijk. *Dietsche Warande en Belfort* 101: 527–536.

Wils, Lode (2003³). *Waarom Vlaanderen Nederlands spreekt*. Leuven: Davidsfonds.

Witte, Els (1993) (ed.). *De Brusselse rand*. Brussel: VUBPress.

Witte, Els & Hugo Baetens Beardsmore (eds.) (1987). *The Interdisciplinary Study of Urban Bilingualism in Brussels*. Clevedon: Multilingual Matters.

Witte Els, Jan Craeybeckx, & Alain Meynen (2009). *Political History of Belgium from 1830*. Brussel: VUBPress.

Witte, Els & Harry van Velthoven (1998). Taalpolitiek en –wetgeving. In *NEVB*, 2994–3034.

Witte, Els & Harry van Velthoven (2010). *Strijden om taal. De Belgische taalkwestie in historisch perspectief*. Kapellen: Pelckmans.

Ytsma, Jehannes (1995). *Frisian as first and second language. Sociolinguistic and socio-psychological aspects of the acquisition of Frisian among Frisian and Dutch primary school children*. Ljouwert: Fryske Akademy.

INDEX